Literature and Pedagogy

Studies in Honour of Bruce Gardiner

Edited by Anthony Cordingley

Figure 0.1 Bruce Gardiner leading a seminar, Colloquium Celebrating the Work of Bev Sherry and Ursula Potter, 27 September 2018. Photo by Huw Griffiths.

Literature and Pedagogy

Studies in Honour of Bruce Gardiner

Edited by Anthony Cordingley

SYDNEY UNIVERSITY PRESS

Sydney University Press
Gadigal Country
Fisher Library F03
University of Sydney NSW 2006
Australia
sup.info@sydney.edu.au
sydneyuniversitypress.com

 A catalogue record for this book is available from the
National Library of Australia.

ISBN 9781761540011 paperback
ISBN 9781761540035 epub
ISBN 9781761540028 pdf

Cover image: Paul Klee, *Once Emerged from the Gray of Night* (1918). ARTGEN / Alamy Stock Photo.
Cover design: Nathan Grice.

We acknowledge the traditional owners of the lands on which Sydney University Press is located, the Gadigal
people of the Eora Nation, and we pay our respects to the knowledge embedded forever within the Aboriginal
Custodianship of Country.

Contents

Introduction: "Follow thy Bruce"   ix
Anthony Cordingley

Part I. Bruce Gardiner *en acte*   1

1   The Antimanager   3
    Nick Riemer

2   Revolutionary Tradition   13
    A.J. Carruthers

3   They Danced by the Light of the Moon: Edward Lear, Bruce Gardiner   21
    and Learning Ways to Mean
    Christopher Richardson

4   Navigating, Networking, Nurturing: The Research, Teaching and   33
    Leadership of Bruce Gardiner
    Adam Gall, Benjamin Miller, Susan E. Thomas

5   Human Voices, and a Bruce Gardiner Lecture   53
    Peter Godfrey-Smith

6   "My Wretched Dragon Is Perplexed": Scenes of Submission and   61
    Response
    Rodney Taveira

7   Marks in the Margin: Reading Benjamin Reading Baudelaire   75
    Brett Neilson

8   The Windhover in Him   89
    Peter Banki

Part II. Imagined Pedagogies: Poetry and Play   99

9   Triptych   101
Toby Fitch

10 Street Library (A–Z)   105
Michelle Kelly

11 Bruce Gardiner's Emily Dickinson   113
Monique Rooney

12 Play as Structure   125
Émile Benveniste (Translated by Jack Cox, writer and translator)

Part III. Bruce Gardiner, Original Teachings   133

13 "To entertain this Starry Stranger": Jane Taylor, William Blake,   135
Edward Lear and Mem Fox in Martha Nussbaum's Classroom
Bruce Gardiner

14 Lectures on Oscar Wilde's Aesthetics in *The Picture of Dorian Gray*   151
Bruce Gardiner

15 Luce Irigaray's *The Forgetting of Air in Martin Heidegger*   165
Bruce Gardiner

Part IV. The Poetics of Pedagogy   183

16 Lyrebirds   185
Alexis Harley

17 The Queer Optimism of Ginsberg's "Kaddish" (for Bruce Gardiner)   199
Kate Lilley

18 Teaching Interpretation: The "Genuine Sense" in Bruce Gardiner's   217
Lectures
Marc Mierowsky

19 The Nonsense of Knowledge: A Reading of George MacDonald's   239
At the Back of the North Wind
Jessica Lim

20 Virtue or Villainy? Mrs. Grose in "The Turn of the Screw" and   255
The Haunting of Bly Manor
Liz Shek-Noble

21 Djuna Barnes' Modernity: Addition, Subtraction, Failure, Fantasy   271
Melissa Hardie

Contents

22 The Last Man: Literature and Survival   283
    Peter J. Hutchings

Contributors   297

Appendix 1. Bruce Gardiner: Educational and Academic History   303

Appendix 2. Bruce Gardiner: Record of Teaching and Supervision,   307
1981–2021

Index   315

Introduction: "Follow thy Bruce"

Anthony Cordingley

Literature and Pedagogy celebrates and builds on the approach to reading literature that Bruce Gardiner pioneered at the University of Sydney and taught for over four decades. This book is not a how-to manual for teaching literature. Yet teachers would do well to heed its lessons, for it explores the ways that literary texts seek to instruct their readers; how they train, seduce and coerce readers into unique ways of knowing and distinct ways of understanding the world.

The inimitable Gardiner is affectionately referred to as "Bruce" by each of this volume's contributors, consisting of his former students and colleagues, and so it seems fitting to engage with him on a first-name basis here as well. "Bruce" is synonymous with a signature teaching style, spellbinding lectures and dazzling erudition; with a singular devotion to students, upon whose work he lavished commentary that, according to Rodney Taveira in his chapter, was "legendary [...] Copious, trenchant and eloquent"; with transformational, meticulous supervision and extreme generosity as a colleague; and with one of the most intransigent defences of academic independence in the face of management hostility that the University of Sydney has ever seen. Bruce refused to publish – on management's terms – and he did not perish. Even though his career at the University of Sydney was under threat – a challenge he faced while suffering health complications due to contracting HIV/AIDS in the 1980s – he continued to inspire multiple generations of students, many of whom have become professionals in the humanities. A collective impulse led to this project, yet it would have been infinitely diminished without Nick Riemer, who not only formed the initial editorial committee but who remained a tireless editorial partner and source of inspiration and wise counsel throughout the whole project. I am indebted also to Alex Houen for his editorial work, particularly for his expertise in sourcing, peer reviewing and editing submissions, and to Peter Banki for his valuable intellectual support. This book was inspired above all by a shared sense of urgency, firstly, to honour Bruce's scholarly ethos, an ethos at risk of disappearing, and secondly, to celebrate his unique approach to reading literature, a sample of the fruits of which are on display in the chapters of this book.

When I was an undergraduate, one research student, now Professor of English, relayed to me – with a twinkle in his eye – advice once passed down to him, "Follow thy Bruce". Bruce's teaching invited students to put the conventions of scholarly rigour to creative use, for both intellectual and aesthetic ends. The method of this approach was taught through modelling, like sowing a potentiality in the mind of a receptive listener. For this reason, the first section of this book, entitled "Bruce Gardiner *en acte*", alludes to the ancient distinction that Aristotle forged between the potential and the act, between *dunamis* (δύναμις) and *energeia* (ἐνέργεια), where what is *actus* – or *en acte*, as the French say – is that which either is in the process of becoming (*energeia*) or has already been fully actualised (*entelechia* [ἐντελέχεια]). In Part I of the book, the *potentia* of Bruce's method is rendered *en acte* through critical witnessing, which details the history and significance of this pedagogy, including its effect on the learning, researching subject. These testimonials also pay subtle tribute to Bruce's famous performativity while teaching, his affection for playing the dandy, and the strength of his convictions in his own scholarly opinions and in the value of his work.

Contributors to Part I draw on their inspiring encounters with Bruce to reflect on the intersections between pedagogy and literary studies. How does a unique pedagogical style change the evolution of a discipline? How does intergenerational transmission between teacher and student play out both within and beyond disciplinary boundaries? Many contributors to this section explore these questions in relation to efforts to resist the neo- liberalisation and neo-conservatism of contemporary academic culture. The four works contained in Part II, entitled "Imagined Pedagogies: Poetry and Play", respond to Bruce's pedagogy through different literary forms: poetry, the lyric essay, and prose translation.

Bruce resisted arriviste academia, publishing his work not for the sake of promotion but when it made sense personally and professionally. As discussed in the subsequent chapters, he took great pleasure in contributing written work to collegial projects, and the three jewels in the crown of this book are found in "Part III Bruce Gardiner, Original Teachings", which consists of material by Bruce himself.

In Part IV of this book, "The Poetics of Pedagogy", the reader is introduced to Gardinerian perspectives on literary texts and other cultural phenomena. These chapters are attuned to the emergence of pedagogical voices and hermeneutic issues in subjects as diverse as ancient Australian fauna, sacred writings, queer texts, Renaissance poetry, Romantic prose, decadent and modernist literatures, and modern American poetry.

Part I. Bruce Gardiner *en acte*

In Chapter 1 "The Antimanager", Nick Riemer affirms that Bruce is "the quintessential *anti*manager", one who incarnates resistance to the neoliberal university and its ascendent cadre of "market hierophants", whom he defines as managers who dictate and constantly redefine the terms of academic work. Riemer argues that Bruce's triumph over an attack on his character and work sets the standard for a necessary defence of university culture, scholarly rigour and modes of professional conduct, all of which remain invisible to management's battery of metrics but are, in fact, the very heart and soul of any university's mission.

In "Revolutionary Tradition" (Chapter 2), Andy Carruthers finds in Bruce's "prophetic mode" an alternative to the market-driven culture of the modern university. While emphasising that Bruce refused to follow a single critical trend or methodology, Carruthers situates Bruce's analytic orientation and pedagogical style in a tradition that sees the prophet performing social criticism, and criticism itself constituting a form of prophecy. Bruce's teaching extends this history of divinatory hermeneutics, which stretches from Friedrich Schleiermacher's modern philology to ideas by more contemporary critics such as Frank Kermode and Tilottama Rajan. Here, divinatory criticism, or visionary reading, is an antidote to "the stupor and confusion of our time", and Bruce's visionary pedagogy is a truth expressed as the "gift" of reading (Carruthers evokes Frank Kermode's terminology here), a legacy that is passed along from one reader to the next. Of course, Bruce was conscious of this lineage, and Carruthers – with access to Bruce's unpublished lectures on Walt Whitman's *Leaves of Grass* – finds that Gardiner's Whitman "comes closest to the prophetic Voice", a voice that also speaks to the revolutionary traditions of Spiritualism, from Swedenborg to the Shakers to Blake, as Bruce observed. Yet the prophetic tradition is not limited to a specific epoch or medium, and Carruthers calls on each of us, as potential prophet–poets and prophet–critics, to share Bruce's gift.

This legacy is also the subject of Chapter 3, "They Danced by the Light of the Moon: Edward Lear, Bruce Gardiner, and Learning Ways to Mean" by the author of fiction for children and young adults, Christopher Richardson. He recalls Bruce awakening him to the horizons that open up when children's writing is taken seriously. In one of the many contributions evoking Edward Lear – the nineteenth-century Englishman famous for his linguistic ingenuity and stylised nonsense verse, a fact which speaks volumes for Bruce's mischievous genius – Richardson quotes W.H. Auden's poem "Edward Lear", which pays respects to the great poet: "children swarmed to him like settlers. He became a land." For Richardson, as for so many students drawn to Bruce's lime green office, its door always open, Bruce also "became a land". In this chapter, Richardson's pea-green boat ranges far and wide, from Stefan Zweig to Lewis Carroll, from Jorge Luis Borges to Jean Baudrillard, and returns to shore with a mindful lesson: "At a time when reading and writing are increasingly reduced to the technology of neoliberalism – assessed in Australian schools through the microscope of standardised testing such as NAPLAN[1] – a Gardinerian re-enchantment is urgently required."

During his career, Bruce applied his extensive knowledge of the history of rhetoric by contributing to courses in Writing and Rhetoric Studies in the English department. Three of his former colleagues, Adam Gall, Benjamin Miller and Susan E. Thomas, bear witness to the extraordinary impact of his research-led teaching in this field. In "Navigating, Networking, Nurturing: The Research, Teaching, and Leadership of Bruce Gardiner" (Chapter 4), they underscore how Bruce's collegiality and engaged teaching epitomised the traditional values of a humanities education. Inspired by his pedagogy, which drew on different modes of storytelling within its argumentation and exegesis, they integrate autoethnography techniques, each offering a personal account of Bruce's method. First, Gall draws a parallel between Bruce's approach to textual scholarship and the classical myth of the maze and the minotaur, simultaneously evoking many of the qualities that made Bruce's teaching so unforgettable: his "metatheoretical confidence", his "willingness to be certain (or almost certain) on some questions", and his "confidence in disagreement", to name a few. Secondly, Miller attests to Bruce's awareness of relational epistemologies within the field of rhetoric studies – which was on full display when, for instance, Bruce dissected the assigned textbook during a guest lecture he gave in Miller's course – and how this informed his professional sociability, the sense he gave students and colleagues alike of the role they play in the networking and production of ideas, each person being "a vital point in a constellation of knowledge". In the third part of the chapter, Thomas reinforces this view in her testimonial of Bruce's steadfast dedication to guiding colleagues and students through the intricacies of international and interdisciplinary traditions. His selflessness is evident in Thomas' moving account of how Bruce reacted to a hate crime that left him hospitalised.

The next four chapters explore the autoethnographic mode, extending it in different directions and combining it with reflections on intellectual history, bibliography, and archival scholarship, three fields for which Bruce had a particular predilection. The first of these contributions, "Human Voices, and a Bruce Gardiner Lecture" (Chapter 5), hearkens back to 1982, when the philosopher Peter Godfrey-Smith was a high school student who had come to the University of Sydney to hear a lecture about T.S. Eliot. The return journey to this seminal encounter was made possible by the fact that – some forty years later, with the impeccable orderliness and utmost care for teaching materials for which he was renowned – Bruce was able to retrieve the script of his lecture from his personal archives. Godfrey-Smith rediscovers Bruce's unconventional critical style and surprising juxtapositions, with a case in point being a comparison between Eliot and Lear in terms of the nonsense found in each author's verse. Reflecting on

---

1   The Australian National Assessment Program – Literacy and Numeracy is an annual assessment for students in years 3, 5, 7 and 9.

the 1982 lecture and his evolving relationship with his erstwhile lecturer, Godfrey-Smith finds a common spirit between Bruce's approach to philosophy and that of the philosopher Richard Rorty, for whom philosophy was "a kind of writing", a mode of inquiry which, however fruitful, cannot ultimately offer answers to the questions it poses. If Godfrey-Smith came to demur from this view, Bruce's elegant demonstration of it nonetheless remains ingrained in the philosopher's thinking as a foil against his own potential follies, illusions and overzealousness.

Traces of Bruce's work, from a separate archive, also emerge in Rodney Taveira's "'My Wretched Dragon Is Perplexed': Scenes of Submission and Response" (Chapter 6), a piece featuring four examples of Bruce's inimitable feedback on work submitted during Taveira's fourth year in the English honours program. If these were the lowest marks Taveira received that year, the teacher's deliberated responses remind Taveira of the extent to which he relished such exchanges and the intellectual ferment of Bruce's classroom. Taveira thinks through various modes of pedagogical influence (the amanuentic, the disciplinary, the intellectual, the maieutic, the resisted, the unrecognised) before turning to perhaps two of Bruce's most relevant works in this regard. The first is "Christ's Parable of the Sower: Intellectual Property Rights in Gossip and Testimony", a 2018 article published in *Literature and Aesthetics*.[2] In this piece, Bruce establishes the difference between gossip and testimony, and Taveira draws on that distinction not only to situate the nature and evolution of his own opinions, between his time as one of Bruce's students and now, but also to assess the originality of these contrasting perspectives. The second work is Bruce's "Theaetetus's Complaint, or Sadomasochism and Your Supervisor: A Select Bibliography", which scaffolded his rather notorious lecture on the supervisor–supervisee relationship, where Bruce conceives the roles of sadist (supervisor) and masochist (student) to gradually inverse over the period of the PhD candidature. He also surveys the literary representation of pedagogical motifs, from Socrates to Joyce, and psychoanalytic attitudes to the scene of instruction, from Sigmund Freud and Jacques Lacan to Shoshana Felman and her contemporaries. For Taveira, Bruce's scholarly but creative approach to genealogical reading prepared him for a career in American Studies, "an interdiscipline, a transdiscipline, even an antidiscipline [...that] demands a willingness to forge historical and geographical bridges, to interrogate and undo borders, to ford aesthetic and generic boundaries, and to attend to scenes of cultural and spiritual discord". "Theaetetus's Complaint" was taught during a seminar for research students embarking on a PhD, and over the years it evolved into a performance that (if gossip is to be believed and shared) became increasingly provocative; in its later iterations, no sooner had Bruce mapped out his genealogy than he would don a leather waistcoat and ask a stunned audience if they had any questions.

---

2   Bruce Gardiner, "Christ's Parable of the Sower: Intellectual Property Rights in Gossip and Testimony", *Literature and Aesthetics* 28 (2018): 193–221.

Chapter 7 ("Marks in the Margin: Reading Benjamin Reading Baudelaire") sees Brett Neilson remembering what he calls Bruce's "knight's move". When approached by the young Neilson, who had just begun his doctoral studies, Bruce lent his new supervisee his personal copy of Walter Benjamin's *Charles Baudelaire: A Lyric Poet in the Era of High Capitalism*. This book was hardly the most obvious text to give someone embarking on a PhD about the twentieth-century, Paris-based English publisher Nancy Cunard; yet for Neilson, the intellectual encounter was transformational. In this chapter, he recalls his intimate relationship with this particular copy of Benjamin's book, how he pored over Bruce's marginal inscriptions, divining the thoughts of his master in their obscure hieroglyphs. Thinking back to that process offers the author the opportunity for metareflection on Benjaminian themes of memory and experience. The intimate and the political become inextricably entwined in this account of witnessing, as Neilson evokes also Bruce the private citizen who conducted unassuming acts of activism and solidarity. He cites such examples as when Bruce wrote letters to the *Sydney Morning Herald* – including his 5 September 1985 reproach to the NSW government for legislation displaying "prejudice against homosexuality and misogynistic hypocrisies about prostitution" – or when he and his partner sheltered young and otherwise homeless HIV-positive men for extended periods of time in their Darlinghurst home.

Peter Banki's personal account of learning from and befriending Bruce reinforces an understanding of how Bruce's commitment to the humanities was not only a professional principle but indeed an ethos he lived beyond the bounds of academia. With its allusion to the title of Hopkins' famous poem, "The Windhover in Him" (Chapter 8) speaks of a spiritual resource that permeates Bruce as much as it inspires Banki. We first glimpse Bruce walking with an "energetic, upbeat" stride to catch a bus, with Banki watching admiringly and thinking to himself: "[T]he work is giving you energy. You have found a relationship to it that is healthy and joyous." Many will recognise this bounce in Bruce's step, his capacity, no matter what the trial, to seemingly transcend the prosaic and the mundane. Banki reminds us also of Bruce's playful erotics of pedagogy, of the teacher who sought not to repress but to acknowledge, with the utmost professionalism, the libidinal dynamics that animate the pedagogical encounter, and to find therein a means for understanding how authors and texts seduce and convert us to their unique ways of knowing. Banki's reflections on the honesty of speech acts lead him to Paul Celan's famous 1967 meeting with Martin Heidegger at the philosopher's cabin in the Black Forest. While Banki felt he could not speak of this scene in his monograph *The Forgiveness to Come: The Holocaust and the Hyper-Ethical* (2017), he turns to it here, through Celan's poem "Todtnauberg" (1970), which bears witness to the meeting and to the unspeakable.

Part II. Imagined Pedagogies: Poetry and Play

Toby Fitch's poem "Triptych" (Chapter 9) responds to Bruce's lecture on Gertrude Stein's two poems "Picasso" and "If I Told Him: A Completed Portrait of Picasso". Fitch's note contextualises his own poem by explaining that, for Bruce, the second of Stein's poems in particular re-envisages the essence and purpose of poetry, with Stein "savouring" three distinctive possibilities for the art: the Platonic (where poetry is representational and mimetic, concerned with achieving precise resemblance – even if, for Socrates, poets ultimately do not live up to such standards and should be banned from the state); the Freudian (where poetry is symbolic, operating through signs, sign systems and their significance); and the Wittgensteinian (where poetry is ludic, engaging in social and intellectual play, albeit a kind of play that is bound by rules). If Bruce's Stein is especially hostile to the first two perspectives, Fitch's poem sets up a dialogue between these views and numerous other influences that are refracted throughout his triptych, such as Marianne Moore's "Poetry", John Ashbery's "And Ut Pictura Poesis Is Her Name", and Stein's own *Autobiography of Alice B. Toklas*.

Michelle Kelly's "Street Library (A–Z)" (Chapter 10) is a poem that guides the reader through the contents and character of street libraries in her local area and further afield. Kelly completed a doctoral thesis under Bruce's supervision on libraries, where she explored the textual phenomena produced by library books, library patronage and fiction classification. In her poem, Kelly continues her conversation with Bruce's teaching, which was ever attentive to the infrastructure of books and the contingencies of the reading experience, by turning her gaze to the adjacent field of textual infrastructure, in particular to the micro-scale sometimes spontaneous sometimes ephemeral community structures designed to house books for sharing. The poet dialogues with these books' patrons and admirers via the social networks that connect and animate these spaces. Comments on Twitter (now X) and Instagram about these street libraries undergird the poem, their italicised words forming a curious abécédaire that nods to Bruce's interpretation of Djuna Barnes' *Creatures in an Alphabet*.[3]

In her lyric chapter "Bruce Gardiner's Emily Dickinson" (Chapter 11), Monique Rooney meditates on what it has meant for her both to read and to teach works of Emily Dickinson after experiencing Bruce's masterful classes on the poet. Bruce once wrote to Rooney that teachers are not, or are not only, authors; they are irritants. Her interest piqued, through a series of aphoristic vignettes, Rooney retraces etymologies of pedagogical praxes in Dickinson's work, from the mimetic to the maieutic, and gauges their affects, such as the aesthetic shocks generated by the poet who relives the epileptic "gunshots" that her brain fired at her own body.

---

3   Bruce Gardiner, "Djuna Barnes's *Creatures in an Alphabet*: From A for Anecdotage to Z for Zoomancy", in *Shattered Objects: Djuna Barnes's Modernism*, ed. Elizabeth Pender and Cathryn Setz (University Park, PA: Pennsylvania State University Press, 2019), 75–94.

Dickinson's poetry is, Rooney surmises, "tasked with the military duty of guarding and protecting a body hostage to a cognitive disorder". Her reading of Dickinson escapes the critical conventions that entrap the female body – epitomised as waif or maid – in order to proffer it redemption or defence. Rather, Rooney draws on a critical symbology and on an attention to variations of metaphor and metonymy indebted to Bruce's instruction; she unearths Bruce's unpublished papers "Where Did That Penis Go?" and "Judith Butler. The Lesbian Phallus and the Morphological Imaginary. A Commentary". Rooney's Gardinerian synapses lead her to attribute to Bruce an idea which is quite possibly her own – namely that the poet Susan Howe's Emily Dickinson "is the [Lacanian] phallus of American Literature". They also lead her to a sense of the contemporary iterations of this idea, an example of which being Louise Bourgeois' impish smile in Robert Mapplethorpe's 1982 portrait of the artist, where Bourgeois is shown from the waist up, wearing a fur coat and cradling *Fillette*, her poodle-sized sculpture of a phallus. The invention of this beguiling trope, with its spectral sower of the seed, underscores the prescience of Bruce's insight, this time cited verbatim from Rooney's correspondence with him: "I'd say that despite their extraordinary power, Heidegger's lecture notes reveal much less about his teaching than do his students' transformation of them, including Lacan's." That's a key performance indicator no managerial metric could measure! In these poetics of irritation, Rooney finds not so much evidence of annoyance that is "minor" and "noncathartic", according to Sianne Ngai's definition of the emotion, as a Gardinerian "structure of transmission through which *unwritten knowledge* is passed from teacher to student" (my emphasis).

The coda for this section is a reflection on the nature of play itself: the novelist Jack Cox offers his translation of Émile Benveniste's 1947 essay "Le jeu comme structure" (Chapter 12). The work makes its English-language publication debut here, as "Play as Structure". In his chapter, Benveniste explores myriad connotations of the French *jeu* (play, game) that foreground structural understandings of play (versus player) as *form*, as opposed to sociological understandings of play as *function*. The project is simple enough at the start: "I shall call play all ordered activity that has its end in itself and does not aim to usefully modify reality." Yet it quickly brims with complexity and paradox. Benveniste retraces the displacement of the Latin *ludus* (a form of training connoted with "competition; game for the arena") by *jocus* (wordplay, a frivolous remark) – so that "play" is now located in words, not only in acts – and the legacy of each notion in the French *jeu*. He considers the relationship of play to "reality", practical vocation, ritual and myth, finding a profound dialectic with the sacred. If Benveniste's play-as-form inhabits politics, religion, war and courts of law as much as it resides in poetry, it is nonetheless "bound up with the predominance of subconscious life [...] it frees up spontaneous activity". As such, it induces in us "a beneficial abandon to forces that real life reigns in and injures", and above all, it awakens our childlike "native representation of things", that "magical understanding, which the real world disappoints at every turn". This incursion from the great linguist offers a wry counterpoint to many of the themes, and indeed forms, of playful reading contained within this book. That all of these acts have been inspired by one person testifies to the power of Bruce's own form, the living heritage of the playful master.

Part III. Bruce Gardiner, Original Teachings

The first of Bruce's three chapters is an unpublished essay entitled "'To entertain this Starry Stranger': Jane Taylor, William Blake, Edward Lear and Mem Fox in Martha Nussbaum's Classroom" (Chapter 13) in which Bruce analyses the curious quartet of Taylor, Blake, Lear and Fox with respect to Nussbaum's ethical paradigm for reading and assessing children's literature. He dissects the way the contemporary philosopher mobilises Taylor's "Twinkle, Twinkle, Little Star" as a vehicle for her own moralistic didacticism on how to read literary works. Nussbaum claims that, when channelled by the benevolent tutelage of a reading parent, the infant's wonder at the star's preternatural sparkle and fancy guides the child's moral imagination. Bruce challenges Nussbaum's affirmation that this reading scene offers an ethical lesson in how to nurture sympathy, where the child is led to understand the little star through prosopopoeia ("How I wonder what you are"), and where the sparkling adamant becomes a lodestar for cultivating the child's emotional palette, from fear to anger to love. For Nussbaum, learning the way of the star will educate the child to empathise with any living creature. However, for Bruce – whose poetic riposte passes through the likes of Blake, Charles Dickens and the bestselling contemporary Australian author of children's literature, Mem Fox – what engages the child's imagination in "Twinkle, Twinkle, Little Star" is not the lullaby's "moral meaning" but rather its "mortal meaning". Bruce's star becomes a "brilliant entelechy" for the child's contemplation, a focus for the consideration of essential human qualities – mortality, mystery, wonder. He interprets Taylor's poem not sociologically, as Nussbaum does (*how you are*) but ontologically ("what you are").

"Lectures on Oscar Wilde's Aesthetics in *The Picture of Dorian Gray*" (Chapter 14) comprises two lectures which set out a core thesis that Bruce advanced in seminars he taught on Wilde's novel from 2007 to 2011 and in lectures he gave on the same book between 2016 and 2020. In both contexts, Bruce brought *Dorian Gray* into a dialogue with Immanuel Kant's *Critique of the Power of Judgment*, G.W.F. Hegel's *Aesthetics*, Walter Pater's *The Renaissance*, John Ruskin's *Modern Painters*, and Henry James' "The Last of the Valerii". The script offered here covers two lectures delivered in November 2020. "Lecture 1" considers the status of the aesthetic for Wilde and his characters, with Bruce examining their beliefs, conscious or otherwise, against the aesthetic theories of Kant, Hegel, Schopenhauer and Ruskin. Bruce draws our attention to the novel's textbook quality, writing that "[w]e as readers are addressed as the fellows of this star-pupil Dorian, as aesthetic novices no less in need than he of elementary lessons in aesthetics". Bruce leads us to perceive the lessons – both avowed and unavowed – contained within the novel's discourse on the art object's relationship to the body and time, the senses and the sensual, and the social order.

"Lecture 2" pivots towards the overlooked, or rather unappreciated, figure of Sibyl Vane, the object of Dorian's sentimental devotion and betrayal. Bruce highlights how Sibyl challenges the misogynistic prism within which she is set by her coterie of male aesthetes and even by Wilde himself. She is defiant of aesthetic expectations in her performance – presented here as a *coup de théâtre* of anti-acting – when she plays the eponymous female lead in Shakespeare's *Romeo and Juliet*, exhorting Dorian "to make the finest distinctions between the artfulness and artlessness of her performance, which he proves incapable of doing". In Bruce's conception, Sibyl emerges in her role as the master, drawing Dorian into "a Shakespearian-cum-Dickensian world of her own making to teach him a lesson about art, specifically her art". This inversion bears the signature of Bruce's critical dramaturgy, and Dorian – Wilde's tragic hero – becomes "a puppet in the melodrama of Sibyl's devising".

"Luce Irigaray's *The Forgetting of Air in Martin Heidegger*" (Chapter 15) was born from an experience no one could have anticipated. Between 2016 and 2020, in a course on twentieth-century literary theory initially required for admission to the English Honours program, Bruce taught seminars on the feminist philosopher Luce Irigaray's 1983 work on Heidegger, each time following seminars on Heidegger's "Language", "The Thing" and "The Origin of the Work of Art". With the onset of the COVID-19 pandemic, and having no appetite for videoconferencing, Bruce spent a full semester conducting his course in a written online environment. He posted his reflections from week to week, and students were initially required to respond with two short critical commentaries, to which Bruce would reply individually before producing a compendium synthesising the different positions that would guide further discussion. Students found the process highly engaging, and despite the mountain of work it generated, Bruce responded with his hallmark attention to every single student commentary. Reproduced in this volume is sample material from this virtual classroom, beginning with Bruce's exegeses of selected chapters of Irigaray's book, followed by the relevant compendia.

The awe that Bruce's lecturing generated owed much to its rhizomatic surprise, when the invisible tendrils underlying ideas, language and tropes across media, cultures and genres emerge before the listener. Bruce's impeccable scholarly genealogies furthermore set a standard against which to reject, as Adam Gall notes in Chapter 4 of this volume, "a hazy historicism that can justify almost any connection via nebulous lines of influence and connection". This quality is on display when Bruce contrasts Irigaray, who is attracted to the physics of the universal ether and the biology of preformationism (specifically ovism), with Heidegger, who is drawn to the physics of the cosmic vacuum and the biology of epigenesis. He discusses Irigaray's critique of what she believes to be Heidegger's patriarchal phenomenology (she calls it "the him"), which denatures and dehumanises, as opposed to a feminine ideal ("the her"), which connects all beings to each other and their environment. Bruce challenges students to think about this gendering of aesthetic representations, and at one point, he tests three of Irigaray's symbols of masculinist oppression – the bridge, the portico and the erection – against the way these figures emerge in the work of different authors. In the first instance, Bruce retraces the ontology of the bridge in "It Is Deep (don't never forget the bridge you crossed over on)" (1969), a poem by the Black American writer Carolyn M. Rodgers. In Bruce's reading, the mother's umbilical cord winds metaphorically into a telephone cord, through which the mother continues, or fails, to reach her daughter before this filament (of the feminine?) is recast anew as bridges which connect the island boroughs of New York City and support her daughter's movements through the metropolis. Second, Bruce discovers a depiction of the mother as portico in Pablo Picasso's *First Steps* (1943), where "the child's body, angular and tense with effort, bursts with energy it draws from its mother, whom it treats as a battery, a reliable source of power, and as a garage, a shelter to which it can return between trips toward an autonomy that imagines it can eventually serve as its own battery and garage". If the mother is the focal point and passage – the portico – in Picasso's painting, Bruce considers the third Irigarayan figure – the erection – in Wallace Stevens' celebrated "Anecdote of the Jar", from *Harmonium* (1923). Bruce discerns a "dialectic of erection and ejaculation" in the poem, and when the speaker seeks to order what he calls the "slovenly wilderness", setting his jar atop the hill with "dominion everywhere", Bruce draws attention to Irigaray's account of "the effect of the architectonic, technocratic power of 'his' [the masculinist and patriarchal] thought and language on 'her' [the feminine, the natural] being". Bruce extends these tropes and ideas with a reading of how Irigaray contrasts "his" and "her" modes of voyaging and self-projection. To be a student in this class is exhilarating, and in these lectures, we encounter Bruce initiating students into a new mode of reading, with this particular demonstration followed by an invitation: "Please read the poem by Constantine Cavafy titled 'Ithaka' (1911) … to determine if and how it exemplifies or contradicts Irigaray's phenomenological description of the voyage."

Bruce interprets Irigaray's challenging notion of seeing as "her", likened to a seeing that perceives beings as "equivocally distinct and yet indistinct in the dusk before sunrise, which is when we sense, through a kind of seeing that is indistinguishable from touching, the 'ever-ajar' interbeing of everything". This kind of seeing leads Bruce as naturally to Plato's *Timaeus* (51e–53d, the χώρα, chôra or khôra, receptacle) as it does to Julia Kristeva's *Revolution in Poetic Language* (1974). He massages the mind one more time: "Please read the poem by Emily Brontë [Ellis Bell], 'Stars' (1846), to determine if and how it exemplifies or contradicts Irigaray's phenomenological description of 'her' way of seeing as opposed to 'his'." No one else teaches like this, and in Bruce's compendia devoted to his students' responses, the intellectual ferment is palpable.

Part IV. The Poetics of Pedagogy

Inspired by Bruce's lifelong interest in birds, and his own anthology of poems featuring hummingbirds that he once brought to class, Alexis Harley (Chapter 16: "Lyrebirds") recalls the twenty-one lyrebirds from mainland Australia that were released in 1934, in Mount Field National Park, Tasmania. Thirty years later, descendants of this settler bird population were heard singing a song associated with the whipbird, a species unknown to the island. Harley considers how this story might attest to the multidimensionality of lyrebird learning and their retention of songs that were handed down from their parents or learned from many contemporary species. But for some ornithologists, Harley notes, the lyrebirds' repertoire was dismissed as an utter absence of learning. This view extended nineteenth-century commentators' descriptions of the lyrebird as "a mimic" (and sometimes "a mocker"): from one generation to the next, its imitation of an imitation of a birdsong, which no extant Tasmanian lyrebird had ever heard, exposed the semantic emptiness of lyrebird song. Harley details how, in writing about these birds, the human settler population of the early colony of New South Wales reproduced a suite of European cultural referents. In the earliest colonial vernacular, the bird was compared to European *Phasianidae* and referred to with names such as a "mountain pheasant", "native-pheasant" or "wood-pheasant". The name "lyrebird", which by the 1830s had become the dominant English vernacular name for the bird, invoked the classical Greek stringed instrument which the bird's tail was supposed to resemble. As the symbol of lyric poetry, the figure of the lyre brought the lyrebird into connection with a literary mode that, in the early nineteenth century, was strongly associated with originality, and often (controversially) defined against mimetic modes. This chapter explores both human and bird learning – as well as, of course, the refusal to learn – in the settler-colonial state. Harley builds on Bruce's extraordinary reflections on the literary history of originality and plagiarism as she considers early nineteenth-century ideas about lyric and mimetic writing as epistemological devices and ways of learning; she elucidates the limitations of such ideas in contexts of cultural and interspecies encounter.

Kate Lilley's "The Queer Optimism of Ginsberg's 'Kaddish' (for Bruce Gardiner)" (Chapter 17) celebrates "Kaddish", Allen Ginsberg's "big elegy" for his mother, Naomi (1894–1956). The poet revisits the "sunny pavement of Greenwich Village" and the downtown precincts he had recently sublimed in "Howl" (1955/6), to recast Manhattan as a scene of diasporic mourning that is at once apocalyptic and everyday. Guided by Shelley's "Adonais", the Hebrew *kaddish*, and the body of his errant, incarcerated, immigrant mother, Ginsberg retraces the interwoven histories of Naomi's life and his own. What emerges is a transnational *visio*: a prophetic dreaming of the aftermath of the Holocaust, the Bomb, and what Ginsberg later called the "Fall of America", all through the eyes of Naomi and, at second distance, through those of her scribe, true heir, and youngest son. A paean and valediction delivered three years after Naomi's death, Ginsberg's elegy narrates a crisis of coming out and coming after, staging a homecoming from afar: dateline "Paris, December 1957–New York, 1959". Lilley zooms in on Ginsberg's "Note" on composition, first published as the liner notes for a 1959 Fantasy album of Ginsberg reading from various texts, including "Howl" and "Kaddish". In the note, Ginsberg described his desire to, in his own words, "write what I wanted to without fear, let my imagination go, open secrecy, and scribble magic lines from my real mind". When Ginsberg then imagines different audiences for his prophecy – his "own soul's ear and a few other golden ears", as opposed to "ghostly Academics in Limbo screeching about form" – Lilley, in her fitting tribute ("(for Bruce Gardiner)"), explores two incompatible pedagogies: "the mirroring pleasures of coterie manuscript circulation" and "the colonisation threatened by these ungendered, inhuman bodysnatchers". She writes about Ginsberg's fantasy of poetic revenge on these predatory paternal ghosts, evoking Ginsberg's "creeps [who] wouldn't know Poetry if it came up and buggered them in broad daylight", and the poet's corollary of what he termed his "scared love" of feminised "forms in [his] own image". In doing so, Lilley affirms, Ginsberg aligns queer poesis with the engulfing creator-mother; in the poet's words, "a poem in the dark–escaped back to Oblivion".

The topoi of hermeneutics remain front and centre in "Teaching Interpretation: The 'Genuine Sense' in Bruce Gardiner's Lectures" (Chapter 18), where Marc Mierowsky revisits Bruce's lecture "What Is Interpretation?". Mierowsky recalls how, in characteristically wide-ranging fashion, Bruce begins with a focus on John Dryden's knowledge of Biblical textual history – the variants, revisions, corruptions and aporias that Dryden accommodated in his vision of the Bible's integrity – and his capacity to incorporate this knowledge into the radically different religious position that accompanied his conversion to Catholicism in 1685. Observing the evident shift between Dryden's poems "Religio Laici" (1682) and "The Hind and the Panther" (1687), Bruce discovers a mode of reading that incorporates the chaos of a text's composition, decomposition and afterlife. The "genuine sense" that Dryden identified as the basis for exposition becomes, in Bruce's hands, a habit of noticing that looks beyond the poem as a hermetic object; it is a form of sustained attention that encourages one to read and cite ecumenically. Mierowsky builds on this analytic technique while picking up on Bruce's claim that, from the Enlightenment onwards, "the resemblance of human and divine authorship grows ever variously closer". He focuses on the problems that this confluence poses for two sets of critics as they attempt to define the function and purpose of criticism. First, Mierowsky contrasts Dryden with Christian Hebraists such as Robert Lowth, who had to contend with a Hebrew-speaking (read: Jewish) God. He then turns to two contemporary Jewish American critics, Cynthia Ozick and Geoffrey Hartman, who were faced with an interpretive tradition which was culturally theirs yet, at the same time, largely co-opted in Lowth's wake by Christianity. Mierowsky therefore brings together two moments in the history of interpretation where, he writes, "the sacred vestiges of textual scholarship confront readers trying to negotiate the value of literature and its relation to their religious identity". His comparative reading celebrates the rigorous generalism of Bruce's method, for Dryden and Ozick each in their own way invoke the idea of a transmitted inheritance which places the past and future in the interpretative moment. Following Bruce's guiding light, Mierowsky finds here "a way to read that resists the neatness of any one system, the limits of a single context, and (not so implicitly) the drive to specialisation that marks the teaching and practice of interpretation today".

In "The Nonsense of Knowledge: A Reading of George MacDonald's *At the Back of the North Wind*" (Chapter 19), Jessica Lim turns her attention to the Scottish novelist, poet and masterly precursor of modern fantasy literature. In MacDonald's 1871 novel, the physically vulnerable protagonist, Diamond, and his mother encounter an abandoned book and are solicited by a nonsense poem found within it. Lim's original reading of this scene integrates Bruce's differentiation between testimony and gossip, and discovers fluid boundaries between these two notions and the ways of knowing that are depicted in MacDonald's work. This discussion expands into a reflection on how Victorian nonsense poetry foregrounds uselessness and excess as central forces in the creative renewal of a capitalist world concerned with scarcity and the efficient allocation of resources; MacDonald's novel explicitly challenges the idea that knowledge transference and skill training represent a sufficient and legitimate model of education. Lim argues that, in MacDonald's work, pedagogy is more akin to twenty-first-century accounts of moral psychology, in which our propensity to agree or disagree with moral propositions is closely linked with modes of cognitive intuition that are grounded in affect and emotion (see, for instance, Jonathan Haidt's *The Righteous Mind*); thus, MacDonald's variety of pedagogy "becomes a reclamation of the origin of the *paedagogium* as a place of hospitality". Here, the nonsensical poem that calls our assumptions of aesthetic value into question is linked to the "nonsensical mode of pedagogy" within MacDonald's work. This mode, in turn, is viewed as a precursor to Makoto Fujimura's "generative thinking", which in Lim's words, "enables creativity, enables the performance of and expectation of generosity, and has impacts that extend beyond one's immediate generation".

Liz Shek-Noble's "Virtue or Villainy? Mrs. Grose in 'The Turn of the Screw' and *The Haunting of Bly Manor*" (Chapter 20) resonates with Bruce's readings of Luce Irigaray's feminist philosophy and of Wilde's Sibyl Vane, as it considers the figure of the governess in Henry James' 1898 horror novella and its recent miniseries adaptation by Mike Flanagan released by Netflix in 2020. Inspired by Bruce's 2018 lecture on "The Turn of the Screw", Shek-Noble counters traditional readings of Mrs. Grose either as unintelligent and subservient or as a "villain" competing with the governess for the children's affections. Shek-Noble builds on Bruce's hypothesis that the governess and Mrs. Grose are "one joint investigative team", the latter playing an essential role in assisting the governess to interpret the central "text" of the novella, namely the actions and words of the children, Miles and Flora. Indeed, Shek-Noble's close reading demonstrates that Mrs. Grose has more than a few arms of rhetoric at her disposal. The chapter then focuses on how such relationships shift in *The Haunting of Bly Manor* (2020). Flanagan's miniseries adaptation reframes the role of Mrs. "Hannah" Grose as a figure who propels an investigation into the reasons why the ghosts first perceive themselves as being alive, and who is tasked with determining the veracity of the governess' account. Mrs. Grose's fate changes dramatically in *The Haunting of Bly Manor*, causing Shek-Noble to reassess this mystery of hermeneutics. She concludes her chapter by returning to Bruce's insight about how scholars should refrain from committing a kind of "critical narcissism" against the characters as much as against the narrator of a tale; we should, more specifically, resist being too readily swayed by "adverse findings" about their competence and reliability, findings which have caused so many to fail to see that Mrs. Grose is the first and sharpest "reader" in "The Turn of the Screw".

In "Djuna Barnes' Modernity: Addition, Subtraction, Failure, Fantasy" (Chapter 21), Melissa Hardie reflects on intersections between the queer and the adulterous in the modernist novel. She begins by considering the (im)possibility of separating "queer modernism" from "modernism", and by contrasting the historical representation of the queer as repressed or closeted, with that of adultery, as visible public disruption and as a dereliction of contractual fidelity. Ultimately, she discovers in Djuna Barnes' *Nightwood* a "queer adultery". This potent, paradoxical conjunction animates Hardie's exploration of what she sees as late modernism's twin drive to historicise the novel and abate the pace of modernist experimentation. Hardie affirms that, for Barnes, history within this aesthetic becomes the site and pretext for formal experimentation, one that includes, ultimately, "unfaithfulness" to one's own writing life, an errant praxis of re/living history. Hardie's exploration of unavowed or indeterminate meanings through her analysis of the tropes and rhetoric associated with (in)fidelity advances a disciplinary precept, namely that hermeneutic strategies aspiring to disciplinary innovation are often faithful, even reducible, to established disciplinary conventions.

In a fitting conclusion to this section, Peter J. Hutchings offers a tribute to Bruce, the euphemistic "last Academic", generating an encounter between Maurice Blanchot and Mary Shelley. "The Last Man: Literature and Survival" (Chapter 22) explores Shelley's 1826 novel, *The Last Man*, the story of Lionel Verney who survives a plague that has killed all of humankind. Verney lives on in the libraries of Rome, dedicating himself to writing the history of the last living person, a book addressed to the dead. *The Last Man* is composed of multiple narratives of survival; indeed, it is introduced as a survival artefact, made up of texts from the past that have been translated in a present of writing which is itself a form of survival for their translator. The novel presents its origins as a process of deciphering and transcription, in keeping with Shelley's presentation of the earlier Frankenstein as the outcome of a "waking dream". Literature here is a project of reading and reinscription, of deep scholarship in the face of bereavement, plagues and disasters. The library becomes the site of survival, not only for the writer but also for the body of literature that the room contains, a body animated by the practices of scholarship and interpretation. This is a very particular understanding of literature and literary inheritance, and of a process of writing which is never distinct from reading. Hutchings' beguiling tribute to Bruce intimates a mode of pedagogy which is understood as a practice of survival and endurance, erudition and imagination.

Appendices

Bruce himself has the last word in this volume, which is nothing less (and yet so much more) than a brief autobiography, and his "Record of Teaching and Supervision, 1981–2021". A testament to Bruce's unquenchable curiosity, these documents telegraph a narrative of intellectual adventure that transported students and colleagues alike for over forty years. Many of those who have contributed to this volume recall Bruce's quiet but firm resistance to the corporatisation of teaching and research during this period, and Bruce's record can be read alongside, for instance, Kate Lilley's testimony (Chapter 17) to the transformation of the culture of the English department at the University of Sydney during Bruce's tenure, a period which also coincided with the turbulent era of the culture wars and the wholesale questioning of the legitimacy of the English literary canon. It is likely that, at the University of Sydney, no other voice for the progressive reform of the canon was better acquainted with it, was so widely read, or was so profoundly committed to the flourishing of that tradition. As the premier literature department in this country – if not the southern hemisphere – over those four decades, the University of Sydney hosted its fair share of academic superstars and literati. None, it is evident, have had a greater or more lasting influence on students of literature than Bruce Gardiner.

Part I. Bruce Gardiner *en acte*

1

The Antimanager

Nick Riemer

The displacement of the "god professor" by the "god manager" at the apex of university hierarchies in recent decades has not left its academic and student victims silent: there has been an outpouring of scholarly analysis and, often more importantly, polemic, from the staff and students whom neoliberal university managers have, over the last thirty or more years, dragged behind them into their relentless austerity spree. It goes without saying that none of this commentary is enough on its own to turn the tide on the managerial ascendancy in universities, particularly given the complicity with it of alarmingly large swathes of the academic profession itself. As the market hierophants who run higher education turn campuses more and more into unrelieved satires of themselves, the rapidly mounting piles of critical literature against the neoliberal university are simultaneously an expression of the enormous disaffection in contemporary academia, incontrovertible evidence of the severe crisis of managerial legitimacy in it, and a sobering reminder of the yawning gap between political analysis and political effect.

Universities obviously need people to help them run; an administrative, as distinct from a managerial, function is a necessary part of the make-up of a university, as it is of any large organisation. Something that characterised Bruce Gardiner over his many years as a member of the English department at the University of Sydney was his close friendship with many of the highly competent and collegial administrative staff who were crucial to the department's smooth running. These staff, some of whom had "manager" in their title, are not the ones in question here, and not those to whom the "antimanagerial" status I will attribute to Bruce should be contrasted. Nor are those enlightened academic managers at the university – a small minority, usually at low levels of the managerial hierarchy, and sometimes only present in an acting capacity – who have respected Bruce's contribution to the English department as much as his colleagues and former students do. What is at issue here, and what makes Bruce the quintessential *anti*manager, are the standing norms of academic management in universities:

the unilateral, coercive direction of scholarly work, as implemented by a class of academic managers – the modern university's Vice-Chancellors, Provosts, Deans, Deputy Vice-Chancellors, along with the more ambitious subordinates who have chosen to make themselves instruments of their policies at lower levels of the academic hierarchy – who must urgently be stripped of their power if universities are to have any chance of fulfilling a remotely democratic or critical purpose.

Academic management in this sense is, or rather should be, an entirely alien function in a university, at least if we conceive of that institution as a self-governing community of scholars and students dedicated to the extension and democratisation of knowledge. The creativity and open-endedness intrinsic to both research and education make both radically incompatible with the accountancy-logic of managerial power. Managers' essential role is to perpetuate authoritarian control of the institution, in the name of safeguarding a budgetary bottom line that is, above all, an ideological construction with no other purpose than a self-reflexive one: justification of austerity-based management practices themselves. Reflecting on the University of Sydney in recent decades, one can hardly fail to be struck by its near-perfect exemplification of the devastating analysis of academic managerialism in Chris Lorenz's classic *Critical Inquiry* essay from over a decade ago.[1] As Lorenz notes, the complete redundancy of the managerial function with respect to universities' prima facie purpose means that "there are scarcely objective constraints on managers' freedom toward their employees"; this, along with the absence of any objective measures of organisational "efficiency", gives managers free rein to impose whatever performance criteria they see fit, and means that their own self-validation becomes the basic rationale of their professional activity. The "pressure, blackmail, divide-and-conquer tactics, and open humiliation" which they deploy to shore up their authority are ultimately guaranteed by their ability to dismiss staff, an eventuality with which Bruce was, as we will see, scandalously threatened in the later portion of his career at the university.[2]

The terms of academic governance ratified by managerial power in universities do not just make a transformatively critical or democratic vision of higher education unthinkable; they militate against almost *any* comprehensive project for the university that might depart, even narrowly, from the reigning consensus. In this regime, the managerial function, typically characterised by incoherent and capricious decision-making, frequent financial profligacy and,

---

1   Chris Lorenz, "If You're So Smart, Why Are You Under Surveillance? Universities, Neoliberalism, and New Public Management", *Critical Inquiry* 38 (2012): 599–629. The ideological character of the budgetary rationales for managerial decisions is clearly exposed by the fact that austerity practices are maintained even in times of plenty. Regardless of how much money universities actually have, managers rigorously starve almost every part of the university of funds, except the managerial function itself and its favourites *du jour*.

2   The other manifestation of this is, of course, the maintenance of structural precarity in the academic workforce through the overuse and exploitation of casual staff. Staff with ongoing jobs are under constant threat of losing them; casuals never get them in the first place, and are forced to work under conditions of intolerable job insecurity, lack of workplace rights, and underpayment.

often, incompetence, is a perpetual-motion engine in which one class of managers fabricates problems for its successors or subordinates to solve, and in which the ideal manager's horizon is limited to permanent compliance and damage control as a mode of career advancement, optionally accompanied, for those without the stomach for overt or only unconvincingly repressed cynicism, by ostentatious and often self-congratulatory performances of progressivism.

Since mystification of the real conditions of universities is essential to keeping the show on the road, senior individual university leaders are rarely shy in articulating what they amusingly present as their distinctive "vision" of higher education, usually couched, with disarming naivety, in predictable and uncritical clichés.[3] For reasons that are mainly material, but which also speak to the considerable reserves of complacency and credulity to be found in white-collar professions, academia included, a remarkably large proportion of the university workforce – largely those who haven't bothered unionising – is only too happy to leave these vapidities unchallenged. Nonetheless, the ideology of managerialism and the policies of particular managers have regularly been the subject of critical analysis, with Thorstein Veblen's *The Higher Learning in America* – a book that inspired Bruce – a striking early instance.[4] Less frequent, however, are accounts of managers' adversaries – the university dissidents working to resist the submission of education to the demands of the managerial class, and to preserve the ideals of scholarship and education in the heart of a system that is determined to crush them whenever possible, one academic, program, department or degree at a time.

This is why there is, hopefully, some point in a few brief and necessarily personal remarks about Bruce Gardiner, whose colleague I had the honour to be from my first arrival at the Sydney English department in 2005 until Bruce's retirement in 2022. I will concentrate on my experience of Bruce as a senior colleague – someone whose room was around the corner from mine, someone I regularly spoke to, drank coffee or ate lunch with, frequently appealed to for advice, asked to read my work, and shared teaching with. Other chapters in this volume give a much better picture than I can of Bruce's qualities as a literary scholar and teacher. Here, it is his presence as a colleague that will be the focus.

It so happens that Bruce's retirement from the university, at the end of the distinguished and distinctive career to which this volume pays tribute, coincided with the outright abolition of the department structure of the Faculty of Arts and Social Sciences at the university, and the dissolution of the previously autonomous departments, including English, into "disciplines" even more heavily under the thumb of academic managers. Designed, as I have written elsewhere, to break academic autonomy as decisively as possible and to sever once and for all the

---

3   Glyn Davis, *The Republic of Learning* (Pymble: ABC Books, 2010); *The Australian Idea of a University* (Carlton: Melbourne University Publishing, 2017).

4   Thorstein Veblen, *The Higher Learning in America. A Memorandum on the Conduct of Universities by Business Men* (Baltimore, MD: Johns Hopkins University Press, [1918] 2015).

link between the university's organisational structure and its intellectual and educational purposes, this was a highly symbolic reform which only confirmed the impression that Bruce's retirement marked a state-change in the nature of the organisation.[5] The reform exemplified university managerialism in an unadulterated state: masterminded by the university Provost, Professor Annamarie Jagose, it is best contextualised as one in a long series of institutional choices by which university management gratified forces from the economic or social right.[6] It was ratified as the first significant decision of "Professor" Mark Scott, the newly appointed university Vice-Chancellor, and, in a consummation of the triumph of managerial form over academic substance, the first non-academic Vice-Chancellor of the university. Scott is a professional bureaucrat, recruited from outside higher education, who lacks any experience in teaching or research, and whose "Professor of Practice" title was conferred on him in a bizarre attempt to keep up the academic appearances which are readily sacrificed almost everywhere else, including in his appointment itself.[7] At the time of his retirement, Bruce was described with great accuracy by the then-head of English as the soul of the department (as it then still was). Its abolition at the time of Bruce's departure meant that that soul had now been lost in more ways than one.

He would no doubt not have defined himself in those terms, but Bruce nonetheless was, and is, an antimanager in every respect. His principles and conduct have constantly put him at odds with the managerial world view and the practices that go along with it, and so with the senior management of the university and the norms they enforce. Never among the crowd of flatterers, he was a permanent reminder of the ideal of erudition, humanism, and the spirit of critique to which academic life in a discipline like English should aspire. But he was more than this. To Stanley Fish's all-too-accurate generalisation about academics, that they "present an irresistible target [to politicians], not simply because they are highly visible, but because, by and large, they will not fight back", he was an unequivocal exception.[8] Just how exceptional he was is best gauged by some anecdotes from the last decade Bruce spent in the department.

In 2014, a point at which he had been in the English department for thirty-three years, Bruce was summoned to a meeting with a senior faculty

---

5   Nick Riemer, "The managed destruction of Australia's oldest Faculty of Arts", *Overland*, 17 November 2021.

6   Jagose is a gender-studies scholar best known outside the university for her award-winning novel *Slow Water,* and more recently, for her preparedness to allow an organisation with very clear links to Western supremacism and the far right to sponsor a degree program in "Western Civilisation" at the university: Annamarie Jagose, *Slow Water* (Milsons Point: Vintage, 2003); Sian Powell, "Sydney Social Sciences Dean open to Ramsay program", *Australian*, 31 October 2018.

7   Jordan Baker, "Mark Scott to be next Vice-Chancellor of Sydney University", *Sydney Morning Herald*, 12 March 2021.

8   Stanley Fish, "The unbearable ugliness of Volvos", in *There's no such thing as free speech ... and it's a good thing too* (NY: Oxford University Press, 1994), 278.

manager, on the subject of his alleged shortcomings in research "performance". This underperformance could ultimately have led to his being dismissed from his position at the university, but in the meantime the proposals being made to redress it were meant to function as a powerful and humiliating mechanism to bring an obviously dissident staff member under managerial control.

I accompanied Bruce to this meeting as a "support person", and witnessed a ferocious and unrelenting attempt to discipline him, discharged by a manager whose academic work is surrounded by a nimbus of intellectual and political radicalism. We were both shaken by this interview, which was harrowing in the manager's sheer investment in correcting a disobedient subordinate. I have never encountered a more principled or honourable resistance to the insolent logics of university managerialism than the one Bruce offered in response. In the face of an outright threat to his integrity as a scholar, to say nothing of his livelihood, he simply *refused* each ultimatum about how he had to work – what and when he had to publish and how he had to do so, contesting the manager's impertinencies with the greatest dignity. In a totalitarian academic environment conditioned into the systematic perversion of terms like "research", this resistance, Bruce's refusal to be timetabled and his insistence that proper work takes the time it takes, was breathtaking in its frankness and oppositional daring. Managerial success in universities is built on compliance and depends on the compliance of subordinates. In the context of a disciplinary procedure dressed up in the cynical euphemisms of collegial "support", "guidance" and "resources", Bruce's refusal to play the game was more than disconcerting, and it deeply rattled the manager in question.

It speaks volumes about the crudeness of managerial culture that this was not the first time that Bruce had been the object of an attempted purge at the University of Sydney. Some years earlier, he had been targeted, along with hundreds of other staff, by a different university manager, Michael Spence – a Vice-Chancellor later notorious for having spent thousands of dollars of university money on renewals of his membership of the Oxford and Cambridge club[9] – and threatened with dismissal for "not pulling his weight". A petition against this dismissal gathered hundreds of signatures, many from luminaries of the scholarly world, and a widely read article on the news website *Crikey* by *Sydney Review of Books* editor Catriona Menzies-Pike called the university to account for its short-sightedness in dismissing him: "I can't imagine," wrote Menzies-Pike, "how [Gardiner's] contribution to his students and colleagues at Sydney, and to the intellectual life of the city could adequately be measured."[10] As in 2014, Bruce was, in the end, spared from any sanction.

In these recurrent efforts to rid themselves of him, the management of the University of Sydney showed its characteristic blindness to everything that gives a

---

9   Fabian Robertson and Christian Holman, "VC splurged thousands of University money on exclusive OxBridge and Australian boys' clubs", *Honi Soit*, 29 August 2022.
10 Catriona Menzies-Pike, "How could you sack this great man, Sydney University?", *Crikey*, 13 December 2011.

university value as an educational and scholarly community, and consolidated Bruce's own status as a beacon of antimanagerialism. When reviewing this sequence of aborted purges, it is hard to know what had more influence in the antidemocratic black box of university processes – the public manifestations of support for Bruce, or his own dogged practices of resistance. My own assessment is that Bruce's principle and lack of compromise was decisive. Public petitions and denunciations are ubiquitous in university life, more often ignored than accepted, and little match for large universities' powerful media and marketing machines; but when they are doubled by intense local resistance on the part of their beneficiary, it is a different story.

These deplorable episodes should be put on the record, but they should not be allowed to overshadow Bruce's remarkable antimanagerial contributions to the department over many decades. As many others have noted, this was nowhere more evident than in his teaching. Bruce always spoke of teaching as the domain which demanded the most intensive effort and originality: his extraordinary, highly memorable lectures, their delivery often punctuated with sips of Diet Coke, rested on an encyclopaedic grasp both of the subject in question and of current scholarship on it, and were intended to provide students with analysis they could find nowhere else, more exhaustive than anything yet available in published form. In a culture conditioned by teaching overwork, the consequent pressure towards minimally prepared, just-in-time and just-good-enough classes, this single-minded devotion to pedagogy was an act of significant dissidence. It was thanks to Bruce that generations of students were exposed to an ideal of erudition, rigour and scholarly imagination that they would rarely have encountered elsewhere.

Managers' contemptuous attitude to academics like Bruce contrasts with his own permanently respectful attitude to his students. As Rodney Taveira discusses in Chapter 6, the comments that Bruce made on students' essays were celebrated for their length and for the seriousness with which he engaged with even lazy and slapdash efforts, in which he was able to identify the flickerings of real ideas. Reading these comments must have been a jolt for many students, and confronted them with the shock, and the compliment, of *actually being taken seriously*. They were certainly extremely memorable. Elias Greig, a former PhD student in the department, says that he now thinks of Bruce every time he marks. In reference to a comment by Bruce on one of his undergraduate essays that he shared on Twitter (as it then was), Elias observed that Bruce's comment "says, essentially, that my essay was under-researched, impressionistic, and wrong – and he [Bruce] loved it".[11] This quality of generosity and attention did not just extend to undergraduate work: Bruce ran the English Honours program for many years – now likely to be another casualty of managerial vandalism[12] – and served for many years as

---

11   Elias Greig, Comment by Bruce Gardiner. Twitter 1 Aug 2022. A photo of the comment in question can be seen in this tweet.
12   Luke Cass, "Discipline-specific Honours units endangered by new proposal", *Honi Soit*, 9 March 2023.

the supervisor of last resort for Masters and doctoral students in the department – those students whom no one else could or would supervise. All research is collective, even when it has a single author, Bruce reminded me once. The research he shepherded into existence with his inimitably rigorous, kind and conscientious supervision constitutes one of his most important contributions to scholarship and to literary culture in Australia and beyond it.

In this as in other aspects of his professional life, Bruce was characterised by a penetrating and mercurial intelligence, driven by a deep commitment to the value of written texts and the ideas they incorporated. This was nowhere more evident than in his syllabuses, which embraced a kaleidoscopic variety of authors, genres and periods. Equally comfortable teaching A.E. Housman, Lacan, history writing in English, or Romantic philosophy of language – to name only a small selection – Bruce seemed at ease across the whole spectrum of European and American literatures and their philosophical and cultural backgrounds. As Adam Gall, Susan Thomas and Ben Miller note in Chapter 4 of this volume, he seemed to know *everything*. He was proud to have taught many Anglo-American, African American and Native American works, and many works by women. One of the most deeply cultured people I have encountered, viscerally attached to music and art – and, in passing, a great connoisseur of the natural world, always able to identify trees or birds – he was also anything but a snob. In *The Intellectuals and the Masses*, John Carey argued that most celebrated Western intellectuals have had a deeply contemptuous attitude to ordinary people.[13] Nothing could have been further from Bruce's sensibility. Equally engaged supervising work on Romantic poetry or fantasy literature, there was no aristocratic veneration of the canon with him, just an intense enthusiasm and respect for the creative intelligence in all its manifestations.

For all its pretence of sober rationality and deliberative decision-making, the managerial function in universities is fundamentally servile, implementing a world view sponsored by politicians, international consultancy firms and higher education employer organisations. It follows that academic managers express, as we have seen, a relentlessly *dirigiste* sensibility. Since power isn't real unless it's arbitrary, this sensibility combines a highly authoritarian exercise of institutional authority with a directionless, continually shifting set of ideas about what the university should be like and what its members should be required to do. Rigidity of the command-and-control structure compensates for a meretricious opportunism and a flagrant absence of principle about the most fundamental questions in academic life. At one moment, research-led teaching is the watchword; at another, teaching and research are to be separated. In one year, academic functions are to be centralised; in the next, they are to be devolved. Structures and processes are hastily erected, only to be pulled down again shortly afterwards. This authoritarian style of management is

---

13   John Carey, *The Intellectuals and the Masses* (London: Faber, 1992).

empty at its core, filled only by managers' overarching commitment to maintaining the hierarchy from which their status derives. Their subordinates, like their students, are, most fundamentally, little more than cells on spreadsheets, objects whose value only lies in their contribution to their managers' KPIs. Bruce exemplified the opposite combination of qualities. Highly committed to his own intellectual and pedagogical principles, and always ready to defend them, his attitude to students and colleagues was libertarian, premised on the conviction that people can, and should, choose their own direction, free of coercion.

As well as its authoritarianism, managerial culture in universities is also, as I have already suggested, highly irrational and very frequently chaotic. This is another point of contrast with Bruce, whose rationality and punctiliousness in all his professional activities were legendary. His dapper sartorial style, in which there was never a thread astray, was mirrored by his meticulous attention to detail in everything he did. Many times, after a conversation, I would find an email sitting in my inbox with a recommendation of an author or text that he – almost invariably rightly – thought it would be useful for me to read. Bruce transformed everyday administrative tasks into art forms. In his hands, ordering books on behalf of the department for the university library became a theoretical project underpinned by a rigorous theory of collection and bibliography; in a similar vein, preparing a guide for students on citation practices and plagiarism resulted in a meticulous and intellectually stimulating treatise.

No portrait of Bruce as antimanager could be complete without mentioning that most of his remarkable and enduring contribution to education and scholarship was made under conditions of debilitating physical illness after he contracted HIV/AIDS in 1987. This event was determinative: it was the likelihood that he did not have long to live that led him to devote himself exclusively to his students. His ability, for so many years, to serve scholarship and education, to resist one managerial attack after another, while all the time enduring significant incapacity, reveal an out-of-the-ordinary fortitude. And, for all his investment in the life of the mind and spirit, he understood that resistance needs to be collective, and concrete. Of all my interactions with him, one image in particular sticks: that of Bruce picketing the entrance to the university on Carillon Avenue during a strike in 2013. Bruce was a loyal member of the National Tertiary Education Union, the only real counter-force to managerial power in Australian universities. Even though he was sick at the time, Bruce joined other union members on strike in defence of better conditions. Most union members content themselves with striking but stay away from pickets, which can often be confrontational. In the course of this campaign, which involved six separate days of strike action, picketing staff and students were assaulted by strike-breakers and members of conservative student organisations and charged by violent riot police. Bruce was sick, but he came anyway. This was typical, and just one of the many reasons for the esteem in which he is so widely held – a sign that, despite everything, managerialism in universities has not triumphed yet, and doesn't have to.

Bibliography

Baker, Jordan. "Mark Scott to be next Vice-Chancellor of Sydney University", *Sydney Morning Herald*, 12 March 2021. https://tinyurl.com/ms4t5zwt.

Carey, John. *The Intellectuals and the Masses*. London: Faber, 1992.

Cass, Luke. "Discipline-specific Honours units endangered by new proposal", *Honi Soit*, 9 March 2023. https://honisoit.com/2023/03/discipline-specific-honours-units-endangered-by-new-proposal/.

Davis, Glyn. *The Australian Idea of a University*. Carlton: Melbourne University Publishing, 2017.

Davis, Glyn. *The Republic of Learning*. Pymble: ABC Books, 2010.

Fish, Stanley. "The unbearable ugliness of Volvos". In *There's No Such Thing as Free Speech ... And It's a Good Thing Too*. NY: Oxford University Press, 1994.

Greig, Elias. Comment on work by Bruce Gardiner, Twitter. 1 Aug 2022. https://x.com/elias_greig/status/1553722592736841730?lang=en.

Jagose, Annamarie. *Slow Water*. Milsons Point: Vintage, 2003.

Lorenz, Chris. "If You're So Smart, Why Are You Under Surveillance? Universities, Neoliberalism, and New Public Management." *Critical Inquiry* 38 (2012): 599–629.

Menzies-Pike, Catriona. "How could you sack this great man, Sydney University?", *Crikey*, 13 December 2011. https://tinyurl.com/22pex796.

Powell, Sian. "Sydney Social Sciences Dean open to Ramsay program", *Australian*, 31 October 2018. https://tinyurl.com/43mdej9u.

Riemer, Nick. "The managed destruction of Australia's oldest Faculty of Arts", *Overland*, 17 November 2021. https://overland.org.au/2021/11/the-managed-destruction-of-australias-oldest-faculty-of-arts/.

Robertson, Fabian and Christian Holman, "VC splurged thousands of University money on exclusive OxBridge and Australian boys' clubs", *Honi Soit*, 29 August 2022. https://tinyurl.com/5n7a42tm.

Veblen, Thorstein. *The Higher Learning in America. A Memorandum on the Conduct of Universities by Business Men*. Baltimore, MD: Johns Hopkins University Press, 2015.

Figure 1.1 Dr Bruce Gardiner protesting funding cuts at the University of Sydney on 5 June 2013. Photo by Sam Ruttyn/Newspix.

2

Revolutionary Tradition

A.J. Carruthers

In contemporary academies more time is spent applying for grants that would allow us to write than doing the writing itself. The imposition of grants leads to all sorts of corruptions; marketisations of "research areas", subordination to mandated research frameworks, outsourcing of teaching for the so-called reclamation of research labour-time, consolidation of accepted or conventionalised networks of citation (like the five- to ten-year rule for "outdated" sources), and degradations in spirit and style in favour of slipshod output. Research has entered the world of speculative capital; the alleged market value of a "project" decided in advance of its completion. Collateral damage is, as Gayatri Spivak has noted, the death of discipline itself, an enforced interdisciplinarity that, so the argument goes, destroys the integrity of the integrated disciplines, and artificial – rather than entrenched – cross-disciplinary relations.[1] Discipline as such is now a threat to research.

Walter Benjamin famously proclaimed that in every era "the attempt must be made to wrest tradition away from a conformism that is about to overpower it".[2] Benjamin takes his civilisational cues from Karl Marx in the *Eighteenth Brumaire of Louis Bonaparte*, who uses the phrase "revolutionäre Überlieferung" in reference to how the Revolution of 1848 parodied that of the period 1793–1795.[3] We have only to recognise that in our time we are losing view of this idea; that revolutions come through traditions, and that tradition, or at least certain traditions, must oppose conformism. For Hans-Georg Gadamer in *Truth and Method*, tradition is one of the four key elements of hermeneutics. Tradition is encapsulated in *Überlieferung*, a word that means something similar to the handing-down from the past.[4] It leads not to the passive attitude but rather the question or self-questioning *from*

---

1   Gayatri Chakravorty Spivak, *Death of a Discipline* (New York: Columbia University Press, 2003).
2   Walter Benjamin, *Illuminations*, trans Harry Zorn (New York: Schocken Books, 1969), 255.
3   Karl Marx, "Der 18te Brumaire des Louis Napoleon (1852)," in *Karl Marx and Friedrich Engels Werke, Band 8* (Berlin: Dietz Verlag, 1960), 115.
4   Hans-Georg Gadamer, *Truth and Method*, trans. Joel Weinsheimer and Donald G. Marshall (London: Bloomsbury, 2013). See Translator's Preface, xv.

an historical position, necessary for hermeneutics to take place. One can see how all this has come to pass in the present, how we have lost our *Überlieferung*, but we must specify too the particular disciplines or traditions of which we speak: criticism. Criticism is the result of revolutions in reading, in the inheritance and alteration of tradition, as difficult as it may be to claim this today. But has it suffered a counter-revolutionary blow? Is that which replaces criticism also (counter)-revolutionary? We may have advocated reform or renovation at least, but alas no longer can this suffice. There are those who claim criticism has been replaced either by theory ("Theory's Empire")[5] or a certain vulgar type or brand of literary historicism (I'm thinking here of Jane Gallop's 2007 essay on the historicisation of literary studies).[6] Either may be true; we can at least say criticism has not been enriched by them. There may have been a time when we could have advocated not overhaul but enrichment. There was a window of opportunity once where history and theory may have worked to the betterment of criticism, not to its destruction. This window is now closed shut; we are left with criticism's destruction in the wake of the neoliberal revolution.

The question of a critical tradition is tied up with the history of criticism within or alongside institutions. Is it a coincidence that the destruction of criticism occurred concomitantly with the destruction of the university? Capitalist modes of production, sometimes advanced, but never profitable on the plane of social relations, ultimately destroyed the contemporary university (to leave problems with the pre-neoliberal university aside), or more exactly, contemporary universities primarily in the capitalist West fell to the neoliberal phase of the capitalist mode of development in a process which arguably began in Chile after the fall of Salvador Allende in 1973 (thus outside the West). There, as Raewyn Connell puts it in *The Good University*, the neoliberal turn was made "at the point of a bayonet".[7] Neoliberalism, at least in the Chilean example, came first as a United States imperialist military exercise. In Chile the phenomenon of "Taxi Professors" – casualised teachers who "rush from university to university to teach different classes" – came as a result of the brutal and bloody military violence that ushered in this new "market regime" imposed by the United States of America.[8] I would go so far as to suggest that the neoliberal phase of capitalist development also led to, or is leading to, the downfall of the critical tradition. For neoliberalism is revolutionary too: it cannot handle traditions of this kind. We may harness critical traditions against it, but its power is immense, and its determination to recognise only one form of value, an arbitrary market value, cannot be underestimated. Tradition in

---

5   Daphne Patai and Wilfrido H. Corral, *Theory's Empire: An Anthology of Dissent* (New York: Columbia University Press, 2005).

6   Jane Gallop, "The Historicization of Literary Studies and the Fate of Close Reading", *Profession* (2007): 181–6.

7   Raewyn Connell, *The Good University: What Universities Actually Do and Why It's Time for Radical Change* (London: Zed Books, 2019), 69.

8   Connell, *The Good University*, 69, 116.

itself may not be much, but contained within it is a peculiar element of the solution for a greater disciplinary independence, since it has now found itself more able to stand "apart from" or "above" the neoliberal behemoth and is, by virtue of its inherent long-term ability to resist conformity, less susceptible to integration into neoliberal forms of value.

I suggest this not to advocate a pure regression of action, as if there is some prior moment to return to that can fix everything. By no means should we hearken after the past and dwell upon what was lost; we need only recognise the revolutionary potential that lies dormant in the critical tradition itself. Not all is lost because a weapon we have is our reading and readings. We cannot stop reading, and readings carry us on into the future. In *The Secular Scripture*, Northrop Frye wrote:

> The word "critic" is connected with the word "crisis," and all the critic's scholarly routines revolve around a critical moment and a critical act, which is always the same moment and act however often it recurs. This act, I have so often urged, is not an act of judgment but of recognition. If the critic is the judge, the community he represents is supreme in authority over the poet; all human creation must conform to the anxieties of human institutions. But if the critic abandons judgment for recognition, the act of recognition liberates something in human creative energy, and thereby helps to give the community the power to judge itself. If the critic is to recognize the prophetic, of course, he needs to be prophetic too: his model is John the Baptist, the greatest prophet of his age, whose critical moment came with recognizing a still greater power than his own.[9]

It might seem well-nigh mad today (a time in which there are so many "crises" that it is hard to tell which crisis it is of which one speaks) to run around proclaiming that criticism is prophetic; but one must experiment with it. We know from all Frye's writings that he meant the critical tradition was linked to the judgemental tradition of social prophecy, of the kind Michael Walzer speaks of in *Interpretation and Social Criticism*.[10] Where the liberation of "human creative energy" is concerned, we are speaking here of something far greater than a superficial "creative-critical" rapprochement we hear a lot about today. On the one hand the critic must be prophetic because of the prophets and prophetic literature, or must become so in order to muster the courage to face the prophetic literature, which I will go into further below in light of Bruce Gardiner's prophetic reading of Walt Whitman. Yet on another register criticism simply passes itself on to the next generation of readers because it offers new or visionary readings and methods of readings for it. Imagine

---

9   Northrop Frye, *The Secular Scripture and Other Writings on Critical Theory, 1976–1991* (Toronto: University of Toronto Press, 2005), 166.

10   Michael Walzer, *Interpretation and Social Criticism* (Cambridge, MA: Harvard University Press, 1987).

claiming to a grant supplier today the necessity of passing a new visionary reading on to a new generation of readers! Yet this is precisely what Bruce Gardiner, who I argue is both a revolutionist and traditionalist, has done for us. Bruce's teaching is necessarily and truly interdisciplinary in that it can connect traditions while recognising that the dialectics of tradition respects to a certain degree disciplinary integrity and depth, and that disciplinary integrity and depth is a crucial precursor to any interdisciplinary contact. Bruce's teaching was and is "useful" as much as "valuable". It can be truly put to use. As such, it is hard to speak of such teaching in terms of "value" under the terms ascribed to it today. Value, particularly social value, must also be rigorously discussed and not readily assumed. Criticism presupposes no value. Criticism unsurprisingly seeks to critique all value, which makes it peculiarly susceptible to condemnation in our time.

If all this is so, if criticism has been overrun by a revolution (or counter-revolution), what has come forth to replace it? Very little has replaced it, to our advantage. The degradation of the situation is such that it is clear; it is of the broadest benefit to bring back the basic tools of criticism, to return to the thrill of enigmas, emendation, divinations of meanings and revelation of countermeanings, to bring forth again the thrill of "English" in more than one language, to borrow from Colin MacCabe's 1984 defence of the trivium.[11] It makes sense in the global arena, far even from the imperial metropoles; in the English departments of the Second[12] and Third Worlds, where such tools are largely still taught due to a belated acquisition of method and a relative insulation from the dynamics of neoliberal austerity in developed metropoles. The deeper value of criticism is surely the broadness of its applicability. It is of benefit to students, readers, teachers, enthusiasts, and possibly even to the livelihood of writing and writers themselves, who may resist criticism yet rely on it more than they are consciously aware. Perhaps we can revive a term used by those who have concentrated some effort on uncovering the divinatory in hermeneutics, from Schleiermacher to Frank Kermode and Tilottama Rajan: divinatory criticism, or visionary reading.[13] Such modes of criticism are arguably the very vein of

---

11   Colin MacCabe, "Towards a Modern Trivium – English Studies Today", *Critical Quarterly* 26, no. 1–2 (March 1984): 69–82.

12   My use of the term "Second World" here is of course regressive and contestable, since after the fall of the Soviet Union and Yugoslavia it is mostly not used now, but I revive it simply to refer to the remainder of the socialist countries, a "buffer zone", which through socialist governance or national liberation movements, can still be said neither to fall geopolitically to the Third, the undeveloped, nor the First, developed, worlds. In Chinese universities, for instance, one cannot earn the disciplinary title "literary critic" without having an encompassing knowledge of the Western and Eastern critical traditions.

13   See Friedrich Daniel Ernst Schleiermacher, *Hermeneutics and Criticism, And Other Writings*, trans. Andrew Bowie (Cambridge: Cambridge University Press, 1998); Frank Kermode, *An Appetite for Poetry* (Cambridge, MA: Harvard University Press, 1989); Tilottama Rajan, *The Supplement of Reading: Figures of Understanding in Romantic Theory and Practice* (Ithaca, NY: Cornell University Press, 1990).

accessibility and access. In the stupor and confusion of our time, visionary reading holds true because it passes what Kermode identifies as the "gift" of reading from one reader to the next. In the teachings of Bruce Gardiner we find the truest expression of revolution within the tradition, a passing-down of the gift.

In Gardiner's final lectures in his posting at the University of Sydney he gave a two-part series on Walt Whitman's prophetic poetics.[14] The question of a prophetic voice that is an American voice is a most difficult one, for an American who speaks from *that* centre, from the country out of which, and under which, a once new, now false "sign of democracy" pullulates, will surely not find those voices alien enough to constitute a prophetic voice. The key here is not America's outsideness as colony, but rather Whitman's outsideness: "No one believed him," Gardiner says. Not even the Americans, at least not at first; what once was anti-literary did not become literary overnight. Being sad and alienated in one's country is of course a necessity for any prophet, but Gardiner reminds us it is both prophecy and scripture. Whitman's prophetic "aspect" is precisely that which is written in the plain or common speech of prophecy, the common speech we primarily identify as prophetic since the literary words of Amos, who spoke against poverty and priesthood in the Northern Kingdom of Israel, and whose very outsideness from the "school of prophets" made him the truest of prophets. Amos set in motion the notion of prophecy as writing, as scripture.

The nature of Whitman's prophetism is thus partial, but still crucial. Extravagant eulogy is also useless. We speak not of any explicit or implicit critique of America that we might find in Whitman, but we can speak of war, or of Whitman's prophetic voice as partly that of a prophet of destruction and war, not just the Civil War but all wars to come. Geoffrey Hartman, in *Minor Prophecies*, could find in the voice of "cultural prophecy" all the worst horrors of national and racial destiny.[15] In an account of Whitman's prophetic voice, Yosefa Raz cites Alicia Ostriker's disavowal (in 1991, the first weeks of the Gulf War) of Whitmanian warmongering in "Drum-Taps"; the grand prophetic voice is culpable, nay condemnable on the level of US geostrategic and geopolitical hegemony.[16] Ultimately, what makes Whitman prophetic must eventually be separated from what makes Whitman American. Whitman's American tradition is not necessarily that of the poetic-prophetic tradition: it could spurn and seed various lines of influence, from Charles Reznikoff's citational realism to Allen Ginsberg's mid-century American Personalism, neither of which are essentially prophetic, though they are American. Nor should it trouble us too much that poet-prophets,

14   I thank Monique Rooney for alerting me to these lectures in 2023: Bruce Gardiner, "Lectures on American poetry" (unpublished scripts), 2020.

15   Geoffrey Hartman, *Minor Prophecies: The Literary Essay in the Culture Wars* (Cambridge, MA: Harvard University Press, 1991). See in particular the stunning final chapter "Literary Criticism and the Future" for various angles on the problem of cultural prophecy.

16   See Yosefa Raz, "Untuning Walt Whitman's Prophetic Voice", *Walt Whitman Quarterly Review* 36, no. 1 (September 2018): 1.

from Blake to Yeats to Whitman, did not prepare for us the foundation of a new religion. For Whitman it was human poetry that was religion enough. Gardiner's interest here is rather on the peculiar nature of prophetic voice, which on the one hand is a singular and stand-out voice, rising above carnage to speak loud and clear, yet on the other hand a collocation of many voices. Irreducible to national democracy, characteristically then it is epic poetry *and* scripture ("script of a preacher's speech"). It is an uncommon summoning of the common voice of the many. Through theophany it reaches us, or the poet, that is: through manifestation. Whitman is ceaselessly in dialogue with what André D. Neher called prophetic silence,[17] most clearly in the 24th section of *Song of Myself*, which emulates the Hebrew prophetic books of the Nevi'im. "Long dumb voices" come through to Whitman, who speaks them into existence.[18]

But it is in discussing the sixth section of *Leaves of Grass* that Gardiner comes closest to the prophetic voice, which arrives through theophany. This does not mean that the poet sits back and receives the divine message without doing anything or putting in any effort. A prophetic poetry is a poetry of guesses just as the critical reading is a criticism of guesses, hints and divinations. It nudges itself into the right position to receive the manifestation, or as Gardiner puts it, "Epiphanies only happen to those primed for them." In section 6 Whitman is guessing at grass and guessing at the child's speech; the guessing of a graminologist – expert in grasses – who investigates as any graminologist should, but in the end

> the grass speaks through the child who in turn speaks through Whitman, their three tongues as one. If the child's speech is an epiphany, then within it the grass's speech is a theophany and echoing it Whitman's speech a prophecy, the line of transmission that secures the truth of scripture.

The securing of the truth of scripture by no means implies a rigid or priestly following of the order. It is precisely the revolutionary out-speaking of the poetic mode of prophecy that secures the transmission. The triplet of epiphany, theophany and prophecy folds voice through voice through voice – the speaking-through jumping portal to portal, from tongue to tongue to tongue. Prophecy comes as a voice from Outside, as Maurice Blanchot well knew.[19] What makes Whitman's guessing at grasses prophetic is not that it predicts anything, but rather that it joins a larger prophetic tradition outside America. Gardiner emphasises that Whitman was urging his prophetic voice forth, speaking precisely to the revolutionary traditions of Spiritualism, from Swedenborg to the Shakers to Blake. As to "what

---

17   André D. Neher, "Speech and Silence in Prophecy", *Dor le Dor* 6, no. 2 (Winter 1977–8): 61–73.
18   Walt Whitman, *Leaves of Grass, Comprehensive Reader's Edition*, ed. Harold W. Blodgett and Sculley Bradley (New York: W.W. Norton & Company, 1965), 52.
19   Maurice Blanchot, *The Book to Come*, trans. Charlotte Mandell (Stanford, CA: Stanford University Press, 2003).

kind of scripture" we speak of, then, it happens to be a broad array of historical influences constituting what Gardiner calls a "great spiritual revival":

> Whitman was deeply influenced by discoveries about electromagnetism, neurology, pre-Darwinian evolutionary biology, pre-Mendelian genetics, and historical linguistics that appeared to suggest that only the flimsiest barriers separated the present from the past and the living from the dead. The spiritual ramifications of these discoveries were first codified in the early 1840s in New York State by several pioneers of what soon became Spiritualism, the most important among them Andrew Jackson Davis, an admirer of the Shakers and follower of the Swedish mystic Emanuel Swedenborg, as was the English religious poet William Blake. Davis believed that "Death is a chemical strainer, a sieve through which individuals are passed on to their stations in the summer land." This is the great spiritual revival to which Whitman so hoped his prophetic poem would give proper voice. And Hooper and Spielberg's *Poltergeist* is a late, despondent echo of this great revival.

From Swedenborg, Yeats too derives a prophetic poetics, but the revival to which Whitman was speaking in Blake is the most striking. Surely there is no Whitmanian America without Blake's America. Blake's America connects to other regions in global hemispheric space – Europe, Africa, Asia – and is prophetic (social-prophetic) precisely because it praises and critiques revolution, carrying within itself a theory and poetic mythos of all revolution inseparable from its prophetism. Yet the transmission of the poet-prophetic tradition, let us not forget, requires recognition, critical recognition in the first place: Gardiner's critical recognition of such a tradition is the first leap towards it. To prophetic literature Gardiner can prophetically speak. This is entirely divorced from canon-making, which cannot conceive of it. We have reason to believe the prophetic tradition as such is not limited to any particular historical age at all, nor any one medium. Gardiner draws Hooper and Spielberg's *Poltergeist* (1982) into the prophetic tradition.[20] Likewise I consider Rochelle Owens a contemporary living example of a poet-prophet who, in poems like "W.C. Fields in French Light" (1986)[21] but also in more recent works of hers, gives full voice to this great revival. We have a tradition to wrest from conformism, not one to conserve.

The prophetic tradition, a revolutionary one and a critical one, is poorly understood in our time, most probably because we don't live in a prophetic age (though we may ever be on the edge of one). It is a tradition which requires revolution to restore its truthful transmission. I wish that all those who have been exposed to the teachings of Bruce Gardiner will carry on the revolutionary traditions they have come into contact with, and that prophet-critics and

---

20   Tobe Hooper (Dir.) and Steven Spielberg (Prod.). *Poltergeist* (Beverly Hills: Metro-Goldwyn-Mayer Studios, 1982).

21   Rochelle Owens, *W.C. Fields in French Light* (New York: Contact II Publications, 1986).

prophet-poets will advance liberally, without bad encumbrance and yet with good moderation, when times call for them to do so. Carried on the tide of these traditions, we have a sure way to the production of new, visionary readings. It will happen between recognition and judgement, between reflection and direct contact. As Frye said in *The Secular Scripture*, and please allow me to repeat it one more time, if the critic is to recognise the prophetic, the critic "needs to be prophetic too". Whether our model is John the Baptist, Amos, Swedenborg, Whitman, Blake, Frye, or indeed Bruce Gardiner, our challenge now is to turn judgement back into recognition, tradition into revolution.

Bibliography

Benjamin, Walter. *Illuminations*. New York: Schocken Books, 1969.

Blanchot, Maurice. *The Book to Come*. Trans. Charlotte Mandell. Stanford, CA: Stanford University Press, 2003.

Connell, Raewyn. *The Good University: What Universities Actually Do and Why It's Time for Radical Change*. London: Zed Books, 2019.

Frye, Northrop. *The Secular Scripture and Other Writings on Critical Theory, 1976–1991*. Toronto: University of Toronto Press, 2005.

Gadamer, Hans-Georg. *Truth and Method*. Trans. Joel Weinsheimer and Donald G. Marshall. London: Continuum, 1975.

Gallop, Jane. "The Historicization of Literary Studies and the Fate of Close Reading." *Profession* (2007): 181–6.

Gardiner, Bruce. "Lectures on American poetry" (unpublished scripts), 2020.

Hartman, Geoffrey. *Minor Prophecies: The Literary Essay in the Culture Wars*. Cambridge, MA: Harvard University Press, 1991.

Hooper, Tobe (Dir.) and Steven Spielberg (Prod.). *Poltergeist*. Beverly Hills: Metro-Goldwyn-Mayer Studios, 1982.

Kermode, Frank. *An Appetite for Poetry*. Cambridge, MA: Harvard University Press, 1989.

MacCabe, Colin. "Towards a Modern Trivium – English Studies Today." *Critical Quarterly* 26, no. 1–2 (March 1984): 69–82.

Marx, Karl. "Der 18te Brumaire des Louis Napoleon (1852)," in *Karl Marx and Friedrich Engels Werke, Band 8*. Berlin: Dietz Verlag, 1960.

Neher, André D. "Speech and Silence in Prophecy." *Dor le Dor* 6.2 (Winter 1977–8): 61–73.

Owens, Rochelle. *W.C. Fields in French Light*. New York: Contact II Publications, 1986.

Patai, Daphne, and Wilfrido H. Corral. *Theory's Empire: An Anthology of Dissent*. New York: Columbia University Press, 2005.

Rajan, Tilottama. *The Supplement of Reading: Figures of Understanding in Romantic Theory and Practice*. Ithaca, NY: Cornell University Press, 1990.

Raz, Yosefa. "Untuning Walt Whitman's Prophetic Voice." *Walt Whitman Quarterly Review* 36, no. 1 (September 2018): 1–26.

Schleiermacher, Friedrich Daniel Ernst. *Hermeneutics and Criticism, And Other Writings*. Trans. Andrew Bowie. Cambridge: Cambridge University Press, 1998.

Spivak, Gayatri Chakravorty. *Death of a Discipline*. New York: Columbia University Press, 2003.

Walzer, Michael. *Interpretation and Social Criticism*. Cambridge, MA: Harvard University Press, 1987.

3

They Danced by the Light of the Moon: Edward Lear, Bruce Gardiner and Learning Ways to Mean

Christopher Richardson

In Stefan Zweig's 1927 novella *Confusion*, a venerable German scholar of literature learns he will be celebrated in a *Festschrift* to mark thirty years of academic teaching. "They meant well, my students and colleagues in the Faculty," Roland ruminates. Perusing the contents of this handsomely bound volume, he adds:

> I now scan these pages with the same pride as did the schoolboy whose report from his teachers first indicated that he had the requisite ability and strength of mind for an academic career. And yet: when I had leafed through the two hundred industrious pages and looked my intellectual reflection in the eye, I couldn't help smiling … I who have spent a lifetime depicting human beings in the light of their work, portraying the intrinsic intellectual structure of their worlds, was made aware again from my own experience of the impenetrability in every human life of the true core of its being, the malleable cell from which all growth proceeds.[1]

Thus begins Roland's spectacular confession, as Zweig's narrator retraces his spiritual and intellectual formation, in particular the influence of his own great mentor and teacher. Unlike our revered narrator Roland, this man – we are told – goes unremembered now, except, of course, in the pages of Roland's testimonial (now in the reader's hands). Zweig's darkly comic novel traces the brief but intense friendship between the two men: the wayward undergraduate and his charismatic teacher. The simmering *eros* of their intellectual union culminates with the young man sleeping with his professor's wife and ends with a cathartic parting kiss between the two. In the final lines of Zweig's novella, Roland confesses to the reader that, "I have more to thank him for than my mother and father before him or my wife and children after him. I have never loved anyone more."[2]

---

1   Stefan Zweig, *Confusion*, trans. Anthea Bell (London: Pushkin Press, 2017), 7–8.
2   Zweig, *Confusion*, 153.

As the Calvinist American author Marilynne Robinson explains in "A Theology of the Present Moment" in the *New York Review of Books*, the seventeenth-century English Puritan theologian and writer John Flavel believed that "we will be judged twice, once when we die and once when everything we have said or done has had its final effect".[3] We understand this idea in a secular sense today, as we reflect upon the impact of our human actions on the fragile health of our environment and climate. Even those without a palpable sense of eschatology may feel Flavel's words ring true when we imagine our lasting impact on family, friends, colleagues, peers, and even strangers. For teachers, this "final effect" is traceable for generations yet to come. Education lifts individuals, families and communities from poverty, increases health and life expectancy, strengthens economies and states. Beyond the gaze of maps, graphs and statistics, teachers daily bring meaning and purpose to human lives. So it was for the two great teachers of Zweig's novella, whether publicly celebrated in a *Festschrift* like Roland, or in the quiet devotion of the old scholar as he recalls the one who kindled the fires of his own understanding. I hope that Bruce will, like Roland, read the pages of his *Festschrift* with schoolboy pride. I would not presume to reveal the impenetrable "true core" of any man, but instead propose to share what Bruce means to me.

In 2001, I commenced my undergraduate studies at the University of Sydney. Against the wishes of my more ambitious high school masters, I spent my substantial Universities Admission Index – as the Australian Tertiary Admission Rank (ATAR) was then known – to enrol in a Bachelor of Arts and majored in English literature, instead of pursuing the Law degree that many of my peers preferred. Many are now happily ex-lawyers and a few became English teachers too. I had been warned to expect less warmth and personal attention from university teachers than I was accustomed to getting from school teachers, and early lectures with hundreds of other similarly lost undergraduates felt much like drowning in cold seas. There were prowling posses of preternaturally assured first-year English students, striding through the John Woolley Building, brandishing the works of Martin Amis and Bret Easton Ellis like talismans of literary masculinity, or extravagantly (re-)reading *Ulysses* in readiness for Bloomsday. Yet soon I found my tribe. I recall sitting in the back row of the lecture theatre and exchanging scribbled lines in Entish with a brilliant young peer who would become Dr Olivia Murphy, one of Australia's great Austen scholars. Soon I would befriend the future Dr Timothy Hanna, Dr Tessa Lunney, Dr Hannah Croke, Dr Phil Johnson, Dr Sascha Morrell. How strange to write these words two decades on and think of all those seeds sown in the minds of our eighteen-year-old selves! Like many of this cohort, I regard my four years in the Woolley Building as among the happiest of my life, and our Honours Year an *annus mirabilis*.

---

3   Marilynne Robinson, "A Theology of the Present Moment", *New York Review of Books*, 22 December 2022.

Lifelong friendships were forged in the Woolley Building's cranial labyrinth, yet it took longer to discern which lecturers and teachers would claim our hearts and minds. I wish I could recall the first time I heard Bruce teach, but I suspect it was when he appeared as a guest lecturer in one of my first-year subjects. Now, as then, I am a hypersensitive learner. Like a young child, restless, even sleepless, at the prospect of a looming birthday party, or a lover restless, sleepless, at the thought of their beloved's return, I still find myself flushed and trembling when I encounter words that move me deeply. At times I hear Young Werther's cry for help, "You ask if you shall send me books. My dear friend, I beseech you, for the love of God, relieve me from such a yoke! I need no more to be guided, agitated, heated."[4] Zweig captures this exhausting rapture, as the ageing scholar Roland recalls the spiritual intoxication and visceral punch of his own beloved teacher's first lecture on Shakespeare and the Elizabethan Stage. Decades later, Roland still recalls how, "I felt I had been pierced to the heart … I felt the blood hot in my veins, my breath came faster, that racing rhythm throbbed through my body, seizing impatiently on every joint in it."[5] Returning to his apartment transformed, the young Roland turned to *Coriolanus* as if for the first time. As he recalled:

> A new world suddenly opened up on the printed page before me, the words moved vigorously towards me as if they had been seeking me for centuries; the verse coursed through my veins in a fiery torrent, carrying me away, inducing the same strange sense of relaxation behind the brow as one feels in a dream of flight. I shook, I trembled, I felt the hot surge of my blood like a fever – I had never had such an experience before, yet I had done nothing but listen to an impassioned lecture … passionate as I was by nature, I had discovered a new passion, one which has remained with me to the present day: a desire to share my enjoyment of all earthly delights in the inspired poetic word.[6]

It was Bruce's rumination on the works of Lewis Carroll that pierced my heart. It sounds strange to write it now, but that was the first time I had heard anyone take writing for children seriously. I recall introducing myself to Bruce at the end of his lecture to offer my thanks. Did he sense the change his words had wrought in me? That night I re-read *Alice's Adventures in Wonderland* with fresh eyes, yearning to discern its mysteries and secrets. Bruce's teaching pushed me to think deeply about the nature and development of children's literature and its relationship to education, psychology, and shifting social and political attitudes to childhood. I devoured Philippe Ariès *Centuries of Childhood* for the first time and delved into the work of Iona and Peter Opie and their delightful "ethnographies" of childhood

---

4   J.W. Goethe, *The Sorrows of Young Werther*, trans. R.D. Boylan (Urbana, IL: Project Gutenberg, [1854] 2009).
5   Zweig, *Confusion*, 30.
6   Zweig, *Confusion*, 36.

through an exploration of schoolyard rhymes and games. Around that time, my first writing for children was published, a series of non-fiction picture books for primary-school aged readers. These books were commissioned works and did not reflect any abiding literary passions, except the thrill of seeing my name in print for the first time. I was also hard at work on a draft of what would become my debut novel for young readers, *Empire of the Waves* (Penguin), although it would take more than a decade to see that book to publication. Captivated and not a little intimidated at that time, I enrolled in the first course I was able to select that came under Bruce's purview. To this day, the Course Reader for Bruce's "Children's Cultures: Learning Ways to Mean" still lies close at hand to my writing desk, not as a memento, but a touchstone and a guide. It was during that course that Bruce transformed my understanding of childhood and the thematic and linguistic possibilities of literature for young people. And it was then that I resolved my "long essay", or "honours thesis" as we portentously preferred to called it, would explore these questions further.

In my maturity I agree with British geologist Herbert Harold Read's dictum that "the best geologist is he who has seen the most rocks". I read widely in the hope of becoming a better reader, writer and teacher. Yet in my subject choices for my undergraduate degree, my youthful prejudices were on spectacular display. With some notable exceptions, writing from the twentieth century was out, especially the latter half of the century, and most especially anything postmodern.

I recall entering Bruce's green office – a place seemingly as immaculate as the man himself and visually at odds with the Woolley Building's uniformly drab aesthetic – to ask whether he would consent to be my supervisor for my honours thesis. And I recall his delighted *yes*. Lewis Carroll was already the subject of a vast body of impressive scholarship, his work fastidiously annotated by the brilliant mathematician and writer Martin Gardiner, so I would explore the works of that other great purveyor of nonsense, Edward Lear, author of *A Book of Nonsense* (1846) and *Nonsense Songs* (1872). Lear had been the subject of biographies by Vivien Noakes and Peter Levi, yet there was soil to be tilled. In his lifetime (1812–1888), Lear had drawn the praise and friendship of the Tennysons and Wilkie Collins and other giants of his age. John Ruskin had named Lear's *A Book of Nonsense* as his favourite book and, as the pre-eminent ornithological draughtsman of his day, Lear was invited to teach young Victoria to paint. During the twentieth century, W.H. Auden, George Orwell, G.K. Chesterton and Anthony Burgess all penned appreciations of Lear. And yet, compared to the kaleidoscopic infinities of Carrolliana, Lear remained largely untouched by academia and Hollywood alike (for which we can be thankful). Even then, the affinities between Bruce and Lear subliminally stirred inside me, although I would not have dared to air them. As Humphrey Carpenter wrote of Lear's revolutionary early writing, "a lone voice was beginning to mutter, chiefly into the ears of children. Its message was that the public world was vindictive and intolerant and that the man of vision, the true artist, must alienate himself from society and pursue a private dream."[7] Like Lear's poetry, Bruce's teaching proved a playful refuge from a vindictive and intolerant public world, yet neither dream would be entirely private. Transcendence from the world is not retreat, as the legion of future teachers who emerged transformed by Bruce's pedagogy will attest.

Challenging the didacticism of popular mid-nineteenth-century English children's literature, Lear had set himself in opposition to the Rev. Isaac Watts and Charles and Mary Lamb. Lear published *A Book of Nonsense* pseudonymously as the "Old Derry Down Derry", a character from the mummers' plays, the first of his many holy fools. Lear did not write to promote the "all-endearing cleanliness" beloved by the Lambs, nor did he yearn to teach children to "love working and reading", like the industrious and pious Watts. Rather, Lear's Derry writes because he "loved to see little folks merry".[8] As Bruce noted in one of our many illuminating conversations about Lear, there were echoes here of William Blake, whose "Laughing Song" in *Songs of Innocence* had portrayed children's laughter resounding in what seems to be the world to come. As Blake writes, "Come live, and be merry, and join with me / To sing the sweet chorus of 'Ha ha he!'".[9] Blake imagines peals of laughter in defiance of the mortal darkness enveloping so many of the children in his poems. Annihilating forces prowl the pages of *A Book of Nonsense*, depicted as an all-seeing and all-judging *They*. In a typical example, the Old Person of Buda is destroyed for his disruptive behaviour.

> There was an Old Person of Buda,
> Whose conduct grew ruder and ruder;
> Till at last, with a hammer, they silenced his clamour.
> By smashing that Person of Buda.[10]

Lear's words offer no details of the Old Person's conduct, yet his illustration depicts the man standing on one leg. For Lear, this simple act was a symbol of all non-conformist behaviour, writing to his friend Fanny Coombe that "the uniform apathetic tone assumed by lofty society irks me *dreadfully* … [there is] nothing I long for half so much as to giggle heartily and to hop on one leg down the great gallery – but I dare not."[11] For no more a crime than this, the Old Person is marked for destruction. Whereas Sir John Tenniel's illustrations meticulously materialised Carroll's world in *Alice's Adventures in Wonderland*, Lear's drawings frequently disrupt his text. He was, like William Blake, a brilliant innovator as an

---

7   Humphrey Carpenter, *Secret Gardens: The Golden Age of Children's Literature* (London: Allen & Unwin, 1985), 11.
8   Vivien Noakes, ed., *Edward Lear: The Complete Verse & Other Nonsense* (London: Penguin Books, 2001), 71.
9   William Blake, *Songs of Innocence and Experience* (Urbana, IL: Project Gutenberg, [1901] 2009).
10   Noakes, ed., *Edward Lear: Complete Verse*, 93.
11   Jackie Wullschläger, *Inventing Wonderland* (London: Methuen, 2001), 72.

author-illustrator. Lear writes, for example, that the Old Man of Ancona "found a small dog with no owner", whilst the dog, as drawn, is terrifyingly large.[12]

If adult language in Victorian England was governed by grammar, decorum and an imperial immutability, then language in Lear's disruptive childhood realm was exuberant, dynamic, malleable and elusive. Notice the disdain on the onlooker's face in Lear's illustration as the Old Person of Wick explodes with a nonsensical, "Tick-a-Tick, Tick-a-Tick / Chickabee, Chickabaw".[13] Lear's characters are doomed to live and die behind the bars of the limerick's claustrophobic five-line structure, scrutinised like specimens in a museum or zoo, whilst the reader becomes complicit in the gaze of the destructive *They*. Consider the fate of the Old Man of Whitehaven, "smashed" because he "danced a quadrille with a Raven".[14] There is no question, of course, where Lear's sympathies lie. Lear's poetry seeks the dignity of the outsider, understanding, like Montaigne, that "what we call monstrosities are not so to God".[15] Perhaps the most peculiar assembly of characters in English literary history, *A Book of Nonsense* constitutes Lear's very own *festum stultorum*, a Rabelaisian jamboree of holy fools and rebels. Lear was sceptical of efforts to "explain" his verse and protested that "critics are very silly to see politics in such bosh",[16] yet the mere creation of Lear's poetry was a revolutionary act in the history of English language children's literature.

Death haunts Lear's limericks, yet there is another side to Lear's nonsense. Equally radical, Lear's later poetry offered up a vision of emancipation. Whereas Blake had moved from innocence to experience, Lear's vision seemed to lighten with the drift of time. Despite his chronically poor physical and mental health, Lear travelled widely in Italy, Malta, Corfu, Albania, Egypt, Greece, Palestine and Lebanon, always sketching, painting, writing and making new friends. Lear's most famous nonsense song, "The Owl and the Pussy-cat", was composed in Cannes, and in 1870 Lear purchased a home in San Remo, where he would pass his final years. Lear's later poetry is drenched in sunlight. Unlike Blake, Lear did not have to wait for the coming of the *eschaton* to dwell in the light of Heaven. To Emily Tennyson in 1865 Lear wrote: "I loathe London by the time [I] have been here a month. The walking – sketching – exploring – noveltyperceiving and beautyappreciating part of the Landscape painter's life is undoubtedly to be envied … the contrast of the moneytrying to get, smokydark London life – fuss – trouble & bustle is wholly odious, & every year more so."[17]

"The Owl and the Pussy-cat" is a tale of star-crossed lovers. One expects less serenading and more carnage. Yet Lear's lovers set sail in a "beautiful pea-green

---

12   Noakes, ed., *Edward Lear: Complete Verse*, 363.
13   Noakes, ed., *Edward Lear: Complete Verse*, 338.
14   Noakes, ed., *Edward Lear: Complete Verse*, 172.
15   Michel de Montaigne, *The Essays of Montaigne*, trans. E.J. Trenchman (London: Oxford University Press, 1927), 161.
16   Vivien Noakes, ed., *Edward Lear: Selected Letters* (Oxford: Oxford University Press, 1988), 228.
17   Noakes, ed., *Edward Lear: Selected Letters*, 204–205.

boat", become engaged, and are married by a Turkey in the "land where the Bong-tree grows".

> They dined on mince, and slices of quince,
> Which they ate with a runcible spoon;
> And hand in hand, on the edge of the sand,
> They danced by the light of the moon,
> The moon,
> The moon,
> They danced by the light of the moon.[18]

Lear's later *Nonsense Songs* brims with such rapturous escapes. Thus does the Quangle Wangle find bliss with his companions upon the Crumpetty Tree, where "at night by the light of the Mulberry moon / They danced to the Flute of the Blue Baboon".[19] Yet even in Lear's later songs, the constricting "They" seeks to reassert its hegemony of good manners. The spirited Nutcrackers and Sugar-tongs are mocked for their "awful delusion" by a scolding Frying-pan,[20] whilst the Jumblies depart home "in spite of all their friends could say".[21] Lear's sieve-as-boat is the ultimate metaphor for the impossible dream made possible by the sheer determination of the dreamer. The revolution, impossible in Lear's limericks, is finally fulfilled. There is something divine in the vision of love and reconciliation in the later songs of Edward Lear, recalling Isaiah's prophesy of that holy day when "the leopard shall lie down with the kid; and the calf and the young lion and the fatling together … the lion shall eat straw like the ox". Reflecting on "The Owl and the Pussy-cat", Anthony Burgess wrote that "[Its] joy is unqualified … the grace of a great light in the sky and an eternal ocean – on whose verge the bridal pair dare to dance – sanctifies all impossibilities. Life is bigger than Victorian England. Nonsense means what we cannot understand. God is nonsense."[22]

There is deep truth in nonsense, so it is unsurprising that many of the most radical and innovative writers of the twentieth century embraced Lear and Carroll. In his essay "The Precession of the Simulacra", Jean Baudrillard recalled Jorge Luis Borges' one-paragraph short story "On Exactitude in Science" in which an imperial power seeks to design a map on a scale of 1 to 1. As Borges writes:

> In that Empire, the Art of Cartography attained such Perfection that the map of a single Province occupied the entirety of a City, and the map of the Empire, the entirety of a Province. In time, those Unconscionable Maps no longer satisfied, and

---

18 Noakes, ed., *Edward Lear: Complete Verse*, 238.
19 Noakes, ed., *Edward Lear: Complete Verse*, 392.
20 Noakes, ed., *Edward Lear: Complete Verse*, 273.
21 Noakes, ed., *Edward Lear: Complete Verse*, 253–256.
22 Anthony Burgess, *Homage to Qwert Yuiop: Selected Journalism 1978–1985* (London: Abacus, 1987), 303.

the Cartographers Guilds struck a Map of the Empire whose size was that of the Empire, and which coincided point for point with it.[23]

Baudrillard called Borges' tale "the finest allegory of simulation", depicting a world in which systems of knowledge and classification replace reality itself.[24] Of course, Baudrillard's frightening contention was that the map today precedes the territory itself, that in our postmodern age there is no longer any underlying truth at all. More hopefully, Borges foresees a time when the map is ultimately deemed "Useless", antithetical to feeling and the complexity of truth. The map is seen as "not without some Pitilessness". Animals and beggars now dwell in the ruins of the map in the barren "Deserts of the West". Borges concludes by noting that "in all the Land there is no other Relic of the Disciplines of Geography".[25] The map lies broken and discarded in the desert sands like Shelley's Ozymandias, the relic of a fallen empire and a once hegemonic way of seeing.

Borges borrowed this striking vision of mapmaking as an instrument of imperial control from Lewis Carroll's 1893 novel *Sylvie and Bruno Concluded*. Meeting a strange Germanic visitor from another world called Mein Herr, Carroll's narrator, the Historian from London, learns of a land where the art of mapmaking has been elevated to the highest science:

> "That's another thing we've learned from your Nation," said Mein Herr, "map-making. But we've carried it much further than you. What do you consider the largest map that would be really useful?"
>
> "About six inches to the mile."
>
> "Only six inches!" exclaimed Mein Herr. "We very soon got to six yards to the mile. Then we tried a hundred yards to the mile. And then came the grandest idea of all! We actually made a map of the country, on the scale of a mile to the mile!"
>
> "Have you used it much?" I enquired.
>
> "It has never been spread out, yet," said Mein Herr: "the farmers objected: they said it would cover the whole country, and shut out the sunlight!"[26]

It is a Romantic notion lingering in Carroll's late Victorian vision of a world consumed with the pursuit of scientific rationality, that the *farmers* might object to the rolling out of this all-seeing map. Writing in the aftermath of the Darwinian revolution, Carroll was also attuned to the dangers of eugenics. It is no coincidence that Mein Herr's world is as preoccupied with the mapping and control of human bodies as it is with the mapping of terrain.

---

23   Jorge Luis Borges, *Collected Fictions*, trans. Andrew Hurley (London: Penguin, 1998), 325.
24   Jean Baudrillard, *Simulations*, trans. Paul Foss, Paul Patton and Philip Beitchman (New York: Semiotext(e), 1983), 1.
25   Borges, *Collected Fictions*, 325.
26   Lewis Carroll, *Sylvie and Bruno Concluded* (Urbana, IL: Project Gutenberg, [1893] 2015), 169.

"In my country," said Mein Herr, "no one is ever drowned."

"Is there no water deep enough?"

"Plenty! But we can't sink. We are all lighter than water. Let me explain," he added, seeing my look of surprise. "Suppose you desire a race of pigeons of a particular shape or colour, do you not select, from year to year, those that are nearest to the shape or colour you want, and keep those, and part with the others?"

"We do," I replied. "We call it 'Artificial Selection.'"

"Exactly so," said Mein Herr. "Well, we have practised that for some centuries – constantly selecting the lightest people: so that, now, everybody is lighter than water."[27]

Mein Herr adds that in a further millennium of scientific breeding, his people expect to be lighter than air itself. That Baudrillard should draw from Borges who drew in turn from Carroll is not surprising. The nonsense of Lewis Carroll and his predecessor Edward Lear remain prophetic. Both exposed the cruelty and hypocrisies of a society that sought – and seeks – to impose its totalising pursuit of knowledge on bodies, minds and language. There is no mercy in the map. To be free, Lear's characters must leave and cross the waves to reach the light of the Jelly Bo Lee and Great Gromboolian Plain, to lands beyond the map itself.

In preparation for my contribution to this *festschrift*, I revisited my honours thesis for the first time in years. I have sought to excavate some key ideas, to close one loop between the present and the past. I find myself writing in the company of my earlier selves, writing in the company of Bruce Gardiner and Edward Lear. One thing that struck me most was the absence of theoretical maps in my thesis, what in my Master's degree and PhD in the social sciences we would call "a framework of analysis". Although there is much secondary literature cited in my thesis – too much I now believe! – that long essay was, above all, a personal encounter between myself and Edward Lear. As Georges Poulet writes of the alchemy of reading:

In short, the extraordinary fact in the case of a book is the falling away of the barriers between you and it. You are inside it; it is inside you; there is no longer either outside or inside … I realise that what I hold in my hands is no longer just an object, or even simply a living thing. I am aware of a rational being, of a consciousness; the consciousness of another, no different from the one I automatically assume in every human being I encounter, except that in this case the consciousness is open to me, welcomes me, lets me look deep inside itself, and even allows me, with unheard-of licence, to think what it thinks and feel what it feels … There is only once place left for this new existence: my innermost self.[28]

---

27 Carroll, *Sylvie and Bruno Concluded*, 165.
28 Georges Poulet, "Phenomenology of Reading", *New Literary History* 1, no. 1 (October 1969): 54.

Not coincidentally, it was Bruce who introduced me to Poulet. Perhaps our words bring us closer to the true core of one another's being than the narrator of Zweig's novella will allow.

So many of Bruce's former students share the memory of the care he took in crafting feedback through his elegantly penned epistles on our papers. He engaged our work as we sought to engage his words and the novels and poems we read together. The loyalty and love that this inspired transformed minds into deeper and more generous thinkers and, I believe, inspired deeper and more generous lives. Such an encounter between consciousness and consciousness is what elevated Bruce's teaching to the sublime. At a time when reading and writing are increasingly reduced to the technology of neoliberalism – assessed in Australian schools through the microscope of standardised testing such as NAPLAN – a Gardinerian re-enchantment is urgently required. The idolatry of data is the madness of the map, as Borges and Carroll understood. The fact that Bruce, of all teachers, was compelled for so many years to actively justify his role at a university obsessed with data instead of the testimony of peers and students sums up the tragedy unfolding in our places of education this century. But if the old seventeenth-century Puritan John Flavel is right and we are judged a final time when all that we have said and done has had its last effect, then Bruce's teaching will keep the light of learning burning for a long time yet. In "Edward Lear", Auden wrote of Lear's flight from the "the legions of cruel inquisitive They". The poet crossed seas to find his peace, then "children swarmed to him like settlers. He became a land."[29] Bruce offered me and so many students an education forged in love, intelligence, integrity, and the opening of one mind to another. For me, as for so many, Bruce too "became a land".

Bibliography

Auden, W.H. *Collected Shorter Poems: 1927–1957*. London: Faber and Faber, 1966.

Baudrillard, Jean. *Simulations*. Trans. Paul Foss, Paul Patton and Philip Beitchman. New York: Semiotext(e), 1983.

Blake, William. *Songs of Innocence and Experience*. Urbana, IL: Project Gutenberg, [1901] 2009. https://www.gutenberg.org/ebooks/1934.

Borges, Jorge Luis. *Collected Fictions*. Trans. Andrew Hurley. London: Penguin, 1998.

Burgess, Anthony. *Homage To Qwert Yuiop: Selected Journalism 1978–1985*. London: Abacus, 1987.

Carpenter, Humphrey. *Secret Gardens: The Golden Age of Children's Literature*. London: Allen & Unwin, 1985.

Carroll, Lewis. *Sylvie and Bruno Concluded*. Urbana, IL: Project Gutenberg, [1893] 2015. https://www.gutenberg.org/ebooks/48795.

Goethe, J.W. *The Sorrows of Young Werther*. Trans. R.D. Boylan. Urbana, IL: Project Gutenberg, [1854] 2009. https://www.gutenberg.org/ebooks/2527.

Montaigne, Michel de. *The Essays of Montaigne*. Trans. E.J. Trenchman. London: Oxford University Press, 1927.

---

29   W.H. Auden, *Collected Shorter Poems: 1927–1957* (London: Faber and Faber, 1966), 127.

Noakes, Vivien, ed. *Edward Lear: Selected Letters*. Oxford: Oxford University Press, 1988.

Noakes, Vivien, ed. *Edward Lear: The Complete Verse & Other Nonsense*. London: Penguin Books, 2001.

Poulet, Georges. "Phenomenology of Reading." *New Literary History* 1, no. 1 (October 1969): 53–68.

Richardson, Christopher. "Hagiography of the Kims and the Childhood of Saints." In *Change and Continuity in North Korean Politics*. Eds. Christopher Green and Adam Cathcart, 123–49. London: Routledge, 2016.

Robinson, Marilynne. "A Theology of the Present Moment." *New York Review of Books*, 22 December 2022.

Wullschläger, Jackie. *Inventing Wonderland*. London: Methuen, 2001.

Zweig, Stefan. *Confusion*. Trans. Anthea Bell. London: Pushkin Press, 2017.

4

Navigating, Networking, Nurturing: The Research, Teaching and Leadership of Bruce Gardiner

Adam Gall, Benjamin Miller, Susan E. Thomas

Introduction

The professionalisation of scholarly careers privileges metrics of success such as published outputs, grant outcomes, citations, teaching evaluation survey results, and rankings, while devaluing human-centred activities such as engaging peers in conversations about research and theory, building collegial and critical networks, and caring for and supporting colleagues. The testimonies presented in this chapter, which use methods of storytelling and cultural rhetorics to recall the impact of Bruce Gardiner's academic career, speak to those forms of scholarly work that are silenced under the dehumanised metrics of neoliberal governance. In the garishly titled *How to be an Academic Superhero*, Iain Hay astutely observes that, within the neoliberalised higher education sector, there is a "rhetoric of success" that measures "success" by focusing "first on research, then on teaching, and then, to a lesser degree, [on] community engagement and service". For Hay, "less attention, if any, is given to other estimations and components of academic success",[1] as he admirably creates a handbook on academic career development that is mindful of the need for collegiality, networking and mentoring, alongside chapters on publishing books, teaching well, and securing funding. In this chapter, we seek to amplify "other estimations" of academic success, both to point to the extraordinary career of Bruce and to highlight the potential for meaningful academic work that does not abandon the best values underpinning the humanities to appease cruel managerialism.

The harsh reality of neoliberal management was on full display in 2011, when the University of Sydney attempted to force Bruce into an "education-focused role" that would strip research time from his workload and replace it with additional teaching. The attempt was based on a crude metric: the number of published

---

1   Iain Hay, *How to be an Academic Superhero: Establishing and Sustaining a Successful Career in the Social Sciences, Arts and Humanities* (Cheltenham: Edward Elgar Publishing, 2017), 4.

articles over a designated period of time. Bruce argued audaciously that his lectures reflected the same intellectual rigour as other colleagues' research outputs, and that his research allocation was necessary to maintain the exceptional quality of his teaching. While meetings were held to discuss Bruce's "value" to the university, rallies, demonstrations, letters and petitions were organised by current and former students and local and international colleagues. The "Save Bruce" campaign ultimately worked, but Bruce faced a similar challenge from management in 2014, again successfully resisting demands to compartmentalise teaching, research and service, and remaining on the standard "40/40/20" academic contract until he retired. This chapter considers the connectedness of teaching, research and mentorship in the exemplary career of Bruce Gardiner.

Context, Method and Outline

The modern university exists under conditions of neoliberalism that increase pressure on staff and drive a sense of hopelessness that the humanities is not marketable and, therefore, has a limited future. While David Shumway cautions that neoliberalism is not the root of all problems in higher education, it simply exacerbates pre-existing problems,[2] many academics see the prevailing practices of neoliberal management – casualisation, workload intensification, increased job precarity (undermining tenure, for example), and economic "value-based" assessment of programs and individuals – simultaneously as the source of workplace anxiety and the catalyst for a modern crisis in the humanities. Zoe Hope Bulaitis describes the shift in university culture under neoliberalism as a change from social service to production:

> Nineteenth-century liberal education sought to cultivate a society of individuals equipped with faculties for making moral choices and living meaningful lives, whereas contemporary neoliberal higher education redefines individuals primarily as consumers of education. There has been a shift whereby the freedom of an individual has been transformed into an individual's freedom of choice, in a free market of economic opportunity.[3]

For staff, the change entails a shift from a vision of academic teachers and researchers as guides, mentors and critics who improve the lives of individuals and communities to an expectation that teachers and researchers produce marketable education and research and attract external funding. Shumway articulates the dire

---

2   David Shumway, "The University, Neoliberalism, and the Humanities: A History", *Humanities (Basel)* 6, no. 4 (2017): 91.

3   Zoe Hope Bulaitis, *Value and the Humanities: The Neoliberal University and Our Victorian Inheritance*, Palgrave Studies in Literature, Culture and Economics (Cham: Springer International, 2020), 8.

effect on humanities as follows: "Because neoliberalism rejects the very idea of 'not-for-profit' and insists that all values must be measured by the market, the humanities appear valueless."[4] Obviously, when we speak of the humanities, we speak both of the range of disciplines, knowledge and methods for investigation and of the people who practise in and develop these fields of study; when the humanities are devalued, so are humanities academics.

While it is difficult to ascribe motivations to widespread economic, political and managerial trends, there is a sense that diminishing the value of research and teaching in the humanities preserves neoliberal ideology. Judith Butler, for example, suggests that:

> The humanities are underfunded precisely because they represent values that challenge the hegemony of neoliberalism and its market metrics. We should perhaps allow that critique to live. And though some skeptics maintain that critique is destructive and purely negative, they tend not to understand the relation between critique and dissent, the power of the imagination to think beyond the status quo, to establish a critical distance on neoliberalism, and to open up possibilities precisely when the felt sense of the world is dire. If we can imagine beyond the fiscal realism of the present, then we are already practitioners of the humanities.[5]

For Butler, the ability of humanities research and scholarship to foster creative thinking is vital for an innovative, free society, and the antithesis of neoliberal management of education. Of course, Butler is not the first to suggest that neoliberalism opposes the kinds of creative thinking fostered by a study of the humanities. In fact, others argue that the style of creativity and analysis encouraged by research and teaching in the humanities can undermine neoliberalism. As Bulaitis recommends, "humanities scholars should be attentive to alternative indicators that might open up new possibilities in the articulation of value".[6] Taken together, the ideas of Butler and Bulaitis suggest that the development of creative approaches to questions of knowledge and value might be, at the same time, the reason neoliberal management strangles the humanities and the saving grace of the humanities.

Any attempt to challenge neoliberal tendencies in the valuation of the humanities – its disciplines and its people – confronts a dominant and powerful ideology. Fortunately, the field of Rhetoric and Writing Studies has for some time been developing and mapping methods for communication that stand against dominant systems. Malea Powell and her colleagues, for example, in a formative article "Constellating Cultural Rhetorics", articulate a new methodology that decentres

---

4   Shumway, "The University, Neoliberalism, and the Humanities: A History", 90.
5   Judith Butler, "The Public Futures of the Humanities", *Daedalus* 151, no. 3 (2022): 49.
6   Bulaitis, *Value and the Humanities*, 113.

dominant status quo discourses. As a methodology, cultural rhetorics led to the creation of a dedicated journal, *Constellations*, and encompasses a range of multimodal, creative, cross-disciplinary, story- and autobiography-based analyses and reflections that question how value is articulated within specific cultures. In the words of Powell and colleagues, cultural rhetorics reveal and recontextualise "power relationships" by identifying how "practices – ways of thinking, ways of problem solving, ways of being in the world – are valued (or not) within specific cultural systems and/or communities".[7] In the context of an analysis of the influence of neoliberalism on how a scholar's career is remembered, the notion that value can be articulated differently in different cultural contexts is particularly pertinent. Further, the use of personal story and critical reflection can decentre traditional ways of writing about scholarly research, teaching and collegiality, thereby articulating the overlapping and intertwined nature of different aspects of academic life.

Key to the method of cultural rhetorics is storytelling. According to Powell and colleagues, "the practice of story is integral to doing cultural rhetorics [...] if you're not practicing story, you're doing it wrong".[8] Storytelling contributes to cultural rhetorics' objectives in many ways. In academic cultural rhetorics research, for example, storytelling techniques can introduce sources (anecdotes, experiences, conversations, sightings, sites, emotions), lines of reasoning (creative, contradictory, allegorical), and affects that are not usually validated in traditional academic writing. This can create space for writers working from various cultural backgrounds where the styles of communication and foundations for knowledge are different from those taught and practised as traditional forms of academic argument (see also Wood 2006 and Knoblauch 2001).[9] Put another way, writing and research through a cultural rhetorics method provides equal privilege to authors from backgrounds that align with dominant values in academic culture and authors whose experiences are not typically valued in academic culture. Breaking with academic conventions through the use of story can also reveal the rules and norms that university culture relies on, revealing them to be subjective, biased and blinkered, despite the appearance of objectivity and universality. In this chapter, the authors will use storytelling as a method to several ends: to decentre typically neoliberal ways of valuing academic work, to value unrecognised academic labour, to give voice to different cultures within higher education, and to add to the chorus of work that seeks to extend academic conversations beyond traditional forms of communication.

Storytelling in scholarly writing is not necessarily new, nor is it restricted to cultural rhetorics work. The genre of autoethnography, for example, has been an important method for anthropologists, feminists, cultural studies scholars and

---

7   Malea Powell, Daisy Levy, Andrea Riley-Mukavets et al., "Our Story Begins Here: Constellating Cultural Rhetorics", *Enculturation* 18 (2014): I.ii.

8   Powell et al., "Our Story Begins Here: Constellating Cultural Rhetorics", I.i.

9   Nancy Wood, *Essentials of Argument* (Saddle River, NJ: Pearson/Prentice Hall, 2006), 315; A. Abby Knoblauch, "A Textbook Argument: Definitions of Argument in Leading Composition Textbooks", *College Composition and Communication* 63, no. 2 (2011): 245.

others to document, explore and share the challenges to emotional wellbeing and career advancement. Ellis, Adams and Bochner define autoethnography as follows:

> an approach to research and writing that seeks to describe and systematically analyze personal experience in order to understand cultural experience. This approach challenges canonical ways of doing research and representing others and treats research as a political, socially-just and socially-conscious act. A researcher uses tenets of autobiography and ethnography to do and write autoethnography. Thus, as a method, autoethnography is both process and product.[10]

Adams, Jones and Ellis add that autoethnography "shows people in the process of figuring out what to do, how to live, and the meaning of their struggles".[11] One powerful outcome of autoethnography is that it creates space for the personal – the subjective – in knowledge making, not only highlighting the subjectivity of all knowledge creation but opening up the possibility of new knowledge based on lived experience.

Storytelling, on the other hand, can refer to a broader kind of alternative rhetoric. For Arthur Frank, story is the product of an inquiry that invites the reader *into* itself to engage at both emotional and rational levels with the narrator's experience.[12] The researcher-as-storyteller understands the story itself as containing analytical techniques, theory, and dialogical structures[13] which can speak for themselves:

> In a narrative analysis, storytellers emphasize that participants' stories of the self are told for the sake of others just as much as for themselves. Hence, the ethical and heartfelt claim is for a dialogic relationship with a listener […] that requires engagement from within, not analysis from outside, the story and narrative identity. Consequently, the goal and responsibility is to evoke and bear witness to a situation […] inviting the reader into a relationship, enticing people to think and feel *with* the story being told as opposed to thinking *about* it.[14]

Similarly, Laura J. Shepherd admonishes us to "bring the wholeness of [our] humanity into [our] work".[15]

---

10 Carolyn Ellis, Tony E. Adams and Arthur P. Bochner, "Autoethnography: An Overview", *Forum: Qualitative Social Research* 12, no. 1 (2011): 1.

11 Tony E. Adams, Stacy Linn Holman Jones and Carolyn Ellis, *Autoethnography*, Series in Understanding Statistics (New York: Oxford University Press, 2015), 2.

12 Arthur W. Frank, "The Standpoint of Storyteller", *Qualitative Health Research* 10, no. 3 (2000): 355.

13 Alan Bleakley, "Stories as Data, Data as Stories: Making Sense of Narrative Inquiry in Clinical Education", *Medical Education* 39, no. 5 (2005); Ellis, Adams and Bochner, "Autoethnography: An Overview", 273–90.

14 Brett Smith and Andrew C. Sparkes, "Narrative Inquiry in Psychology: Exploring the Tensions Within", *Qualitative Research in Psychology* 3, no. 3 (2006): 169–192.

It is well known that Bruce Gardiner is a teacher and scholar extraordinaire. It is less well known that he is a master storyteller, with each of his narratives serving as a portal to discovery – of knowledge, yes, but just as often as a vehicle for self-discovery, for finding some personal aspect of ourselves that informs our scholarly practice. By evoking and bearing witness to situations, Bruce invites his participants into a relationship, enticing them to think and feel *with* the story being told as opposed to thinking *about* it. The authors of this chapter, therefore, find the method of storytelling an appropriate way to honour Bruce while critiquing the prevailing academic culture that tends to devalue much of what made Bruce so influential for his students and peers.

As scholars of Rhetoric, Writing Studies, and allied fields, we are choosing a less iconised path in using a storytelling methodology, built on narrative reflection, rather than a deductive approach to argumentation. One justification can be found in Bruce's own pedagogical approach to modern and contemporary rhetoric (to which each of us has borne witness through his masterful lectures), which relies on storytelling as well as argumentation and exegesis. Another can be seen in the rhetorical theory of Chaïm Perelman and Lucie Olbrechts-Tyteca, on whose work Bruce is expert. Since our purpose here is epideictic (that is, pertaining to the present negotiation and assignation of value), we follow the lead of New Rhetoric scholars who value a broader range of argumentative techniques. As Perelman and Olbrechts-Tyteca suggest, in epideictic rhetoric, "every device of literary art is appropriate".[16] Yet, we cannot take these isolated points of reference – however authoritative – as our only cues.

One way to frame the narratives each of the authors contributes is as story-based texts that invite contemplation and consideration of the way we, as peers and colleagues, value academic work in the humanities. In inviting contemplation, we follow Bruce's own theories of analysis, prompting our readers to enter into the "maze" of textual interpretation and analysis. To posit a text as a "maze" might seem a misleading analogy given the assumed linear unfolding of text or speech before reader or audience. Yet Bruce's own suggestive choice, in an early published review,[17] of just this term illuminates something important about his own methodology as a scholar of language and literature, as well as an entry point for our own reflections as scholars of Rhetoric and Writing Studies. Bruce's choice of "maze" and not "labyrinth" suggests a pointed difference with certain other approaches to literary and rhetorical criticism, a methodological decision which we appreciate and whose implications we seek to follow. While these words are often used interchangeably, there is a persistent, if fine, distinction: a labyrinth, although

15 Laura J. Shepherd, *The Self, and Other Stories: Being, Knowing, Writing* (Blue Ridge Summit: Rowman & Littlefield Unlimited Model, 2023), xi.

16 Chaïm Perelman and Lucie Olbrechts-Tyteca, *The New Rhetoric: A Treatise on Argumentation* (Notre Dame: University of Notre Dame Press, 1969), 50.

17 See Bruce Gardiner, "E. Warwick Slinn, *Browning and the Fictions of Identity* (Book Review)" (Melbourne: Australasian Universities Language and Literature Association, 1983).

sometimes disorienting, traces a single path; a maze implies multiplicity. Because the labyrinth combines a unicursal path with turns and counter-turns, repetition with development, critics have often found in it a useful figure to associate with narrative text. Ruskin, for example, affirms this in *Fors Clavigera*, noting that Daedalus' labyrinth "has set the pattern of almost everything linear and complex".[18] Later, J. Hillis Miller links this "oxymoronic" idea of linear complexity – "the line which is not simply linear" – to realist narrative.[19]

Bruce, by contrast, wants to entertain a fuller set of possibilities for reading, scholarship, and the negotiation of meaning in general. In this, his work anticipates a wider shift towards methods of storytelling, since these methods assume a maze-like proliferation of texts and complex, situated experiences of textual practice.[20] For Bruce, these are constitutive features of communication, even if the individual reader or scholar must be more decisive about textual meaning. Indeed, in his own more direct contribution to Rhetoric and Writing Studies scholarship (an important essay on digital rhetoric from 2007), he would go on to argue that any text "is intrinsically a network of many orders"[21] and that our mental experience of this "vexed"[22] object is one variously of "play" and "assemblage". More recent innovations in digital delivery would seem to change our relationship to textuality, but these merely make more visible what was already the case (though they do, he notes, affect the material economies of text production and reception). The text, then, is more maze-like than labyrinthine; the role of the scholar or critic is more demanding than simply following a single thread, however often or sharply it turns. This also suggests a paradoxical freedom: while it is certainly possible to take numerous wrong turns and lose one's way, there is likely more than one path into and through the network. In this chapter we suggest at least three by offering three different stories of our own. The first, by Adam Gall, extends the maze (and minotaur) metaphor to examine Bruce's approaches to textual scholarship more broadly. The second, by Benjamin Miller, considers Bruce's commitment to collaborative pedagogies and guiding colleagues through the maze of professional networks. The third, by Susan Thomas, recounts Bruce's unwavering commitment to mentoring colleagues and students and helping them negotiate international and interdisciplinary mazes. Taken together, these stories work against standard

---

18 John Ruskin, *Fors Clavigera (Volume 1 of 8) Letters to the Workmen and Labourers of Great Britain* (Urbana, IL: Project Gutenberg, [1871] 2019), 407.

19 J. Hillis Miller, *Ariadne's Thread: Story Lines* (New Haven, CT: Yale University Press, 1992), 157.

20 See, for example, Ebony Elizabeth Thomas and Amy Stornaiuolo, "Restorying the Self: Bending toward Textual Justice", *Harvard Educational Review* 86, no. 3 (2016); and Anna De Fina and Sabina Perrino, *Storytelling in the Digital World (Benjamins Current Topics)* 104 (Amsterdam: John Benjamins Publishing Company, 2019).

21 Bruce Gardiner, "What's New and How New Is It? Contemporary Rhetoric, the Enlightenment, Hypertext and the Unconscious", in *What Is the New Rhetoric?*, ed. Susan E. Thomas (Newcastle-upon-Tyne: Cambridge Scholars Publishing, 2007), 35.

22 Gardiner, "What's New and How New Is It?", 37.

discourses of academic value to amplify the alternative and powerful ways of being in academia, with their myriad, divergent pathways.

Stories about Bruce Gardiner

Adam's Reflection

As a serial contract teacher and non-career researcher, my encounter with the Gardinerian method (and with Bruce's personal generosity) came later than my co-authors'. By the time I was able to work with Bruce, I had traversed several institutions and disciplines, arriving in Rhetoric and Writing Studies as a place where my interests in textual scholarship, contemporary public and popular culture, and representations of history could be brought together productively for a few semesters. After witnessing a single lecture for undergraduates, I found Bruce's perspective compelling enough to immediately want to learn more. Attending as many of his lectures as collegial decorum would allow, I also read back into Bruce's published work, which, while telling only part of his story, added a desirable bibliographic dimension to my burgeoning fandom. An early reference to the role of theory in textual inquiry (also mentioned in our introduction) frames my reflection. I will explore some dimensions of Bruce's meta-theory for textual scholarship – his approach to theory and theorising – and what it has meant for my practice as a scholar and writer.

The reference in question comes from a review of Slinn's *Browning and the Fictions of Identity*, in which Bruce firmly cautions against the resistance to theory. His reminder to Slinn (and to us): "But theory, left untended, doesn't depart. It remains as the minotaur in the maze, an ideology which will announce itself as close to the end as it can."[23] When one finds oneself in the maze of textual research (something akin, perhaps, to being alone in a dark wood at night, but somehow more urbane) it is theory that will appear as the minotaur: theory is inevitable and has a dramatic role that can't – and should not – be denied. This role in the textual drama evinces a narrative logic ("as close to the end as possible"), a logic of suspense that sets theory in an anticipatable place in the work of the scholarly reader of texts, though not in a definitely known place (that is, not "at the end"). At the same time, this narrative positioning points to theory as a likely source of pleasure – both narrative pleasure and, perhaps, other kinds of textual pleasure as well. Although a minotaur is not generally a figure of fun, the generic quality of the encounter, its structured anticipatory (yet somewhat uncertain) quality, point in this direction. Finding theory "close to" the end of the maze ensures it preserves its awful necessity, but it also guarantees complex pleasures in the encounter. Like Barthes' reader in *The Pleasure of the Text*, the minotaur of theory must be sought

---

23   Gardiner, "E. Warwick Slinn, *Browning and the Fictions of Identity* (Book Review)", 315–16.

(maybe even "cruised") in our scholarly practice; one is driven inward and through the maze to find him.

Bearing witness to such encounters is another source of pleasure, another form of encounter, and a model for participation. As mentioned, my own first opportunity to see Bruce in this light came very late: he gave a lecture to senior undergraduates in a course on contemporary rhetoric in which I was a lecturer and seminar leader; his topics were the rhetorical kinds and his theory of intellectual property. Bruce began by outlining his interpretation of Aristotle's *Rhetoric* contra the normative emphasis of contemporary philosophical interpretations. Characteristically, Bruce offered students (and other fortunate witnesses) a key insight in the paratext by referring students to a digital copy of Eugene Garver's "Deliberative Rhetoric and Ethical Deliberation" (2013) with the comment that his own view on Aristotle's rhetorical kinds is contrary to the dominant one among scholars (as represented by Garver). For Garver (as for other contemporary Aristotelian scholars), only those speeches which reach a certain threshold of quality may be seen as belonging to the kinds (or genres). Garver suggests that while "the art of rhetoric can be used to get someone to take his medicine, or in courtship and seduction [...] the art operates *fully* in its three genres".[24] In other words, for Garver, Aristotle's kinds only fully apply to communication that meets some threshold of quality. Further, Garver argues that Aristotle "makes deliberation the centre of the art of rhetoric",[25] confirming the secondariness of the epideictic among modern critics.

Bruce vigorously denied both points, exhibiting a tolerance for certainty that is rare among contemporary scholars, especially in a pedagogical mode. His lecture script reads: "I will argue that *all verbal communication is of only three kinds*, which Aristotle names deliberative, forensic and epideictic rhetoric."[26] Following Perelman and Olbrechts-Tyteca, Bruce also treats the epideictic as the prevalent form; as a proponent of modern psychology[27] he gives a developmental account to explain this: "at first our entire experience of communication is exclusively epideictic".[28] He then refreshes our views of the deliberative and forensic branches by sharing a wide array of examples and linking them to theories of textuality in Barthes (deliberative: what matter who's speaking?) and Heidegger (forensic: the interrogation of what is spoken, by whom). Bruce's astute distinction of his own ideas of intellectual property[29] and his decision against scholarly consensus in

---

24   Eugene Garver, "Deliberative Rhetoric and Ethical Deliberation", *Polis* 30, no. 2 (2013): 207.

25   Garver, "Deliberative Rhetoric and Ethical Deliberation", 193.

26   Bruce Gardiner, "An Aristotelian Rhetoric of Intellectual Property" (2019), 1, my emphasis.

27   Gardiner's commentary and published work is rich with psychological reference, often, though not exclusively, neo-Freudian.

28   Gardiner, "An Aristotelian Rhetoric of Intellectual Property", 2, lecture 1.

29   A published version of this theory, as it pertains to authorial and personal forms of intellectual property, is given in Bruce Gardiner, "Christ's Parable of the Sower: Intellectual Property Rights in Gossip and Testimony", *Literature and Aesthetics* 28 (2018): 193–220. In that text, the connection to Aristotle is noted but not fully elaborated.

this matter were together accompanied by a pedagogical gesture towards the best representative of that consensus. There is perhaps some irony in promoting the view that all texts could be worthy of attention (contra Garver) when every text of Bruce's is of such high quality. There is an intellectual generosity that is, in some important way, lacking in self-regard.

I am interested here not so much in the finer points of Aristotelianism in rhetorical theory – nor necessarily the theories of intellectual property (or of gossip – though I am *very* interested in that, in general) – but in their metatheoretical underpinnings. To a one-time student of Cultural Studies, this theoretical undertaking was impressive (it has been noted by McKenzie Wark and others that contemporary scholars, in a kind of venerational scholasticism, don't tend to *do* theory: Bruce's account of epideictic rhetoric is indisputably a theory – he encounters the minotaur). Bruce's metatheoretical confidence, a willingness to be certain (or almost certain) on some questions, is also the product of labour sometimes invisible to his students and colleagues (and to university administrators); yet it is also a promise. What commended this explication to me, and still does, is Bruce's confidence in disagreement. In Garver and Gardiner are two models of careful, practised scholarship; yet the latter more determinedly advances a commitment to theorising as a creative encounter. At the same time, this was never a lecture as would-be conference paper: Bruce's whole approach really did help students (and me) to better understand the rhetorical kinds.

My second anecdote is more concise; it also hinges on well-earned theoretical confidence and generosity *sui generis*. Bruce and I were at lunch at the quietly excellent Rubyos on King Street in Newtown (his shout), talking about, yes, cultural theory. Over diverse tapas, the conversation turned to Bourdieu, about whom I enthused a connection to Heidegger. I proffered that connection in the kind of loose and fuzzy way that some speculative humanities scholarship might around concepts such as embodiment or ethos.[30] Bruce firmly, yet without a hint of disparagement, pointed out that the two theories – and theorists – were not at all alike. There was no glibness, nor was this a whimsical dismissal: Bruce took (and takes) Bourdieu at his word;[31] I took (and take) Bruce at his word. His is neither a "toolkit" model of theory, nor a hazy historicism that can justify almost any connection via nebulous lines of influence and connection. Bruce's other students and colleagues (are we not always already both?) will recognise this form of encounter: a dead end in the maze, as firm as it is reassuring, as pleasurable in its way as finding the minotaur.

---

30 See Bryan S. Turner et al., *Routledge Handbook of Body Studies*, Routledge International Handbooks (Florence: Routledge, 2012); or James S. Baumlin and Craig A. Meyer, *Histories of Ethos: World Perspectives on Rhetoric* (Basel: MDPI, 2022), as examples of the kind of thing I mean in two fields in which I have participated.

31 See, for example, Pierre Bourdieu, *The Political Ontology of Martin Heidegger* (Stanford, CA: Stanford University Press, 1991).

Ben's Reflection

I came to the University of Sydney as somewhat of an outsider – I had completed a PhD and taught elsewhere in Sydney before becoming the second academic hired to develop and teach in a new program in Rhetoric and Writing Studies at the University of Sydney. As a new academic in a new faculty-based program of teaching and research at the university, I was isolated from the usual onboarding, induction and introductions that staff in established schools and departments might receive. But I did receive one warm and generous welcoming email – from Bruce Gardiner. As an outsider, I interpreted the email without a sense of its author's reputation. Had I known then what I know now, I would have recognised Bruce immediately as an opinionated and generous literary critic (as Adam's story highlights), as a wide and considerate reader, and a demanding and good-humoured teacher. Had I been aware of Bruce's reputation among students, I would not have been surprised by his care and support for someone new to the university. But my ignorance of these things did not prevent a favourable reading of the email. Bruce welcomed me to the university (something senior managers and administrators had not done beyond a template letter from the HR department) and invited me to present at an upcoming forum he had organised on approaches to Indigenous literature. I knew immediately that Bruce was an open-minded and innovative academic with a mind as much intrigued by the latest trends in cross-cultural textual analysis as by traditional literary theories.

Upon my arrival at the forum, as guests and participants were making tea and registering for the day's events, Bruce made a beeline for me and swiftly began introducing me to people: "Here's Professor Giles – you and he share an interest in … And you should meet Dr Minter – you both work on … and let's chat to Professor Teuton, the scholar I'm hosting from UBC …" This was more than polite networking. There was the sense that Bruce had taken the time to know our research areas and that he cared about our ability to share ideas and connect. The plenary speaker at the forum was Chris Teuton, whose book *Deep Waters: The Textual Continuum in American Indian Literature* had recently been published, and Bruce was clearly a fan. In the following years, as I taught alongside Bruce in the university's Rhetoric and Writing Studies curriculum, his enjoyment of Teuton's work became obvious to me. Teuton argues that Native American literature has three main drives: the oral impulse, the graphic impulse, and the critical impulse.[32] For Teuton, literature by Native American writers continues and innovates long traditions of speaking, writing and theorising. Although Bruce, who presented a paper on "Tribal Intellectual Property" that began with a photo of his five-year-old self dressed as an "Indian", his brother as a cowboy (see Figure 4.1), before masterfully unpacking a range of ethical considerations of property

---

32   Chris Teuton, *Deep Waters: The Textual Continuum in American Indian Literature* (Lincoln: University of Nebraska Press, 2010), xiv.

Figure 4.1 John Gardiner and Bruce Gardiner (left) playing cowboys and Indians.

ownership and frontier representations, was extremely mindful of the politics of appropriation, his own scholarly commitment to something akin to Teuton's triumvirate was renowned. Bruce's lectures were a demonstration of expert oratory, creating a strong sense of occasion in the classroom; his writing was full of wisdom and wit; and he was, in all things, critical. This is not to confuse criticism with pessimism or derision, but to say that Bruce was critical in the classical scholarly sense in that he was committed to testing and refining ideas, knowledge, and the limits of our communication. And, as with Teuton's theory of Native American literature, nothing is to be achieved by isolating and separating these strands of work.

A few years later, when I first coordinated a senior-level undergraduate course, I asked Bruce to come and speak about rhetorical traditions. Early on a Thursday morning he arrived for his first guest lecture, removed his famous hat, and pulled out the course textbook, George Pullman's *Persuasion: History, Theory, Practice.* "Who is George Pullman?", he asked as if he had never encountered the author before. Students were immediately hooked on the mystery, or perhaps they were intrigued by the idea of a lecturer who had not read the course textbook. Over the next hour, Bruce dissected the textbook – he had clearly done his homework – tracing and mapping the citations, interpreting the index, and painting a picture of Pullman's critical network. Pullman, to Bruce, was an Aristotelian with an interest in the new rhetoric who had less time for Cicero and the Romans and no time for critical theory that, to Bruce's mind, was deeply rhetorical. Needless to say, students and teachers who witnessed the lecture were elevated beyond the local concerns of a particular chapter or concept and found themselves with a transhistorical and worldly view of the context for their learning. And perhaps more importantly, students began to consider how their own scholarly connections – flagged in citations, references, quotes and mentions – might signify their own identity. I think of this as early work in the study of what has become known as "the politics of citation", which is increasingly present in feminist, critical race, and Indigenous studies (see Mott and Cockayne for a discussion in feminist studies, Somerville or Ohri for a consideration of Indigenous studies, Chakravartty et al. for an application in critical race studies, and Kim for a more general overview).

In reflecting on these anecdotes, the care and attention to networking is interwoven throughout Bruce's teaching, research and collegiality. In all of these areas of work, Bruce connected students to their fields of study, fostered collaborations among peers, mapped the relationship between ideas, and helped people understand themselves as a vital point in a constellation of knowledge. In fact, a relational understanding and practice of rhetoric, such as Bruce's, is a revolutionary concept. According to Rodriguez: "A relational worldview gives us the beginnings of a new rhetoric that can help us remove the violence that is destroying and disfiguring the world, and, ultimately, destroying and disfiguring so much of us."[33] Rodriguez is talking here about a new rhetoric for a decolonial world, where connectivity between people should be prioritised in everyday and academic communication, and where generosity, even for those we strongly disagree with, is necessary to stop the continuation of colonial violence. For Bruce, decolonisation was important – clearly, as he supported scholars like Teuton and theorised about Indigenous intellectual property rights. But Bruce's relational practice in academic culture also stood firm against an academic culture that increasingly attempts to isolate teaching, research and leadership into separate and quantifiable categories. Stories such as those in this collection, at a minimum, reveal a different kind of value for a career such as Bruce's, and, more optimistically, continue to prompt our own institutions to better recognise the importance of unquantifiable aspects of academic work. For example, how can we possibly (or should we even) define or categorise the impact of a form of collegiality that so authentically springs from caring and respectful scholarship, teaching and mentoring?

Susan's Reflection

In January 2004, I reported for my first day of work in the English department. With the ink barely dry on my American thesis (and passport stamp), I was still

---

33   Amardo Rodriguez, "A New Rhetoric for a Decolonial World", *Postcolonial Studies* 20, no. 2 (2017): 179.

acclimating to life in Australia and wondering how my expertise in Rhetoric and Writing Studies would be received in a literature-centric department. I nervously expected a crowd of unfamiliar faces, not knowing then about the scarcity of academics in the Woolley building in January. As I powered up my computer, a slight well-dressed gentleman, seemingly from a bygone, more genteel era, appeared in my doorway. Expecting to have to explain myself as a "rhetoric specialist" (distinct from "bullshit artist") to an audience unfamiliar with the mostly-American discipline of Rhetoric, I took a deep breath and prepared to deliver my spiel. But no sooner than I'd said Aristotle, Bruce launched into an impromptu lecture on Aristotle's influence on modern theorists, particularly Heidegger, as well as his own philosophy of teaching. It became clear quickly that I would never need to explain *anything* to Bruce Gardiner.

Over the next twenty years, these exchanges became pleasantly routine, leading to professional mentoring, teaching collaborations, and a steadfast friendship. Like most who've been lucky enough to have Bruce for a colleague, I soon realised that he knew something about practically everything – and that he knew far more about my own discipline than I did. He is, undoubtedly "a part of all that [he has] met".[34] However, as both Adam and Ben attest in their reflections, Bruce's kindness, magnanimity and gentleness meant that I never felt intimidated. On the contrary, I felt encouraged and eager to learn more, and would soon come to realise that this was precisely the effect Bruce had on his students.

In thoughtful preparation for my arrival in the English department, Bruce had read not only my staff profile, but my entire thesis, and, foreseeing the struggles I would face in having writing units accredited by the English department, had some ideas on how I could contribute to the department beyond the writing curriculum I'd been hired to develop. Upon Bruce's suggestion, inspired by his stories of English department colleagues interested in Rhetoric, I hosted the "What is the New Rhetoric" conference in Sydney in 2005. The call for papers invited contributors to ponder how rhetorical study has influenced their own work. Not only did Bruce assist in reviewing conference proposals and editing subsequent submissions for the eponymous collection of conference papers, including his own, he taught my classes for two weeks so that I could attend to conference administration. I note this occurred long before the implementation of the university's eventual workload policy, and despite being on a 40/40/20 contract, I was (like other colleagues) teaching upwards of twelve face-to-face hours per week in those days, which Bruce happily assumed, on top of his own staggering teaching load.

Thanks to Bruce's generosity, the conference was a resounding success, as affirmed by the appreciative and congratulatory notes received afterwards. Whether from postgraduate students or distinguished professors, including keynote speaker Andrea Lunsford from Stanford University, each reflection bore a common thread:

---

34 Britannica, T. Editors of Encyclopaedia. "Ulysses", *Encyclopedia Britannica*, 4 August 2017. https://www.britannica.com/topic/Ulysses-poem-by-Tennyson.

admiration for Bruce as "the most impressive" figure at the conference. He had made a particularly favourable impression on tentative undergraduate presenters, attending their sessions, asking questions, and chatting with them during the tea breaks, offering advice and assistance. Epitomising simultaneously Aristotle's ideals of ethos and aretê, Quintilian's "good man [sic] skilled in speaking" and Cicero's "citizen orator", Bruce's best lessons were taught by personal example, and they were not lost on two outstanding undergraduate conference presenters who went on to successful careers in academia and journalism, respectively. This calls to mind the lesson in Christ's parable of the sower, which Bruce cited often in his own research and teaching:

> But that on the good ground are they, which in an honest and good heart, having heard the word, keep it, and bring forth fruit with patience.
> No man, when he hath lighted a candle, covereth it with a vessel, or putteth it under a bed; but setteth it on a candlestick, that they which enter in may see the light.[35]

Shortly after the conference, Bruce was the victim of a random hate crime, being senselessly bashed as he walked a city street. When news reached the Department of English, Bruce's condition and prognosis were unclear. In a state of shock and disbelief, I left my assembled class and caught a cab to St. Vincent's Hospital. Nothing could have prepared me for what I was about to witness, and the image of my beloved colleague's swollen, bloodied and bruised face will no doubt remain with me forever. Still young and somewhat naive to the propensity of human beings to inflict such brazen acts of cruelty and intolerance upon each other, I stood by Bruce's bedside in disbelief. How could anyone wittingly inflict pain and suffering on such a gentle soul? But in true Bruce fashion, even lying in a hospital bed in the critical care unit, his thoughts were for others rather than himself. He calmly assured me he would be okay and that I shouldn't worry – but that I *should* get back to my students.

When I think of all I have learned from Bruce, one admonishment rings truer than the rest. "*Nothing matters more than students*". Bruce said this to me on the first day we met and reiterated it on many occasions. Even when barely conscious and breathing through a tube, his first thought was for the students I'd abandoned in my mad dash to the hospital. It is because of Bruce that I am more generous with student feedback and more patient with students in general. It is because of Bruce that I take a more scholarly approach to my teaching, aiming to deliver, as Bruce did, what educational theorist George Kuh calls "seamless learning".[36] And it is because of Bruce that I encourage my students to ask more questions, be

---

35   Luke 8:15–16 (Bible, King James Version).
36   George D. Kuh, "Guiding Principles for Creating Seamless Learning Environments for Undergraduates", *Journal of College Student Development* 37, no. 2 (1996): 135–48.

more observant, find humour in unlikely places, and take more risks, both in their arguments and their lives.

I used to lament having missed out on being Bruce's student, but have since realised that I have benefited from his instruction for the past twenty years. In that time, institutional trends and agendas have come and gone, but Bruce has remained a steadfast presence in a kaleidoscopic higher education sector. Even without one of those trendy "WWJD" (What would Jesus do?) neon bracelets to remind me, I often ask myself "What would Bruce do?" And while it's impossible to know exactly what he would *do* in particular situations, his rationale is ever-clear: *nothing* is more important than students.

Conclusion

Bruce's methodological cues are not limited to the maze analogy outlined at the outset of this discussion, ramifying as it does the paradoxes of narrative (or argument), and the networked quality of text. They extend to intellectual networks and intertextual connections. His dissertation establishes a method of contributing to social and intellectual history by modelling a "simple procedure" for identifying "certain ideals and tactics" among his chosen milieu (The Rhymers' Club) and their "undercurrents of agreement",[37] discovered by examining their works and correspondence. Bruce thus gestures towards an *argument in a network* of texts. His understated representation of the (probably) intense labour of his own scholarship is elaborated with a diagrammatic "embryology of prior associations". That diagram, maze-like, represents Bruce's networked method for conducting the intellectual and social history of texts, developed and refined across his career. It also gives visual form to Bruce's tolerance for both certainty (or near-certainty) and uncertainty through its deployment of solid and broken lines marking connections between participants (a tolerance also evident in Bruce's approach to the problematic of theory, as we have seen).

As far as we are able to present an argument about the significance and importance of a career such as Bruce's, we have sought to use storytelling and critical reflection to reveal a maze-like network of influence. Throughout the narratives presented here, it is clear Bruce's impact cannot be reduced to a number of publications or numerical scores on a teaching survey when his pastoral support for students and colleagues continues to influence academics working in student support and teaching, or when his research-informed teaching has provided a model for others. Further, it speaks to the authenticity of Bruce's approach to academic life that his own research into maze-like networks of textuality provides a more appropriate way to understand the influence of his scholarly life. Our own

---

37   Bruce Gardiner, "The Rhymers' Club: A Social and Intellectual History", PhD thesis (Princeton University, 1983): 3–4. The associative "embryology" is given on page 21.

approach is admittedly less ambitious than Bruce's in "The Rhymers' Club", or even in his important essay on digital rhetoric. However, we share his interest in networks of real and possible connections among texts, writers and readers, and in noticing some points of adhesion along the way.

As we reflect now on Bruce's career, it is remarkable that he was able to withstand the harsh measurements of the neoliberal university. His career perhaps speaks to the kind of arguments that need to be made time and again as the value of the humanities comes into question, or as professional managers try to replace research time with teaching hours. Bruce might respond by arguing for the value of research-informed teaching, or for the importance of our teaching-informed scholarly networks. Larger questions appear in such a consideration of Bruce's career, such as how a neoliberal university can continue its traditional purpose – to produce research, to improve society, or to engage students in the process of testing and creating knowledge – under modern conditions, or how tools of measurement might erode collegiality, research potential, or teaching quality. For Bruce, we believe, navigating the modern university requires us to be networked – connected to one another in a consideration of how ideas are related and interwoven. And it is our scholarly networks that will nurture and sustain us through predictable, but no less devastating, attacks on the humanities. For the authors of this chapter, Bruce Gardiner is an exemplary academic, whose impact and significance will continue to be understood in the many favourable stories that abound, as the seeds he has sown continue to bear fruit.

Bibliography

Adams, Tony E., Stacy Linn Holman Jones, and Carolyn Ellis. *Autoethnography.* Series in Understanding Statistics. New York: Oxford University Press, 2015.

Baumlin, James S., and Craig A. Meyer. *Histories of Ethos: World Perspectives on Rhetoric.* Basel: MDPI, 2022. https://doi.org/10.3390/books978-3-0365-1699-8.

Bleakley, Alan. "Stories as Data, Data as Stories: Making Sense of Narrative Inquiry in Clinical Education." *Medical Education* 39, no. 5 (2005): 534–40. https://doi.org/10.1111/j.1365-2929.2005.02126.x.

Bourdieu, Pierre. *The Political Ontology of Martin Heidegger.* Stanford, CA: Stanford University Press, 1991.

Britannica, T. Editors of Encyclopaedia. "Ulysses." *Encyclopaedia Britannica*, 4 August 2017. https://www.britannica.com/topic/Ulysses-poem-by-Tennyson.

Bulaitis, Zoe Hope. *Value and the Humanities: The Neoliberal University and Our Victorian Inheritance.* Palgrave Studies in Literature, Culture and Economics. Cham: Springer International, 2020.

Butler, Judith. "The Public Futures of the Humanities." *Daedalus* 151, no. 3 (2022): 40–53. https://doi.org/10.1162/daed_a_01927.

Chakravartty, Paula, Rachel Kuo, Victoria Grubbs, and Charlton McIlwain. "CommunicationSoWhite." *Journal of Communication* 68, no. 2 (2018): 254–66. https://doi.org/10.1093/joc/jqy003.

De Fina, Anna, and Sabina Perrino. *Storytelling in the Digital World*. Amsterdam: John Benjamins Publishing Company, 2019.

Ellis, Carolyn. "Compassionate Research: Interviewing and Storytelling from a Relational Ethics of Care." *The Routledge International Handbook on Narrative and Life History*. Eds. Ivor Goodson, Molly Andrews, and Ari Antikainen. New York: Routledge, 2004.

Ellis, Carolyn, Tony E. Adams, and Arthur P. Bochner. "Autoethnography: An Overview." *Forum, Qualitative Social Research* 12, no. 1 (2011).

Frank, Arthur W. "The Standpoint of Storyteller." *Qualitative Health Research* 10, no. 3 (2000): 354–65. https://doi.org/10.1177/104973200129118499.

Gardiner, Bruce. "An Aristotelian Rhetoric of Intellectual Property." Lecture, 2019.

Gardiner, Bruce. "E. Warwick Slinn, *Browning and the Fictions of Identity* (Book Review)", 315. Melbourne: Australasian Universities Language and Literature Association, 1983.

Gardiner, Bruce. "The Rhymers' Club: A Social and Intellectual History", PhD Thesis, Princeton University, 1983.

Gardiner, Bruce. "What's New and How New Is It? Contemporary Rhetoric, the Enlightenment, Hypertext and the Unconscious." In *What Is the New Rhetoric?*. Ed. Susan E. Thomas, 29–45. Newcastle-upon-Tyne: Cambridge Scholars Publishing, 2007.

Gardiner, Bruce. "Christ's Parable of the Sower: Intellectual Property Rights in Gossip and Testimony." *Literature and Aesthetics* 28 (2018): 193–220.

Garver, Eugene. "Deliberative Rhetoric and Ethical Deliberation." *Polis* 30, no. 2 (2013): 189–209. https://doi.org/10.1163/20512996-90000538.

Hay, Iain. *How to Be an Academic Superhero: Establishing and Sustaining a Successful Career in the Social Sciences, Arts and Humanities*. Cheltenham: Edward Elgar Publishing, 2017. https://doi.org/10.4337/9781786438126.

Kim, Annabel L. "The Politics of Citation." *Diacritics* 48, no. 3 (2020): 4–9. https://doi.org/10.1353/dia.2020.0016.

Knoblauch, A. Abby. "A Textbook Argument: Definitions of Argument in Leading Composition Textbooks," *College Composition and Communication* 63, no. 2 (2011): 244–68.

Kuh, George D. "Guiding Principles for Creating Seamless Learning Environments for Undergraduates." *Journal of College Student Development* 37, no. 2 (1996): 135–48.

Miller, J. Hillis. *Ariadne's Thread: Story Lines*. New Haven, CT: Yale University Press, 1992.

Mott, Carrie, and Daniel Cockayne. "Citation Matters: Mobilizing the Politics of Citation Toward a Practice of 'Conscientious Engagement'." *Gender, Place and Culture: A Journal of Feminist Geography* 24, no. 7 (2017): 954–73. https://doi.org/10.1080/0966369X.2017.1339022.

Ochsner, Kevin M., and James J. Gross. "The Cognitive Control of Emotion." *Trends in Cognitive Sciences* 9, no. 5 (2005): 242–49.

Ohri, Indu. "Sara Ahmed's Politics of Citation and Student Scholarship: Uncovering Indigenous Coauthors of British Folklore Collections." *Victorian Studies* 64, no. 2 (2022): 292–96. https://doi.org/10.2979/victorianstudies.64.2.12.

Perelman, Chaïm, and Lucie Olbrechts-Tyteca. *The New Rhetoric: A Treatise on Argumentation*. Notre Dame, IN: University of Notre Dame Press, 1969.

Powell, Malea, Daisy Levy, Andrea Riley-Mukavetz, Marilee Brooks-Gillies, Maria Novotny, and Jennifer Fisch-Ferguson. "Our Story Begins Here: Constellating Cultural Rhetorics." *Enculturation: A Journal of Rhetoric, Writing, and Culture* 18 (2014). https://enculturation.net/our-story-begins-here.

Pullman, George. *Persuasion: History, Theory, Practice*. Indianapolis, IN: Hackett, 2013.

Rodriguez, Amardo. "A New Rhetoric for a Decolonial World." *Postcolonial Studies* 20, no. 2 (2017): 176–86. https://doi.org/10.1080/13688790.2017.1361309.

Ruskin, John. *Fors Clavigera (Volume 1 of 8) Letters to the Workmen and Labourers of Great Britain*. Project Gutenberg, [1871] 2019. https://www.gutenberg.org/ebooks/59456.

Shepherd, Laura J. *The Self, and Other Stories: Being, Knowing, Writing*. Blue Ridge Summit, PA: Rowman & Littlefield Unlimited Model, 2023.

Shumway, David. "The University, Neoliberalism, and the Humanities: A History." *Humanities (Basel)* 6, no. 4 (2017): 83. https://doi.org/10.3390/h6040083.

Smith, Brett, and Andrew C. Sparkes. "Narrative Inquiry in Psychology: Exploring the Tensions Within." *Qualitative Research in Psychology* 3, no. 3 (2006): 169–92. https://doi.org/10.1191/1478088706qrp068oa.

Somerville, Alice Te Punga. "Unpacking Our Libraries: Landlocked, Waterlogged, and Expansive Bookshelves." *American Quarterly* 67, no. 3 (2015): 645–52. https://doi.org/10.1353/aq.2015.0056.

Teuton, Chris. *Deep Waters: The Textual Continuum in American Indian Literature*. Lincoln: University of Nebraska Press, 2010.

Thomas, Ebony Elizabeth, and Amy Stornaiuolo. "Restorying the Self: Bending toward Textual Justice." *Harvard Educational Review* 86, no. 3 (2016): 313–38. https://doi.org/10.17763/1943-5045-86.3.313.

Turner, Bryan S., Kathy Davis, Mary Evans, Victoria Pitts, Darin Weinberg, and Whang Soon-Hee. *Routledge Handbook of Body Studies*. Florence: Routledge, 2012. https://doi.org/10.4324/9780203842096.

Wood, Nancy. *Essentials of Argument*. Saddle River, NJ: Pearson/Prentice Hall, 2006.

5

Human Voices, and a Bruce Gardiner Lecture

Peter Godfrey-Smith

1982, June. The University of Sydney back then had days when high school students in their final year, coming up to their Higher School Certificate examinations, would make their way into the city to see a handful of special lectures by university academics.[1] The aim was to give us a taste of university-level work, also to supplement what we had been doing in preparation for our exams. I don't know how many university departments did this and how many schools took part, but the English department put on some of these lectures, so my classmates and I trooped in from the suburbs one day and crowded the Wallace Lecture Theatre.

English literature was my main interest back then, and I'd read a lot, I imagined, about the works on the syllabus that year – Conrad, Shakespeare, Eliot. I'd dipped into academic journals and supposed I had a sense of how the business of responding to a text could go – a sense of the nature and scope of the enterprise, and what was more-or-less possible. Then a slender man with a particular energy, Bruce Gardiner, appeared at the podium and gave a lecture about "The Love Song of J. Alfred Prufrock".

I didn't think too much of the poem beforehand (was more of a Ted Hughes man, then and now). But the lecture gave me an instant jolt, and shifted, I think, my view of poems, books and critical projects.

Hauling 1982 up from the recollective well, my response back then was partly to the ideas and partly to the person. He had such an acrobatic mind, was uncovering paths and introducing possibilities that would never have occurred to me but were each immediately apt, and that would each be replaced before I had time to fully take them in, let alone scribble onto foolscap. The lecture felt like a ride in a very fast open-top car.

I turned up at university next summer in 1983, and took first-year English. Lecturers came and went from the Wallace Lecture Theatre to handle particular

---

1   When did these stop? According to Nick Riemer, they were still going in the late-80s and early 90s. They were sponsored by the English Association rather than by the university.

works: Penny Gay on *Twelfth Night*, Gerald Wilkes on *A Portrait of the Artist as a Young Man* – it says a lot about the 1980s department and university that I remember individual lectures in this way – and Bruce on a kindred spirit, Oscar Wilde, and *The Importance of Being Earnest*.

When I approached Bruce in person, he was generous from the start. I began visiting him in his office, and kept doing so long after I'd abandoned English to concentrate on philosophy. For me, Bruce in those years came to be an ongoing point of contact with a more freewheeling, subversive intellectual style.

We both had an interest in Richard Rorty's work, a writer positioned between Bruce's world and the one I was making my way into. Rorty in print and Bruce in person represented a critique of the pretensions of system-building naturalistic philosophy – a gentler critique in Bruce's case than Rorty's. Rorty would mount explicit criticisms and offer pointed caricatures of the kind of systematic work that I was starting to do, exposing its history and sometimes asking, directly, what people in such a field could reasonably take themselves to be attempting.[2] Bruce nudged in the same direction, but did so more by example, by treating philosophy as one more interesting body of writing, rather than any kind of putative intellectual overseer.

Rorty has an essay on Derrida, from around that period, that is called "Philosophy as a Kind of Writing".[3]

> Philosophy is best seen as a kind of writing. It is delimited, as is any literary genre, not by form or matter, but by tradition – a family romance involving, e.g., Father Parmenides, honest old Uncle Kant, and bad brother Derrida. (143)

> Non-Kantian philosophers like Heidegger and Derrida are emblematic figures who not only do not solve problems, they do not have arguments or theses. They are connected with their predecessors not by common subjects or methods but in the "family resemblance" way in which latecomers in a sequence of commentators on commentators are connected with older members of the same sequence. (143)

> Derrida's point is that no one can make sense of the notion of a last commentary, a last discussion note, a good piece of writing which is not an occasion for a better piece. (159)

Philosophy was part of Bruce's omnivorous interest, and I think he saw that tradition in something like the way seen here in Rorty – as a sequence of works that comment on each other (and on other writings), exercises that try out new directions, provide resources for further rounds of writing, but can't sensibly offer

---

2   In my favourite of his unkind descriptions, some years later, Rorty referred to epistemology as a "collapsed circus tent" under which people were still thrashing about (in "Charles Taylor on Truth", in *Truth and Progress: Philosophical Papers* (Cambridge: Cambridge University Press, 1998), 93).

3   Richard Rorty, "Philosophy as a Kind of Writing", *New Literary History* 10, no. 1 (1978): 141–60, reprinted in his collection *Consequences of Pragmatism*, which came out in 1982.

final answers to the questions being addressed. And that is fine, not something to regret, because the tradition of commentary on commentary is a valuable thing in itself, and something that can serve good humanistic ends.

Derrida, the ostensible topic of that Rorty essay, was also of considerable interest to Bruce, and the early 1980s was the time when Derrida's work well and truly arrived in Australia. He became a topic and a resource in many discussions, including the latest round of internal ructions and ruptures within – not *the* philosophy department, but – the *two* philosophy departments at the University of Sydney, departments that had split over an earlier round of disagreement about the nature and boundaries of the field. I shared the common analytic philosopher's view of Derrida as a showman at best, a somewhat empty figure and one with a mostly malign influence. This was not Rorty's or Bruce's view, though Rorty in that essay did distinguish the better and worse sides of Derrida, where the better side transcended the misguided project of general philosophical theorising about language and the worse side fell into it.[4]

I resisted, and still resist, the "kind of writing" view of philosophy, even when shorn of pretension and made coherent in the way Rorty did sometimes succeed in making it. I'd not be doing philosophy unless I thought it could make progress on answering some of its unwieldy traditional questions, where "answering" I understand in a way that has a fair bit in common with scientific question-answering, as opposed to a project of endlessly offering new pictures and interpretations. But I have always taken the other view seriously as a challenge; that critique of philosophy's ambitions has always sat there in my mental background, including the way that Bruce seemed to expect to get the same sort of fruits from good systematic philosophy as he would from a poem.

* * *

When I'm writing about Bruce, most of the material above is written from memory, looking back forty years. The 1982 Prufrock hour left its mark, but what was in it? What did Bruce say? I must admit that the content had faded, leaving just an imprint that I knew mattered. But Bruce's meticulous filing practices meant that he was able to send me a copy of the typescript of the lecture (in Courier, with its dark stamped apostrophes and underlines), which I read in the sun last week.[5] Bruce's accompanying note said that he did not think it was one of his best lectures, but I can see why it had the effect on me that it had in '82.

The lecture shows no deference whatsoever to Eliot – to the revolutionary, the modernist innovator, and to what was, and still is, one of the most famous poems in English (perhaps the most actually remembered poem) from that century. Much

---

4   Rorty did something similar for Dewey, in an essay called "Dewey's Metaphysics", which is also in the collection *Consequences of Pragmatism*.

5   "Last week" when I wrote this part of the chapter. Many thanks to the editors of this collection for their patience as I slowly wrote the rest.

of the lecture has the feel of Bruce steadily calling Eliot's bluff. He begins by reading an entire poem by Edward Lear. Lear wrote "nonsense poetry", which has an effect despite its lack of ordinary sense. It succeeds, when it works, in establishing a sort of contact, presenting not ideas but a voice. Bruce then works through the voices presented in quick succession in Eliot's poem, asking what sort of voice each seems to be and what effect it has, without needing to ask what that voice was determinately *saying*, and without worrying too much about why these voices, rather than others, are the ones we confront.

A good deal of what arrives in this stream of voices is nonsense, Bruce says, roughly as in Lear. Passages that invite a careful interpretation – much-discussed passages that might tell us something specific about Prufrock's frame of mind, such as the women talking of Michelangelo, are presented by Bruce as things that have lodged in Prufrock's mind for no apparent reason, or no reason other than their vague atmosphere and some echoing phonetics, like those fragments of graffiti glimpsed in the street that can settle and reverberate unexpectedly in consciousness.

Bruce handles the "I am not Prince Hamlet" passage at the end of the poem, fleshes out this particular voice, not primarily by describing it, but by addition – by interpolating extra lines of interior monologue that provide a rationale, of sorts, for the written lines. These additions offer a mixture of self-doubt, vague affirmation, and idle thought. The "trousers rolled" and "eat a peach" passages of this part of the poem are handled by presenting them as a bit of Learian rhyming nonsense in the former case, and as an attempt to distract by arbitrarily introducing something wholesome in the second.

This avoidance of questions of meaning was the opposite of what I was used to with literature. An internet search directed at the poem today still yields candidate meanings for all sorts of passages. The yellow fog – is it a symbol of love? A symbol of something else? Can we work out roughly what "overwhelming question" Prufrock contemplates asking? Is it a personal question that Prufrock might ask a woman, or something more general and philosophical? All this is the sort of thing that Bruce saw as a mistake, something he was trying to steer us away from. Familiar ways of trying to understand what is going on in the poem, the sort of thing I was doing with great intensity in my last year of high school, were pointless because they were being deliberately thwarted by Eliot. If we insisted on finding a meaning, it would be like being fooled by Lear. We would be missing the boat.

Decades on, what do I think of the poem, and Bruce's interpretation, now? I think that his response to it is mostly right. And – or *but* – I mean this in a way that is perhaps at odds with what I take to be Bruce's own meta-theory, his overall picture of the situation. I wonder if the rightness of his 1982 lecture is a bit realer or firmer than he might say.

I think this is in part because of some external facts, some external evidence. Prufrock, the poem, used to be a fair bit longer. It used to include a 40-line passage called "Prufrock's Pervigilium" that was cut, except for two lines, and not included in the 1915 published version. This passage was eventually published in 1996 as part of a notebook of early works and scraps that Eliot had sold to John Quinn, a collector and patron, in 1922. Eliot said that a condition for the sale was that the works in the notebook were never to be printed, but they eventually were.[6]

If these extra lines are included, if the poem is read including them, they give the whole quite a different character. Ostensibly, they fill out the picture of Prufrock's streets and his experience of them, in a way with a dark paranoid flavour.

> Then I have gone at night through narrow streets,
> Where evil houses leaning all together
> Pointed a ribald finger at me in the darkness
> Whispering all together, chuckled at me in the darkness.

It goes on like this, with good doses of sexual anxiety, alienation and insomnia. (The darkness itself "leapt to the floor and made a sudden hiss".)

These lines do not give a new overall "meaning" to the poem, but they unify the voices, and give context to the unstable sequence charted in Bruce's lecture. The whole becomes darker, more definite, less enigmatic – more definitively unhinged. (The phrase "my Madness" appears twice in the deleted passage.) When the poem includes this material, the lines that *were* published take on a more definite cast as neurotic fragments, as nonsensical, as echoes and misfirings. They are products of a mind that is presented more explicitly, that is drawn more sharply, in the

---

6   They are published in T.S. Eliot, *Inventions of the March Hare: Poems 1909–17*, ed. Christopher Ricks (London: Harcourt Brace, 1996). An internet search will also turn up unauthorised publications on blogs and the like.
From a *Los Angeles Times* review:

> One would think that an author has a right to decide what is to be published as his (considered and finished) work and to have his drafts or the early work that he cannibalized to make the great poems discarded (or disregarded). However, author's [sic] wishes now are frequently ignored either in the interest of the academic English literature business (and readers' understandable wish to know more about an author's development) or in the quest for profit. In this case, the manuscript, which had ended in the collections of the New York Public Library, had since 1968 been available to scholars, who nonetheless were not permitted to quote the contents. It is Valerie Eliot who commissioned this publication, and Ricks [the editor] observes that she "is the best judge of what her husband would have wished in changed cultural circumstances."

> The word "Pervigilium" is translated as *eve* or *vigil*; the *Pervigilium Veneris* is a Latin poem from the second to fourth century. See *Inventions of the March Hare*.

Pervigilium, which was then cut. The unifying voice was deleted and we are left with a sort of shell.[7] Once the *Pervigilium* is gone, a Learian carapace remains.

I am endorsing Bruce's 1982 interpretation, but I am not sure if the form of my appeal to an external fact, the deleted material, is in accordance with his mindset at all. There are two ways (at least) of handling this sort of extra material. One way is to treat it as generating a new object, the longer version of the poem, which can be considered in the same sort of way that one treats the shorter one, with commentary layered on commentary. Another way is to see the material as, in a stronger sense, uncovering something about Prufrock, as *showing* something about the poem. But then some further details about this material also matter. Eliot himself said that the *Pervigilium* was written a bit after the rest – 1912 rather than 1910–11 – and that Conrad Aiken, another poet, suggested that the extra material was inferior and should be cut. (Aiken later said he had no recollection of this.)[8] If the extra material was added later and then removed, can it really be important in the second, more revelatory way distinguished above? It can contribute to the ever-growing garden of commentary, but can it do more than that? I am not sure, but I note in reply that the chronology is not so straightforward in any case. According to Eliot's biographer Lyndall Gordon, Eliot in his 1911 manuscript of the poem "deliberately left four pages in the middle of the poem blank which suggests he had a rough draft of the 'Pervigilium' which awaited completion".[9]

All this might be a thoroughly non-Gardinerian, or *contra*-Gardinerian, defence of Bruce's 1982 lecture. I want to end by expressing my gratitude to Bruce, whose audacity and intellectual omnivory, as well as generosity, were such wonderful things to encounter on those first forays into university life.

---

7   I wonder also about the role of a particular feature of Eliot's writing, as described by Hugh Kenner, a critic Bruce credits in the endnotes to his lecture:

> On the rare occasions when we have the opportunity of inspecting Eliot's procedures in action, we discover a tendency of short, highly finished passages to be borne into the eddies of the poem by some rhythmic current, and to lodge there because the writer doesn't want to give them up.

> This is the opposite of my way of writing anything at all, and it certainly seems bound to give rise to poems that thwart attempts to find meaning. This is in Kenner's *The Invisible Poet: T.S. Eliot* (New York: McDowell, Obolensk, 1959). Kenner also notes Eliot's high regard for Lear.

8   All these chronological matters are discussed in Ricks' notes in *Inventions of the March Hare*.

9   Lyndall Gordon, *Eliot's Early Years* (Oxford and New York: Oxford University Press, 1977), also quoted in *Inventions of the March Hare*.

Bibliography

Eliot, T.S. *Inventions of the March Hare: Poems 1909–17*. Ed. Christopher Ricks. London: Harcourt Brace, 1996.

Gardiner, Bruce. "A Prufrock Primer," lecture on T. S. Eliot's "The Love Song of J. Alfred Prufrock," Higher School Certificate study day, Saturday 19 June 1982.

Gordon, Lyndall *Eliot's Early Years*. Oxford and New York: Oxford University Press, 1977, 45.

Kenner, Hugh. *The Invisible Poet: T.S. Eliot*. New York: McDowell, Obolensk, 1959, 37.

Pfaff, William. "Inventions of the March Hare: Poems 1909–1917. By T.S. Eliot", *Los Angeles Times*, 20 April 1997. https://www.latimes.com/archives/la-xpm-1997-04-20-bk-50506-story.html.

Rorty, Richard. *Consequences of Pragmatism: Essays, 1972–1980*. Minneapolis: University of Minnesota Press, 1982.

Rorty, Richard. "Philosophy as a Kind of Writing". *New Literary History* 10, no. 1 (1978): 141–60.

Rorty, Richard. *Truth and Progress: Philosophical Papers*. Cambridge: Cambridge University Press, 1998.

6

"My Wretched Dragon Is Perplexed": Scenes of Submission and Response

Rodney Taveira

"How, in the most general terms, do we respond to what we read and hear?" asks Bruce Gardiner at the beginning of his brilliant essay, "Christ's Parable of the Sower: Intellectual Property Rights in Gossip and Testimony", published in *Literature and Aesthetics* in 2018.[1] Less courageous and capable than Bruce, I limit what follows to how we respond to what we read and hear in terms of instruction, grading and feedback; Bruce's legendary responses to student papers provide the grist I will mill. Copious, trenchant and eloquent, with nary a cross-out or erasure, the page of handwritten commentary that met students on their papers' returns indicate Bruce's generosity, which takes seriously an encounter, or even a fight, between reading selves. This chapter reflects on these scenes of reading by framing them in terms of submission and response, where influence is both enacted and explicitly interrogated. I follow Bruce by taking seriously – but also fondly and playfully – the paratextual elements to and by which student essays are directed, returning to institutional documents that govern the production and reception of these essays, and I consider the question of pedagogical influence, whether that be, among other things, amanuentic, disciplinary, intellectual, maieutic, resisted or unrecognised.

This return is also, of course, a return to the position of a student, a position that is at once eternal and left behind as, for example, I graduated from being an Honours and PhD student in English at the University of Sydney to later take up a faculty position alongside whom Bruce dazzled undergraduates (and me) with virtuosic readings of Walt Whitman and Harriet Jacobs in an American Studies course I coordinated. To make these returns, I unearth a personal archive by re-reading several undergraduate essays written for Bruce and reproducing and re-attending to the feedback.[2] I parse these encounters as models of instruction, care, and literary production against the subjects of the essays and in response

---

1 Bruce Gardiner, "Christ's Parable of the Sower: Intellectual Property Rights in Gossip and Testimony", *Literature & Aesthetics* 28 (2018): 193.
2 I also adhere to the word limit of those essays.

to "Theaetetus's Complaint, or Sadomasochism and Your Supervisor", a "Select Bibliography" and an accompanying handout of excerpts, titled "UNDER INSTRUCTION",[3] which Bruce curated for first-year PhD students that supplemented a seminar on the supervisor–supervisee relationship.

∗ ∗ ∗

> That is the decisive difference; and yet, whatever kind of movement it may be which the New Testament writings introduced into phenomenal observation, the essential point is this: the deep subsurface layers, which were static for the observers of classical antiquity, began to move.[4]
> Erich Auerbach, *Mimesis*

Before moving to my commentary on Bruce's feedback and his discussion of testimony and gossip, I will offer an account of "Theaetetus's Complaint" in order to trace the historical, generic, international and modal depth to Bruce's pedagogy. Bruce's selection from Plato's *Theaetetus* finds Theaetetus complaining about the confusion and uncertainty he feels about knowledge and truth. Socrates asks him what he believes knowledge to be. Theaetetus struggles to provide a clear and satisfactory definition. Throughout the dialogue, Theaetetus expresses frustration with his inability to arrive at a solid understanding of knowledge. He grants that he has been taught different definitions by various philosophers, but none of them seem to capture fully its essence. He suggests that knowledge is perception, but Socrates points out the flaws in this idea; perception can be deceptive. Theaetetus bemoans "battling with shadows" (2) in his quest for understanding. Despite Theaetetus' protests, Socrates encourages him to continue seeking knowledge and understanding.

As I re-read my student essays, it becomes apparent that I had something against allegory and analogy. (It is clear that I have gotten over whatever this was!) Nonetheless, it is tempting to make the connection, or even analogy, to Theaetetus struggling with the field of knowledge and its political economy – its production, its distribution, its affirmation – and my undergraduate years, where Bruce enters the scene. I majored in Biology and Psychology as well as Film Studies and English, dabbled in Mathematics until it became too difficult, failed at Sociology. Who or where or how – my undergraduate itinerary moans – to believe, to know? My discipline hopping betrays a similar epistemological dissatisfaction to Theaetetus' but, nonetheless, I attempted to instrumentalise these hops to the advantage of my WAM (weighted average mark). I used a definition from my BIOL1001 textbook

---

3   Bruce Gardiner, "UNDER INSTRUCTION", ten-page photocopied document, University of Sydney, received by the author, March 2005. Future references to this document are to this manuscript, and will be cited parenthetically by page number, unless quoted directly, in which case the reference to the original source is also provided.

4   Erich Auerbach, *Mimesis: The Representation of Reality in Western Literature*, trans. Willard R. Trask (Princeton, NJ: Princeton University Press, 2003), 45.

in an "evolution of language" essay for Bruce, even dictating the process of DNA transcription – an amanuensis pretending to maieusis – where the subject matter – it strikes me now, and likely then – wants to add factitious weight to the performance. I even pondered epigenetic heritability. The intended reader was not, however, bamboozled.

The section of *Theaetetus* that has informed much of my thinking here, and that explains my references to maieusis (and from there, perhaps by contrived visual similarity and *Greekness*, to amanuensis), follows next. Bruce's selection offers an image of Socrates as a self-proclaimed midwife (and the son of a midwife), who explains that midwives have had children (experience required!) but are past child-bearing age (and so resemble Artemis, the childless patroness of birth). They are the best at detecting a pregnancy. With their "drugs and incantations" they can bring on the pains of childbirth, allay them, or even abort a pregnancy. Socrates notes further that midwives are the most skilled at pairing mates to produce the best offspring.

In a striking pairing with Plato, Gardiner's "Theaetetus's Complaint" begins with a 1972 newspaper cartoon from Bruce Petty that depicts Christopher Columbus getting kicked out of class for breaking the rules. "I don't care where you go," yells the teacher in the final cell, "so long as it's as far away as possible!" (1). I once posted a picture of Columbus' Tomb in the Seville Cathedral as what I captioned the "Tomb of Admiral of the Ocean Sea and past president of the American Studies Association, Christopher Columbus". While Gardiner adduces across antiquity, Asia, Albion, the Americas and *The Age*, I merely hear America singing. The easy grab here (and I will take it) is to the method and wide-ranging archive of Walter Benjamin's *Arcades Project*, and it is there that Benjamin declares "Literature submits to montage in the feuilleton".[5] I have gone on to a career in American Studies (a submission to montage, or the feuilleton, or both?), and while the New World existed long before its newness, and it is a long way from the Potomac to Acheron and from the Theatre of Dionysus to Broadway, the cursory, curious and continual responses I had and have to Bruce's selections map onto the combination or montage of art, literature, critical reviews, and impressions of the city that irked writers such as Karl Krauss and Hermann Hesse when they looked at the kind of *Reader's Digest* versions of the modern and modernist city created by the feuilleton sections of newspapers. An interdiscipline, a transdiscipline, even an antidiscipline, I have found American Studies demands a willingness to forge historical and geographical bridges, to interrogate and undo borders, to ford aesthetic and generic boundaries, and to attend to scenes of cultural and spiritual discord.

From Socrates the midwife, "Theaetetus's Complaint" jumps two millennia to James Joyce's *A Portrait of the Artist as a Young Man* (1916), where Bruce excerpts a Platonic dialogue between the Dean of Studies, a Jesuit, and Stephen Daedalus,

---

5   Walter Benjamin, *The Arcades Project*, trans. Howard Eiland and Kevin McLaughlin (Cambridge, MA: Harvard University Press, 1999), 13.

the artist, a young man, on what is beautiful and good, over the practical work of lighting a fire. Remaining in Joyce's homeland, William Butler Yeats invokes Irish mythology in his poem "Michael Robartes and the Dancer" (1918). Telling a story of a knight, a lady and a dragon (the wretched and perplexed dragon that titles this chapter) that he derives from images on an altar-piece, Robartes interprets the dragon as a figuration of the Dancer's thoughts, her self-knowledge. He laments that there is something hidden in this figuration, which does not contain a transcriptive fidelity because it is not directed to a mirror but to and by a mythical beast. Robartes wishes her to turn to the mirror so that he himself "would grow wise" (4) in the apprehension of apprehension.

Reproduced on the same page as the poem by Yeats, Ezra Pound's "Canto XIII" (1924) offers unique access to East Asia. As in *Theaetetus*, various interlocutors offer critiques and counterviews to the subject under discussion. Kung (Confucius) renders an image that reflects the reading list I will discuss below, an imaginary or fantastic private ledger, a pliant placeholder, where slots are set aside or given over to others to enter into a field of instruction and authority.

> And even I can remember
> A day when historians left blanks in their writings,
> I mean for things they didn't know,
> But that time seems to be passing. (4)[6]

The final line vibrates with the functionalisation of contemporary pedagogy, where less and less time is given over to dialogue between student and teacher. The generous and transformative feedback that Bruce delivers resists this instrumentalisation. Even when the technology of submission and response changed, Bruce used a workaround. When online, soft-copy assessment submission was introduced, Bruce printed out each student essay, produced his customary handwritten feedback, scanned the handwritten pages, and uploaded them to each student. These responses, despite these extra layers of production and reproduction, become even more intimate and direct because they stand starkly against the software-generated, generic streamlining of efficiency-focused feedback. Bruce's distinctive penmanship and what it pens reminds the student that in this pedagogical scene of submission and response they are led and judged by a human intelligence and not (only) an institutional machine of credentialing.

Before roving from north-eastern China to South Asia, with images of pedagogical inter-penetration in "A Teacher's Prayer" from the Upanishads, we leap epochs and technologies to analogous images from Billy Wilder's *Double Indemnity* (1944), where Keyes (Edward G. Robinson) describes the job of an insurance claims officer to a dubious Walter Neff (Fred MacMurray):

---

6   Ezra Pound, Canto XIII, *The Cantos of Ezra Pound*, (New York: New Directions, 1972), 60.

> To me a claims man is a surgeon, and that desk is an operating table, and those pencils are scalpels and bone chisels. And those papers are not just form and statistics and claims for compensation. They're alive, they're packed with drama, with twisted hopes and crooked dreams. A claims man, Walter, is a doctor and a bloodhound and a cop and a judge and a jury and a father confessor, all in one. (5)

In other words: claims man as Socratic midwife.

The movement from mythology, religion and antiquity is completed by a poem by Randall Jarrell, written in response to a letter sent to him from the English Office at the University of Texas, Austin, remonstrating that students cannot find him for office hour consultation.

> Learn for yourself (if you are made to learn)
> That you must haunt an hourless, nameless door
> Before you find – not me, but anything. (5a)[7]

Plays provide scenes of the erotic charges of pedagogy. Eugene Ionesco's *La Leçon* (1951) humorously depicts a bumbling, middle-aged male professor faced with a dull, lovely, rich female pupil, while David Mamet's *Oleanna* (1992) finds the student schooling the professor in the changing norms and consequences of intimacy and solicitation in the institutional scene of pedagogy that is described in the selection from (Bruce's future colleague) John Frow's "Discipline and Discipleship":

> The master-disciple relation, whether in a focused or a diffuse form, is a mechanism – archaic and clumsy – for investing the process of transmission of knowledge with a productive intensity. It is a politically fraught mechanism; and it remains, directly or indirectly, the horizon of all our disciplinary transactions. (8)[8]

The allowance of a dialogue between the student and teacher is emphasised by the inclusion of Shoshana Felman's *Jacques Lacan and the Adventure of Insight*. She claims that ignorance is "an integral part of the very structure of knowledge" (7) – it is not simply opposed to knowledge. Noting that Freud was taught by his patients, by their dreams, and by his dreams, she writes:

> Unlike Hegelian philosophy, which *believes it knows all there is to know*; unlike Socratic (or contemporary post-Nietzschean philosophy), which *believes it knows it does not know* – literature, for its part, *knows it knows but does not know the meaning of its knowledge*, does not know *what* it knows. (7, emphasis original.)[9]

---

7   Randall Jarrell, "Office Hours 10-11", *Complete Poems*, (New York: Farrar, Strauss & Giroux, 1969), 463.
8   John Frow, "Discipline and discipleship", *Textual Practice*, 2(3), 1988. 321.
9   Shoshana Felman, *Jacques Lacan and the Adventure of Insight*. (Cambridge, MA: Harvard University Press, 1987), 92.

Rather than hiding among the discourses of other disciplines, separated by degree award programs, learning spaces, and their different means of making claims about the world, Bruce's feedback becomes not only Socratic but, I have come to see, a catalyst that transforms the student essay into a kind of parabasis. Often used in ancient Greek drama, where the chorus or one of the actors steps out of character to address the audience directly, parabasis is used to convey the playwright's personal opinions or to remark on current events. It offers direct commentary to the audience, and it is up to the audience whether they simply leave it at that, use it to inform their understanding of the play in which the parabasis takes place, or remove it from its contiguous context and place it against, for example, other works or parabases by the playwright or works or parabases by other playwrights.

* * *

Pedagogic side of this undertaking: "To educate the image-making medium within us, raising it to a stereoscopic and dimensional seeing into the depths of historical shadows." The words are Rudolf Borchardt's in *Epilegomena zu Dante*, vol. 1 (Berlin, 1923), pp. 56–57.[10]
Walter Benjamin, *The Arcades Project*.

"I define gossip and testimony as follows," declares Bruce in "Christ's Parable of the Sower":

If a message would bear the same interest for those party to it had another sender sent it, then that message is the basic unit of gossip. If it could not bear the same interest for those party to it had another sent it, then it is the basic unit of testimony. The salient distinction is whether one sender serves as well as another. If one does, then the message betokens the representative standing of the sender, but if one does not, it betokens the difference of that sender from all others. … Gossip generates and sustains our indiscriminate sociability, testimony our irreducible autonomy.[11]

Bruce's feedback functions as testimony – it would not bear the same value for the student had another scholar sent it. But this value is only obvious *after* the student reads Bruce's feedback (at least the first time). While one could easily imagine a rote response that uses standard phrases (phrases that may even await the grader in a software program ready to be dragged-and-dropped into a comment box) and judges submissions on criteria plainly articulated by a rubric (to which the student may direct their essay), and can thus be categorised as gossip, one grader serving as

---

10   Benjamin, Walter. "From N [On the Theory of Knowledge, Theory of Progress]", *The Arcades Project*, 458.
11   Gardiner, "Christ's Parable of the Sower", 194.

well as another, this image is supplanted by Bruce's singular response, a singularity that exists at the level of form and content, and the materiality of the message. The effortless effort of Bruce's handwriting – sometimes difficult to discern – prompts *more*: more reading, more ideas, more thought, more time.

To return to this chapter's opening query, how, then, do we respond to guidance, feedback and criticism? To begin at an end, if we exclude the page number, journal title, issue number and year of publication for Bruce's "Christ's Parable of the Sower", the final two words of the document, in a footnote Bruce uses to "thank all who offered me such excellent advice when I asked them for it", are my name.[12] I must admit my surprise at coming across this paratextual cameo as I re-read Bruce's essay despite reading drafts and offering whatever feedback I could, knowing Bruce's propriety in *all* matters (my name is the last because of Bruce's alphabetical ordering of influence), and, most pertinently, reading the finished article in this very form soon after its publication.

It is precisely these moments of overlooking and all-too-humanness that Bruce makes apparent and delights in, what he turns over in his essay, working through the different versions of the parable across the Gospels, where Christ "wonders … how some of us can ignore or forget the very words that others recognise as of world transforming import".[13] Analysing Christ's parable in terms of intellectual property, Bruce draws a distinction between two kinds of listener, "those who take the message to heart and those who do not" – that is, those who cast or broadcast the message as testimony or as gossip.[14] This distinction seems most apposite for *Festschriften*, where testimony – Bruce's "Christ's Parable of the Sower" and the reproductions of "Theaetetus's Complaint" – and gossip – my "behind-the-scenes" and "after-the-fact" commentary – mingle as the influence of the honoured scholar is celebrated. The response to feedback, it seems, is not linear, but follows organic or peripatetic patterns of development, dormancy and regression, where, in line with Felman's argument, forgetting and ignorance nonetheless provide a shape and structure for knowledge.

* * *

Even a private xerographic copy can be a primary record if a person who used it becomes a subject of historical inquiry – or, of course, if one's topic is the history of reproductions.[15]
G. Thomas Tanselle, *Literature and Artifacts*.

---

12   Gardiner, "Christ's Parable of the Sower", 222, fn 72. *Literature and Aesthetics* does not require a bibliography; footnotes suffice.
13   Gardiner, "Christ's Parable of the Sower", 193.
14   Gardiner, "Christ's Parable of the Sower", 194.
15   G. Thomas Tanselle, *Literature and Artifacts* (Charlottesville: Bibliographic Society of the University of Virginia, 1998), 100.

The generous reader does not necessarily award high marks. Indeed, when I look at my English Honours record, the mark I received for Bruce's "The Learned and the Literary" seminar was the lowest of my six grades that year. High marks are what the student seeks in their submissions, but Bruce's responses, his reading, demonstrate that those high marks are desired merely "among other things", things that his responses bring to light or – to begin the archival exploration – midwife, like Socrates, or germinate, like Christ as the Sower, for the student.

It is rather bracing to re-read my essay on "Hume's 'Of the Standard of Taste'" and the judgement it was given. Reproducing here Bruce's least impressed feedback returns me to a position somewhere between amanuensis and maieusis. Where the former refers to dictation or transcription and thus some mimetic capacity to record and perhaps disseminate the thoughts, words and ideas of another person, the latter bespeaks a vital hand in the process of creation and reproduction. Rather than regurgitating whatever I thought I might have gleaned from lectures and tutorial discussion, I attempted to demonstrate originality by adducing an unexpected regime of knowledge. This more creative or productive practice is described by Bruce as my "being so understandably entranced by psychology" (see Figure 6.1). This entrancement fails not so much because it was my own entrancement with the discipline – I abandoned Psychology in favour of English when deciding upon which Honours program to take after completing a BSc and a BA – but, rather, in my attempt to entrance the reader by venturing what I assumed was far afield. Surely, I suspect I reasoned to myself, references to p-values and the Central Limit Theorem will convince Dr Gardiner that I am offering something new and superior about Hume's standard – or obfuscate my incomprehension.[16] But "Hume's aesthetics are fundamentally ethical rather than psychological – about the ought, not the is". My contrived punning on *standard* reaps shrivelled fruit. "With Hume's imprimatur, I'll thank you for such a quixotic effort, meaning thereby to praise it" (see Figure 6.1). I fundamentally mistook Hume's argument. Or at least Dr Gardiner said so, and I believe him, still.

The next encounter is that between Bruce and an essay I titled grandiloquently, "Darwin and Müller and the meaning of life". Again, I turned away from English and to the history and philosophy of science, though at least here the two subjects of inquiry justify adducing this field. And I can re-invoke the practice and figure of amanuensis because it appears in the production of Charles Darwin's work, as he often relied on amanuenses throughout his life of chronic ill health. He employed several people to assist him in transcribing his work, quite often his wife, Emma, and his two daughters. Darwin's use of amanuenses indicates that it is never a matter of simple transcription and perfect reproduction.

---

16   Revising this chapter, I remember that I have "developed", in one of my recent lectures, a "Central Limit Theorem of Humour".

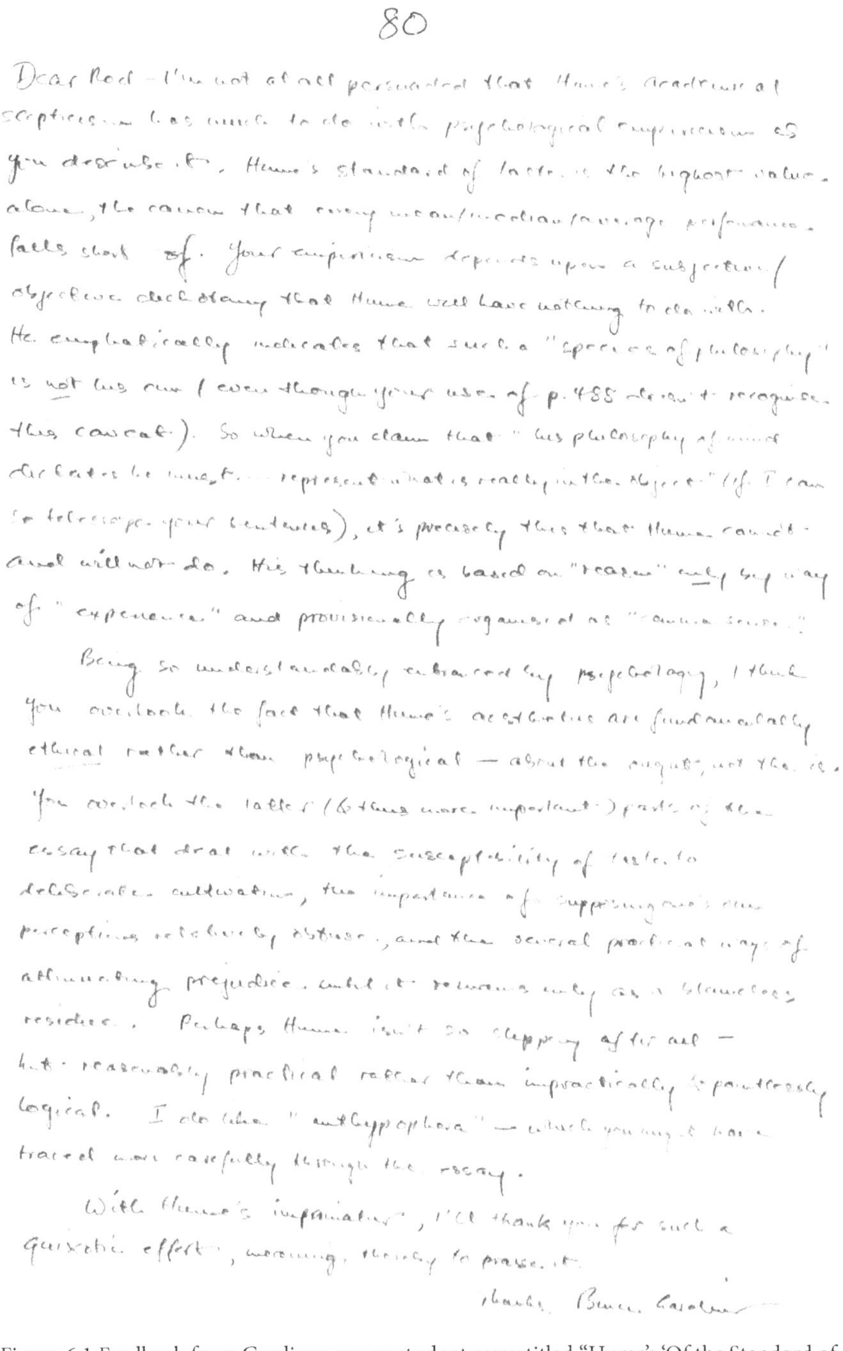

80

Dear Rod – I'm not at all persuaded that Hume's academical scepticism has much to do with psychological empiricism as you describe it. Hume's standard of taste is the highest value alone, the canon that every unconventional average performance falls short of. Your empiricism depends upon a subjective/ objective dichotomy that Hume will have nothing to do with. He emphatically indicates that such a "species of philosophy" is not his own (even though your use of p. 488 seems to recognise this caveat). So when you claim that "his philosophy of mind dictates he must ... represent what is really in the object" (if I can so telescope your sentences), it's precisely this that Hume could and will not do. His thinking is based on "reason" only by way of "experience" and provisionally organised as "common sense."

Being so understandably embraced by psychology, I think you overlook the fact that Hume's academics are fundamentally ethical rather than psychological — about the auguste, not the etc. You overlook the latter (& thus more important) parts of the essay that deal with the susceptibility of taste to deliberate cultivation, the importance of suppressing one's own perceptions rather by distrust, and the several practical ways of attenuating prejudice, until it remains only as a blameless residue. Perhaps Hume isn't so slippery after all — but reasonably practical rather than impractically & pointlessly logical. I do like "antihypophora" — which you might have traced more carefully through the essay.

With Hume's imprimatur, I'll thank you for such a quixotic effort, meaning, thereby to praise it.

thanks, Bruce Gardiner —

Figure 6.1 Feedback from Gardiner on my student essay titled "Hume's 'Of the Standard of Taste'" (2003).

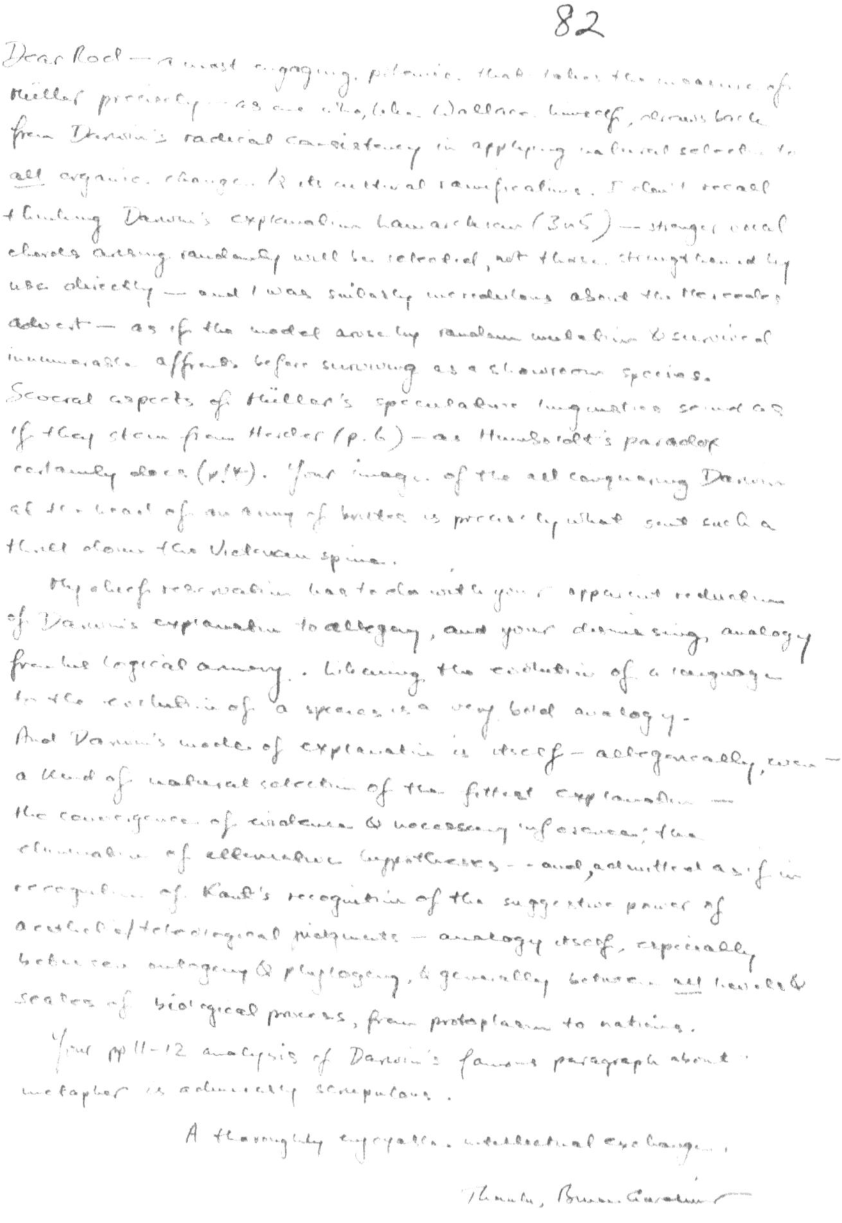
82

Dear Rod — a most engaging polemic, that takes the measure of Müller precisely — as one who, like Wallace himself, draws back from Darwin's radical consistency in applying natural selection to all organic change & its cultural ramifications. I don't recall thinking Darwin's explanation Lamarckian (3n5) — stronger vocal chords arising randomly will be selected, not those strengthened by use directly — and I was similarly incredulous about the Meccano's advent — as if the model arose by random mutation & survival of innumerable affronts before surviving as a showroom species. Several aspects of Müller's speculative linguistics sound as if they stem from Herder (p. 6) — as Humboldt's paradox certainly does (p.14). Your image of the all conquering Darwin at the head of an army of brutes is precisely what sent such a thrill down the Victorian spine.

My chief reservation has to do with your apparent reduction of Darwin's explanation to allegory, and your dismissing analogy from his logical armory. Likening the evolution of a language to the evolution of a species is a very bold analogy. And Darwin's mode of explanation is itself — allegorically, even — a kind of natural selection of the fittest explanation — the convergence of evidence & necessary inference; the elimination of alternative hypotheses — and, admitted as if in recognition of Kant's recognition of the suggestive power of aesthetic/teleological judgements — analogy itself, especially between ontogeny & phylogeny, & generally between all levels & scales of biological process, from protoplasm to nations.

Your pp 11-12 analysis of Darwin's famous paragraph about metaphor is admirably scrupulous.

A thoroughly enjoyable intellectual exchange.

Thanks, Brian Gardiner

Figure 6.2 Feedback from Gardiner on my student essay titled "Darwin and Müller and the meaning of life" (2004).

> Utterly devoted to his interests, she [Emma Darwin] created and preserved the orderly, quiet, entirely domestic environment Darwin desperately craved for his work and health … Emma was ready to read aloud to him during his periods of rest on the indispensable sofa, write letters at his dictation … She helped proof the *Origin*; transcribed many of Darwin's notes, manuscripts, and letters; and, along with their children and servants, dutifully watched over his experiments.[17]

These relations of wife, mother and offspring reveal that amanuensis is not merely a mimetic copy of the thoughts and words divorced from the social scene of writing and reading; the practice and very presence of the amanuensis brings – even births – the thoughts and words into the world.

Similarly, maieusis is important in the work of Friedrich Max Müller, the philologist and Orientalist whom we read historiographically for his contributions to the study of linguistics and to the history of religion at a time when Darwin's work was being published, and for Müller's critiques of Darwin's theories. Müller believed that the study of language was a key to understanding the development of human culture and thought. He argued that the emergence of new languages and new forms of expression was a process of maieusis, in which new ideas and concepts were brought into the world through dialogue and mixture, but without a governing mechanism such as natural selection. I garner this summary from reading my essay, and I stick with it, because Bruce says I "take the measure of Müller precisely" (see Figure 6.2).

In Bruce's response to an essay, "Of what consequence is a theory of the *evolution* of language to a theory of the *nature* of language?" one might infer the suggestion that I cribbed Herder: "Dear Rod, intriguingly, several of your most persuasive points are anticipated by Herder" (see Figure 6.3). But I was not informed enough to know to pilfer Herder's writings, so the possibly inflammatory suggestion instead becomes high praise once I worked out Herder's status and placed the suggestion within the *gestalt*: "Overall, you offer a very lucid argument, enlivened with astute interpretations of your guides" (see Figure 6.3). While I suggest that Bruce's feedback functions in the realm of testimony, it has the intellectually enlivening effect of turning the student's work into gossip. The student wishes to distinguish themselves from their peers, chasing credit and distinction, by demonstrating, among other things, a novel approach and original mentation, but Bruce places the student and their work into a centuries- and even millennia-long intellectual discourse, which, like the matrimonial, convalescent, loving and parturitional scenes of Darwin's work, has a necessarily social dimension, full of coincidence, history, accommodation, jealousy, rivalry and ignorance. The student comes to operate among Herder, Müller, Darwin and Hume; each sender serves as well as another. But rather than a diminution

---

17   Evelleen Richards, *Darwin and the Making of Sexual Selection* (Chicago, IL: University of Chicago Press, 2017), 47.

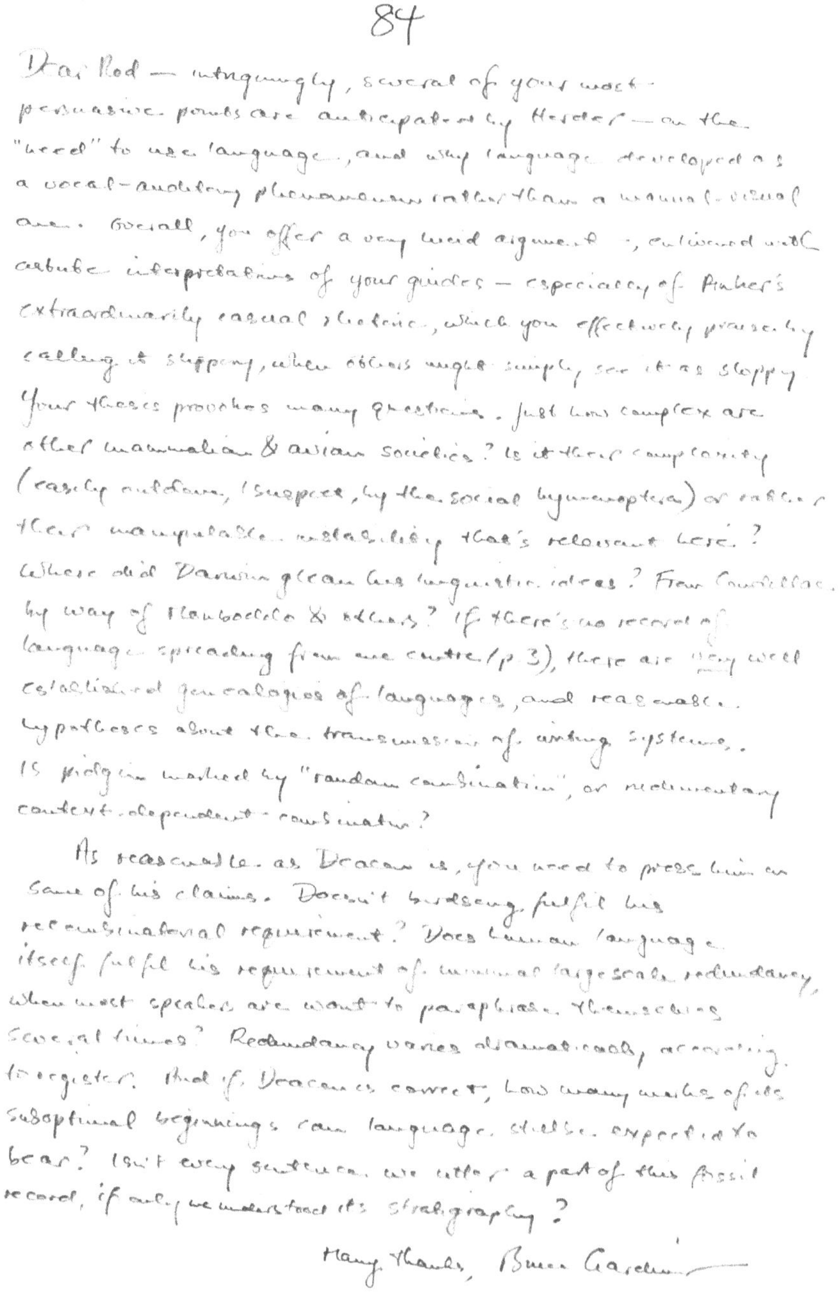
84

Dear Rod — intriguingly, several of your most persuasive points are anticipated by Herder — on the "need" to use language, and why language developed as a vocal-auditory phenomenon rather than a manual-visual one. Overall, you offer a very lucid argument, enlivened with astute interpretations of your guides — especially of Pinker's extraordinarily casual rhetoric, which you effectively praise by calling it skipping, when others might simply see it as sloppy. Your theses provoke many questions. Just how complex are other mammalian & avian societies? Is it their complexity (easily outdone, I suspect, by the social hymenoptera) or rather their manipulable instability that's relevant here? Where did Darwin glean his linguistic ideas? From Condillac, by way of Humboldt & others? If there's no record of language spreading from one centre (p. 3), there are very well established genealogies of languages, and reasonable hypotheses about the transmission of writing systems. Is pidgin marked by "random combination", or rudimentary context-dependent combination?

As reasonable as Deacon is, you need to press him on some of his claims. Doesn't birdsong fulfil his recombinatorial requirement? Does human language itself fulfil his requirement of minimal large-scale redundancy, when most speakers are wont to paraphrase themselves several times? Redundancy varies dramatically, according to register. And if Deacon is correct, how many marks of its suboptimal beginnings can language still be expected to bear? Isn't every sentence we utter a part of this fossil record, if only we understood its stratigraphy?

Many thanks, Bruce Gardiner

Figure 6.3 Feedback from Gardiner on my student essay titled "Of what consequence is a theory of the *evolution* of language to a theory of the *nature* of language?" (2003).

of some notion of individuality or the realisation of some unique potential, the student is lofted, "sharing intellectual property that is everyone's generally, no one's particularly, and anyone's representatively".[18]

While the becoming-gossip of student submissions generated by Bruce's responses indicates that amanuensis is always maieutic, amanuentic tics endure. In years past, I would emulate Bruce's page of feedback with my own word-processed response. While my ugly penmanship was one reason for choosing to type and print my feedback instead of writing it directly on the reverse of the final page, the main reason was to allow myself the best chance of producing a pellucid comment; I could delete and modify as much as I wanted as I approached the Gardinerian ideal of my own undergraduate years. I have frequent recourse to "My chief reservation …" (see Figure 6.2) in my own grading. I also sign off "Thanks" or "Many thanks", the more emphatic emerging in response to when I suspect the submitter has given the piece of writing a lot of time and thought, no matter the final, numerical grade. I have adopted Bruce's "Dear ___," in my email correspondence with students, and I smile when it is adopted by my correspondents.

Bruce delivered the courteously condensed comment of Figure 6.4 when acting as second marker for a seminar called "American Romance". Shorter but not attenuated, it manages to capture the implications of the argument, correct or guide them, draw in medieval High Romance, offer a psychoanalytic interpretation, and add another book for my reading list (see Figure 6.4).

What, finally, is this reading list? A powerful, ongoing placeholder – recall Kung's "day when historians left blanks in their writings" from the selection from Ezra Pound – it contains books read and not read, and, most importantly in this context, books read by others. It is also a list to which Bruce's feedback gives the student entrée, admitting them into this realm where their work converses with that of others, a kind of intellectual gossip, akin to the seeds scattered in Christ's Parable of the Sower. While the different probabilities, imperatives and motivations of the brothers for trying to germinate the seeds in their different situations are instructive, here it is merely presenting the seeds themselves that is most significant. Once the student is made aware of them, it takes a strong act of wilful, antisocial forgetting to undo or refuse the introduction. But this is not to say that the student and intellectual conversation is only one of gossip. Its ongoingness betokens a temporality that asks, even demands, that the student testify, that they exercise their intelligence for, to and against the reading list to which Bruce admits.

In the end, I take succour that the handout that accompanies "Theaetetus's Complaint, or Sadomasochism and Your Supervisor" is given the temporally indeterminate or at least ongoing title, "UNDER INSTRUCTION". I hope it is clear that Bruce has remained an important interlocutor and guide, and that this chapter has added some small measure of testimony to Bruce's influence. It is precisely his

---

18   Gardiner, "Christ's Parable of the Sower", 194.

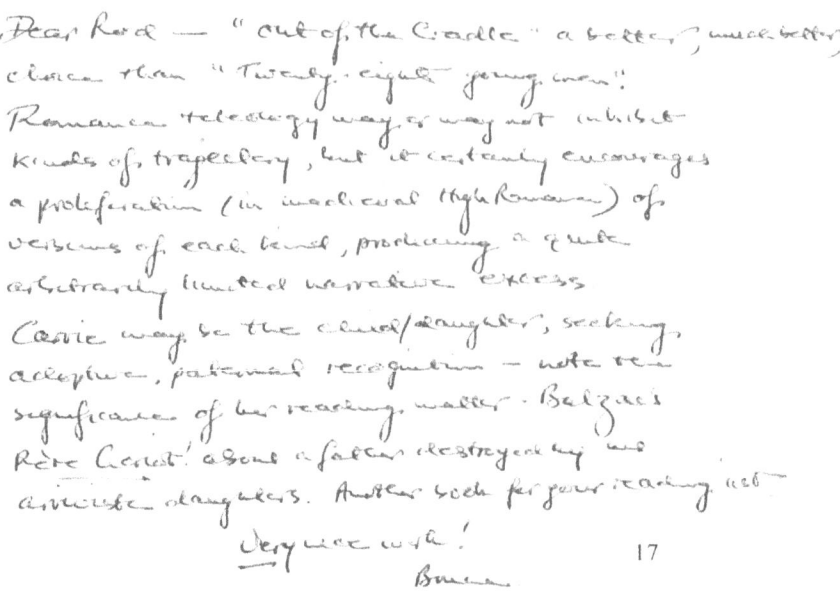

Figure 6.4 Feedback from Gardiner on my student essay titled "'The Bygone Heroine of Romance': Sister Carrie and The Awakening" (2004).

conversance with a wide domain of knowledge production, comfortable enough in many disciplines to articulate his discomfort with many of their claims, which has continued to allow me to pose questions in my own scholarship, for these questions to be answered (both insufficiently and sufficiently), to be ignored for stretches of time, to be worried, to be repressed, to be ever-present.

Bibliography

Auerbach, Erich. *Mimesis: The Representation of Reality in Western Literature*. Trans. Willard R. Trask. Princeton, NJ: Princeton University Press, 2003.

Benjamin, Walter. *The Arcades Project*. Trans. Howard Eiland, and Kevin McLaughlin. Cambridge, MA: Harvard University Press, 1999.

Felman, Shoshana. *Jacques Lacan and the Adventure of Insight*. Cambridge, MA: Harvard University Press, 1987.

Frow, John. Discipline and discipleship. *Textual Practice*, 2(3), (1988). 307–323. ttps://doi.org/10.1080/09502368808582038.

Gardiner, Bruce. "UNDER INSTRUCTION." Ten-page photocopied document, University of Sydney. Received by the author, March 2005.

Gardiner, Bruce. "Christ's Parable of the Sower: Intellectual Property Rights in Gossip and Testimony." *Literature & Aesthetics* 28 (2018): 193–220.

Jarrell, Randall. "Office Hours 10-11", *Complete Poems*, (New York: Farrar, Strauss & Giroux, 1969).

Pound, Ezra. Canto XIII, *The Cantos of Ezra Pound*, New York: New Directions, 1972.

Richards, Evelleen. *Darwin and the Making of Sexual Selection*. Chicago, IL: University of Chicago Press, 2017.

Tanselle, G. Thomas. *Literature and Artifacts*. Charlottesville: Bibliographic Society of the University of Virginia, 1998.

7

Marks in the Margin: Reading Benjamin Reading Baudelaire

Brett Neilson

In 1986, Bruce Gardiner lent me his copy of Walter Benjamin's *Charles Baudelaire: A Lyric Poet in the Era of High Capitalism*. From memory, it was the 1983 Verso paperback edition, a reprint of the 1973 translation by Harry Zohn, featuring Étienne Carjat's 1862 photographic portrait of Baudelaire on the cover. I remember that Bruce wrote my name and the title of the volume in a slim book he kept in his office drawer. It was an act that struck me with fear, as if the prospect that I might not return the book was a reality. I could see but did not recognise the names of other students written in this ledger. I assumed they were doctoral candidates, but I wasn't sure. In any case, it felt like an initiation. Under Bruce's supervision, I was embarking on an Honours thesis about Nancy Cunard, a notorious British-American socialite, exile and muse who was also a little-known modernist poet. Introducing me to Benjamin's writings was a knight's move. What I encountered was not a literary reading in the traditional sense. Rather than being anchored in the early twentieth-century Anglo-American context, which provided the background for the project I was about to start, Benjamin's text, as is well known, offered a broad panorama of modern urban life. Centred on mid-nineteenth-century Paris and engaging Baudelaire's poetry as a thread around which to weave observations on the city, the commodity, and the development of capitalism, the essays I read extended literary study in ways that previously had not been evident to me. In retrospect, this encounter was a formative moment.

This chapter reconstructs my experience of reading Benjamin's texts on Baudelaire. I pay particular attention to my recollection of the pencil markings that I encountered during this reading. I cannot be sure, but my presumption is that these marks were made by Bruce. There was no underlining. The inscriptions consisted of precise delineations of sentences or clauses, marked by two dots in the margin joined with a line, exact but hand drawn. It was my first encounter with Benjamin's writings, but my experience was marked by the knowledge that another reader had come before me. Bruce had literally sliced the text, placing, if I recall correctly, an exclamation mark next to passages that stood out. The sense I make of these marks relates not to the passages or phrases highlighted, which, lacking the book that Bruce lent me, I would now struggle to identify. Rather I take my memory of these marks as an occasion to reflect upon learning from Bruce, as I embark upon a reading of the same text. I understand the marks as indices of Bruce's pedagogy, like a footprint is an index for Charles Sanders Peirce, a sign that Bruce had been there. But I also approach them as icons of a teaching style, marked by precision on the one hand and glee on the other, a sense that attentive reading should not destroy the pleasure of the text.

In re-reading Benjamin's essays in the same 1983 Verso edition, I consider my own intellectual development and Bruce's early role in setting its trajectory. The critical practice I now pursue has moved away from literary study, insofar as it deals with questions of society, culture and politics that do not necessarily elicit an engagement with literary production, history, reception or analysis. Nonetheless, I count reading, understood as an interpretive art deeply connected to the structures of power and social value that shape human life, as a crucial part of this practice. Reading again Benjamin's writings on Baudelaire, after over thirty-five years, offers an opportunity to take stock of the course of my work. I assess the extent to which the style and ambit of Benjamin's essays gave impetus to my own interest to extend interpretive practice beyond the literary object. My re-reading of Benjamin aims to recall and gauge the impact of an earlier reading. In so doing, it exhibits a dynamic of *Nachträglichkeit* or the revision of memories to accord new experiences. The situation is further complicated by the changing position of literary studies in the human sciences since the 1980s. I take Benjamin's own reflections on memory and experience as an occasion to remember the influence of Bruce's teaching, and to reflect on how my literary education has drifted towards the reading of social realities.

The Passer-By

At a crucial moment of the essay entitled "The Flâneur", Benjamin takes the rare step of quoting one of Baudelaire's poems in full. The piece in question is the sonnet "À une passant", one of the most famous in the *Fleurs du mal*. Benjamin reproduces the French original and the Verso edition adds an English translation by E.F. MacIntyre. Notably, this same pattern of quotations is repeated in the expanded version of "The Flâneur", "Some Motifs in Baudelaire", which offers a much more truncated reading of the poem. In the original essay, Benjamin comes as near to offering a close reading of Baudelaire's verse as he does anywhere in the pieces collected and translated in the Verso volume:

> The *never* marks the high point of the encounter, when the poet's passion seems to be frustrated but in reality burns out of him like a flame. He burns in this flame, but no Phoenix arises from it. The rebirth in the first tercet reveals a view of the

occurrence which in the light of the preceding stanza seems very problematical. What makes his body twitch spasmodically is not the excitement of a man in whom an image has taken possession of every fibre of his being; it partakes more of the shock with which an imperious desire suddenly overcomes a lonely man. The phrase *comme un extravagant* almost expresses this; the poet's emphasis on the fact that the female apparition is in mourning is not designed to conceal it. In reality there is a profound gulf between the quatrains which present the occurrence and the tercets that transfigure it.[1]

I stress the anomaly of this approach because it is not usual for Benjamin to attend closely to the workings of literary or poetic text. The focus here on phrasing, transfiguration and the relations among quatrains and tercets is not the typical mode of analysis to which Benjamin subjects Baudelaire's poetry. More often, he is interested in how Baudelaire's verse registers the social transformations of its day, or, to paraphrase the title of the volume in which he planned to collect his essays on the poet, how Baudelaire's lyricism relates to *Hochkapitalismus*. In this regard, the emphasis on shock is pertinent as it connects this reading of "À une passant" to the wider themes of urban life that Benjamin explores by engaging with texts and objects as diverse as Edgar Allan Poe's story "The Man of the Crowd", Georg Simmel's essays on the metropolis, and the urban redesign program of Georges-Eugène Haussmann. Indeed, the more condensed reading of the sonnet in the later version of the essay, "Some Motifs in Baudelaire", moves directly to these concerns. As Benjamin revised his essays on Baudelaire, the kind of close literary analysis conducted in the passage above was systematically ironed out.

As an undergraduate reading Benjamin's text, I noticed this tendency and wondered about the possibilities it held. I was also confused. Was I allowed to write like this? Why had Bruce offered me a critical work that seemed to break one of the cardinal rules of literary study – always ground wider cultural and social analysis in close textual reading? The precision of the marks left by Bruce in the margins of the book seemed to register how his own practice at once adhered to this approach and stretched it to a breaking point. I felt preceded by a reader who had looked at Benjamin's text through a microscope, even picking out phrases from the volume's dense footnotes, as if preparing for a virtuoso reading. I knew from Bruce's lectures his ability to work a reading into a crescendo, embellished with literary terms, excessive but accurate, at once erudite and exultant. My memory does not stretch to specific occasions on which Bruce displayed this aptitude, but I recall that they were common. Looking back at his writings, the following snippet from a 2011 review article captures something of this flair:

---

1   Walter Benjamin, *Charles Baudelaire: A Lyric Poet in the Era of High Capitalism*, trans. Harry Zohn (London: Verso, 1983), 45–46.

Field's nine quatorzains are in effect anti-sonnets, sestet pre-empting octet, trochee overthrowing iambus, tetrameter displacing pentameter. In each quatorzain, the sole trochaic trimeter of the penultimate line trumps the sole iambic pentameter of the third, the octet's choric couplets supplant the sestet's colloquial interlaced rhyme, and incantatory catalectic trochaic lines extirpate more meditative iambic lines after two attempts in the sestet.[2]

Bruce's exuberance for the form and metre of Michael Field's poem "The Sleeping Venus" can hardly be contained. As in Benjamin's reading of "À une passant", the economy of stanzas is an important factor in the poesis at play. However, Bruce finds an intricate play of rhyme and metre to exceed the break between Field's sestets and octets, "pre-empting", trumping and extirpating any kind of absence around which the poem might revolve. The piece is one of around forty works penned collaboratively under the pseudonym of Field by two female authors, Katherine Bradley and Edith Cooper. Field's poem presents no "high point", like the *never* in Baudelaire's lyric, which, for Benjamin, carries the frustrated passion of the male gaze. Rather, the quatorzains engage Giorgione's painting "The Sleeping Venus" to conjure a woman "who masturbates herself into being".[3] At stake is "an arousal that defines the literary as the essential fecundity of language".[4] And, for Bruce, it is precisely this "extravagant power" of language that Hilary Fraser misses in an interpretation of the poem that provides a foil for his own.[5] Fraser's reading gives only an "impressionistic description" of Field's poetic technique, and, as such, fails "to face the most radical formal and substantive issues" raised by "literary and aesthetic inquiry".[6]

Although written twenty-five years after I had moved on from working with Bruce, I recognise the moves of this reading. Most notably, they recall the interpretative brio Bruce displayed regularly in the Honours seminar titled "Masculine and Feminine", which he taught with Penny Gay. The course covered works from Christina Rosetti, Oscar Wilde, Virginia Woolf and James Joyce among others. In offering readings that stayed close to text, Bruce broached issues of body, sexuality and language in ways that seemed more pressing than the theories of desire I was encountering in theory books by Julia Kristeva or Gilles Deleuze and Félix Guattari. In analogy to the way he describes Field's quatorzains as anti-sonnets, I remember these interpretative acts as anti-close readings. Bruce was

---

2   Bruce Gardiner, "Talking of Michelangelo: Routine and Radical Inquiry into Literature and Aesthetics", *Literature and Aesthetics* 22, no. 2 (2011): 180–98.
3   Gardiner, "Talking of Michelangelo", 182.
4   Gardiner, "Talking of Michelangelo", 181.
5   Gardiner, "Talking of Michelangelo", 185; Hilary Fraser, "Through the Looking-Glass: Looking Like a Woman in the Nineteenth Century", in *Strange Sisters: Literature and Aesthetics in the Nineteenth Century*, ed. Francesca Orestano and Francesca Frigeri (Oxford: Peter Lang, 2009), 189–211.
6   Gardiner, "Talking of Michelangelo", 186.

never content to approach a text as a staid urn. For him, literature was simply too exciting, and when he entered the classroom, there was mischief to be had. Staying close to text almost always meant showing how a literary work was bursting at its seams, crowded, moving beyond itself, extending into a network of other texts and realities, feelings and representations. To this extent, there was something Benjaminian about Bruce's readings, even if the commitment to close analysis was constitutive and could never be abandoned.

In this period, I read several times Bruce's *Southern Review* essay titled "Decadence: Its Construction and Contexts".[7] Before swerving to a history and appraisal of late nineteenth-century British literary decadence, the article rehearses theories of decadence as developed by authors such as Richard Drake, Richard Gilman and Carl E. Schorske. Bruce finds the decadent aesthetic to be characterised by "a claustrophobia of collapsed perspectives" that makes it "no longer clear what is authentic or inauthentic, actual or fanciful, moral or immoral".[8] At stake is a "stylistic overloading" that trammels over any textual economy punctuated by a *punctum* or single climactic point.[9] Moreover, decadence attests "a massive shortcircuiting of the transmission of patriarchal power and responsibility from one generation to another".[10] Bruce's critical and pedagogical practice reflected this concern with the "loss of the father".[11] He refused any model of pedagogy as the handing of knowledge and power down a male line. His teaching advanced an aesthetic of reading that curved towards a sweet spot, not a pivot around which to leverage anxieties of agon and misprision but the site of a pleasure reducible to neither the erotic nor the hermeneutic. This mode of literary engagement was not beyond the sugar hit, as attested by the following paragraph from the *Southern Review* essay, which lists entities and experiences that attract the qualification of decadence:

> The word is exceptionally sticky, promiscuously qualifying individuals; their aggregations, such as races, classes, couples, cocktail parties, cities, states and empires; their epochs, from weekends to millennia; their appearance; their behaviour, whether political, economic or sexual; their poetry and pornography; and, as my digestion can testify, their desserts. (A Chocolate Decadence can be enjoyed at a certain Sydney cafe, for only $2.)[12]

How many times did Bruce's students speculate as to the location of the establishment that purveyed this cheap delight? We were spared the wondering of streets and browsing of menus by the fact that Bruce was serving up treats weekly in the

---

7   Bruce Gardiner, "Decadence: Its Construction and Contexts", *Southern Review* 18, March (1985), 22–43.
8   Gardiner, "Decadence", 22.
9   Gardiner, "Decadence", 23.
10 Gardiner, "Decadence", 24.
11 Gardiner, "Decadence", 24.
12 Gardiner, "Decadence", 26.

classroom, of the literary rather than the culinary kind. However, the urge to stroll, to orient oneself in the world of commodities and price tags, was not disconnected from the reading experiences to which we were exposed. This is the lesson of Benjamin, for whom Baudelaire's identification of the flâneur as the central figure of modern life provides a key for the interpretation of the lyric poet's verse.

Benjamin understood Baudelaire's poems to record the ambulatory gaze of the flâneur on Paris. However, this insight was not turned primarily, or even secondarily, to an analysis of Baudelaire's poetic language. As Susan Buck-Morss writes, "Benjamin treated Baudelaire's poetry as a social object, not a literary one."[13] He read away from the poems instead of into them, seeking not to excavate Baudelaire's aesthetic intentions or delve into the workings of literary form, but to relate the flâneur's vision of the city to diverse philosophical and social issues. These matters include the impact of shock on the human psyche, the transcience of fashion and modernity, the positions of the prostitute and the gambler in commodity society, the politics of urban space, the ethos of heroism, the relation of literary montage to the work of the ragpicker, the advent of photography, and the dynamics of memory, just to name a few of Benjamin's more prominent concerns. Ultimately, for me, this mode of analysis would prove more seductive than sticking with careful readings of literary text. But I still had several rounds of grappling with the proclivities and technicalities of literary language before I was confident enough to make this break.

The Dandy

One day in 1985, Bruce walked into the Woolley Building's N395 lecture theatre wearing a pair of high-top basketball boots. Although I can't recall the lecture's content, it seems to me that the shoes were red and white in colour. By the mid-1980s, the clothing preferences of university lecturers had shifted beyond the dourness of tweed, although not completely among senior members of the English department. However, Bruce's footwear was out of the ordinary. To me, it signified Blackness, athleticism and the United States. Doubtless, it had been chosen artfully. Yet this was work attire. It was difficult to picture Bruce shooting hoops, but he was certainly no idler. The care and detail with which he crammed his lectures suggested that he was working with a zeal befitting the Presbyterian origins of the New Jersey institution from which he had recently obtained his doctorate. Dandyism, for him, was an object of professional investigation, part of his interest in the aesthetics and politics of decadence. While he flirted with the dandy's sense of artificiality and exaggerated refinement, his engagement was professedly critical and analytical. Besides, it was not the time to be aestheticising sickliness or declaiming nature's perversity in the

---

13 Susan Buck-Morss, *The Dialectics of Seeing: Walter Benjamin and the Arcades Project* (Cambridge, MA: The MIT Press, 1989), 57.

manner of late nineteenth-century decadents such as Karl-Joris Huysmans, when public discourse and policy were at every turn mobilising these same tropes to pathologise same-sex desire.

By 1985, some 4,500 people had contracted HIV/AIDS in Australia, many of them homosexual men in inner-city Sydney and Melbourne. Although these were not the only communities in which the syndrome circulated, the public perception that AIDS was a gay illness was quickly entrenched. Apart from threatening lives, there were indications, and fears, that the spread of the virus would offer a pretext for a formal crackdown on recently won social freedoms, such as the decriminalisation of homosexual sex, which in New South Wales had only been achieved in 1984. As many commentators point out, the epidemic was not only a medical phenomenon but also a cultural one. Mainstream media and opinion made the illness synonymous with collective memories about pathogenic bodies – homosexuals, drug users, prostitutes – until recently perceived as deviant. With the advent of testing in 1985, the NSW government proposed legislation that would make positive results notifiable and criminalise the nondisclosure of positive status before sexual activity. Passed in December, these laws engrained the perception of so-called carriers as polluters who, by opening the floodgates of promiscuity, placed the general public at risk. On 5 September, the *Sydney Morning Herald* published the following letter:

> SIR: Delicate adjustments of principle to the exigencies of power are the hallmark of the NSW Labor Government. But this complex calculus sometimes runs amok, as it has over its proposed AIDS legislation (*Herald*, August 28).
>
> However unintentionally, the Government's explanations indicate that it is acting only because it believes hitherto tolerated unfortunates, such as prostitutes and homosexuals, now threaten to contaminate the apparently innocent and pure heterosexual public. The real threat is precisely the reverse. The most prominent disease vectors are not the virus or its victims, but prejudice against homosexuality and misogynistic hypocrisies about prostitution, both of which the proposed legislation would effectively endorse.
>
> The legislation will not placate uninformed hysteria. It legitimises it. It panders to it, whether it means to or not.
>
> On behalf of those stigmatised and threatened by the Government's uncharacteristic recklessness, I plead with it to come to its senses and drop the legislation immediately.
>
> Bruce Gardiner,
> Womerah Avenue,
> Darlinghurst[14]

---

14   Bruce Gardiner, "A Reckless Move", *Sydney Morning Herald*, 5 September 1985, 10.

Bruce's letter, which he signs as a private citizen, gives insight into the personal and political issues that informed his professional and intellectual work. It was only a year later that I learned that Bruce and his partner Mark were giving shelter to young and otherwise homeless HIV-positive men in their Darlinghurst home. This act of solidarity and generosity was a strike against the very prejudice and hypocrisy that his letter to the *Sydney Morning Herald* found the public health legislation to endorse. Yet, despite Bruce putting his name on the line, this hospitality was grounded in an ethics that did not invite publicity. While the basketball boots and flashy readings were part of the mix, the politics necessitated by contagious vectors of social prejudice and homophobia were remote from the nonchalance and affectlessness of dandyism.

Doubtless, Bruce's critical interest in decadence, fashioned in advance of the AIDS epidemic, had been inflected by the fact that this same epithet was being turned by mainstream and conservative voices against the community of which he was part. The moral panic that surrounded the circulation of HIV gave Bruce's work new urgency. In this light, the hyperglycaemic aspects of his practice might rightly be seen as a reclamation of pleasure in the face of adversity, much as some of the first poster campaigns devised within the gay community offered messages such as "Great Sex! Don't Let AIDS Stop It".[15] That the lens of the present refracts literary history and criticism is no revelation. This observation applies equally to Benjamin's reading of Baudelaire as to Bruce's recuperation of literary decadence. Yet, insofar as Baudelaire was a crucial figure in the history of modern decadence, Benjamin's engagement with his poetry provides a sounding board against which to assess the perils and gratifications of such a retrieval.

Importantly, for Benjamin, the flâneur is not the dandy, although the two can certainly coexist in the same body. The flâneur is the observer of modern life, who prefers to view the city from the anonymity of the crowd and maintains a watchfulness analogous to that of the detective, journalist or even social scientist. The dandy, by contrast, fashions the self for public display but is simultaneously indifferent to external influences. Benjamin finds this paradoxical aspect of the dandy to register particular historical conditions. For him, Baudelaire is mistaken to see the dandy as a last hero in the face of modern destitution. Rather than being the belated heir of the classical hero, the dandy's origins are recent and English, caught up in the contradictions of imperialism, finance, trade and the marketplace:

> To Baudelaire the dandy appeared to be a descendant of great ancestors. For him dandyism was "the last shimmer of the heroic in times of decadence". It pleased him to discover in Chateaubriand a reference to Indian dandies – evidence of a past flowering of those tribes. In truth it must be recognized that the features which are combined in the dandy bear a very definite historical stamp. The dandy

---

15   L.K. Chan and Raymond Donovan, "Safer Sex Messages: Australian HIV/AIDS Campaigns 1985–2014", *HIV Australia* 12, no. 3 (2014), 9.

is a creation of the English who were leaders in world trade. The trade network that spans the globe was in the hands of the London stock-exchange people; its meshes felt the most varied, most frequent, most unforeseeable tremors. A merchant had to react to these, but he could not display publicly his reactions. The dandies took charge of the conflicts thus created. They developed the ingenious training that was necessary to overcome these conflicts. They combined an extremely quick reaction with a relaxed, even slack demeanour and facial expression.[16]

I can't recall whether Bruce had marked this passage, but I wouldn't be surprised if he did so. Benjamin links the dandy's emergence to England's position as the world's primary trading nation, the global reach of the London stock market, and the unpredictable tremors of imperial finance. As is well known, the 1890s were a period of financial turbulence, marked by deflationary pressures that affected the value of bonds issued to build the railways, canals, ports and steamship lines that enabled England's global commercial dominance. In 1890, Argentinean bond defaults precipitated the Baring Bank crisis, which led to a bailout funded by London financiers. Events such as the collapse of property values in Australia, the US financial panic of 1893, and the rush on South African mining shares in the late 1890s triggered many failures on the London stock market. By understanding the dandy's insouciance as a response to these fluctuations, Benjamin positions this figure at the heart of empire's meshes. There is something dialectical in this image of the dandy, whose demeanour overcomes the conflicts established by an increasingly financialised capitalism. However, the dandy does not reconcile or sublate these contradictions. Rather, in signifying neither revealed surface nor concealed truth, he leaves these dissonances in suspension and comes to represent the fissure in the historical reality that gave birth to him.

Reading Benjamin as an undergraduate, this kind of analysis was dizzying and thrilling. In retrospect I realised there were gaps to fill if I was to understand or replicate the logic of this stretch from a facial expression to the tremors of world capitalism. The reading I undertook in the years immediately after working with Bruce, say before 1990, helped to fill this gap. Among the works in question were writings by Immanuel Wallerstein and Giovanni Arrighi on world systems theory, the postcolonial theory of Gayatri Chakravorty Spivak and Homi Bhabha, and Fredric Jameson's explorations of the relations between capitalism and cultural form. However, Bruce's emphasis on the sexual and aesthetic politics of decadence provided me with another angle to make sense of Benjamin's writings on the dandy and flâneur.

In many ways, my Honours thesis on Nancy Cunard was an attempt to come to terms with the gendered dimension of the figures of the dandy and flâneur. To what extent was it possible to apply the terms of Benjamin's analysis to the feminist revision of modernism? If, for the flâneur, a certain visual mastery

---

16   Benjamin, *Charles Baudelaire*, 96.

provides a means to negotiate the spectacular conditions of modernity, what of the female subject positioned as a vital, metonymic part of this spectacle? Cunard strove to control this visual field, posing for photographers such as Man Ray and Cecil Beaton as well as inspiring Constantin Brâncuși's sculpture *La jeune fille sophistiquée*. She was the paramour and patron of male literary figures. However, she also wrote her own poetry, much of which I could only obtain by writing to her biographer Hugh Ford, who generously sent copies of original publications and unpublished works. As the archetypal flapper, Cunard flouted sexual, racial and class boundaries, fashioning a subjectivity reducible to that of neither the flâneur nor the dandy. Yet she was also a privileged socialite, enmeshed by empire's financial and infrastructural webs as the heiress of a fortune amassed by running steamships across the Atlantic. This knot of gendered, economic, literary and visual relations offered fertile ground for a critical engagement with Benjamin's essays on Baudelaire, pointing to the limits of flânerie and dandyism as heuristic instruments for coming to terms with modernity's plural forms.

The Commodity

What then are the limits of Benjamin's rendering of modernism and urban modernity, and how do I see these limits now as opposed to when I first read the essays on Baudelaire? Responding to this question requires recognition of the multiple efforts of translation and commentary that have enhanced our knowledge of Benjamin's writings since 1986. Already in 1998, Peter Osborne noted that "Benjamin's prose breeds commentary like vaccine in a lab".[17] Howard Eiland and Kevin McLaughlin's translation of Rolf Tiedemann's edited volume *Das Passagen-Werk* appeared in 1999, offering English language readers a vista on the wider, unfinished and fragmentary project of which the essays on Baudelaire are a part.[18] By basing this chapter in a re-reading of translations that many would consider redundant, I do not mean to sideline the prodigious work that has clarified the relation of the writings in question to Benjamin's convoluted and complexly assembled oeuvre. Nor, however, do I seek to make this commentary a primary object of investigation. My interest is more in the faded memory of a past reading than in the reclamation or updating of perspectives made on its basis.

In this sense, my approach resonates with that of Benjamin's 1931 essay "Unpacking My Library", which associates the encounter with forgotten books with

---

17   Peter Osborne, "Philosophizing Beyond Philosophy: Walter Benjamin Reviewed", *Radical Philosophy* 88 (1998): 28.

18   Walter Benjamin, *Das Passagen-Werk*, ed. Rolf Tiedemann (Frankfurt: Suhrkamp Verlag, 1982); Walter Benjamin, *The Arcades Project*, trans. Howard Eiland and Kevin McLaughlin (Cambridge, MA: The Belknap Press of Harvard University Press, 1999).

"not thoughts but images, memories".[19] The questions of experience and memory return throughout Benjamin's writings, beginning with his early essays on Immanuel Kant. In *Charles Baudelaire*, these themes are most prominent in those sections that deal with the experience of shock, drawn from Baudelaire's account of the flâneur's negotiation of the crowd and made to link the machine, film and the game of chance. Theoretically, Benjamin explores a series of correspondences between Proust's "involuntary memory" and Freud's theory of consciousness. This investigation is part of his strategy of reading Baudelaire's portrayal of the modern symptomatically, as a way of reflecting on his own twentieth-century present and uncovering the experience of the transformation of historical time by the commodity form:

> The *flâneur* is someone abandoned in the crowd. In this he shares the situation of the commodity. He is not aware of this special situation, but this does not diminish its effect on him and it permeates him blissfully like a narcotic that can compensate him for many humiliations. The intoxication to which the *flâneur* surrenders is the intoxication of the commodity around which surges the stream of customers.[20]

Baudelaire's response to this intoxication was to attempt to distil the eternal or heroic within it, working primarily from a juxtaposition with the ancient and maintaining the anachronistic poetic form of the lyric. By contrast, Benjamin emphasised the shock of the new and the formal structure of sameness involved in its repetition, particularly in fashion, boredom and technical reproduction. By transforming the new into the self-same, the commodity refigures the possibilities for the experience of history. On the one hand, it de-historicises experience and breaks its relation to a successive or progressive notion of historical time. On the other, its restless sameness opens experience to something outside of time, a Messianic break, associated with the interruptive stasis of the image and the futural promise of revolution. In this double movement, the writings on Baudelaire open towards that most gnomic of Benjamin's late fragmentary texts, "Theses on the Philosophy of History".[21]

My first encounter with Benjamin's essays on Baudelaire was shaped by an engagement with the writings of two commentators, both of whom emphasised the commodity form. The first was Marshall Berman, who in *All That is Solid Melts into Air* characterises Benjamin as at once drawn by the commodity's fetishism and wrenched from its temptation by his Marxist sensibilities: "he wants to be saved, but not now".[22] The second was Terry Eagleton, whose *Walter Benjamin or Towards a Revolutionary Criticism* was published under the same Verso imprint as

---

19   Walter Benjamin, "Unpacking My Library: A Talk About Book Collecting", in *Illuminations*, ed. Hannah Arendt, trans. Harry Zohn (New York: Schocken Books, 1969), 67.
20   Benjamin, *Charles Baudelaire*, 55.
21   Walter Benjamin, "Theses on the Philosophy of History", in *Illuminations*, ed. Hannah Arendt, trans. Harry Zohn (New York: Schocken Books, 1969), 253–64.

the volume Bruce had lent me. Eagleton, in particular, zeroed in on the commodity, exploring its obfuscation of "the traces of its production", its capture in "the frozen dialectic of history", and its relation to "the modern semiotic signifier".[23] In so doing, Eagleton found in Benjamin's work "more than a strong echo of Georg Lukács's *History and Class Consciousness*, which in similar idealist fashion sees the reduction of the proletariat to the paradigmatic commodity as the prelude to its emancipation".[24] Although these commentaries bear the marks of their time, I still think it is important to stress the role of the commodity in Benjamin's thought. The point is not to dramatise the vacillations of the bourgeois intellectual, as does Berman, but to situate Benjamin's focus on the commodity in a global context that accounts for uneven development and variegated forms of capitalism.

Benjamin makes no secret that his study of Baudelaire has a distinct spatial and temporal location; Paris in the age of *Hochkapitalismus*. But the philosophical and theological underpinnings of his thought cut through this particularism and bring it into relation with more universalising tendencies. In this regard, it is important to situate Benjamin's thought within wider currents of historical materialism and critical theory. In broad terms, Benjamin's work is part of Western Marxism. This name is a label given by the Soviets to distinguish their own discussions from Lukács' *History and Class Consciousness*, a text that Benjamin studied assiduously during his stay on the Italian island of Capri in the mid-1920s. In the view of the Soviets, Lukács' work embodied a shift away from concerns with labour and production to a focus on how the commodity form structures thought and culture. As Harry Harootunian suggests, this "tendency has become so hegemonic or commonsense ... that it has managed to mask its own cultural and politically specific origins and run the risk of making its claims complicit with capitalism's self-representations".[25] At stake is the assumption that the commodity relation has been achieved everywhere, leading to the realisation of what Marx termed "real subsumption" and registering the final completion of capitalism's domination of everyday life. Continued through the work of the Frankfurt School, this line of thought is strongly upheld in Benjamin's writings of the 1930s, which perhaps more than others produced at the time, make the commodity form central to the structuring of modern social life and, in particular, to the operations of culture.

Undoubtedly, this feature recommended Benjamin's work to those who began to rescue and reconstruct it in the 1960s. However, in bringing the commodity form to the centre of his analysis, Benjamin is perhaps insufficiently attentive to variegations of capitalism outside Europe and the West, where the encounter with

---

22 Marshall Berman, *All That is Solid Melts into Air: The Experience of Modernity* (New York: Simon & Schuster, 1982), 146.

23 Terry Eagleton, *Walter Benjamin or Towards a Revolutionary Criticism* (London: Verso, 1981), 26, 28 and 30.

24 Eagleton, *Walter Benjamin*, 22.

25 Harry Harootunian, *Marx After Marx: History and Time in the Expansion of Capitalism* (New York: Columbia University Press, 2015).

heterogeneous forms of production, social organisation and culture often entails not real subsumption but the need for capital to reckon with its outsides through continuing processes of primitive accumulation or extraction. For Benjamin, as the earlier quoted passage about the dandy sitting at the centre of world trade and financial networks attests, the tremors of empire refract back upon the metropole. But what would it mean to analyse these interruptions at their source? For Harootunian, the "capacity to situate practices from earlier modes alongside newer ones under the command of capital" constitutes "the force of temporal interruption, unevenness, fracturing, and heterogeneity" that upsets capital's "homogenous, unitary, and linear trajectory of time".[26] Can, as this language suggests, the Benjaminian aesthetic of shock and temporal disruption be turned away from theological tropes of prophecy and towards an apprehension of how practices of solidarity and translation across different times and spaces might challenge the multiple and varied forms of capitalism? How to adapt Benjamin's insights for a contemporary world in which the transformation of historical time folds into the problem of the unity and disjunction of social space at the global level?

I cannot pretend to answer these questions here, although they inform much of the work I have done in recent times. My writings with Sandro Mezzadra grapple with the question of how capitalism operates across the different times that constitute the contemporary and within the social spaces in which these times are embedded and articulated.[27] This is not work that takes the literary as its primary object, but insofar as it traces mutations of politics and economics through modernity's multiple forms, it is perhaps not so far from the use I made of Benjamin under Bruce's instruction. Re-reading Benjamin's essays on Baudelaire as a means of charting changes in my own practice has dramatised a moment in the return of the same. But the repetitions at stake are not without punctuation. Bruce's lesson stands like an exclamation mark in the margin.

Bibliography

Benjamin, Walter. "Theses on the Philosophy of History." In *Illuminations*. Ed. Hannah Arendt. Trans. Harry Zohn, 253–64. New York: Schocken Books, 1969.

Benjamin, Walter. "Unpacking My Library: A Talk About Book Collecting." In *Illuminations*. Ed. Hannah Arendt. Trans. Harry Zohn, 59–67. New York: Schocken Books, 1969.

Benjamin, Walter. *Das Passagen-Werk*. Ed. Rolf Tiedemann. Frankfurt: Suhrkamp Verlag, 1982.

Benjamin, Walter. *Charles Baudelaire: A Lyric Poet in the Era of High Capitalism*. Trans. Harry Zohn. London: Verso, 1983.

Benjamin, Walter. *The Arcades Project*. Trans. Howard Eiland and Kevin McLaughlin. Cambridge, MA: The Belknap Press of Harvard University Press, 1999.

---

26 Harootunian, *Marx After Marx*, 64.

27 Sandro Mezzadra and Brett Neilson, *The Politics of Operations: Excavating Contemporary Capitalism* (Durham, NC: Duke University Press, 2019); Sandro Mezzadra and Brett Neilson, *The Rest and the West: Capital and Power in a Multipolar World* (London: Verso, 2024).

Berman, Marshall. *All That is Solid Melts into Air: The Experience of Modernity*. New York: Simon & Schuster, 1982.

Buck-Morss, Susan. *The Dialectics of Seeing: Walter Benjamin and the Arcades Project*. Cambridge, MA: The MIT Press, 1989.

Chan, L.K., and Raymond Donovan. "Safer Sex Messages: Australian HIV/AIDS Campaigns 1985–2014." *HIV Australia* 12, no. 3 (2014), 9.

Eagleton, Terry. *Walter Benjamin or Towards a Revolutionary Criticism*. London: Verso, 1981.

Fraser, Hilary. "Through the Looking-Glass: Looking Like a Woman in the Nineteenth Century." In *Strange Sisters: Literature and Aesthetics in the Nineteenth Century*. Ed. Francesca Orestano and Francesca Frigeri, 189–211. Oxford: Peter Lang, 2009.

Gardiner, Bruce. "Decadence: Its Construction and Contexts." *Southern Review* 18, March (1985), 22–43.

Gardiner, Bruce. "A Reckless Move." *Sydney Morning Herald*. 5 September 1985, 10.

Gardiner, Bruce. "Talking of Michelangelo: Routine and Radical Inquiry into Literature and Aesthetics." *Literature and Aesthetics* 22, no. 2 (2011), 180–98.

Harootunian, Harry. *Marx After Marx: History and Time in the Expansion of Capitalism*. New York: Columbia University Press, 2015.

Mezzadra, Sandro, and Brett Neilson. *The Politics of Operations: Excavating Contemporary Capitalism*. Durham, NC: Duke University Press, 2019.

Mezzadra, Sandro, and Brett Neilson. *The Rest and the West: Capital and Power in a Multipolar World*. London: Verso, 2024.

Osborne, Peter. "Philosophizing Beyond Philosophy: Walter Benjamin Reviewed." *Radical Philosophy* 88 (1998), 28–37.

8

The Windhover in Him

Peter Banki

Introduction

As a younger man, I remember watching you one day walk to the bus stop after a seminar and I noticed the way you walked. It was energetic, upbeat. I dare say, you were light and happy. And I thought to myself, the work of reading and teaching is giving you energy. You have found a relationship to it that is healthy and joyous. No mean feat. I had recently come back from Europe, and I had seen so many of us suffering, myself included, maybe unconsciously using the work as an alibi for this suffering.

This was perhaps a projection, a fiction I created for myself. But it has inspired me deeply. This bound me to you, as if you had a secret. You, who have experienced more adversity than most in life, whose mortal survival will have been due, you told me once, to sheer chance, who have lost – a lot, and lived so close to death, you have found some alliance with life, with pleasure, sensuality, eroticism through the reading of so many poems and books. Who ever knew there was so much poetry?

I remember sitting in your seminar with a poem in front of me, as if it were a primal scene. Sitting with confusion learning to read, to listen and speak with curiosity and pleasure.

How does one thank a teacher? By thinking, I'm told. But you will have been more than a teacher, I have been blessed also with a closeness. Am I allowed to say that I had a bit of a crush?

I never received what is called an academic appointment, which is often the destination of good students, even while I remember you telling me once that some of your best students didn't continue in the profession. As we all know, there are not enough jobs. Despite never having succeeded in joining the profession, I still feel a responsibility for scholarship and the values that sustain it. It lives in me, like so many ghosts.

But how does one even manage to do scholarly work today without institutional support? How even to access scholarly articles, if not by subterfuge, by using a friend's login details?

While remaining in the institution for over forty years you admirably resisted managerial coercion. You did not submit to the contract: publish or lose your job. And you were not fired. You had trouble sleeping, you told me, for a long time. We can't sleep when we don't feel safe. What I thought as a young man concerning the promise of an academic career was perhaps a mistake, that is, that you could have the security of a job and do what you believed to be most important. In his draft for the University of Berlin at the beginning of the nineteenth century, Wilhelm von Humboldt defined the modern idea of the university as a sanctuary (*Freistätte*), a refuge both from the state and market forces. He wrote:

> The idea of an academy must be noted as the highest and last free place [*Freistätte*] of science [*Wissenschaft*: a term, which includes the Humanities and Sciences] and as the corporation most independent from the state …
>
> Since these institutions can thus achieve their purpose only if each one, as much as possible, faces the pure idea of science (*Wissenschaft*), solitariness and freedom are the predominant principles in their circle. But since the intellectual work within humanity flourishes only as co-operation … the internal organization of these institutions must bring forth and sustain a collaboration that is uninterrupted, constantly self-renewing, but *unforced and without specific purpose*.[1]

As compromised and improbable as Humboldt's "inherently lovely and beneficial"[2] idea has become in the twenty-first century, at what cost today do we give up on it? You told me once you could not have grown into the scholar and teacher you became without the supportive conditions of continuous employment.

Keeping Promises

As a young man you told me you had once written to Patrick White, asking him if one could be both a writer and a literary critic. He wrote back a long letter to you, ultimately saying: "No, one has to choose." This is not a view that Friedrich Schlegel or Friedrich Hölderlin would have accepted. For me, your scholarship, while remaining rigorous, is also very artistic. When asked if he thought it necessary to make a firm distinction between literature and literary criticism, Jacques Derrida responded once:

---

1   Wilhelm von Humboldt, "On the Internal and External Organization of the Higher Scientific Institutions in Berlin" [1810], trans. Thomas Dunlap, 1; emphasis mine.

2   von Humboldt, "On the Internal and External Organization", 5.

I'm not sure … I don't feel at ease either with a rigorous distinction between "literature" and "literary criticism" or with a confusion of the two. What would the rigorous limit between them be? "Good" literary criticism, the only worthwhile kind, implies an act, a literary signature or counter-signature, an inventive experience of language, in language, an inscription of the act of reading in the field of the text that is read … At any rate I wouldn't distinguish between "literature" and "literary criticism," but I wouldn't assimilate all forms of writing or reading. These new distinctions ought to give up on the purity and linearity of frontiers.[3]

Whether or not we can keep our promises, Derrida says elsewhere, the promise itself is an affirmation, a commitment (*engagement*) to the future:

I believe one ought to be able to say that, beyond determined promises, all language acts entail a certain structure of the promise, even if they do something else at the same time. All language is addressed to the other in order to promise him or her to speak to him or her in some way […] Before I even decide what I am going to say, I promise to speak to you, I respond to the promise to speak, I respond. I respond to you as soon as I speak and consequently I commit or pledge myself.[4]

It took me forever to finish my PhD. But I always thought I had this responsibility to you (and others) to finish it, even though you were not my advisor or even worked in the same field. I was also accountable to you. That it could take a long time and that it was okay that it took a long time. I am still accountable. The credit account is still open.

Unlike the others, you acknowledged and took interest in the erotics of teaching, even, dare I say, in its homoerotic and sadomasochist aspects. Scrupulously ethical and never crossing the line of physical contact or professional boundaries, you gave hospitality to erotic play in and as the study of literature. Never too much, but in a manner that was honest about what may be going on psychically between teachers and students, or supervisors and supervisees. This hospitality to erotic play tickled me and even made me feel safe, because you acknowledged what is so often unspeakable. To illustrate what a supervisor sometimes has to do, I remember once that during an induction for doctoral candidates you rather theatrically put on some leather.

---

3   Jacques Derrida, "This Strange Institution Called Literature: An Interview with Jacques Derrida", trans. Geoffrey Bennington and Rachel Bowlby. In *Acts of Literature*, ed. Derek Attridge (New York: Routledge, 1992), 49.

4   Jacques Derrida, "Passages From Traumatism to Promise", in *Points…: Interviews 1974–1994*, trans. Peggy Kamuf and others, ed. Elisabeth Weber (Stanford, CA: Stanford University Press, 1992), 384. See also Jacques Derrida, *Mémoires for Paul de Man*, trans. Cecile Lindsay, Jonathan Culler, Eduardo Cadava and Peggy Kamuf (New York: Columbia University Press, 1989), 94f.

While undoubtedly there are possibilities of abuse if boundaries are crossed in hierarchically-structured workplaces, I think it is also dangerous not to acknowledge erotic dynamics and play, because doing so feeds into the shame, fear and ignorance about sexuality that remains so prevalent in our culture and its institutions. How does one acknowledge such dynamics and their diverse effects, while also emphasising that for good reason professional boundaries remain?[5]

Babbling with Heidegger and Paul Celan

After failing to finish a PhD in philosophy at the University of Sydney, in my early thirties I received a grant to enrol in another PhD program in the German department at New York University. I learned German and eventually wrote a dissertation, which became a book entitled *The Forgiveness to Come: The Holocaust and the Hyper-Ethical*.[6] You scrupulously read and commented on the dissertation and also helped me through the publication process. The book was concerned with the impasses of forgiveness, especially in relation to the legacies of Nazi crimes against humanity. I tried to articulate a thought of forgiveness that would not imply closure of the infinite wounds of the past, that would not amount to any kind of "moving on" or amnesia. I wrote:

> If there were such a thing as forgiveness, it would require as a condition that the place of the unforgivable be left empty and/or unspoken. No definition of the unforgivable should be presupposed nor any definite criteria given as to how it could be judged. Only by resisting translation of the injury into a statement of an ontotheological kind (such as "this is unforgivable," or even at the limit, "this is wrong"), only by questioning the necessity of such a translation, can giving and forgiving continue to be possible.[7]

This thought of leaving empty the empty place was inspired by a line from the twentieth-century author and literary theorist Maurice Blanchot, who in *The Writing of Disaster* wrote counter-intuitively:

---

5   "Zealous to exclude the sexual from the pedagogical, many believe teacher-student relations should be neither social nor personal. Although I can see that a 'strictly business' approach is probably the best way to guard against the sexual, I envision an enormous pedagogical loss from prohibiting interaction with the student as a person. ... While I recognized the recently understood dangers of such liaisons, I was nonetheless concerned that an entire stretch of experience was being denied, consigned to silence." Jane Gallop, "Sex and Sexism: Feminism and Harassment Policy", *Academe*: 16–23. See also Jane Gallop, *Feminist Accused of Sexual Harassment* (Durham, NC: Duke University Press, 1997).
6   Peter Banki, *The Forgiveness to Come: The Holocaust and the Hyper-Ethical* (New York: Fordham University Press, 2018).
7   Banki, *The Forgiveness to Come*, 112.

Do not forgive. Forgiveness accuses before it forgives. By accusing, by stating the injury, it makes the wrong irredeemable [*irremissible*]. It carries the blow all the way to culpability. [*Il porte le coup jusqu'à la culpabilité.*] Thus, all becomes irreparable; giving and forgiving cease to be possible.[8]

In the book I decided not to include a reading of Paul Celan's famous poem "Todtnauberg" (1970), which bears witness to his meeting with Martin Heidegger in the philosopher's cabin in the Black Forest in 1967. But because the topos of this meeting was so closely related to my project's, at the very least I had to justify this decision in a footnote. I gave the excuse that I felt I have nothing to add to the fine studies which already exist. But even if one has nothing to add, maybe the path and the pain through the encounter with this poem is ineluctable, if one wants to study German poetry and philosophy responsibly.

Several contemporary readings of the poem, including that of Jacques Derrida, have questioned the priority given to the theme of the poet's disappointed expectation for a word from Heidegger about the Shoah and have focused rather on the motif of the gift of the poem as of a forgiveness asked for, granted and/or to come. For Derrida, there is already a gesture of forgiveness inscribed in the act of addressing oneself and speaking to another, just as there is one also inscribed in the act of listening. "Forgiveness", he says, "is implied in the very first speech act. I cannot perform what I would like to perform. That is why things happen."[9] From this point of view, the poet's expectation must have been disappointed, even if Heidegger had made a public declaration repudiating the resurgence of Nazism. Derrida says I cannot perform what I would like to perform because language – or what he calls "trace" and later "cinders" also in memory of the Holocaust – do not permit self-identity and self-presence. The trace, cinders or ash differ and defer themselves. They are iterable. As a consequence, what I consciously wish or intend to perform is never what I do perform, there will always be *différance*: spacing and temporisation.[10] Speaking, writing, reading and listening are never identical with themselves, and thus in a sense never take place as something that I, as a subject, can simply perform. In order for things to happen, therefore, there is always implicitly, silently, a forgiveness requested and/or granted. This event of forgiveness happens, as it were, automatically, without the subject consciously intending it and, moreover, as something that is undecidedly equivocal, heterogenous to the order of presentable knowledge in the present.

---

8   Maurice Blanchot, *The Writing of Disaster*, trans. Ann Smock (Lincoln: University of Nebraska Press, 1995), 105; Maurice Blanchot, *L'écriture du désastre* (Paris: Gallimard, 1980), 89. See also Sara Guyer's reading of this passage in "The Pardon of the Disaster", *Sub-Stance* 35, no.1 (2006): 85–105.

9   Jacques Derrida, "On Forgiveness: A Roundtable Discussion with Jacques Derrida", in *Questioning God*, ed. John D. Caputo et al. (Bloomington: Indiana University Press, 2001), 56.

10   Jacques Derrida, "Differance", in *Margins of Philosophy*, trans. Alan Bass (Chicago, IL: Chicago University Press, 1986), 1–27.

Todtnauberg	Todtnauberg
Arnika, Augentrost, der Trunk aus dem Brunnen mit dem Sternwürfel drauf,	Arnica, eyebright, the draft from the well with the starred die above it,
in der Hütte,	in the hut,
die in das Buch – wessen Namen nahms auf vor dem meinen? –, die in dies Buch geschriebene Zeile von einer Hoffnung, heute, auf eines Denkenden kommendes Wort im Herzen,	the line – whose name did the book register before mine? –, the line inscribed in that book about a hope, today, for a thinking man's coming word in the heart,
Waldwasen, uneingeebnet, Orchis und Orchis, einzeln,	woodland sward, unlevelled, orchid and orchid, single,
Krudes, später, im Fahren, deutlich,	coarse stuff, later, clear, in passing,
der uns fährt, der Mensch, der's mit anhört,	he who drives us, the man, who listens in,
die halb- beschrittenen Knüppel- pfade im Hochmoor,	the half- trodden wretched tracks through the high moors,
Feuchtes, viel.	dampness, much.[11]

Now the question this thinking leaves open is whether an experience of forgiveness is inscribed not only in speech, but also in silence? Can silence be addressed to the other as a promise, affirmation, commitment, pledge? Can silence be a cinder of forgiveness asked for, granted, and/or to come?

Maybe the first thing to say about the poem "Todtnauberg" is what it does not say. It does not give a transparent and univocal narration of what happened, if such were possible. Even while it mentions "*Krudes, später, im Fahren, deutlich*"

---

11   Paul Celan, *Gesammelte Werke*, Band 2 (Frankfurt: Suhrkamp, 1983), 255–6; Paul Celan, "Todtnauberg", trans. Michael Hamberger, in *Poems of Paul Celan* (New York: Persea Books, 1989), 292–3.

("crudeness later clearly while on the road"[12]), it does not name what this crudeness refers to or who utters it. The proximity of the two words "crudeness" and "clearly" even suggests that clarity may itself be crudeness in this context. The letter of the poem and its ellipsis complicate any simple narrative such as the form: "Celan came, Heidegger did not ask the Jews for forgiveness in the name of the Germans. Celan who was waiting for a word of forgiveness left disappointed and he made a poem of it. He recorded it."

Even to the point where it is scarcely intelligible, Celan's language resists the logic of univocal representation. This is probably one of the reasons why his poetry is so important in relation to the questions I raised above. I would even go so far as to suggest that it is possible to read Celan's poetry without necessarily referring to the Holocaust, that the poetry is legible without this reference, such that in its dialogue with Hölderlin, for example, it could have been written in the nineteenth century, even if the Shoah had never happened.

In relation to the letter and ellipsis of the poem, many scholars have sought to determine its meaning by referring to the biographical details and testimonies given in correspondence with Celan, including that of Martin Heidegger. This witnessing is probably indispensable to the reading of the poem, but it is also supplementary inasmuch as the poem still speaks without it. There is a double imperative, reminiscent of those who testified to the camps: "Know what happened, do not forget, but at the same time never will you know."[13] A lot of Celan's poetry is similar in this regard. In his famous reading of Paul Celan's *Du Liegst*, a poem on the murder of Rosa Luxemburg and Karl Liebknecht, Peter Szondi argues that if one was not a witness at the exact time and place in which the events happened, one will never know to what the poem is exactly bearing witness.[14]

In the summer of 1967 Paul Celan visited Martin Heidegger in his cabin in the Black Forest. The previous night Celan gave a poetry reading at the invitation of Gerhart Baumann, Ordinarius for Germanistik at Freiburg University, in an auditorium packed with well over a thousand listeners. Heidegger sat in the first row as Celan read. Afterwards at dinner, when Celan expressed the wish to see the nearby moorland, invited him to see the Horbacher Moor the next day and, while in the area, to visit his cabin near Todtnauberg, a Black Forest village southeast of Freiburg.[15]

Celan, who during their meeting before his reading had brusquely refused to be photographed with Heidegger, reluctantly accepted the invitation. It was, as he explained to Baumann, difficult for him to come together with a man whose

---

12   All unattributed translations are mine.

13   Blanchot, *The Writing of Disaster*, 153.

14   Peter Szondi, "Eden", in *Celan Studies*, trans. Susan Bernofsky with Harvey Mendelsohn (Stanford, CA: Stanford University Press), 88.

15   Werner Hamacher and Heidi Hart, "Wasen: On Celan's 'Todtnauberg'", *The Yearbook of Comparative Literature* 57 (2011): 18. Hamacher's account follows the narrative given in Gerhart Baumann, *Erinnerungen an Paul Celan* (Frankfurt: Suhrkamp, 1986 and 1992), 59–80.

history he could not forget. He spent the morning before the group lunch with Heidegger near Todtnauberg. Baumann's assistant, Gerhard Neumann, was with them both in Heidegger's cabin and on a walk on the moor, soon interrupted by wet weather.

During their time in the cabin, Celan inscribed these lines in the guest book:

Into the hut-book, with the view of the well-star / with hope for a coming word in the heart. / On July 25, 1967 / Paul Celan.[16]

Just a few days after this visit, on 1 August, Celan wrote the poem titled "Todtnauberg" in Frankfurt; it contains an almost word-for-word rendering of the words he had written in the guest book. Returning to Paris the next day, 2 August, Celan reported to his wife:

Heidegger approached me – the day after my reading I went, with M. Neumann, the friend of Elmar [Tophoven], to Heidegger's cabin in the Black Forest. Afterwards there was a serious conversation in the car, with very clear words on my part. M. Neumann, who witnessed this, told me afterwards that the conversation held an epochal aspect for him. I hope that Heidegger takes up his pen and writes some responsive, warning pages that repudiate the resurgence of Nazism.[17]

Against this backdrop, the poem can be read as a fixing of impressions that struck Celan during the morning gathering at Heidegger's cabin. It appears on the surface to recapitulate and recall an historic event, an epochal meeting, and to recognise the "obvious proof" of Celan's "painful disappointment, perhaps also adamant rejection of Heidegger".

On 2 November 1967, three months after the transcription of "Todtnauberg", Celan turned to Robert Altmann, the publisher of Éditions Brunidor, and proposed that the poem appear in a single, limited edition. On 12 January 1968 the Brunidor edition of "Todtnauberg" appeared in an edition of fifty copies, the first of which was sent to Heidegger. Two weeks later, in a letter to Celan, Heidegger responded:

The word of the poet who says "Todtnauberg," who names place and landscape where a thought tried to take a step back into baseness (*wo ein Denken den Schritt zurück ins Geringe versuchte*) – the word of the poet, which is at once encouragement and warning and which preserves a memento of a Black Forest day of many moods (*vielfältig gestimmten Tag im Schwarzwald aufbewahrt*). But it happened already in the evening of your unforgettable reading at the first greeting

---

16 "Ins Hüttenbuch, mit dem Blick auf den Brunnenstern / mit einer Hoffnung auf ein kommendes Wort im Herzen / am 25. Juli 1967 / Paul Celan." Cited in Werner Hamacher and Heide Hart, "Wasen: On Celan's 'Todtnauberg'", 28.

17 *Paul Celan-Gisèle Celan-Lestrange: Correspondence I.*, eds. Bertrand Badiou and Eric Celan (Paris: Seuil, 2001), 550, cited in W. Hamacher, "Wasen: On Celan's 'Todtnauberg'", 18–19.

at the hotel. Since then we have left much unsaid to each other (*Vieles einander zugeschwiegen*). I think that there is still a day in which to talk about the unspoken (*daß einiges noch eines Tages im Gespräch aus dem Ungesprochenen gelöst wird*).[18]

The rare verb in Heidegger's letter, *zuschweigen*, is hardly translatable; it corresponds to *zusprechen* and *zusagen*, which both mean various forms of addressing the other (to promise or to affirm, to speak forwardly and so on), but *zuschweigen* means to address silence to someone; not exactly to address something by silence to someone, but to address silence to someone.

Celan read again in Freiburg several months after Heidegger's letter, in June 1968, and undertook another excursion on the moor with Heidegger. Two years later, in March 1970, when Celan was more ill than ever, a third and final meeting between the two occurred in Freiburg; they made arrangements for another in Donautal. A month later, in April, Celan took his own life in the Seine.

Bibliography

Banki, Peter. *The Forgiveness to Come: The Holocaust and the Hyper-Ethical*. New York: Fordham University Press, 2018.

Blanchot, Maurice. *The Writing of Disaster*. Trans. Ann Smock. Lincoln: University of Nebraska Press, 1995.

Celan, Paul. *Paul Celan-Gisèle Celan-Lestrange: Correspondence I*. Ed. Bertrand Badiou and Eric Celan. Paris: Seuil, 2001, 550, cited in Hamacher, "Wasen: On Celan's 'Todtnauberg'", 18–19.

Derrida, Jacques. "On Forgiveness: A Roundtable Discussion with Jacques Derrida", in *Questioning God*. Ed. John D. Caputo et al. Bloomington: Indiana University Press, 2001.

Derrida, Jacques. "Differance", in *Margins of Philosophy*. Trans. Alan Bass. Chicago, IL: Chicago University Press, 1986, 1–27.

Derrida, Jacques. "This Strange Institution Called Literature: An Interview with Jacques Derrida". Trans. Geoffrey Bennington and Rachel Bowlby, in *Acts of Literature*. Ed. Derek Attridge. New York: Routledge, 1992, 49.

Hamacher, Werner and Heidi Hart, "Wasen: On Celan's 'Todtnauberg'", *The Yearbook of Comparative Literature* 57 (2011): 15–54.

Lyon, James K. *Paul Celan and Martin Heidegger: An Unresolved Conversation, 1951–1970*. Baltimore, MD: Johns Hopkins University Press, 2006, 240.

Szondi, Peter. "Eden", in *Celan Studies*. Trans. Susan Bernofsky with Harvey Mendelsohn. Stanford, CA: Stanford University Press, 83–92.

von Humboldt, Wilhelm. "On the Internal and External Organization of the Higher Scientific Institutions in Berlin". Trans. Thomas Dunlap. Accessed 1 June 2023. Original source: Wilhelm von Humboldt, *Werke in fünf Bänden* [*Works in Five Volumes*]. Ed. Andreas Flitner and Klaus Giel, 4: *Schriften zur Politik und zum Bildungswesen* [*Writings on Politics and Education*]. Darmstadt: Wissenschaftliche Buchgesellschaft, 3rd ed., 1982, 253–65. https://ghdi.ghi-dc.org/sub_document.cfm?document_id=3642.

---

18   James K. Lyon, *Paul Celan and Martin Heidegger: An Unresolved Conversation, 1951–1970* (Baltimore, MD: Johns Hopkins University Press, 2006), 240.

Part II. Imagined Pedagogies: Poetry and Play

9

Triptych

For Bruce Gardiner

Toby Fitch

1

Did Picasso do Stein or did Stein do Picasso.
Would this be the definitive public image, or would that
be too wooden, her face rendered as if detached and stuck
through a hole in a circus board. Would her word be ruse
or rose. I do and I dote as echo chamber, yet still

poem and painting converse. Just how that came about is a little
vague in everybody's mind. Like a brushstroke the truth broke
and posed to me ninety times for this portrait. Would that be
to divide, to outstroke or outbrush one another. To what end this
is becoming yourself. As winter went on pulling down curtains

slow as a Swiss glacier. During these long walks and poses
I mediated, made sentences like a seesaw. Painting and poem
converge despite everyone's interference. I, too, dislike it – my face –
but somehow it adheres, indifferent as an echo. I can't see you
any longer when I look. All the same it is all there.

2

Not all there. Lights out. I'm taking a bath, listening
to the sonar pealings of a bat, which is arcing above

the trainline looking for things to chop up and chomp
down on. The bath water's an *Architect's Table*,

a phantasmal, shallow space churning with glacial,
three-dimensional colours, impossible to know

in the dark. I project its textures beneath my fingers
of hammered metal, chiselled stone, tiled brick,

stucco, cut paper and glass, while the noise of two
trains, my legs, ploughs through the water. All these

phenomena leap out at me. Other parallels look in.
But how to round them up or down. A little whorl

descends beneath the surface of the water while the
bat's shadow ascends a wall, through two-dimensional

tree shadows, into the stuck night sky. My mind's a flat
circle from certain angles, dropping traces of its leaving

into the choppy waters of *MA JOLIE* – my oval face reflecting
and projecting its appeal – as its desire branches out, as if

to sweep the sky, perceiving. And wouldn't that mean,
or wouldn't that be, to make of poiesis a batsign.

3

Is water ludic. Would it make me a luddite to think that. There is light inside it. And utter it in liquid time. Really. What a to-do in the gutter. Meanwhile, a reel of toads, or frogs, teems unruly in my garden.

Re gardening, I would like to speak magnolias to my beloved rogue planet, the plural of France, but … (I'm getting the films mixed up) she's a Celtic melon from first to last (reel), raining birds.

Should this be mean, or not mean, be. Does being mean to speak more freely when sampled and meanly sober, or does being merely *libre* in reverse misread, for example, a glass of red mist as the exemplary train of thought pouring through it, shattering Earth into a billion shards.

Do jests test the limits of admissible, the. In this are we just being miserable, or does melancholia miss us, being the finest jest of all, as in becoming who we may as well remain for the rest of our lives. And wouldn't that leave me abject, and our curls feeling sick (without a beloved lemon).

So much for self-banalysis. For words such as (these) delphiniums (I hand you) detonate into larkspur! With luck, doing both (with lemon) will unstick us from this broth, so that understanding may begin, and in doing so be undone.

Back in my bath, a vast broth of chaotic echoes, you and my text reassemble beneath our touch, suggesting a pattern of diamonds or lozenges, according to the trains. Or chess from a bat's-eye point of view. Or prison if we're in a bad mood. Or at last a lucid cave to see us through to the end of time in, budding with new chiasmata as if to (dis)integrate glass in its prism.

Through that would light not scintillate.

Note: In Bruce Gardiner's lecture on Gertrude Stein's two poems "Picasso" and "If I Told Him: A Completed Portrait of Picasso", Gardiner arrives at the notion that the latter of the two poems in particular "reconceives the nature and function of poetry, savouring three possibilities in turn. First, is poetry representational, as Plato thinks, concerned with exact resemblance? Second, is it symbolic, as Freud thinks, concerned with signs and their significance? And third, is it ludic, as Ludwig Wittgenstein thinks, concerned with rule-bound social and intellectual play? Stein is certainly anti-Platonic and anti-Freudian." My "Triptych" plays on these three questions regarding the nature and function of poetry, while shards of Gardiner's lecture, Stein's poems, Marianne Moore's poem "Poetry", John Ashbery's "And *Ut Pictura Poiesis* Is Her Name" and Gertrude Stein's *Autobiography of Alice B. Toklas* are refracted throughout.

10
Street Library (A–Z)

Michelle Kelly

I started on the street but moved to the screen

Like social media free libraries are

> *Always* open for browsing, day or night

In the angled light strewn by my phone I learn the street library on Oxford Street

> started w– an old *bookcase* & a *bag of books*

The photo shows a bookcase against a wall painted with a beam spreading from shelves to

the stars – like a beacon; a siren call to

> *Come* find your story

I sink into the pool of light and it holds me; a world of books and not a scrap of paper in my

hand

*

In Newtown, someone surveyed a street library and noticed

> One of these books was about *decluttering*, very apt

In Marrickville, Petty Cash consider its collection

> an *extension* of the cafe and we lovingly curate and stock it daily

In Amsterdam, a photographer documents

> novel ways of storing books outside, ranging from an old Coca-Cola *fridge* to a retired
>
> phone kiosk

Boys hold books and stand tall outside a New Lambton home and I learn

> Street Library is a great project to do with your family during a *global* pandemic

*

a tiny vestibule of literary *happiness*
a symbol of trust and *hope*

*

A street library can be built from a flat-pack but
     It ain't *ikea*
In a construction workshop someone's congratulated for
     most accurate *joins* and neat cuts on the day!
At school a year 11 class built
     the *kit* version of The Shed
A pitched roof is retained in a new model for those who prefer
     a more traditional *look* and a storybook feel
A cottage industry in several senses
Site in the structure
The mode of production within the build

*

Little library | Bigger on the inside
More metonymy still
The pool of light within the book

*

Street librarians may be reverent but also not:
     You know your Street Library is getting well used when it gets *MESSY*!
An alphabet too can be
     something of a *mess...*

Its elements are as found, and their use as plastic as may sustain the happy rivalry

through which they define one another's usefulness

An alphabet is *not* a logical system

And yet

The impulse to put things in *order*, as Immanuel Kant insists, is irrepressible

*

One street library in the inner city is

set amongst an edible, *organic* garden

Of course! Because

Street Libraries are beautiful homes for books, *planted* in your front yard

(A book is like a little garden carried in your *pocket*)

(A real green thumb says they

always carry a box of great books with me to "*pollinate*" any little libraries I find)

Some street libraries are topiary with all the trimmings, but we're drawn in too by what grows over:

Grab a book, find a *quiet* spot in the park, and have a read under a shady tree

*

The impulse to repeat:

irresistable, cannot be *resisted* when contemplating a site designed for flow

Some street libraries are

replenished regularly

Some custodians aim

to *refresh* the contents weekly

Elsewhere,

It doesn't take long for a book share to become part of local's *routines*

A street librarian sits on her porch to check out

our *regulars*

including

The *runner* who stops every time to check for new books

and

      Little kids crowding around on their walk home from *school*

One structure is made

      from *second-hand and salvaged* materials

and is accompanied by a box

      stocked with fresh and dried herbs from the garden

*

      The *street* is the giver

*

It was a passion for literacy that inspired one educator to establish a street library:

      Helping children learn to read and enjoy books is one of the greatest moments for a
      teacher

It is axiomatic too that the teacher is the giver

*

      Use edges and *value* the marginal

is a permaculture principle, I learn; high words to shape worthy deeds

One person established their library guided by a declaration they recalled from a book:

      You must do something to make your *world* more beautiful

A customised bicycle, the *XYZ CARGO MOBILE LIBRARY*, inspires the incredible

Borgesian prospect of enabling access to

      all the necessary books without limits

A coastal street library, decorated with writing, displays

      a hundred titles that have given me great pleasure over the *years*

*

Zero means none

reads the *Macquarie Children's Dictionary* I picked up from the free library in a local bowling club. The dictionary is otherwise jauntily illustrated but the image for zero is a plump black "O"

A "Z" in a circle, in a square, in a far from elementary alphabet, traces

endless movement through a world that never moves...

circling through the same twenty-four hours or twenty-six letters again

Or through one trillion pixels

And papered dreams; the drowning scroll; or

The boxes that yield and receive

The loop of text and the pool of light

Source notes

Indented text are quotations drawn from Twitter and Instagram, predominantly posts accompanying photographs of street libraries, and other sources as noted. The quotations are unaltered except for the addition of italics. Date and time stamps are as they appeared to me.

Always: Fiske Street Little Library [@FiskeLittle], Twitter, 21 June 2021, 11:33am.

Bookcase/bag of books: Place Partners [@PlacePartners], Twitter, 26 February 2016, 10:31pm.

Come: Fiske Street Little Library [@FiskeLittle], Twitter, 7 February 2022, 7:48am.

Decluttering: Alison Byrne [@alisonmarybyrne], Instagram, 18 April 2016.

Extension: Petty Cash Cafe [@pettycashcafe], Instagram, 19 July 2021.

Fridge: Eglė [@egleskl], Instagram, 10 February 2022.

Global: "Street Librarian", cited on Street Library Australia [@streetlibraryau], Instagram, 19 February 2022.

Happiness/hope: Street Library Australia, "What is a Street Library?". Accessed 1 June 2023. https://streetlibrary.org.au/what-is-a-street-library/. I have transposed the sequence of phrases in the statement.

Ikea: StreetLibrary [@streetlibraryau], Twitter, 24 August 2017, 10:08am.

Joins: StreetLibrary [@streetlibraryau], Twitter, 30 November 2015, 11:19am.

Kit: Street Library Australia [@streetlibraryau], Instagram, 7 December 2020.

Look/little: Street Library Australia [@streetlibraryau], Instagram, 28 September 2022; Fiske Street Little Library [@FiskeLittle], Twitter bio at 10 February 2022.

Messy/mess: The Markets Wanniassa [@themarketswanniassa], Instagram, 30 June 2019; Bruce Gardiner, "Djuna Barnes's *Creatures in an Alphabet*: From A for Anecdotage to Z for Zoomancy", in *Shattered Objects: Djuna Barnes's Modernism*. Eds. Elizabeth Pender and Cathryn Setz, University Park, PA: Pennsylvania State University Press, 2019, 75.

Not: Gardiner, "Djuna Barnes's *Creatures in an Alphabet*", 75.

Order/organic: Gardiner, "Djuna Barnes's *Creatures in an Alphabet*", 89 (Here Gardiner refers the reader to Immanuel Kant "on teleological judgments generally" in *The Critique of the Power of Judgment*); Beth Herbert [@bethwacreative], Instagram, 27 July 2019.

Planted/pocket/pollinate: StreetLibrary Australia [@streetlibraryau], Twitter bio at 30 May 2023; "Street Librarian", cited on Street Library Australia [@streetlibraryau], Instagram, 4 April 2022; Crystal [@books_inthewild], Instagram, 20 July 2022.

Quiet: Whiteman Park [@whitemanpark], Instagram, 21 November 2019.

Replenished regularly/refresh/routines/regulars/runner: Our Lady of Mercy College, Burraneer [@olmcburraneer], Instagram, 16 June 2020; Rhoda [@booksbakesandbrooches], Instagram, 18 January 2020; StreetLibrary [@streetlibraryau], Twitter, 13 November 2016, 1:49pm; Leslie Paige [@homelorelibrary], Instagram, 6 January 2022; Leslie Paige [@homelorelibrary], Instagram, 6 January 2022.

School/second-hand and salvaged/stocked/street: Leslie Paige [@homelorelibrary], Instagram, 6 January 2022; "Shani", cited on Permaculture Australia [@permacultureaustraliaofficial], Instagram, 17 November 2020; "Shani" cited on Permaculture Australia [@permacultureaustraliaofficial], Instagram, 17 November 2020; Josephine Pennicott [@talepeddlerJo], Twitter, 6 February 2022, 3:25pm.

Teacher: Street Library Australia [@streetlibraryau], Instagram, 3 April 2022.

Use/value: "Shani", cited on Permaculture Australia, [@permacultureaustraliaofficial], Instagram, 17 November 2020.

World: Little Free Library® [@LtlFreeLibrary], Twitter, 20 June 2021, 9:40am. The book referred to is *Miss Rumphius*.

XYZ: V-A-C Foundation [@vacfoundation], Instagram, 9 July 2021. The name of the bicycle was sourced from: http://n55.dk/NEWS/omninews.html. Accessed 31 May 2023.

Years: "Street Librarian", cited on Street Library Australia [@streetlibraryau], Instagram, 27 December 2021.

Zero/Z: Macquarie Library, in association with Ashton Scholastic, *The Macquarie Children's Dictionary*, illustrated by Louis Silvestro, McMahons Point: Macquarie Library, 1983 (reprinted 1985), 108; Gardiner, "Djuna Barnes's *Creatures in an Alphabet*", 88–89.

11

Bruce Gardiner's Emily Dickinson

Monique Rooney

Part One: My and We; Girl and Gun

My We

> It is the women above all – there never have been women, save pioneer Katies; not
> one in flower save some moonflower Poe may have seen or an unripe child. Poets?
> Where? They are the test. But a true woman in flower, never. Emily Dickinson,
> starving of passion in her father's garden, is the very nearest we have ever been –
> starving.
> Never a woman: never a poet. That's an axiom. Never a poet saw sun here.
> William Carlos Williams, *In the American Grain*

In the above quotation, which is the epigraph to Susan Howe's *My Emily Dickinson*,
there are only two pronouns – a "they" and a "we". The quotation stands alone on
a page of Howe's text; turn the page to her introduction, and you'll see that the
first word of her first sentence is "My". "My book is a contradiction of its epigraph,"
she writes.[1] With this beginning, Howe stakes her territory, suggesting that she will
be reading her book's poet against the grain of an American great. She thus takes
Williams' Dickinson from her place in his textual garden, where she is "starving"
while being subject to the starvation of "we who have ever been – starving".

> My Life had stood – a Loaded Gun –
> In Corners – till a Day –
> The owner passed – identified –
> And carried Me away –

---

1   Susan Howe, *My Emily Dickinson* (New York: New Directions Press, 2007 [1985]), Loc. 140.

Howe's *My Emily Dickinson* is itself a loaded gun, one that affords power and greatness to its owner or user. The "My" of both the book's opening sentence and its title recurs throughout the text, including in ways that explicitly undercut the idea of possession. For example, Howe writes that the transmission of "My voice" to a page incurs loss of authority, autonomy and ownership:

> My voice formed from my life belongs to no one else. What I put into words is no longer my possession. Possibility has opened. The future will forget, erase, or recollect and deconstruct every poem. There is a mystic separation between poetic vision and ordinary living. The conditions for poetry rest outside each life at a miraculous reach indifferent to worldly chronology.[2]

Thus can we understand Howe's possession – the reach of her book *My Emily Dickinson* – as the writing of a life ("My Life"). This life that "had stood – a Loaded Gun – / In Corners – till a Day –" inscribes a voice that echoes:

> And every time I speak for Him
> The Mountains straight reply –

Does Howe, like Dickinson before her, merely echo "Him" who comes before all things?

Emily Dickinson is the Phallus

"Howe's Emily Dickinson *is* the [Lacanian] phallus of American Literature." This is my recollection of words spoken by Bruce Gardiner in a 1992 class I attended and that have returned unbidden to my mind each time I've since prepared classes on Dickinson's poems. The words returned as I listened in 2020 to two of Bruce's recorded lectures. These were not the 1992 lectures of my aforementioned recall, but rather two on Dickinson from Bruce's "Six Lectures on Four American Poets" that he had delivered in 2020 and shared with me. In these lectures, Bruce's Dickinson is an unflinchingly unsentimental writer whose attention to death concentrates poetic powers that deliver her enjoyment of solitude. While a poem such as "I'm Nobody! Who are You?" "sets us thinking about the social and cultural power of the proper name",[3] Bruce's Dickinson also intensifies a stony individuality whose singularity he entirely sets apart from Whitman and his poetry of *we* and *they* – "His body is as theirs; their voices are as his."[4] Anticipating my contribution to this volume, I email Bruce to ask if he remembers describing Howe's Dickinson as the "phallus of American Literature". In his reply, Bruce does not discount the

---

2   Howe, *My Emily Dickinson*, Loc. 220.
3   Bruce Gardiner, "Six Lectures on Four American Poets", Lecture One.
4   Gardiner, "Six Lectures on Four American Poets", Lectures One and Three.

possibility that he spoke those words, and he later sends me photocopies of those very lectures. Did I "forget, erase, or recollect and deconstruct" words that may have been spoken rather than written down for class? Or did I attribute that voice and ear to him?

Giddy Pride in Her Own Power of Utterance

In an email reply sent to me in November of 2021, Bruce wrote:

> I recall teaching "My Life had stood – a Loaded Gun –" in several classes, most vividly in those on [James Fenimore] Cooper's *The Deerslayer*, in which I took it to epitomise the predicament of Judith Hutter, reduced at the end (in Chapter 32) to her gun, dubbed Killdeer, festooned with her ribbon, and that of her sword-wielding Biblical namesake. I happen to have turned my seminar notes on Cooper into lectures, which I could send you. I cannot find my notes on Susan Howe, even though I have now sorted through all forty years' worth of my files, but they may be pinned to other notes on citation. The gun certainly possesses the symbolic physiology of the phallus: a thumb (thumbs up or down, under the thumb, giving the thumb), a mouth (of eruptive, ballistic force), an eye (sovereign, predatory), a rigidity (inorganic, mechanical), and an impersonality with which a person must equip him or herself to hold sway. The poet gleefully recounts the many pleasures (equivalent to powers) of such weaponry to allay her belatedly admitted dread of dependency, defining the psychology of delegated power, which is the phallic economy.
>
> I especially like the parity of the mountainous powers of world and gun, which suggest to me that the poet thinks in terms of her uterine power to populate and dominate this or that place, to subdue duck and doe with her daughters and sons, evoking not only the uterine competitions of the Book of Genesis but also Cadmus sowing dragon's teeth. The phallic register admits a giddy pride in her own power of utterance, perhaps comparable to an arresting song by Bret Harte, "What the Bullet Sang," which I found in John Hollander's wonderful anthology of *American Poetry: The Nineteenth Century*. Having not then read much Lacan, I did not explain matters in terms of having versus being the phallus.[5]

What is the Proper Name of the "Nobody!"?

"Exposed as you have been in this schoolroom to ["I'm Nobody! Who are You?"], what do you make of Adrienne Rich's condescension to little girls ... and of her assumption that the poet's seclusion is strange?" Bruce puts this question to his

---

5   Bruce Gardiner, email to author, 29 November 2021.

listeners at the end of the first of his "Six Lectures on Four American Poets", in which he equips his students with four traditional motivations for why one might want to keep one's poetry to oneself: 1) feminine modesty; 2) religious scruple; 3) psychological trauma or madness; and 4) aristocratic privilege and diplomacy.[6] In this lecture, Bruce reads Dickinson's "I'm Nobody! Who are You?" according to its unconventional uptake of the ballad form, which, deriving from early English and Anglo-Scots traditions, had been the source of private devotional hymns derived from popular culture. Bruce also states that Dickinson's poems were originally written for women in her family, who, soon after Dickinson's death, both readied and released them in time for the Christmas trade in gift books. He hints at the idea that Dickinson's poetry honours the popular – rather than strictly religious – roots of the ballad when he notes the movement of Dickinson's poems from the poet's private hands to intimates to the commercial market. Throughout his close reading of certain of the poem's formal elements, Bruce inimitably dramatises aspects of her poetry's metrical and rhythmic character. Introducing both conventional and unconventional syllabic stresses and beats of the poem to new ears, Bruce compels his listener to hear Dickinson's lyrical "Nobody!"

Gunshots From the Brain into Her Body

Biographer Lyndall Gordon gathers evidence from letters, journals and medical books to propose that Dickinson endured epilepsy, which condition, she argues in turn, influenced her poetry. In making this argument, Gordon notes the nineteenth-century stigmatisation of epilepsy as a "form of demonic possession" that led to certain victims being incarcerated "in asylums". Gender and illness are not so much categories conditioning the passivity of the suffering female poet as they are obstacles to be heroically transgressed. "Females especially provoked genteel aversion as they broke the rules of ladylike control," writes Gordon as she genders Dickinson's epilepsy as a disability that the poet suffers and then overcomes:

> What's clear, on the evidence of Dickinson's writing and the sheer volume of her output, is that she coped inventively with gunshots from the brain into her body. In "My Life had stood – a Loaded Gun –," the power to kill makes the gun a "deadly foe," but since this gun outlives its Master it's no ordinary gun. Can it be the poet's art? …
>
> So it was that art and life converge at this point, when poetic immortality is certain. Poetry is not only celebrated for its explosiveness; it's also the protective gun that guards the "head" by night (art's ability to protect against outbreaks of sickness), and this guardianship is preferable to the shared pillow of matrimony. …

---

6   Gardiner, "Six Lectures on Four American Poets", Lecture One.

In this way, "My Life had stood – a Loaded Gun –" turns an explosive sickness, its recurrent dramas of "Revolver" and "Gun", into well-armed art.[7]

Gordon departs somewhat from readings by Adrienne Rich and others that emphasise Dickinson's poetry as evidence of the poet's gendered victimhood or self-diminution, presenting the poetry instead as certain of its own "immortality" and greatness. Were it not for Gordon's presentation of the poet's own body as the battleground, her reading would amount to a shift in the terms of a longstanding gender war in which women are either maids or waifs to be either redeemed or defended. The loaded gun of Dickinson's poem is read by Gordon as a literal manifestation of a neural shot from Dickinson's brain that racks her body. Great poetry is here tasked with the military duty of guarding and protecting a body hostage to a cognitive disorder.

Stepping Carefully as "Lightning Punches Darkness"

At the end of his Lecture Two of "Six Lectures on Four American Poets", Bruce cautions his students against a "widespread impulse" to read Dickinson "autobiographically and pathologically, as if she were incapable of writing about anyone or anything other than herself and her own life". He continues:

> Now, reading imaginative literature as a form of pathological self-disclosure discounts or dispenses with what I will call the literariness of literature, including its supra-personal, self-abstracting power, its aesthetic and ideational freedom to play however it likes with whatever it likes, notably with what is least like us and most remote from us.[8]

Explicitly echoing the French writer Christiane Rocheforte, Bruce alerts his students to a tendency to read women writers "below the belt, personally" and according to a tradition in which male writers tend to be read at the "glorious level of the brain". "A woman writer arousing our interest as a patient; a male writer arousing our interest as a diagnostician." In place of reading the "I felt" of "I felt a Funeral, in my Brain" as an instance of the poet feeling or emoting, Bruce proffers an alternative meaning of the verb "to feel" as the act of examining or investigating something cautiously, as in "feeling one's way" or "feeling one's pulse", before suggesting to his students that "feeling one's way" is also a way to poetry. "To feel poetically is to step carefully from one word to another close by" and these "small poetic steps are *metonyms* and *metaphors*". Drawing further on the language of "I felt a Funeral, in my Brain", Bruce advises that metonyms "tread

---

7   Lyndall Gordon, *Lives Like Loaded Guns* (New York: Viking, 2010), 136.
8   Gardiner, "Six Lectures on Four American Poets", Lecture Two.

and creak cautiously across thresholds" while metaphors "break through and drop down, causing us to lose our footing as when 'a Plank in Reason, broke' and to lose our orientation when 'Space – began to toll'". The latter are mistakes that reveal a hidden truth, as "lightning punches darkness".[9]

My Tinnitus

> The most delicate, the most fragile thing that exists is to be encroached upon and brought into conjunction with bustle and commotion, when part of the ideal of lyric poetry, at least in its traditional sense, is to remain unaffected by bustle and commotion …
>
> … Until we have either broadened it historically or turned it critically against the sphere of individualism, however, our conception of lyric poetry has a moment of discontinuity in it – all the more so, the more pure it claims to be. The "I" whose voice is heard in the lyric is an "I" that defines and expresses itself as something opposed to the collective, to objectivity; it is not immediately at one with the nature to which its expression refers. It has lost it, as it were, and attempts to restore it through animation, through immersion in the "I" itself. It is only through humanization that nature is to be restored the rights that human domination took from it. Even lyric works in which no trace of conventional and concrete existence, no crude materiality remains, the greatest lyric works in our language, owe their quality to the force with which the "I" creates the illusion of nature emerging from alienation. Their pure subjectivity, the aspect of them that appears seamless and harmonious, bears witness to its opposite, to suffering in an existence alien to the subject and to love for it as well – indeed their harmoniousness is actually nothing but the mutual accord of this suffering and this love.[10]

I am excited after listening to Bruce's lecture on "I felt a Funeral in My Brain", in which Bruce delivers his "extravagantly anachronistic analogy" that Dickinson is a head-banging, heavy metal rock chick who experiences the "psycho-physiological ecstasy" of music "followed by swooning disengagement and mortification that the music is over".[11] I write to Bruce to congratulate him and to broach my thoughts about Dickinson and tinnitus. It is not simply that my tinnitus comes to mind as I read the poem after listening to Bruce's lecture. I also think about what heavy metal's characteristically ear-piercing volume has meant for both its musicians and fans. I've been unable to locate the email concerned, but my recollection is that in Bruce's reply he reiterated a point that is also a key takeaway of his lectures: it is neither necessary nor desirable to understand Dickinson's poetry by identifying a

---

9   Gardiner, "Six Lectures on Four American Poets", Lecture Two.
10   Theodor Adorno, "On Lyric Poetry and Society", in *Notes to Literature, Volume 1*. Ed Rolf Tiedemann, trans Sherry Weber Nicholson. (New York: Columbia University Press, 1991), 37, 42.
11   Gardiner, "Six Lectures on Four American Poets", Lecture Three.

personal condition – whether of epilepsy or tinnitus or other. To read Dickinson or any other poet in this way is to overlook what he calls the "literariness of literature, including its supra-personal, self-abstracting power".[12]

My excitement turns to irritation, not because Bruce's reply doesn't strike me as true. It does! Rather, it irritates because it awakens me to the missteps and imprecisions of my hazarded email. My point had not been to read Dickinson autobiographically or pathologically. Instead, I had meant to communicate my ambivalent experience of tinnitus as something that is at once solitary (no one else can hear it!) and intrusive (it has at times distracted me to the point of disequilibrium). How might this contradiction awaken one to a "felt" sense of an elusive object? Like the consideration of lightning punching through darkness or the attempt to imagine the unheard frogs croaking in the miring bog of "I'm Nobody! Who are You?", such thought about tinnitus might be analogous to attempting to catch the meaning of the lyric "I", as Theodor Adorno elucidates this process in the quotation above. This is an "I" that is resonant – it resonates with the buzzes and rings of the external world – while learning to be unaffected by such ephemeral sounds, as well as sights and textures. Emerging out of "bustle and commotion", Adorno's lyric "I" defines itself in opposition to such distracting noise even while expressing a solitude that ultimately "restore[s]" rather than rejects the turbulence of the everyday.

Part Two: Irritation and Imitation

"the most exact portrayals of things we do not like to see in real life, the lowest animals, for instance, or corpses."

Poetry, I believe has two over-all causes, both of them natural:

a) *Mimesis* is innate in human beings from childhood – indeed we differ from the other animals in being most given to *mimesis* and in making our first steps in learning through it – and pleasure in instances of mimesis is equally general. This we can see from the facts: we enjoy looking at the most exact portrayals of things we do not like to see in real life, the lowest animals, for instance, or corpses. This is because not only philosophers, but all men, enjoy getting to understand something, though it is true that most people feel this pleasure only to a slight degree; therefore they like to see these pictures, because in looking at them they come to understand something and can infer what each thing is, can say, for instance, "This man in the picture is so-and-so." If you happen not to have seen the original, the picture will not produce its pleasure *qua* instance of mimesis, but because of its technical finish or colour or for some other reason.

---

12   Gardiner, "Six Lectures on Four American Poets", Lecture Three.

b) As well as mimesis, harmony and rhythm are natural to us, and verses are obviously definite sections of rhythm.[13]

Seeing and Hearing, Reading and Listening to Bruce Teach

Thought of the pleasure integral to Aristotle's idea of mimesis comes to mind in a paragraph of Bruce's lecture "The Chic, the Out-There, the To-Die-For: Modern and Contemporary Haute Couture, Aesthetics and Writing", in which he gives his students a way to understand aesthetics. While in Aristotle's *Poetics*, mimetic pleasure extends to the vulgar, the low and the grotesque, Bruce emphasises pleasure in beautiful things when he elaborates on the "scope" of aesthetic considerations:

> The scope of such aesthetic considerations is extensive. **First**, aesthetics is the study of the senses of sight and hearing and of the pleasures we take in them, including the pleasures we take in reading and listening to words. **Second**, aesthetics is the study of how and why *les beaux arts*, the visual and performing arts, and *les belles lettres*, the literary and verbal arts, evoke and savour the beauty of things and thinghood, including persons and personhood, whether they be beautiful by design or by accident. **Third**, aesthetics is the study of the cultural and historical significance of our susceptibility to beauty and our cultivation of it, its relation to moral, economic, and political interests, and most contentiously whether our sense of the beautiful is simply a function of these interests or if it remains in some way impervious to them.[14]

I listen again to Bruce's lecture on "I'm Nobody! Who Are You?" towards the end of which he offers a reading of Dickinson's signature dashes, which were deleted from the first editions of her poems and which were reinserted in Thomas H. Johnson's 1956 publication and other scholarly editions of her poems. "I once attended a conference," says Bruce, "at which the keynote speaker, having developed his habit over decades, punctuated every point he made with a loud snort [Bruce demonstrably snorts]. Are Dickinson's dashes a habit of this kind?" Bruce's loud snort at the relevant moment punctuates his point that Dickinson's dashes can be understood as a quirky mannerism or tic.[15] Removed by editors that Dickinson herself had chosen, the dash that is read by Bruce as analogous to a snort entertainingly dramatises his point "that we condescend to these first editors at our literary and moral peril". For this listener, the pleasure of hearing an erudite teacher

---

13 Aristotle, *Poetics*, trans. M.E. Hubbard. In *Classical Literary Criticism*, ed. D.A. Russell and M. Winterbottom (Oxford and New York: Oxford University Press, 2008), 54–55.
14 Bruce Gardiner, "The Chic, the Out-There, the To-Die-For: Modern and Contemporary Haute Couture, Aesthetics and Writing". Lecture Script, Unpublished, October 2020.
15 Gardiner, "Six Lectures on Four American Poets", Lecture One.

snort has something to do with Aristotle's point about mimesis – a commonplace pleasure emanating from a mutual recognition of a likeness, especially when the thing being reproduced is as lowly as a pig or a frog in a bog.

Solids Becoming Voids and Voids Becoming Solids

Where did that penis go?

I would say that Butler presents sufficient evidence from Freud's text to undermine her argument about the allegedly indisputable privilege of the penis. Freud's picture of the body is surreal, a game of pin-the-penis on the body wherever spot-fires of desire sporadically break out on it or just inside it, in which cavities metamorphose into projections that fit into them, and projections into the cavities into which they fit, decades before Lacan applied to Freud's texts the lessons Salvador Dalí taught about solids becoming voids and voids becoming solids in his paintings of hallucinatory optical illusions, in which the absence of objects is indistinguishable from their presence. The phallus is essentially an exclamation mark (!) or a manicule (☞) pointing to any focus of erotic interest, pressing the hapless penis into symbolic service perhaps because the penis is more obviously than other parts of human bodies (which unlike donkey bodies lack a tail) a little body, a little person in its own right, a corpuscle of the corpse. Surely Freud's fascination with Wilhelm Busch's surreal image of "the jaw tooth's aching hole" indicates that the exclamation mark can be inverted, as in Spanish (¡), poking in as much as poking out, an impression and expression of desire, the vaginal and penile as inverse replicas of each other and every other cavity and protuberance of the arousable body.

Figure 11.1 Screenshot of "Where did that penis go?" in Bruce Gardiner, "Judith Butler: 'The Lesbian Phallus and the Morphological Imaginary': A Commentary." Unpublished Text.

I look at symbols Bruce has included in his unpublished paper, "Where did that penis go?" – the second section of his unpublished text, "Judith Butler. The Lesbian Phallus and the Morphological Imaginary. A Commentary". As I consider the symbols indicating an exclamation mark, an inverted exclamation mark and a manicule (see Figure 11.1), the image of a black and white photograph comes to mind. It is Robert Mapplethorpe's portrait " Louise Bourgeois" 1982, printed in 1991. In the image, the sculptor stands at a slight angle to the camera. Her fur-coated body appears from the waist up only. While she stands in a boldly upright posture, her eyes are caught in a sideways glance, as if having been frozen in a moment of playful movement with the camera that watches her, just as she watches it. The coat she wears is of jet black fur and its coarse, hairy tufts ruffle near the lined skin of her face while inching close to her one, visible hand. This right hand holds the pointed tip of an object, the erect shaft of which is tucked under her furry arm. The object she cradles is a large sculpted penis. Except for its much-larger-than-ordinary size, the object is characterised by anatomic correctness. It is tubular, it has a glans, which is held firmly in place by Bourgeois' gentle hand, and it has two stony testicles. In their rocky hardness, Bourgeois' testicles are obdurately there, seeming to proclaim their status as spherical things, despite the buoyancy with which they appear to float on the far side of the sculptor's fur jacket. Like the results of a lesson taught by Salvador Dalí, the balls evoke the sense of a void as much as a solid, transcendence as much as thingness.

In the days preceding each of Bruce's 1992 American Literature classes, I looked forward to seeing my teacher's attire. For example, in the week in which we read writers from the cold Northeast, Bruce wore a shirt imprinted with tall, green pines, the height of which reached from the implied forest floor of the shirt's waist to its treetop shoulders.

Only an Irritant

I write to Bruce to invite him to contribute to a special issue of *Australian Humanities Review* I am editing, which gathers together a range of scholarly and teacherly perspectives on Rachel Sagner Buurma and Laura Heffernan's *The Teaching Archive* (2020). Bruce responds:

> Although their book sounds very good, Buurma and Heffernan's view of teaching isn't mine. For instance, I'd say that despite their extraordinary power, Heidegger's lecture notes reveal much less about his teaching than do his students' transformation of them, including Lacan's. Buurma and Heffernan appear to regard the teacher as some kind of author, whereas I'd say that a teacher is not only not an author but only an irritant that spurs her/his students to evolve their own authentic and authoritative speech, as Socrates contends in the maieutic theory he ventures in Plato's Theaetetus. My favourite epitome of such a figure is Ammonius Saccus, apparently the teacher of both Plotinus and Origen.[16]

Solitaries Who Go in Company

Bruce was a singular teacher. While attending his classes, I was taking in elements of the teachings of others. Kate Lilley's Susan Howe is house and book, walls and pages, ground and figure, biological family and literary genealogy, visual artist and writer, domesticity and *détournement*, a writer who scales up (fame; esteem) in order to scale down (from private house as installation space to book). She is at once ventriloquist and original, simultaneously "inimitable and derived from many sources", a writer of "solitaries who go in company".[17]

---

16   Bruce Gardiner, email to author, 18 February 2021.
17   Kate Lilley, "Black Work: On Susan Howe's *The Midnight*." In *Poetry and the Trace*, eds. Ann Vickery and John Hawke (Sydney: Puncher and Wattmann, 2013), 254–68; and "This L=A=N=G=U=A=G=E", *Jacket* 2, 1998. http://jacketmagazine.com/02/lilley02.html.

Susan Howe's "My Life had stood – a Loaded Gun –"

My Life: A Soul finding God.

My Life: A Soul finding herself.

My Life: A poet's admiring heart born into voice by idealizing a precursor poet's song.

My Life: Dickinson herself writing in corners of neglect for Higginson to recognize her ability and help her to join the ranks of other published American poets.

My Life: The American continent and its wayward moving frontier. Two centuries of pioneer literature and myth had insistently compared the land to a virgin woman (bride and queen). Exploration and settlement were pictured in terms of masculine erotic discovery and domination of alluring/threatening feminine territory.

My Life: The savage source of American myth.

My Life: The United States in the grip of violence that threatened to break apart its original union.

My Life: A woman taken captive by Indians.

My Life: A slave.

My Life: An unmarried woman (Emily Brontë's Catherine Earnshaw) waiting to be chosen (identified) by her Lover-Husband-Owner (Edgar Linton).

My Life: A frontiersman's gun.[18]

Eclectic Irritations

The word maieutic is cognate with the French *maïeutique* and derives from "the ancient Greek μαιευτικός (lit. 'obstetric'; used figuratively by Socrates in Plato Theaetetus 161 E) [and] μαιεύεσθαι to act as a midwife".[19]

Sianne Ngai conceptualises irritation as one of several "noncathartic feelings" central to texts studied in her 2015 book *Ugly Feelings*.[20] With Harlem Renaissance novelist Nella Larsen's *Quicksand* (1928) as her exemplar, Ngai presents irritation as an ideologeme enabling expression of categories registered textually and at the level of the epidermis.[21] A "minor feeling", irritation here indicates the over-determining function of identity categories as these condition imaginations of everyday life.

For Bruce, irritation is not so much a minor feeling as a structure of transmission through which unwritten knowledge is passed from teacher to student. The word maieutic speaks to the role of teacher as facilitator of life-giving knowledge rather than identifiable expert or authority. Very little is known about Ammonius Saccus, the "epitome" of the "maieutic theory" Bruce had mentioned in

---

18 Howe, *My Emily Dickinson*, Loc 1228.
19 *Oxford English Dictionary*, 2nd ed. (1989), under "maieutic".
20 Sianne Ngai, *Ugly Feelings* (Cambridge, MA: Harvard University Press, 2005), 6.
21 Ngai, *Ugly Feelings*, 207.

the email to me, and whose teachings were not written down. It is said that he lived circa 2 BCE, that he was raised by poor Christian parents, and that he left his job as sack bearer (hence his name Saccus) to become a philosopher. One of the first of the so-called Eclectic philosophers, he opened a school that drew disciples Origen, Heurenius and Plotinus. Eclecticism embraces no particular system but selects and takes from other systems – including the teachings of *both* Plato and Aristotle – those ideas that best comport with the truth.[22]

Bibliography

Adorno, Theodor. "On Lyric Poetry and Society." In *Notes to Literature, Volume One*. Ed. Rolf Tiedeman. Trans. Shierry Weber Nicholson. New York: Columbia University Press, 1991, 37–54.

Roberts, Jonathan M. *Antiquity Unveiled: Ancient Voices from the Spirit Realms*. Philadelphia, PA: Oriental Publishing Company, 1894.

Aristotle. *Poetics*. Trans. M.E. Hubbard. In *Classical Literary Criticism*. Ed. D.A. Russell and M. Winterbottom. Oxford and New York: Oxford University Press, 2008, 51–90.

Gardiner, Bruce. "Judith Butler: 'The Lesbian Phallus and the Morphological Imaginary': A Commentary." Unpublished Text.

Gardiner, Bruce. "The Chic, the Out-There, the To-Die-For: Modern and Contemporary Haute Couture, Aesthetics and Writing." Lecture Script, Unpublished, October 2020.

Gardiner, Bruce. "Six Lectures on Four American Poets." Unpublished audio files, 2020.

Gordon, Lyndall. *Lives Like Loaded Guns: Emily Dickinson and Her Family's Feuds*. New York: Viking, 2010.

Howe, Susan. *My Emily Dickinson*. New York: New Directions Press, 2007 [1985]. Kindle edition.

Lilley, Kate. "Black Work: On Susan Howe's *The Midnight*." In *Poetry and the Trace*. Ed. Ann Vickery and John Hawke. Sydney: Puncher and Wattmann, 2013, 254–68.

Lilley, Kate. "This L=A=N=G=U=A=G=E." *Jacket 2*, 1998. Accessed 16 May 2022. http://jacketmagazine.com/02/lilley02.html.

Mapplethorpe, Robert. "Louise Bourgeois," 1982, printed 1991. Tate Gallery. Accessed May 2022. https://www.tate.org.uk/art/artworks/mapplethorpe-louise-bourgeois-ar00215.

Ngai, Sianne. *Ugly Feelings*. Cambridge, MA: Harvard University Press, 2005.

Oxford English Dictionary, 2nd edition. Oxford: Oxford University Press, 1989.

---

22 *Biographie Universelle*, quoted in *Antiquity Unveiled* (Philadelphia, PA: Oriental Publishing Company, 1894), 75–6.

12

Play as Structure

Émile Benveniste[1] (Translated by Jack Cox, writer and translator)

The domain of play is immense. So varied are its forms that there is no part of our behaviour, speech or thinking that does not belong to it in some measure; forms so incompatible that it is surprising to see them designated under the same name. The origin of the infinitely diverse manifestations belonging to this domain, and which make play appear more as a *modality* of all human activity rather than one activity in particular, has been sought after above all in some biopsychological tendency supposed to exercise and satisfy itself in it. I shall not be following this path here: I am concerned with play, not with the player. Working in the opposite direction, I shall regard play, *qua* form, as a fact, so as to try to uncover the elements that furnish its structure and to attempt a definition of the function it fulfils.

To begin with, a minimal definition of play can be proposed that highlights its basic characteristics, those without which it does not exist. I shall call play all regulated activity that has its end in itself and does not aim to usefully modify reality.

From this definition, the principal traits that distinguish play can already be seen: the fact that it is an activity that takes place in the world, but is heedles of the conditions of "reality", since it deliberately abstracts these; the fact that it "serves no purpose" and appears as a series of forms whose intentionality cannot be oriented towards the useful and which find their end in their own accomplishment; finally, the formal and regulated nature of play, which must take place within a rigorous set of limits and conditions and constitutes a closed totality. It must be said that all these features set play apart from the "reality" in which human will, in thrall to utility, everywhere runs up against events, incoherencies, arbitrariness, where nothing turns out as planned nor according to the accepted rules, where the only certitude man possesses – that of his final end – appears to him both iniquitous and absurd. Play escapes all these limitations, in that it is first and foremost *form*.

---

1   Émile Benveniste, "Le jeu comme structure", *Deucalion: Cahiers de philosophie*, no. 2 (1947): 161–7. This English translation is forthcoming in a new edition of Émile Benveniste's *Problèmes de linguistique générale, I* with HAU Books.

To say that play and the rule-bound games that are a part of it are a "form" is to contrast them with a "content" that would be reality itself. But from this it does not follow that play is an empty form, the production of meaningless acts. On the contrary, the coherence of its structure and its internal purpose imply a meaning that is as if inherent to its form and always extraneous to any practical aim. This meaning is produced by the very arbitrariness of the conditions that limit play and through which, passing from one to the next, this is carried out; the being of play is entirely bound up in the convention governing it. If a single one of the rules maintaining a given game outside of "reality" is violated, the game ceases and the player reverts to reality. The condition of the participants is thus also necessarily arbitrary; they strip themselves of their ordinary personality in order to take on only that assigned to them by the requirements of the game. Their only function is to allow the game to realise itself. And it must be realised as action, being the transcription of a scheme given in advance that exists for itself up until its conclusion. Hence it is the game that determines the players, not the other way around. It creates its actors, it gives them place, rank and figure; it regulates their bearing, their physical appearance, it even renders them, as the case may be, alive or dead. Everything is conditioned by the way the game unfolds, internal to those conditions that constitute the game.

It is not enough to say that this second reality into which play inducts us and in which we are held for as long as the game lasts is different from "true" reality. With the help of the expressions that we apply to it, we can characterise it more precisely. The extension given to the word *jeu* sheds light on the representation that we make of it. We talk of a *jeu de cartes*, of the *jeu de paume*, as well as the *jeu* of a piston, the *jeu* of state institutions, and the *jeu* of a musician or an actor. We say that an actor *joue* and that a door *joue*. We employ expressions as wide-ranging as *entrer en jeu, mettre en jeu, donner du jeu, se faire un jeu de*, etc.[2] The same term seems to signify at once movement and constraint and artifice and ease and exercise. All this apparent dissimilarity, even contradictoriness, is full of instruction, though first and foremost about ourselves; the testimony of words elucidates *our* conception of play. There is no fixed notion in such a matter as this: where we see only varieties of a single species – a children's game and an athletic game – the Greeks distinguished two independent realities (παίγνιον and ἆθλος) that it would never have crossed their minds to conflate. Many languages make the same distinction. With this proviso, the consistent features of a definition are discernible in the multiple uses to which we put the word. The fact that has brought about this semantic proliferation is that all collective activities, all "representations", all figurations are now seen

---

2   The extension of this key word is wider than that of English "play" or "game". The examples cited here elicit the following varied translations: a *deck* of cards, the *game* of handball, the *action* of a piston, the *workings* of state institutions, and a musician's or an actor's *style*; an actor who *acts* (*plays* a role) and a door whose wood *swells and contracts* with the effect of the atmosphere; as well as the equivalent expressions *come into play; bring into play; give slack; child's play*. [Trans.]

as "play", as "non-serious" imitations of reality. It is their fictive side that is thus emphasised. The soldier being drilled, the wrestler in the ring, the actor on the stage make none but the gestures pertaining to their role, and they do so until they have exhausted them. All behaviour that reproduces the outer appearance of a concerted action, that imitates its motions and development, is characterised as play. By extension, an operation considered from the outside, in its regular movement, without regard for the result obtained, is designated accordingly: hence we speak of the movement [jeu] of the muscles, a formal mechanism, the way the parts link together in the whole that commands them, but whose function we do not keep in view. Our representation of play is thus unified in the terms that convey it. This representation was formed once, in Latin, *jocus* (which has given us our word *jeu*) supplanted *ludus*. *Jocus* is wordplay, frivolous remarks, jokes; *ludus* is properly "training" in all of its forms: training for study (whence *ludus* "class, school") and training for combat, military exercise (whence *ludus* "competition; game for the arena"). The replacement of *ludus* with *jocus*, which alone survived, sanctioned a change in attitude towards these exercises and demarcations, now demoted to the rank of simple "games".

We are thus able to measure the area of this representation. But we are no better informed as to its nature. We learn only this: that play is increasingly clearly specified as being distinct from reality, as "non-serious". And yet play is also, in its own way, a reality. Since it is separated by its conventions from reality and everyday life, play must have its own reality. Indeed there is an equally specific reality proper to play, with its laws, its necessity, its logic, its code, and even its language. What is the nature of this distinctive reality, and what is its relationship to the other reality, which it excludes?

The form of play found in a game realises, through the intermediary of the participants, a sort of complete drama, generally agonistic in form, consisting in the struggle for the possession of an object, instrument, or symbol of victory. It is played in a closed group – a team, circle, club, troupe, class, etc. – which only exists for the sake of the game and is entirely dedicated to carrying it out. A game can forge a tie between the members of such a group that is stronger than that of blood. It creates the very keen feeling of a community that draws its mission, its honour, its symbols from it. The players each have an identity that belongs to the game, often a disguise. All this helps to define the type of reality that the game inhabits: it is a mystical reality that borrows from the realm of the sacred some of its most salient characteristics.

This conclusion agrees with those deduced by sociologists from contemporary forms of play. Numerous studies on the origin and signification of most of our games point to more or less clear remainders of ancient dances, combats, masquerades and sacred ceremonies. Ball games dramatise ancient tribal myths. Wedding rites find a continuation in children's games and dances. Games of chance are meant for interrogating or influencing fate. There are competitive games in which the memory of agrarian cults is still recognisable. The spinning top is an ancient divinatory teetotum, etc. There thus appears everywhere a deep relationship between play and the sacred.[3] And it is all the more tempting to identify the two essences given the way the player's passion, which removes him from the real world, often resembles the ecstasy of the worshipper when he is in contact with the sacred. It is the same exaltation, the same pathos, a frenzy that can lead to murder or suicide.

And yet underneath this undeniable lineage, certain fundamental differences can be discerned, the principal instances of which must be brought to light. The sacred supposes a reality, that of the divine; through ritual, the worshipper is brought into a separate world, more real than the real world. Play, on the contrary, deliberately separates itself from reality. It can be said that the sacred is super-real [*sur-réel*], while play is extra-real. Moreover, the sacred operation has a practical aim, which is to render the terrestrial world inhabitable, to repel hostile forces, to organise society, to procure subsistence or victory. Play has in itself no practical purpose; its essence lies in its very gratuitousness. For the aim of play can't be said to be to provoke the emotions it arouses; these emotions are merely consequences and do not concern the nature of the phenomenon. Finally, in the realm of the sacred, each of the very strict rules of the ceremony has its own efficacy in and of itself; it must provoke the intervention of the divinity through direct appeal and at the same time make it possible for men to safely endure the terrible and malefic contact of the sacred. In games, the rules are nothing in isolation and everything when combined with each other, which clearly exhibits their structuralising property; they serve to delimit the spatial and temporal frame, the "conventions", and at the same time they themselves constitute the entire game. This is why ultimately the sacred is all tension and anxiety, while play is all exaltation and deliverance.

Play and the sacred are, then, opposed in every way. And yet in every way they are also akin to one another. Doubtless their true connection lies in this dialectical relationship. Indeed, they share a symmetrical but opposed structure. This homology defines play and the sacred by way of certain common

---

3   Here I converge with – though in order to contradict them – some of the claims made by J. Huizinga in his otherwise remarkable book, *Homo Ludens: A Study of the Play-Element in Culture* (Routledge, 1949). The present reflections had already been composed when I encountered this work, in which anyway I would only have found arguments *against* the thesis he puts forward. Huizinga annexes absolutely all regulated human activity to play. It is no longer possible to see what play would be opposed to, nor, as a consequence, what it would consist of. The fundamental question of the relationships existing between play and the sacred is thus, as I see it, entirely distorted, and yet this is the heart of the problem. Huizinga nonetheless has succeeded in bringing new light to the analysis of major cultural phenomena, showing in an often highly evocative way the importance at least of the various forms of play. (M. Roger Caillois, who was able to read this article in manuscript, was so kind as to indicate to me a study of his own [published in *Confluences* 10 (1946), pp. 66–77], in which he penetratingly analyses and discusses this same work by J. Huizinga. Despite a difference in point of view, his remarks anticipate some of my conclusions in respect to the relationships between play and the sacred.)

characteristics together with a contrary orientation. Whereas the sacred raises man up to the divine, which is a "given" and is the source of all reality, play safely brings the divine down to the level of man, and through a set of conventions, makes it immediately accessible to him. Play is thus fundamentally nothing but a *desacralising operation*. Play is so much inverted sacredness and the rules of the game serve solely to secure this inversion. This will appear in a clearer light if we see what this transmutation consists in and how it comes about.

The sacred is the seat of supreme efficacy, the primordial condition of human efficacy. Our acts attain nothing and remain forever futile if their power has not first been guaranteed by the ceremony in which the officiant performed them in the prescribed forms, and evoked their divine prototype. Now, the power of this sacred "act" lies precisely in the conjunction of the *myth* that utters the story and the *ritual* that reproduces it. If we compare this schema with that of a game, the difference appears essential: in a game, only the "ritual" survives, all that is preserved is the *form* of the sacred drama in which all things are posited anew each time. But the "myth", the pregnantly worded tale that confers meaning and power on the acts, has been forgotten or abolished. Cut off from its myth, the ritual is reduced to a regulated set of now inefficacious acts, a harmless reproduction of the ceremony, a pure "game". Of the divine struggle for the possession of the sun there remains a ball game in which the player may with impunity (did any god ever enjoy such a privilege?) take possession of the solar disc at will. Such is *ludus*.

Jocus presents the same structure but reversed. It is words and no longer acts that constitute this form of play, but words that dispose of their own power only; they are spoken "as if" they expressed a reality, but according to the convention – accepted by all the participants – that they have in fact no true content. *Jocus* is characterised by the deliberately fictive character of the reality it alludes to, but this is not a forged reality, one that would simply be a lie; lies suppose or create the same kind of reality as truthfulness, whereas wordplay and jokes refer to a different reality, one that is admitted as such. It appears then that, contrary to *ludus*, and in a symmetrical way, *jocus* consists in a pure "myth", without a corresponding "ritual" giving it purchase on reality.

In summary, we possess the elements of a definition of play as structure. It originates in the sacred, of which it offers up an inverted, broken image. If the sacred can be defined by the consubstantial unity of myth and ritual, we can say that there is play when only half of the sacred operation is performed, either by conveying the myth alone in words or the ritual alone in acts. We are thus outside of the divine and human sphere of efficacy. Play understood in this way comprises two varieties: jocular when the myth is reduced to its own content and separated from its ritual, and ludic when the ritual is practised for its own sake and separated from its myth. Under this double guise, play embodies each of the two halves into which the sacred ceremony has been split. Moreover, it is in the nature of play to fictitiously recompose in each of its two forms the missing half: in wordplay, we speak as if a factual reality were to follow; in physical games, we act as if they were motivated by a reasoned reality. This fiction makes it possible for these acts and words to be coherent with themselves, in an autonomous world removed by a set of conventions from the inevitabilities of reality.

Pursuing this definition further, for the purposes of verification, it can be argued that it furnishes the necessary and sufficient conditions for the production of play of any sort, for converting any regulated activity into a game. Indeed, for such an activity to switch over into play, it is necessary and sufficient for it to be viewed according to its organised structure without taking into account the "real" end that it sets itself: law courts with their immutable rituals and ceremonies become play when we overlook the case under judgement; politics, which is engaged in amidst so many forms and rules, becomes play if we are not concerned with the government of men; poetry, an arrangement of tightly regulated, arbitrary forms, becomes play if we disregard the feeling that is being expressed; religion, the most regulated of things, becomes play if we separate it from the myths it actualises; war becomes play … etc. Every coherent and regulated manifestation of collective and individual life can be transposed into play once we subtract the reasoned or factual motivation that lends it efficacy.

Perhaps we are now in a position to discern what in ourselves invites play and finds satisfaction there. Play as structure undoubtably relates to a human structure that, having fashioned it, adapts itself to it. Viewing play from a very general standpoint in respect to man, it is first of all noticeable that it is bound up with the predominance of subconscious life, of which it is a vital manifestation from the earliest age. Precisely in that it frees up spontaneous activity, it corresponds to a deep instinct. When the child acquires his first notion of reality, when he understands that the "useful" world is made up of dangers, illogicalities and prohibitions, he finds refuge in play and in so doing compensates the tiring effort that his apprenticeship in reality imposes on his mind. And at any age, whether we let ourselves get caught up in it or whether we seek it out, play signifies a forgetting of the useful, a beneficial surrender to forces that real life reins in and injures. In group play, there is, beyond the individual unconscious, a strong collective unconscious that finds satisfaction. For children's playful activity corresponds to their native representation of things, which is essentially *magical*. This magical understanding, which the real world disappoints at every turn and ever more inflexibly, is the same that play allows the child to *experience*: he may identify with anyone, create whatever he wants, shatter the reign of the possible and the impossible. From one age to the next, the charm of play is the same: suspension. The rigour of the fictive subverts reality. It is enough to become the figure required by the game and to embrace the prescribed risks for a satisfying and intelligible world to emerge from out of its own rules.

This antinomy of the mind and the "real" world must be posited in order for the authenticity of the life of play and its function to come to the fore. Play makes it possible to resolve or abolish the conflict in which the relationship of consciousness to the world is encapsulated. Consciousness is condemned to painfully grope about in a reality that it can neither experience immediately nor completely embrace, for while it often manages to modify it, it is never capable of understanding it. Such is its fate. In order to realise itself according to its deepest tendency, consciousness must *unrealise itself* according to the universe. This is where play comes in: it represents one of the most revealing modalities of this unrealising to which the subconscious aspires. This is why play means free expansion. It is not the only expression of this impulse – the imagination, dreams and art are others. But play and play alone allows consciousness to *experience* its unrealising in a world adapted to it and in which unrealising is law.

We thus find ourselves at the point where a need issuing from consciousness meets with a form proposed by play. The need to unrealise ourselves flourishes in this pre-given, complete structure. It will not find the same satisfaction anywhere else – not in the sacred, for instance; for all its separateness, the sacred is nonetheless aligned with real life, which it commands. The sacred alone gives reality and consistency to what is real, and the power of shaping and governing this to men. The distinction between the sacred and the profane thus in no way overlaps with that between play and reality, it is merely parallel. In preserving only the form of the sacred and projecting this outside of reality, play secures for itself at once the magic of the unreal and the consistency of the human, the joy of free expansion and the writ of safety. We may each of us then, in proportion with our own imaginations and passions, valorise it anew and even re-sacralise it according to a personal myth.

Part III. Bruce Gardiner, Original Teachings

13

"To entertain this Starry Stranger"[1]: Jane Taylor, William Blake, Edward Lear and Mem Fox in Martha Nussbaum's Classroom

Bruce Gardiner

Jane Taylor's "Twinkle, twinkle, little star," when mentioned early in Charles Dickens' *Hard Times*, strikes Martha Nussbaum as epitomising the fancy and wonder that most reliably spark and guide whatever moral imagination a child comes to own. Nussbaum explains that

> When a child and a parent begin to tell stories together, the child is acquiring essential moral capacities. Even a simple nursery rhyme such as "twinkle, twinkle little star, how I wonder what you are" [sic] leads children to feel wonder – a sense of mystery that mingles curiosity with awe. Children wonder about the little star. In so doing they learn to imagine that a mere shape in the heavens has an inner world, in some ways mysterious, in some ways like their own. … A child deprived of stories is deprived, as well, of certain ways of viewing other people. For the insides of people, like the insides of stars, are not open to view. They must be wondered about. … But the wonder involved in storytelling also makes evident the limits of each person's access to every other. "How I wonder what you are," goes the rhyme. In that simple expression is an acknowledgement of the lack of completeness in one's grasp of the fear, the love, the sympathy, the anger, of the little star, or of any other creature or person.[2]

---

1   Richard Crashaw, "An Hymne of the Nativity", line 88, in *Steps to the Temple* (1648), in *The Complete Poetry of Richard Crashaw*, ed. George Williams (New York: Norton, 1974), 81.
2   Jane Taylor, "The Star", in Ann and Jane Taylor, *Rhymes for the Nursery* (1806); Charles Dickens, *Hard Times* (1854), ed. George Ford and Silvère Monod (New York: Norton, 1966); Martha Nussbaum, *Cultivating Humanity: A Classical Defense of Reform in Liberal Education* (Cambridge, MA: Harvard University Press, 1997), 89–90.

The infant's fancy of the star's inner life portends its maturer supposition of another person's inner life. Both feats are imperative because all things and persons are from the beginning so unlike and so remote from each other that only fancy and wonder can leap the abysses between, securing each line of communication by a grappling hook of compassion that conducts sympathy, like moral electricity, from positive to negative pole. But Nussbaum and Dickens miss the poem's meaning in their haste to make it serve an immediate instructive need. What they see as its moral meaning eclipses its mortal meaning, its disclosure of a basic way of being human that we seldom note even though it informs every way of our being this or that particular human being caught in this or that particular situation, including this or that moral dilemma examined by Nussbaum or Dickens.

"Twinkle, twinkle, little star" first draws the child's notice to the star not as a person or an object in itself but as a sign, twinkling as if to advertise its significance.[3] If love be involved, it is love for a sign whose capacity and care to signify we cherish. Cherishing something as a sign involves imputing to it a capacity to communicate with us, a feat of prosopopoeia, and discerning its likeness or unlikeness to another sign, a feat of metonymy or metaphor. This is a personal matter because a person is the kind of being to whom signs address themselves and who addresses him or herself to them and shares them with other persons. This sharing and interfusion of signs is of a more primordial character than the obdurate separateness of individuals on which Nussbaum and Dickens insist, which is, however recalcitrant, contingent on particular circumstances, as pertain in *A Tale of Two Cities*: "A wonderful fact to reflect upon, that every human creature is constituted to be that profound secret and mystery to every other."[4]

"Let them be for signs" says Genesis of the stars, about which the prophet Jeremiah bids us "be not dismayed". Knowingly or not, Jane Taylor follows to the letter Mosaic and Neoplatonic teaching in her reading of the heavens, as before her do the Metaphysical poets, Henry Vaughan noting that stars "As beauteous shapes, we know not why, / Command and guide the eye."[5] In effect, the child's

---

3   *OED*, twinkle, v.1: (b) emit (radiance, flashes, or beams) rapidly and intermittently; communicate (a message or signal) in this way; (d) guide or light to some place by twinkling. Taylor's depiction of the star's twinkling ignores but does not contradict Isaac Newton's explanation of it in his *Opticks* (4th ed., London: William Innys, 1730), Proposition 8, Problem 2, 98.

4   Charles Dickens, *A Tale of Two Cities* [1859], ed. George Woodcock (Harmondsworth: Penguin, 1970), ch. 3, 44.

5   Genesis 1.14; Jeremiah 10.2 (Authorised Version both); Origen, *Commentary on Genesis* (c.229 CE), in *Origen*, trans. Joseph Trigg (London: Routledge, 1998), 87–102; Plotinus, *Enneads* 3.5–6 (c. 250 CE), trans. S. Mackenna and B. Page (Internet Classics Archive, ed. Daniel Stevenson, MIT, 1994–2009, http://classics.mit.edu/Plotinus/enneads.3.third.html) (Origen and Plotinus both following their teacher Ammonius Saccus); Henry Vaughan, "The Starre", lines 23–4, in *Silex Scintillans* (1650), in *The Complete Poetry of Henry Vaughan*, ed. French Fogle (New York: Norton, 1969), 278. The profusion of stars in Vaughan's poems makes him the Joan Miró of the Metaphysicals or makes Miró the Henry Vaughan of the Surrealists. Few poets and painters depict stars so often.

attention is drawn to an asterisk marking an especially important matter in the language of the heavens, to twinkling starlight that attracts us as do flickering fire and rippling water in whose patterns, according to Immanuel Kant, we suspect meanings as deep as those in the rhythmical patterns of language. The star is a citation, a punctuation mark, marking off one phenomenon from all others as Johann Gottfried von Herder imagines language does from the beginning.[6]

By encouraging the infant to fall in love with the signs of sleep the singer hopes it may fall in love with sleep itself. As a lullaby, the poem tries to persuade to sleep a child reluctant or unable to. Sleep it explains as a state in which the child will lose sense of itself and of its caregivers for a while but not forever, reassuring the child that sleep differs from the death it resembles and foreshadows, a difference that the caregiver will feel more or less keenly as particular threats and general mortality rates wax and wane. The lullaby means immediately to smooth the child's way to sleep and ultimately its way to death after as long as possible a postponement by assuring it that it will wake up next day, with its sense of itself, now briefly in jeopardy, punctually and reliably revived.

The singer tells the child that its consciousness will come and go, outshining all else during the day, shrinking almost to nothing at night. Its consciousness will twinkle, its incessant fluctuations like a star's and its own eyes'. A year after Taylor's poem appeared, a sleepless Wordsworth published three sonnets about sleep in which he compares such "twinklings of oblivion" to a fly skittering over the "fretful stream" of time and calls sleep the "blessed barrier between day and day".[7] The lullaby tries to persuade the child that unconsciousness, so close to nothingness, is not only not inferior to consciousness but for hours at a time superior to it, its trustee, even progenitor, certainly not its thief.[8] The child is "the traveller in the dark" grateful for "the tiny spark" of its own being that persists during every lapse of its own sense of it. To the "little star" and its fellows is entrusted the child's being, whenever the child cannot care for itself and however its being transcends self-care, "Like a diamond in the sky". Taylor might, following Milton, have written "Adamantine in the sky", or less musically but

---

6   Immanuel Kant, *Critique of the Power of Judgment* (1790, rev. 1793), trans. Paul Guyer and Eric Matthews (Cambridge: Cambridge University Press, 2000), [5: 243–4,] 127; Johann Gottfried von Herder, *Treatise on the Origin of Language* (1772), in *Philosophical Writings*, trans. Michael Forster (Cambridge: Cambridge University Press, 2002), 87–9. In *Hard Times*, Louisa Gradgrind longs to read her destiny in the flickering patterns of the hearth fire, as Nussbaum notes in *Poetic Justice: The Literary Imagination and Public Life* (Boston: Beacon, 1995), 36.

7   William Wordsworth, "O Gentle Sleep! Do they belong to thee", first of a set of three sonnets addressed to sleep published together in 1807, in *Poetical Works*, ed. Thomas Hutchinson and Ernest de Selincourt (London: Oxford University Press, 1969), 201–2.

8   For Gottfried Wilhelm Leibniz, the mind never stops thinking during sleep, in *New Essays on Human Understanding* (written 1704), trans. Peter Remnant and Jonathan Bennett (Cambridge: Cambridge University Press, 1996), 109–19; for Emily Brontë, nocturnal unconsciousness is paradisal but diurnal consciousness infernal, the sun blinding eyes that see clearly only in starlight, in "Stars" (1846), in *The Complete Poems*, ed. Janet Gezari (Harmondsworth: Penguin, 1992), 5–6, 226–7.

more bluntly "Adamantly in the sky", as "diamond" still echoes, however faintly, its Greek antecedent meaning "unconquerable", endowing the infant's organic being with mineral durability.[9] The vagaries of the child's circadian rhythm are steadied and synchronised with the twenty-four-hour cycle (the nycthemeron) through which all worldly phenomena move. That the sign to which the child is attracted is "Like a diamond" affirms the surpassing beauty of its being. If we may hear "die" *sotto voce* in "diamond", the prospect of the darkness of death is thereby transfigured into a brilliant entelechy, which the child cannot comprehend until death, before which it can only "wonder" but "know not what you are". Nussbaum mistakes "what you are" as "how you are", whereas the child is invited to wonder ontologically about its own and its world's "whatness", not sociologically about someone else's "howness".

The star guides the sleeper, a kind of traveller, through the night in which it twinkles continuously. The child can shut its eye because the star never shuts its, peeping through the curtains of the child's chamber as through the lids of the child's eye, with which the child entrusts it, the vigilance of one enabling the somnolence of the other. One's being abides with its bailees and trustees. Simultaneously, the sun between its setting and rising shines upon nothing, as the sleeper becomes such a nothing, yet still somehow, though only just, someone. The star is both a diminution of the blazing light of consciousness and a magnification of the infinitesimal spark within unconsciousness, a kind of contranym binding them together. By assuring the child that this difference sustains its psychic integrity rather than triggers its disintegration, the caregiver singing the lullaby obeys an ethical imperative to equip it for life by acquainting it with the nothingness at the heart of its somethingness,[10] an imperative far removed from the lesson in civic virtue to which Nussbaum would reduce it:

> The kind of thinking a small child does when she asks, "Twinkle twinkle, little star, how I wonder what you are," has a crucial role to play in the life of a citizen. We see personlike shapes all around us: but how do we relate to them?[11]

---

9   *OED*, diamond, n.: Classical Greek *adamantos*; Classical Latin *adamantis*; Late Latin *diamantis*. Preferring poetic precedent to scientific, Taylor ignores Antoine Lavoisier's 1772 discovery that diamond is simply an allotrope of charcoal, one crystalline, the other amorphous carbon. Until the later eighteenth century, the noun "adamant" could also refer to a loadstone, which attracts and orients magnetised materials towards it.

10 The nature of this "nothing" intrigues Timothy Morton in "'Twinkle, Twinkle, Little Star' as an Ambient Poem: A Study of a Dialectical Image", *Romantic Circles: Praxis Series* (November 2001), paragraph 54; and Jean-Luc Nancy in *The Fall of Sleep* (2007), trans. Charlotte Mandell (New York: Fordham University Press, 2009), ch. 6: "Lullaby", 29–33. My reading of "The Star" addresses few of Morton's concerns and is thoroughly at odds with many of Nancy's reflections on sleep, which also contradict Emily Brontë's in "Stars".

11 Martha Nussbaum, "Exactly and Responsibly: A Defense of Ethical Criticism", *Philosophy and Literature* 22, no.2 (1998): 350.

Nussbaum reduces prosopopoeia to anthropomorphism and metonymy to representation. But the child comes to see in "The Star" the "personlike" shape of itself, without which insight it can know no one else. The monad of the psyche's own society eludes Nussbaum, though not Dickens, who peers into Stephen Blackpool's soul in the very part of *Hard Times* in which starlight figures most brilliantly, Rachael his Star of Bethlehem unnoticed by Nussbaum.[12]

The poem highlights the rhythmical repetition and variation of words, sounds and similes, the diamond-like twinkling of every facet of its language, each element of which flashes, vanishes, then flashes again. In this, the poem's catalectic trochaic tetrameter plays a crucial part. All but two of its lines are in this meter, supplying at the end of each a pause we come to expect and to relish. This consistently repeated absence of sound is interrupted by the poem's only two iambic tetrameter lines ("He could not see …" and "And often through …"), which will disappoint us by the very continuity of the duple rhythm that joins them to their antecedents because we have come to enjoy the repetitious intermittency introduced by the pervasive catalexis. We come to hear sound as the absence of silence, to which we ascribe a positive value and substance. Nussbaum will not allow herself to be distracted by this twinkling of language, even though its intermittences, of many kinds and at many scales, sensitise us to the tempi of our being. Proud of her tin ear, Nussbaum denigrates the very poet most devoted to the twinkling of the English language. Conceding that "there are features of rhythm and sound that play a large part" in lyric poetry and "that these are to some degree separable from the representation of human beings and human life", Nussbaum concludes that

> (We really don't admire Edgar Allen [sic] Poe today, because that is all he offers us.) Beyond this, I'm inclined to say that great lyric poetry is found great because it offers us something to think about in the area of human life and how it might be lived, and thus has a moral element in the broad sense of "moral" that I use throughout my writings.[13]

The rhymes of the poem's final couplet, its tenth, echo those of its first in reverse. Likewise, the rhymes of its penultimate couplet echo those of its fifth in reverse. But the rhymes of its third last couplet echo those of its second in their original order. Two of these three echoes evoke a contrast. Wonder in the second line gives way to ignorance in the penultimate (nineteenth); the diamond in the fourth line gives way to the sun in the sixteenth. Only the fifth and ninth couplets are in complete

---

12 In *Poetic Justice*, Nussbaum mentions Stephen on 29, 33, and 129, and Rachael (misspelt "Rachel") on 33, associating both with "grave flaws", "sentimentality", and "an odd failure in basic literary technique". Nussbaum notes Stephen's political diffidence but not his marital martyrdom. Wendy Jacobson notices all the stars that Nussbaum misses, especially those in Book 1, Chapter 13, and Book 3, Chapter 6, in "The Muddle and the Star: *Hard Times*", *Dickensian* 103 (2007): 144–56.

13 Nussbaum, "Exactly and Responsibly", 357, note 21.

accord, the reciprocity between the star's tiny spark and the traveller in the dark confirmed, the traveller taking the initiative in the fifth, the tiny star taking it in the ninth. Largely on the evidence of these "features of rhythm and sound", duality and dichotomy shape equally the psyche's sense of itself and its world. Furthermore, the diphthong **aɪ** occurs four times in the first and last stanzas, twice in the second, once in the third, and thrice in the fourth, ensuring that "I" and its rhymes resound at the outset and the end. The vowel **u:** occurs once in the first, second and last stanzas, twice in the third, and four times in the fourth, ensuring that "you" and its rhymes resound just before the end as it subsides in favour of **aɪ**. Finally, the vowel **ɑ:** occurs twice in the first and third stanzas, not even once in the second, once in the fourth, and four times in the last, ensuring that the "star" or "spark" resounds as loudly as does "I" at the end, the asterisk settling finally on what it will enduringly mark, concluding the dance through which the persons of the psyche move to the lullaby's tune. These "features of rhythm and sound" tell us exactly "How I wonder", referring as much to the degree to which, as to the way in which, wonder works on the mind. Aptly enough, Taylor's brother Isaac recalls that she composed many of her poems in an attic study whose "window commanded a view of the country, and a 'tract of the sky', as a field for that nightly soaring of the fancy of which she was so fond", catching in them, according to her nephew Josiah Gilbert, the natural world's "infinite suggestiveness" in the "contemplative, and curiously inquiring manner" she shared with Isaac.[14]

Teaching *Hard Times* to a law school class, Nussbaum solicited and received from a student a response to "Twinkle, twinkle, little star" she took to corroborate her view that literature fosters liberality and liberalism in its students:

> [The student] began to describe – with a Dickensian poetry I cannot begin to recapture – the image he used to see of a sky beautifully blazing with stars and bands of bright color. This wonderful sight somehow, he said, led him to look in a new way at his cocker spaniel. He would look into the dog's eyes and wonder what the dog was really feeling and thinking, ... All this, in turn, he said, led to new ways of thinking about his parents and about other children.
>
> Why did [the student] think that the starry sky was benign and not malevolent? Why did it lead him to attribute love and goodness to his cocker spaniel, rather than devilishness and sadism? ... the nursery song itself, like other such songs, nourishes the ascription of humanity, and the prospect of friendship, rather than paranoid sentiments of being persecuted by a hateful being in the sky. It tells the child to regard the star as "like a diamond," not like a missile of destruction, and also not like a machine good only for production and consumption.[15]

---

14 Isaac Taylor, *Memoirs, Correspondence, and Poetical Remains of Jane Taylor* (London: Holdsworth and Ball, 1831), 75–6; Josiah Gilbert, *Autobiography and Other Memorials of Mrs. Gilbert (formerly Ann Taylor)* (London: H.S. King, 1874), 210.

The student speaks to the entire genre of which "The Star" is for him less mesmerising an instance than others. His description is closer to Stephen Blackpool's in *Hard Times* of Rachael as the Star of Bethlehem and to Don McLean's in his song "Vincent" of a night sky colourfully ablaze with stars than to Taylor's tiny spark.[16] By grafting the star's spark into the eyes of his cocker spaniel, the student tethers and domesticates a free and airy being, in effect reducing the Dog Star, brightest in the sky, to a dog, and elevating himself to the status of Orion, hunter worthy to be so spanieled. The student does not so much discover his pet dog's devotion as demand of it such devotion as its proper way of being with him, teaching it tort law. Neither Nussbaum nor the student wonders if the star's vigilance or the dog's does not endow them with their humanity, both presuming they possess the privilege of endowing others with humanity rather than the privilege of receiving theirs as an endowment from others. Neither concedes that their being may be heteronomous, given significance only by a whole world, the "dark blue sky" asterisked by the "little star".

To interpret star and sky thus is to admit the possibility that they may be otherwise, to forfend oneself against the very persecutory paranoia Nussbaum dismisses when insisting that the diamond-like star offers "the prospect of friendship" rather than presaging "a missile of destruction", ignoring the world-perturbing power that stars have always wielded, to which the prophet Jeremiah bids us inure ourselves. Children's bedtime stories and lullabies try to excite such paranoia almost as often as they try to allay it. The reassurance offered by Taylor's "The Star", William Miller's "Wee Willie Winkie", James Ferguson's "Auld Daddy Darkness" and Eugene Field's "Wynken, Blynken, and Nod" is countered by the exhilarating dread inculcated by Johann Wolfgang von Goethe's "The Elf-King" and E.T.A. Hoffman's "The Sandman".[17] Tempering nerves of steel, the nursery rhyme "Now I lay me down to sleep" suggests children quietly accept the possibility

---

15   Nussbaum, *Poetic Justice*, 39. The student would not be the first to reply as his teacher would like, if, as Jacques Lacan insists, such "dyadic complicity" is rife, in "The Freudian Thing" (1955), in *Écrits*, trans. Bruce Fink (New York: Norton, 2006), 434. Tellingly, Nussbaum asks the student his views "before I made any observations of my own", which the student, thus animated by prosopopoeia, makes for her, in *Poetic Justice*, 38. Harbouring misgivings about Nussbaum identifying the student by name, although we must presume he consents to her doing so, I suppress it, especially because I doubt their joint finding and separate being.

16   Don McLean, "Vincent" (United Artists, 1972), its first line, "Starry, starry night", referring to Vincent van Gogh, *The Starry Night* (1889), oil on canvas, Museum of Modern Art, New York City.

17   The four lullabies appear in *The Oxford Book of Children's Verse*, ed. Iona and Peter Opie (Oxford: Clarendon, 1973), 122–3, 172–3, 275–6, 303–4; Goethe's ballad, trans. Matthew Lewis, in *The New Oxford Book of Romantic Period Verse*, ed. Jerome McGann (Oxford: Oxford University Press, 1994), 129; Hoffmann's story in *Tales of Hoffmann*, trans. R.J. Hollingdale (Harmondsworth: Penguin, 1982), 85–125. Marina Warner examines this dichotomy in "'Hush-a-bye Baby': Death and Violence in the Lullaby", *Raritan* 18, no.1 (1998): 93–114. Anglican and Protestant hymnals include reassuring evening hymns for children, such as Sabine Baring-Gould's "Now the day is over". The Opies' text of "The Star" departs in two significant instances from the first edition: "'Tis your bright and tiny spark" becomes "As your bright and tiny spark", and "trav'ller" (trochee) becomes "traveller" (trochee or dactyl).

of death every time they fall asleep.[18] Although Nussbaum contends that "the moral and social aspects of [the] literary scenarios" presented to older children become "increasingly complex and full of distinctions",[19] the complexity and subtlety of "The Star" and of volumes of verse addressed to infants and very young children such as Blake's *Songs of Innocence*, Christina Rossetti's *Sing-Song* and R.L. Stevenson's *A Child's Garden of Verses* can hardly be surpassed.

To regard "The Star" and its like primarily as lessons in moral and civic virtue is more than to mistake the cart for the horse. It is to miss the horse and mistake the cart for it. That these poems can be dragooned into such service indicates that the capacity of prosopopoeia and metaphor to shape us has been impressed so deeply into us that it disappears into intuitive immediacy. This is so even and especially in lullabies that appear to address us in moral and civic terms, as does William Blake's "A Dream", which among other poems in *Songs of Innocence and of Experience* may inform Jane Taylor's poems.[20]

We can easily enough take or mistake "A Dream" as a parable of charity recalling Christ's of the good Samaritan and anticipating fables such as the children's night-time voyage in Charles Laughton's *The Night of the Hunter*[21] only because, immediately and intuitively, we already understand its more basic evocation of the nature of our worldly being. The star that helps "light the ground" as we "look abroad to see" while wandering "wildered and forlorn" through the night is at once a teardrop and a glow-worm, anthropomorphic and zoomorphic forms of the sense of sight localised in a glistening eye, the "watchman of the night" who comes to our rescue when we lose our way like the emmet,[22] whose calls for help elicit calls in reply that together direct the wanderer home like sonar, imagined as "the beetles hum". The acoustic field is that of the sense of hearing localised in an echo-filled ear, which comes to our rescue when bidden by the voice embedded in a mouth guarded by a spirit (Angel) and moved by a dream that becomes ours.

To our usual way of thinking, this kind of ontological psyche-analysis may seem laborious and tendentious, but, on the contrary, our usual way of thinking is more intractably so. The prosopopoeic and metonymic liaison of eye, tear and

---

18   *The Oxford Dictionary of Nursery Rhymes*, ed. Iona and Peter Opie (Oxford: Clarendon, 1952), 254, in its original, bluntest form.

19   Nussbaum, *Cultivating Humanity*, 90.

20   William Blake, "A Dream", *Songs of Innocence* (1789), preferring two particular copies, both coloured in 1826: Fitzwilliam Museum (Cambridge) copy AA, with one star to the left of the "A" of the title, beyond tendrils that resemble living quotation marks, and another star to the right of "me"; Library of Congress (Rosenwald Collection) Copy Z, with a star to the left of each word of the title, a third to the right of "see", and a fourth to the right of "me" (as in AA). Delineated equally well in both are the glow-worm to the right of "tear" and the human or angelic watchman bottom right. John Hampsey judiciously assesses the tantalising circumstantial evidence of an association between Blake and the Taylor family in "Innocence ... and Irony?: The Poetry of Jane Taylor", *European Romantic Review* 8, no.3 (1997): 262–3, 272.

21   Charles Laughton, dir. *The Night of the Hunter* (United Artists, 1955).

22   *OED*, emmet; ant, n.1: OE æmætte; ME amete / amte / ampte / anpte / ante.

glow-worm, of crying mother and humming beetle, and of one call and caller with all other calls and callers is the elementary stuff of the poem, from which any further significance, of whatever kind, must be drawn or extorted. "A Dream" reveals that each of us is an ensemble of members bound together in conjugal intimacy and genial fellowship, caught in a recurring cycle of discomposure ("All heart-broke") and re-composure, much like the composite persons depicted by Giuseppe Arcimboldo and Salvador Dalí, and in a manner that anticipates Dalí's paranoiac-critical method.[23]

Yet, recruiting lullabies and nursery rhymes to her cause, Nussbaum warns that

> The basis for civic imagining must be laid early in life. As children explore stories, rhymes, and songs – especially in the company of the adults they love – they are led to notice the sufferings of other living creatures with a new keenness. At this point, stories can then begin to confront children more plainly with the uneven fortunes of life, convincing them emotionally of their urgency and importance.[24]

To imagine compassion is not to feel it; to introduce "the compassionate imagination" as a theme rather than to bestow it as a companion is nugatory; and to manipulate children's sympathies rather than respect unreservedly their intellectual autonomy, which one must presume to equal or exceed one's own, is to betray one's calling.

Better be taught, as were Lord Stanley's children and grandchildren, by Edward Lear than by a teacher following Nussbaum's curriculum. In limericks such as "There was an Old Man with a gong" and "There was an Old Man with a poker", children contemplate with perfect equanimity the violent propensities of individuals who attack groups, and of groups that attack individuals, whose behaviour is annoying or offensive enough to serve as pretext for an attack first verbal then physical.[25] Individuals' mere individuality is enough to provoke groups' taunts, each equally likely to triumph physically over the other in play, as the limericks and their accompanying cartoons are jokes, in which human relations

---

23 Giuseppe Arcimboldo, paired portraits of *Eve* and *Adam* (1578), oil on canvas, private collection, Basel; Salvador Dalí, *The Great Paranoiac* (1936), oil on canvas, Boymans-van-Beuningen Museum, Rotterdam. The surreal licence of prosopopoeic and metonymic exchange on which I insist eludes and quite undermines the distinctions between species, territories and milieus on which Gilles Deleuze and Félix Guattari insist in their account of lullabies in *A Thousand Plateaus* (1980), trans. Brian Massumi (1987; London: Continuum, 2004), ch. 11: "1837: On the Refrain", 342–86, 608–14. Their ethological theory of language is at odds with the expressly anti-ethological theories from which I derive mine, in Herder, *Treatise on the Origin of Language*, and Martin Heidegger, *The Fundamental Concepts of Metaphysics* (1929–1930), trans. William McNeill and Nicholas Walker (Bloomington: Indiana University Press, 1995), 169–273.

24 Nussbaum, *Cultivating Humanity*, 93, introducing a passage on "Literature and the Compassionate Imagination".

25 Edward Lear, *A Book of Nonsense* (1861), in *The Complete Verse and Other Nonsense*, ed. Vivien Noakes (London: Penguin, 2001), 160, 167.

can be contemplated repeatedly, safely and freely, not hobbled by any peremptory demand that sympathy decide the issue before the issue can be savoured in all its possible forms with all possible outcomes. For Lear, sympathy is the child's sovereign right to bestow or not as it pleases, not the teacher's to coax or extort from it by appealing to sentiment. Lear treats the Stanley children's rhadamanthine proclivities as jokes, seizing household objects such as gongs and pokers as "missiles of destruction" in mimic, metonymic battles in which identical rhymes, like scare-quotes, estrange things from themselves and their quotidian significance. Exceeding the bounds of identification and representation to which Nussbaum would restrict them, Lear's licentious prosopopoeia and metonymy evoke the disinterestedness of the "Kantian and post-Kantian formalist tradition" of aesthetics and anticipate the "moral relativism deriving from French postmodernist philosophy" that Nussbaum deplores.[26]

Citing "The Star" in *Hard Times*, Nussbaum wonders what happens "When a child and a parent begin to tell stories together". Had she wondered what happens when a child and a *grandparent* begin to tell stories together, her reflections would apply with equal accuracy to Mem Fox's *The Tiny Star*, especially if we heed Fox's account of its composition. Fox recalls that she and her grandchild

> became so attached to each other that the thought of my dying and leaving him bereft made me want to sob. I still get a lump in my throat at the very thought of it. Which is where my latest book was born: *The Tiny Star*, a life-cycle story of tenderness and comfort for any child or adult whose aged grandparents or parents are, all [at] once, no longer here. It does have a happy ending, I promise![27]

Nussbaum and Fox agree on the primacy of ascribing humanity to strangers and strange things, offering them sympathy, joining one's neighbours in doing so, realising one's own humanity by such acts, and coming to understand them as the foundation of moral and civic virtue. Yet although writers may be moved to write and readers moved to read in this way, no story's compositional and interpretive history can adequately account for it or regulate it.

Throughout *The Tiny Star*, the star resists personification. Invariably designated "it", it serves as a sign of personhood rather than of any particular person.[28] It characterises personhood as a heavenly condensate, come from afar and soon to recede afar, conferred by general acclamation, and not (primarily or at all) a biological fact. As such, the tiny star leads us along a string of metonyms: the

---

26   Nussbaum, *Cultivating Humanity*, 102, 108.
27   Mem Fox (letterpress) and Freya Blackwood (illustrations), *The Tiny Star* (North Sydney: Puffin, 2019), lacking page numbers, cited by line number from 1 through 54; Mem Fox, "The Story behind the Story of *The Tiny Star*: On Being a Grandparent" (posted 15 October 2019).
28   "It" and "its" refer to the tiny star twenty-four times, or twenty-five if we include the phrase "What a sensation it was" (line 46), in which "it" may refer either to the star or to the sensation it caused.

foundling whose bright disposition enlivens its adoptive kith and kin; the Star of Bethlehem signalling Christ's Incarnation; the starry apotheosis conferred on the illustrious dead; the path of a hyperbolic comet; and the nucleosynthetic origin of the chemical elements or "stardust" of which the human body is composed. The tiny star serves as the asterisk for this train of thought about human being.[29]

The Tiny Star is an ephemeris of an astronomical entity, tracking its variable magnitude (tiny, rounder, smaller, tiny once more), declination (taller), trajectory (falling to earth, returning to the heavens), and occultation (vanishing and then twinkling again).[30] The most important character of its earthly transit is given it by its finders, who take it home

> and wrapped it warmly
> in a quilt all covered with stars.

This ceremony of robing is important enough to be repeated verbatim later in the star's mundane life.[31] The quilt figures in fourteen of the eighteen illustrations of the incarnate star, one of which is of a framed photograph reminiscent of the Holy Family, and in two illustrations on its own after the star's apotheosis, reminiscent of the Girdle of Thomas left behind after the Assumption of the Virgin. Emphatically covered "all" over with stars, the quilt is an earthly miniature of the Milky Way swaddling the whole world, identifying the tiny star, and hence a human being, as a monad, an element of the cosmos that contains within it the entire cosmos. Invested with constellating power, the star transforms everyone's relations with everyone else around it, serving as their palladium and perhaps capable of serving as their vexillum as well, had they need of one, like the Star of David. The star emerges from its cosmic quilt and then recedes back into it as a sign comes to mind and then slips from it. As the public cloak of the tiny star, the quilt also renders visible during the day the cosmos of which sunlight deprives us, as a sign reminds us of what we cannot see.

The wonder evinced by *The Tiny Star* in the nature and power of signs transcends the immediate needs of the civics lesson to which a teacher such as Nussbaum would apply it and inspires Fox's *Radical Reflections*, in which she insists

---

29 This kind of foundling is usually female, including Esther in Charles Dickens' *Bleak House* (1852) and Eppie in George Eliot's *Silas Marner* (1861), and is pictured as such in Freya Blackwood's illustrations of *The Tiny Star*, to be distinguished from the foundling as changeling, such as Heathcliff in Emily Brontë's *Wuthering Heights* (1847), and the foundling as hero, such as Oedipus and Moses. In Byzantine icons and Renaissance paintings of the Nativity, Star and Saviour may glow alike, as in Geertgen tot Sint Jans' *Nativity at Night* (c.1490), oil on oak, National Gallery, London. For readers of Fox's age the most memorable comet would be Kohoutek of 1973. The stellar origins of the human body's chemical elements, first understood by George Gamow in the 1940s, had become the stuff of popular wonder by the 1960s, as in Joni Mitchell's song "Woodstock" (1970), "We are stardust / Billion year old carbon / We are golden."
30 Fox, *The Tiny Star*, lines 2, 10–1, and 32–6; 12–3; 2 and 44; 36–7 and 43–7.
31 Fox, *The Tiny Star*, lines 6–7 and 29–30.

that the "power of words, *the heat of meaning*, depends to a great extent on where words are placed" according to "the right rhythm" that fosters and sustains the mind's ability to shape its thoughts.[32] In *The Tiny Star*, the star's expansion and contraction evoke, in the form of anaphora, the mind's power of circumspection and, in the form of epistrophe, its power of concentration. Its associative energy evokes, in the form of the quantifiers "each" and "every", the mind's power of individuation. Its accumulation of qualities evokes, in the form of the coordinate conjunction, the mind's powers of combination.[33] The story exercises the grammar of thinking rather than inculcating any one thought. Were we to ascribe one thought to it, Kant's wonder at the parity of the starry heavens and the moral law might do it least injustice but would miss the ampler story of signs and signification that, according to Origen and Plotinus, underlies it and all other lessons.[34]

Most of Nussbaum's pedagogical polemic concerns university students reading novels, not infants and young children listening to lullabies and nursery rhymes. Nussbaum's most eminent antagonists, focusing on the novels she considers, fault her chiefly for a "temporal parochialism" that assumes a "moral superiority" over most but not all other periods and parishes, inclining instead to an ideal of disinterest close to David Hume's in "Of the Standard of Taste".[35] But Nussbaum's brief reflections on lullabies and nursery rhymes disclose a greater problem than can be resolved by Hume's multicultural and transhistorical generosity of view, characterised most decisively by Martin Heidegger as the problem of attempting to understand human beings psychologically and anthropologically before one has even begun to understand human being ontologically:

> With special regard to the interpretation of Da-sein, the opinion may now arise that understanding the most alien cultures and "synthesising" them with one's own may lead to Da-sein's becoming for the first time thoroughly and genuinely enlightened about itself. Versatile curiosity and restlessly "knowing it all" masquerade as a universal understanding of Da-sein. But at bottom it remains

---

32 Mem Fox, *Radical Reflections: Passionate Opinions on Teaching, Learning and Living* (Sydney: Harcourt Brace, 1993), ch. 8: "Conveying the Inexplicit", 110, 114.

33 Fox, *The Tiny Star*, anaphora in lines 4–6 and 48–9; epistrophe in lines 38–42; quantifiers "each" and "every" in lines 8, 39–42, 48–50; coordinate conjunctions in lines 16–20. On the coordinate conjunction, see William Gass, "And: A Meditation on the Most Familiar Connective", *Harper's Magazine* 268 (February 1984): 54–61.

34 Immanuel Kant, *Critique of Practical Reason* (1788), in *Practical Philosophy*, ed. and trans. Mary Gregor (Cambridge: Cambridge University Press, 1996), "Conclusion", [5:161–3,] 269–71, on the heavenly warrant of human being and human fellowship.

35 Richard Posner, "Against Ethical Criticism", *Philosophy and Literature* 21, no.1 (1997): 1–27, crediting fellow legal scholar Stephen Holmes with the phrase, on 8. See also its sequel, "Against Ethical Criticism: Part 2", *Philosophy and Literature* 22, no.2 (1998): 394–412; Hilary Putnam, "Taking Rules Seriously: A Response to Martha Nussbaum", *New Literary History* 15, no.1 (1983): 193–200; and, cited by neither, David Hume, "Of the Standard of Taste", *Four Dissertations* (London: A. Millar, 1757).

indefinite *what* is really to be understood, and the question has not even been asked.[36]

Nussbaum's thesis that literary texts help us "see the lives of the different with more than a casual tourist's eye – with involvement and sympathetic understanding" and "transport us, while remaining ourselves, into the life of another" is abjectly vulnerable to Heidegger's critique.[37]

Infants and young children listen to lullabies and nursery rhymes because their words disclose a world, not because they point a lesson or help them begin to form their own character, even though the world they disclose is one of keeping score and forming character and all that countervails these projects. Infants and young children as well as their caregivers take a lifetime to understand the ontological gift these texts and those that purport to supersede them bear. In the words of the young Scheherazade-like protagonist of Catherynne Valente's *The Orphan's Tales*:

> A spirit came into my cradle … and … touched my face, and left there many tales and spells, like the tattoos of sailors. The verses and songs were so great in number and so closely written that they appeared as one long, unbroken streak of jet on my eyelids. … Together they make a great magic, and when the tales are all read out, and heard end to shining end, to the last syllable, the spirit will return and judge me.[38]

"Like the tattoos of sailors", one of a myriad of similes that twinkle throughout Valente's work, hints at a long-postponed reconciliation of accounts such as finally unites Odysseus and Penelope, for so long each other's starry stranger.

Bibliography

Arcimboldo, Giuseppe. *Eve* and *Adam*. Paired portraits. Oil on canvas. 1578. Basel. Private collection.

Blake, William. "A Dream." *Songs of Innocence*. 1789. In two 1826 copies of *Songs of Innocence and of Experience*: Copy AA, Fitzwilliam Museum, Cambridge; Copy Z, Rosenwald Collection, Library of Congress.

Brontë, Emily. *The Complete Poems*. Ed. Janet Gezari. Harmondsworth: Penguin, 1992.

Crashaw, Richard. *The Complete Poetry*. Ed. George Williams. New York: Norton, 1974.

Dalí, Salvador. *The Great Paranoiac*. Oil on canvas. 1936. Rotterdam. Boymans-van-Beuningen Museum.

Deleuze, Gilles, and Félix Guattari. *A Thousand Plateaus*. 1980. Trans. Brian Massumi. 1987. London: Continuum, 2004.

---

36   Martin Heidegger, *Being and Time* [1927], trans. John Macquarrie and Edward Robinson (1962; Oxford: Blackwell, 1996), ¶38, [178,] 222.

37   Nussbaum, *Cultivating Humanity*, 88, 111.

38   Catherynne Valente, *The Orphan's Tale, Volume One: In the Night Garden* (New York: Bantam Dell, 2006), 5.

Dickens, Charles. *Hard Times*. [1854]. Ed. George Ford and Silvère Monod. New York: Norton, 1966.

Dickens, Charles. *A Tale of Two Cities*. [1859]. Ed. George Woodcock. Harmondsworth: Penguin, 1970.

Fox, Mem. *Radical Reflections: Passionate Opinions on Teaching, Learning and Living*. Sydney: Harcourt Brace, 1993.

Fox, Mem. "The Story behind the Story of *The Tiny Star*: On Being a Grandparent." On *Mem Fox*. Website. Posted 15 October 2019.
    https://memfox.com/gossip-behind-mems-books/the-story-behind-the-story-of-the-tiny-star/.

Fox, Mem. *The Tiny Star*. Illus. Freya Blackwood. North Sydney: Puffin, 2019.

Gass, William. "And: A Meditation on the Most Familiar Connective." *Harper's Magazine* 268 (February 1984): 54–61.

Geertgen tot Sint Jans. *Nativity at Night*. Oil on oak. c.1490. London. National Gallery.
    https://www.nationalgallery.org.uk/paintings/geertgen-tot-sint-jans-the-nativity-at-night.

Hampsey, John. "Innocence … and Irony?: The Poetry of Jane Taylor." *European Romantic Review* 8, no.3 (1997): 262–73.

Heidegger, Martin. *Being and Time*. 1927. Trans. John Macquarrie and Edward Robinson. 1962. Oxford: Blackwell, 1996.

Heidegger, Martin. *The Fundamental Concepts of Metaphysics*. 1929–1930. Trans. William McNeill and Nicholas Walker. Bloomington: Indiana University Press, 1995.

Herder, Johann Gottfried von. *Treatise on the Origin of Language*. 1772. In *Philosophical Writings*. Trans. Michael Forster. Cambridge: Cambridge University Press, 2002. 65–164.

Hoffmann, E.T.A. "The Sandman." In *Tales of Hoffmann*. Trans. R.J. Hollingdale. Harmondsworth: Penguin, 1982. 85–125.

Hume, David. "Of the Standard of Taste." In *Four Dissertations*. London: A. Millar, 1757. 203–40.

Jacobson, Wendy. "The Muddle and the Star: *Hard Times*." *Dickensian* 103 (2007): 144–56.

Kant, Immanuel. "Critique of Practical Reason". 1788. In *Practical Philosophy*. Ed. and trans. Mary Gregor. Cambridge: Cambridge University Press, 1996. 137–271.

Kant, Immanuel. *Critique of the Power of Judgment*. 1790. Rev. 1793. Trans. Paul Guyer and Eric Matthews. Cambridge: Cambridge University Press, 2000.

Lacan, Jacques. "The Freudian Thing." 1955. In *Écrits*. Trans. Bruce Fink. New York: Norton, 2006. 334–63.

Laughton, Charles. Dir. *The Night of the Hunter*. United Artists. 1955.

Lear, Edward. *The Complete Verse and Other Nonsense*. Ed. Vivien Noakes. London: Penguin, 2001.

Leibniz, Gottfried Wilhelm. *New Essays on Human Understanding*. Written 1704. Trans. Peter Remnant and Jonathan Bennett. Cambridge: Cambridge University Press, 1996.

McGann, Jerome. Ed. *The New Oxford Book of Romantic Period Verse*. Oxford: Oxford University Press, 1994.

McLean, Don. "Vincent" ["Starry, starry night"]. *American Pie*. United Artists. Vinyl LP. UAS 5535. 1971.

Mitchell, Joni. "Woodstock" ["We are stardust"]. *Ladies of the Canyon*. Reprise. Vinyl LP. RS 6376. 1970.

Morton, Timothy. "'Twinkle, Twinkle, Little Star' as an Ambient Poem: A Study of a Dialectical Image." *Romantic Circles: Praxis Series*. November 2001.
    https://romantic-circles.org/praxis/ecology/morton/morton.html.

Nancy, Jean-Luc. *The Fall of Sleep*. 2007. Trans. Charlotte Mandell. New York: Fordham University Press, 2009.

Newton, Isaac. *Opticks: or, a Treatise of the Reflections, Refractions, Inflections and Colours of Light*. 4th ed. London: William Innys, 1730.

Nussbaum, Martha. *Cultivating Humanity: A Classical Defense of Reform in Liberal Education*. Cambridge, MA: Harvard University Press, 1997.

Nussbaum, Martha. "Exactly and Responsibly: A Defense of Ethical Criticism." *Philosophy and Literature* 22, no.2 (1998): 343–65.

Nussbaum, Martha. *Poetic Justice: The Literary Imagination and Public Life*. Boston: Beacon, 1995.

Opie, Iona, and Peter Opie. Ed. *The Oxford Book of Children's Verse*. Oxford: Clarendon, 1973.

Opie, Iona, and Peter Opie. Ed. *The Oxford Dictionary of Nursery Rhymes*. Oxford: Clarendon, 1952.

Origen. *Commentary on Genesis*. In *Origen*. Trans. Joseph Trigg. London: Routledge, 1998. 86–102.

Plotinus. *Enneads*. Trans. S. Mackenna and B. Page. In *Internet Classics Archive*. Ed. Daniel Stevenson. Cambridge, MA: MIT, 1994–2009. https://classics.mit.edu/Plotinus/enneads.html.

Posner, Richard. "Against Ethical Criticism." *Philosophy and Literature* 21, no.1 (1997): 1–27.

Posner, Richard. "Against Ethical Criticism: Part 2." *Philosophy and Literature* 22, no.2 (1998): 394–412.

Putnam, Hilary. "Taking Rules Seriously: A Response to Martha Nussbaum." *New Literary History* 15, no.1 (1983): 193–200.

Taylor, Ann. *Autobiography and Other Memorials of Mrs. Gilbert, formerly Ann Taylor*. Ed. Josiah Gilbert. 2 vols. London: H. S. King, 1874.

Taylor, Isaac. *Memoirs, Correspondence and Poetical Remains of Jane Taylor*. London: Holdsworth and Ball, 1831.

Taylor, Jane, and Ann Taylor. *Rhymes for the Nursery*. London: Darton and Harvey, 1806. https://www.bl.uk/collection-items/first-publication-of-twinkle-twinkle-little-star.

Valente, Catherynne. *The Orphan's Tale. Vol. 1: In the Night Garden*. New York: Bantam Dell, 2006.

Van Gogh, Vincent. *The Starry Night*. Oil on canvas. 1889. New York City. Museum of Modern Art.

Vaughan, Henry. *The Complete Poetry*. Ed. French Fogle. New York: Norton, 1969.

Warner, Marina. "'Hush-a-bye Baby': Death and Violence in the Lullaby." *Raritan* 18, no.1 (1998): 93–114.

Wordsworth, William. *Poetical Works*. Ed. Thomas Hutchinson and Ernest de Selincourt. London: Oxford University Press, 1969.

14

Lectures on Oscar Wilde's Aesthetics in *The Picture of Dorian Gray*

Bruce Gardiner

I taught seminars on *The Picture of Dorian Gray* from 2007 to 2011 and lectured on it from 2016 to 2020, every time in relation to Immanuel Kant's *Critique of the Power of Judgment*, G.W.F. Hegel's *Aesthetics*, Walter Pater's *The Renaissance*, John Ruskin's *Modern Painters*, and Henry James' "The Last of the Valerii". The script is of two lectures I gave in November 2020, in which I quote from the 1891 version of the novel, as edited by Michael Gillespie (New York: Norton, 2007).

Lecture 1

"Withered, wrinkled, and loathsome of visage" is how Dorian's portrait and then Dorian's corpse finally look. In Dorian's mind, and in his approach to beauty, his body is a time bomb that will surely disfigure and kill him, however much it may seduce and divert him for a time from its murderous intent. Insofar as Wilde's aesthetic thinking mirrors Dorian's, time and beauty are inimical and immiscible, contradicting every one of the theorists of aesthetics we have reviewed so far. According to Kant, the ontological indifference or neutrality of the imagination affords us as plastic a relation to time as possible. According to Hegel, our creation of beautiful tokens with which to think transforms our sensible subjection to time into our intellectual mastery of it. According to Ruskin, because the passage of time confirms our persistence in time, time beautifies all that it carries along with it, including us. Perhaps most remarkably, according to Pater, all time is immanent within the present moment, allowing us to relish its Darwinian whimsy as a kind of Hegelian totality.

Time completely unnerves and terrifies the narrator and protagonist of *The Picture of Dorian Gray*, both describing it as "horrible", the novel's most frequently repeated descriptor. Henry Wotton warns the teenage Dorian Gray that he will one day become "old and wrinkled and ugly" (Chapter 2), a collocation of terms unimaginable in Ruskin. Hiding the portrait that ages so that he need not, Dorian reflects that "it might escape the hideousness of sin, but the hideousness of age was in store for it" (Chapter 10, echoed in Chapter 11), the future a boobytrap eluded only by the decoy of art. As Dorian later broods on his treasured "poisonous book", he reflects on "the ruin that Time brought on beautiful and wonderful things" (Chapter 11), his use of the term "ruin" as derogatory as Ruskin's is laudatory. Even later, as he recalls his life as it was in his thirties, he muses that "Memory, like a horrible malady, was eating his Soul away" (Chapter 16). Finally, haunted by the deaths of James and Sibyl Vane and Basil Hallward, when Dorian contemplates his much-altered portrait, "Out of the black Cave of Time, terrible and swathed in scarlet, rose the image of his sin" (Chapter 18).

In his ever-greater antipathy to time, Dorian inclines increasingly to the aesthetic theory of Arthur Schopenhauer, whose response to the ontological neutrality of Kant's aesthetics is the obverse of Ruskin's. Whereas for Ruskin being is inherently beautiful in proportion to its persistence, for Schopenhauer, in *The World as Will and Representation* (1818, augmented 1844), being human is hardly compatible with being beautiful. I quote him at some length:

> When we say that a thing is beautiful, we thereby assert that it is an object of our aesthetic contemplation, and this has a double meaning; on the one hand it means that the sight of the thing makes us objective, that is to say, that in contemplating it we are no longer conscious of ourselves as individuals, but as pure will-less subjects of knowledge; and on the other hand it means that we recognise in the object, not the particular thing, but an Idea ... For the Idea and the pure subject of knowledge always appear at once in consciousness as necessary correlatives, and on their appearance all distinction of time vanishes ... Therefore, if, for example, I contemplate a tree aesthetically, that is, with artistic eyes, and thus recognise, not it, but its Idea, it becomes at once of no consequence whether it is this tree or its predecessor which flourished a thousand years ago, and whether the observer is this individual or any other that lived anywhere and at any time ... And the Idea dispenses not only with time, but also with space, for the Idea proper is not this special form which appears before me but its expression, its pure significance, its inner being, which discloses itself to me and appeals to me, and which may be quite the same though the spatial relations of its form be very different. (Book 3, §41, trans. Haldane and Kemp [1909])

> With the disappearance of volition from consciousness, the individuality also, and with it its suffering and misery, is really abolished. Therefore I have described the pure subject of knowledge which then remains over as the eternal eye of the world, which, although with very different degrees of clearness, looks forth from all living creatures, untouched by their appearing and passing away, ... while the individual subject, whose knowledge is clouded by the individuality which springs from the will, has only particular things as its object, and is as transitory as these themselves. In the sense here indicated a double existence may be attributed to everyone. As

will, and therefore as individual, he is only one, and this one exclusively, which gives him enough to do and to suffer. As the purely objective perceiver, he is the pure subject of knowledge in whose consciousness alone the objective world has its existence; as such he is all things so far as he perceives them, and in him is their existence without burden or inconvenience. (Supplements to Book 3, Chapter 30)

Schopenhauer's thesis that our aesthetic sense abstracts us from the here and now to which we are tied, as Orpheus' lyre briefly frees Ixion from the rolling wheel of fire to which he is bound, sounds something like Kant's. But Schopenhauer transforms Kant's notion of the ontological indeterminacy of aesthetic judgements into an actual ontological state into which we may enter briefly as if into a Parmenidean eternity, a specific experiential ideal rather than the basis of all possible experience. Whereas for Ruskin, our aesthetic sense reveals and certifies the beauty of time, for Schopenhauer it reveals and saves us from the hideousness and terror of time. For Ruskin, the natural is beautiful; for Schopenhauer, Wilde and Dorian Gray, only the unnatural and the artful are beautiful. Nature is irredeemably nasty; it causes us to suffer and kills us. The body and its appetites must be denatured and pressed to serve unnatural, untimely, unsettling, and inevitably immoral ends, insofar as morality serves to bind us to nature. In brief, one's body and one's biography must be transformed into artworks. As Henry Wotton explains to Dorian, "now and then a complex personality took the place and assumed the office of art, was indeed, in its way, a real work of art, life having its elaborate masterpieces, just as poetry has, or sculpture, or painting" (Chapter 4), taking his cue from the Romantic idea of character formation and Pater's idea of human speciation.

In this respect, Dorian's aesthetic credo is antithetical to the complementary ideals embodied by Alan Campbell and Basil Hallward. Dorian commandeers Alan's scientific, biological expertise, doubtless by blackmailing him on account of his biological, sexual susceptibilities, to destroy the corpse of the painter-*cum*-moraliser whose portrait of him proves lethally misleading, albeit from a biological-*cum*-moralistic viewpoint. In the world that Dorian creates, initially under the auspices of Henry Wotton and chiefly over the two decades covered in Chapter 11, the organic is excised from time by being mineralised, volatilised, and textualised. Note, in Chapter 1, the prominence of silk derived from insects, lacquerware from insects and plants, carpets from sheep, nicotine and opium from plants, and in Chapter 11, gemstones, vestments, cosmetics and embroideries, all donned and displayed like so many amulets to disarm and divert the evil eye of time with its invidious designs on the aesthete's body. Even more crucial is the temporising power of conversation and reading, of all human behaviours those most facilely able to free the mind from the here and now, even and especially when the topic of the conversation or the text is the here and now itself. The novel's narrator and characters are unusually given to being mesmerised and mesmerising each other in conversation and when reading and writing. We as readers are also likely so charmed that we completely forget the time and even time itself. Most wonderfully, Dorian manages to forget completely that he has just murdered Basil when he starts reading Théophile Gautier's collection of poems, *Émaux et Camées* [*Enamels and Cameos*] (1852), the title of which suggests the immortalisation by mineralisation to which Dorian aspires in his own life.

Moreover, the human mind may dislodge itself from its timebound biology, if only for a time, by disrupting its circadian rhythms: waking up and staying awake when it is more natural to fall sleep and *vice versa*. Such temporal derangement produces what may be the most surreally beautiful episode in Dorian's life, just after he witnesses Sibyl Vane's atrociously artless theatre performance:

> As the dawn was just breaking he found himself close to Covent Garden. The darkness lifted, and, flushed with faint fires, the sky hollowed itself into a perfect pearl. Huge carts filled with nodding lilies rumbled slowly down the polished empty street. The air was heavy with the perfume of the flowers, and their beauty seemed to bring him an anodyne for his pain. He followed into the market, and watched the men unloading their wagons. A white-smocked carter offered him some cherries. He thanked him, wondered why he refused to accept any money for them, and began to eat them listlessly. They had been plucked at midnight, and the coldness of the moon had entered into them. A long line of boys carrying crates of striped tulips, and of yellow and red roses, defiled in front of him, threading their way through the huge, jade-green piles of vegetables. Under the portico, with its grey sun-bleached pillars, loitered a troop of draggled bareheaded girls, waiting for the auction to be over. Others crowded round the swinging doors of the coffee-house in the Piazza. The heavy cart-horses slipped and stamped upon the rough stones, shaking their bells and trappings. Some of the drivers were lying asleep on a pile of sacks. Iris-necked and pink-footed, the pigeons ran about picking up seeds. (Chapter 7)

The scene, of London's vegetable, fruit and flower market, strikes Dorian as a work of art, incised, whether intaglio or in cameo, on a pearl shell, and as a vision in a dream, especially because a figure within it, a white-smocked carter, responds to Dorian as if he, conversely, were a vision in the carter's dream, their mutual sexual arousal freed from all biological and moral constraint. The lilies generously relieve Dorian of his drowsiness and the flowers dispense their perfume to relieve him of the pain that binds him to his body, as everything around him offers itself to his connoisseurship. Everywhere nature is transformed into art, by horticulture, floriculture, perfumery and jewellery. Even the vegetables are "jade-green", endowed with the gemstone's beauty and durability, complementing the pearlescence of the sky. Most surreally, as if in dreamy confusion, the fronted adjectival phrases "Iris-necked, and pink-footed" appear at first to refer to the sleeping drivers rather than the pigeons.

Surely only Wilde's indulgence of Dorian's aesthetic disdain of time can adequately excuse a flagrant anachronism in Chapter 11. Dorian, as the narrator tells us, was "Saddened by the reflection of the ruin that time brought on beautiful and wonderful things" as he indulges in several *ubi sunt* meditations, among which is this:

> Where [now was] the huge velarium that Nero had stretched across the Colosseum at Rome, that Titan sail of purple on which was represented the starry sky, and Apollo driving a chariot drawn by white, gilt-reined steeds? (Chapter 11)

A huge sail or awning transforms sidereal time into an artwork, purportedly under the Emperor Nero's auspices. But the Colosseum was built by Vespasian after Nero's death on the site of Nero's demolished palace, the Golden House, to which Dorian refers a little later. Clearly it is imperative that Nero be associated with this time-and-cosmos-conquering canvas, however time and the cosmos might actually object. What better way to declare that art transcends time than by blatant anachronism? Nero has already been mentioned a little earlier when Petronius Arbiter, author of *The Satyricon*, is placed in "imperial Neronian Rome". Pliny the Elder in his *Natural History* characterises the pleasure that Nero takes in watching bloody spectacles in the Circus (which Dorian has obviously mistaken as the Colosseum) in the sentence, *Gladiatorum pugnas spectabat smaragdo*, he used to watch the gladiatorial fights with an emerald, either reflected off a gem's cabochon surface or transmitted through a laminar emerald glass, or as Dorian paraphrases Pliny more poetically a little later on, he "peered through a clear emerald at the red shambles of the Circus". The novel challenges us to follow Nero in looking at nature *smaragdo*, through the lens of art, to relish as beautiful a story of suffering and savagery so appalling that only art can redeem us from a destiny no different from it.

The novel is a bloody mess. Dorian murders Basil. He is implicated in the suicides of Sibyl Vane, Alan Campbell, a young guardsman, and perhaps Hetty Merton; in the accidental death of James Vane; and in the mental derangement and social ignominy of Henry Ashton, Adrian Singleton, the son of Lord Kent, the Duke of Perth, Henry Wotton's sister, Lord Gloucester's wife, and who knows how many others. In the end he commits suicide. The novel challenges us to suppress our natural impulse to sympathise with those who suffer and instead relish art's capacity to overcome suffering in representing it so beautifully, as in Shakespearian tragedy. Let us contemplate the body and history as Nero contemplated them by transforming them into something as beautiful as a gemstone. Dorian longs for the Neronian capacity to do this, implicitly recalling the emperor's supposed last words, *Qualis artifex pereo*, what an artist perishes here. To this end, a large part of the novel is a textbook, emphatically, perhaps too emphatically, not about *The Joy of Sex* but *The Joy of Aesthetics*, of the kind that W.B. Yeats advocates in "Lapis Lazuli", as I explained in an earlier lecture, and that Nero had obviously mastered.

The first four chapters depict the immaculate conception of an aesthete, the rescue of an orphaned "son of love and death" at an age at which he is just reaching his maximal plasticity and ductility before maturation, so that "there was nothing that one could not do with him" in trying to free him from the biological curse he would otherwise suffer as his beautiful mother's son. Dorian is reborn by means of the non-biological congress of two aesthetes, not so much of different sexes as of different aesthetic sensibilities, one an artist of the eye and the other of the ear, as the conjoint gestures of the one's painterly hand and the other's articulate tongue shape their gorgeous progeny:

> Dorian Gray stepped up on the dais, with the air of a young Greek martyr, and made a little *moue* of discontent to Lord Henry, to whom he had rather taken a fancy. He was so unlike Basil. They made a delightful contrast. And he had such a beautiful voice. After a few moments he said to him, "Have you really a very bad influence, Lord Henry? As bad as Basil says?" …
>
> For nearly ten minutes he stood there, motionless, with parted lips, and eyes strangely bright. He was dimly conscious that entirely fresh influences were at work within him. Yet they seemed to him to have come really from himself. The few words that Basil's friend had said to him – words spoken by chance, no doubt, and with wilful paradox in them – had touched some secret chord that had never been touched before, but that he felt was now vibrating and throbbing to curious pulses …
>
> "Basil, I am tired of standing," cried Dorian Gray suddenly. "I must go out and sit in the garden. The air is stifling here."
>
> "My dear fellow, I am so sorry. When I am painting, I can't think of anything else. But you never sat better. You were perfectly still. And I have caught the effect I wanted – the half-parted lips, and the bright look in the eyes. I don't know what Harry has been saying to you, but he has certainly made you have the most wonderful expression. I suppose he has been paying you compliments. You mustn't believe a word that he says." (Chapter 2)

Dorian thus emerges from the painter's womb within which he is transformed by the conversationalist's seminal fancy and from which he is freed by that same conversationalist's maieutic skill. Dorian as image and artwork supersedes Dorian the scion of mother nature, or so all three believe. Basil and Henry endow Dorian not only with a beauty inherited from them but also an autonomous creativity that neither of them ever fully appreciates. Basil is sympathetic, discreet and ethical; Henry is heartless, indiscreet and unethical; Dorian is equivocally like both and like neither. Dorian's aesthetic parentage wars with his natural parentage. The trio's intimacies are beyond the order of nature. Wilde would surely be contemptuous of the tendency among the public defenders of homosexuality then as now to declare it natural, when for Wilde its opposition to nature is of its essence. In any case, aesthetic intercourse comprehensively outdoes sexual intercourse.

Basil's spirit presides over the graphic, descriptive, figurative and metaphoric dimensions of the narrative. Henry's spirit presides over its auditory, conversational, epigrammatic and prosopopoeic dimensions. Henry's voice most informs the Preface and the postprandial debates of Chapters 3, 15 and 17. Basil's writing most informs the book's elaborately visualised episodes and Chapter 11. The two styles vie with each other like a married couple who never come to see eye to eye. One of the novel's most highly wrought passages gives us a vivid description, in Basil's manner, of Henry's insinuatingly powerful conversation, as the two together give birth to the new Dorian:

> Dorian Gray listened, open-eyed and wondering. The spray of lilac fell from his hand upon the gravel. A furry bee came and buzzed round it for a moment. Then it began to scramble all over the oval stellated globe of the tiny blossoms. He watched it with that strange interest in trivial things that we try to develop when things of high import make us afraid, or when we are stirred by some new emotion for which we cannot find expression, or when some thought that terrifies us lays sudden siege to the brain and calls on us to yield. After a time the bee flew away. He saw it creeping into the stained trumpet of a Tyrian convolvulus. The flower seemed to quiver, and then swayed gently to and fro. (Chapter 2)

Insofar as the bee represents the human eye, its scrambling and creeping evoke the chaotic distractibility that guarantees our comprehension of everything in our field of vision. Insofar as the bee represents by its buzzing the musicality of the voice, its exploration of the convolvulus evokes the word's procreative penetration of the ear, the miracle of auricular or annunciatory conception, of being deflowered by another's voice, copulation by audition.

The passage begins with Dorian "listening, open-eyed", aptly enough for an exacting and pedantic lesson about how an aesthete should listen and look, as for instance at "the oval stellated globe of the tiny blossoms" of the spray of lilac. Dorian is not the sole student attending this lesson. Note the phrasing of "*we may try to develop*", "make *us* afraid", "*we* are stirred", "*we cannot find*", "terrifies *us*" and "calls on *us*". We as readers are addressed as the fellows of this star-pupil Dorian, as aesthetic novices no less in need than he of elementary lessons in aesthetics. The novel is a textbook in aesthetics, pedantically and redundantly explanatory, solicitous of our inexperience, reassuring us as we struggle with the radical disruption that aestheticism must introduce into our experience of our senses and social relations. From the Preface onward, the lessons of aestheticism are distilled and debated at what must often seem tediously exhaustive length. Only after the elementary stage of our aesthetic education is completed, in Dorian's case by his relationship with Sibyl Vane, is a more advanced textbook prescribed, the "poisonous book" that Henry gives Dorian and that Dorian spends about twenty years studying, in Chapter 11.

If instead of reading this particular scene in the garden as I have read it, we were to take it as a highly euphemistic account of Dorian's sexual initiation, of the arousal of his oval globes and the penetration of his convolvulus, we would simply reveal ourselves as nature's dunderheads interested only in smut. The novel repeatedly provokes us into making just such a mistake in order to persuade us that it is always a mistake to read it so. Sexual activity is only a meagre, lacklustre travesty of aesthetic activity, at best a fumbling preamble to the ecstasies of aesthetic pleasure, or so the novel hopes until it can no longer do so.

Lecture 2

So far, the account I have offered of *The Picture of Dorian Gray* is by and large that of its original 1890 serialised version. It is not yet an adequate account of the much-augmented version Wilde published as a book in 1891, which added to the original thirteen chapters a Preface, greatly magnifying the stridency of the book's aestheticism, and six extra chapters, now numbered 3, 5, and 15 through 18, four of which drastically magnify the importance of Sibyl Vane, her brother James, and their mother. Without the extra chapters, Dorian's murder of Basil far outweighs in importance his part in prompting Sibyl to commit suicide; but with the extra chapters, the two deaths are equally central and more closely entangled.

Wilde must have felt that his original version either begged crucial questions about Sibyl or at least answered them awry. In the original version, she appears as no more than incidental and exemplary. Yet even as Wilde originally conceived her, there is something patently unsatisfactory about thinking of Sibyl in this way, and his revisionary dreamwork lifts much into view that the original work repressed. In the revised version, which deconstructs the first, the hitherto marginal comes to occupy the centre, and perhaps the hitherto central is relegated to the margins. The first version mistakes Sibyl as the subject of a portrait in the sentimental manner, whereas the second version suggests, albeit surreptitiously and equivocally, that she is a major artist and militant aesthete in her own right, and that the book could as justly be titled *The Picture of Sibyl Vane*. Sibyl may even supersede Basil and Henry as the painter of Dorian's portrait, deftly retouching it after her predecessors have lost touch with Dorian as both artwork and artist. Even if we acquiesce in Wilde's title, we should perhaps add to it a subtitle, *The Picture of Dorian Gray Painted by Sibyl Vane*. Basil seems not quite to know what moves him to portray Dorian as he does, offering a touching but puzzling account of his motives in Chapter 9. Basil may be little more than the unwitting amanuensis of a psychic force that Sibyl more fully understands and masters.

Dorian's dealings with Sibyl occupy Chapters 4 through 10. As an actress, she performs Shakespearian roles that in Shakespeare's day were performed only by boys who, as beings of pluripotent promise, portrayed indifferently every possibility of sexual difference and sexual preference. This is how Dorian describes her to Henry:

> "Well, I can't help going to see Sibyl play," he cried, "even if it is only for a single act. I get hungry for her presence; and when I think of the wonderful soul that is hidden away in that little ivory body, I am filled with awe."
>
> "You can dine with me to-night, Dorian, can't you?"
>
> He shook his head. "To-night she is Imogen," he answered, "and to-morrow night she will be Juliet."
>
> "When is she Sibyl Vane?"
>
> "Never."
>
> "I congratulate you."
>
> "How horrid you are! She is all the great heroines of the world in one. She is more than an individual. You laugh, but I tell you she has genius. I love her, and I must make her love me. You, who know all the secrets of life, tell me how to charm Sibyl Vane to love me! I want to make Romeo jealous. I want the dead lovers of the world to hear our laughter and grow sad. I want a breath of our passion to stir their dust into consciousness, to wake their ashes into pain. My God, Harry, how I worship her!" … He was terribly excited. (Chapter 4)

Thus is the fan smitten by the diva. For Dorian, Sibyl is wholly a creature of art, with no personality of her own, only the personalities with which Shakespeare's art invests her. Her regard for Dorian is no less a matter of art. By calling him Prince Charming, Sibyl absorbs him into her world of art, he also thereby ceasing to be whom he would otherwise naturally be. Sibyl inveigles Dorian out of nature as Shakespeare inveigles her. In the wake of this conversation, Henry envisages Dorian's personality as an "aesthetic masterpiece" and complacently reflects that he, Henry, is largely its creator and curator, the youngster's Svengali. Henry's reveries are obtuse in two ways, both stemming from his misogyny. First, Henry cannot think that Sibyl exerts over Dorian anything like the influence that Basil and he have done. Second, he cannot conceive that Sibyl herself may be an aesthetic masterpiece either Dorian's equal or his superior. What Henry regards as the logical consequence of his thoughts is, on more fair-minded inspection, a series on non sequiturs concerning women always as creatures of art but never its creators.

Throughout both versions of the novel, Henry Wotton is ever so wittily and chivalrously misogynistic. Even when he pictures Dorian as "one of those gracious figures in a pageant or a play" (Chapter 4), he cannot picture Sibyl in the same way. Yet Henry depends abjectly on women as his chief audiences, patrons, and partners in repartee, particularly Lady Narborough in Chapter 15 and the Duchess of Monmouth in Chapter 17. Moreover, he appears discreetly but utterly crestfallen when his wife Victoria moves to divorce him in Chapter 19. It is as if his politely misogynistic banter is a blustering protest at this dependence on women, as if he fears being stigmatised as a superannuated Cherubino, ashamed that his aestheticism effeminises him. He may refuse to take women seriously in protest that men do not take him seriously.

Unlike Henry, Basil appears to have no current relations of any kind with women, given to ardent, Platonic same-sex intimacies in the manner of his heroes, Michelangelo, Montaigne and Winckelmann, mentioned in Chapter 10. So, for quite different reasons, both Basil and Henry overlook the possibility of female aesthetes. Therefore, the narrator must, as a matter of dreamlike compulsion, do everything he can to contradict Basil and Henry by conjuring up a female aesthete from source material that the male aesthetes would most likely dismiss, which is a Dickensian melodrama about the plebeian adoration of Shakespeare in London's East End and further east in the docklands, told in a luridly Gothic way. As if inspired by Pip's visit to a performance of Hamlet in Dickens' *Great Expectations* (1861), Sibyl draws Dorian into a Shakespearian-*cum*-Dickensian world of her own making to teach him a lesson about art, specifically her art.

In Chapter 5, added to the novel in 1891, we see Sibyl with her mother and brother James, neither of whom appears to understand her, and both of whom think her defenceless and in need of her brother's protective cudgel and her mother's exploitive cunning, Dorian looming ambiguously as both her protector and predator. To Sibyl, her brother and mother appear as puppets unconscious of the *commedia dell'arte* roles in which they are trapped, which only she can see for what they are: "Jim – you are like one of the heroes of those silly melodramas mother used to be so fond of acting in." Although her brother and mother see Sibyl as a victim, we on the contrary see them as victims. The Vane family triangle eerily echoes that between Basil, Henry and Dorian. Witness the earnestness of Basil and James, the devious wit of Henry and Mrs Vane, and the beauty of Dorian and Sibyl, each family the parody of the other, as if the question were, whose folks are weirder?

Dorian asks Basil, "I have been right, haven't I, … to find my wife in Shakespeare's plays?" (Chapter 6), as Sibyl casts him in a neo-Shakespearian love tragedy of her own making. Two aesthetes cast each other in plays they wish to direct, each treating themselves as director and the other as their star performer. Dorian's reading of the "poisonous book" in Chapter 11 not only prolongs for twenty years the intermission between the acts of Sibyl's play in which he has no choice but to act, but also tests our credentials as their fellow aesthetes. If we find the chapter tedious, we must be philistines, not aesthetes.

The most disconcerting observation in the entire book opens Chapter 7: "For some reason or other, the house was crowded that night." The night is that on which Basil and Henry accompany Dorian to see Sibyl perform the role of Juliet in Shakespeare's *Romeo and Juliet*. Why "for some reason or other"? The novelist decides not to decide that which is his sole prerogative to decide, suggesting that it is not important, or that he has not looked into it, or that it is not worth looking into, or that he has decided actively to avoid looking into the matter. We cannot tell how casual or careful the observation is, and a similar uncertainty reigns throughout the chapter, complicating our assessment of Sibyl's acting, or failing to act, or acting to persuade her audience that she is not acting. A "common uneducated audience" ensures that the theatre is "crowded that night", a crowd from which the three aesthetes are doubtless keen to distinguish themselves, thinking the Philistines around them aesthetically obtuse. But I would say that the trio entirely fail to distinguish themselves from the crowd among whom they sit and fail completely to understand that Sibyl may most artfully be acting as if she were artlessly failing to act.

Sibyl gives a performance of Juliet that the whole audience, aesthetes included, think woeful. When Dorian rushes to her dressing room afterward to excoriate her, Sibyl explains in her defence:

"Dorian, Dorian," she cried, "before I knew you, acting was the one reality of my life. It was only in the theatre that I lived. I thought that it was all true. I was Rosalind one night, and Portia the other. The joy of Beatrice was my joy, and the sorrows of Cordelia were mine also. I believed in everything. The common people who acted with me seemed to me to be godlike. The painted scenes were my world. I knew nothing but shadows, and I thought them real. You came – oh, my beautiful love! – and you freed my soul from prison. You taught me what reality really is. To-night, for the first time in my life, I saw through the hollowness, the sham, the silliness of the empty pageant in which I had always played. To-night, for the first time, I became conscious that the Romeo was hideous, and old, and painted, that the moonlight in the orchard was false, that the scenery was vulgar, and that the words I had to speak were unreal, were not my words, were not what I wanted to say. You had brought me something higher, something of which all art is but a reflection. You had made me understand what love really is. My love! My love! Prince Charming! Prince of life! I have grown sick of shadows. You are more to me than all art can ever be. What have I to do with the puppets of a play? When I came on to-night, I could not understand how it was that everything had gone from me. I thought that I was going to be wonderful. I found that I could do nothing. Suddenly it dawned on my soul what it all meant. The knowledge was exquisite to me. I heard them hissing, and I smiled. What could they know of love such as ours? Take me away, Dorian – take me away with you, where we can be quite alone. I hate the stage. I might mimic a passion that I do not feel, but I cannot mimic one that burns me like fire. Oh, Dorian, Dorian, you understand now what it signifies? Even if I could do it, it would be profanation for me to play at being in love. You have made me see that." (Chapter 7)

In defiance of the crowded house, Sibyl decides to play a part for Dorian only, whose understanding, which she repeatedly appeals to, is at issue. Her apology is a bravura performance about failing to give a bravura performance, a diva's stagey farewell to the stage, indeed a quintessentially Shakespearian lament about the artifice of the theatre, as well as a free paraphrase of Juliet's declaration of love, to all elements of which Dorian proves as deaf as he is blind to the transfiguration Sibyl undergoes during her apology. He, and perhaps we, hear neither the provocative tautology of "how reality really is" nor the patent absurdity of the claim that Shakespeare's own words are "unreal" and his plays hollow and silly shams. Sibyl challenges Dorian to make the finest distinctions between the artfulness and artlessness of her performance, which he proves incapable of doing. Sibyl also invokes Victorian melodrama, against which Dorian harbours a hapless and thoughtless prejudice, and he cannot read her meaning even when she finally exclaims, "Oh! Don't go away from me. My Brother … No, never mind. He didn't mean it. He was in jest," whereby she sets in motion her brother James as the nemesis that will destroy Dorian. From this point on, Dorian has no choice but to act like a puppet in the melodrama of Sibyl's devising, as James circumnavigates the world for twenty years before returning to London to kill him. Dorian is as witless as Dickens' Pip in not knowing what to make of the play in which he is now caught. Immediately afterward, in Chapter 8, Sibyl continues her bravura performance by committing suicide, as well she might in her Baz Luhrmann inspired spinoff of *Romeo and Juliet*, a tragedy that mandates a double suicide, as occurs in Wilde's novel.

If one is an aesthete, shaping one's life so that it is as little disfigured by nature's artless crudities as possible, then one will especially want to shape one's own death, otherwise nature's crudest and most artless insult, and make an art of dying sublimely, as we may when trying to imagine our own admirable obituary. I do not doubt that a certain aestheticism lies at the heart of the practice of Voluntary Assisted Dying, as the newly approved style of suicide is called. So, Sibyl's suicide, like that of Shakespeare's Cleopatra, may demonstrate her aesthetic autonomy rather than the abject victimhood on which everyone else in the novel insists, in so vulgarly sentimental, presumptuous, and thus entirely unpersuasive a way. Everyone including Dorian all too quickly decides that Dorian is responsible for Sibyl's suicide, denying her the slightest agency. "I have murdered Sibyl Vane," laments Dorian as he and Henry shape Sibyl's story into a neo-Jacobean tragedy they suppose of their own devising, presuming Sibyl herself oblivious of the aesthetic significance they alone may confer on her. As Henry tells Dorian in no uncertain terms,

> But women never know when the curtain has fallen. They always want a sixth act, and as soon as the interest of the play is entirely over, they propose to continue it. If they were allowed their own way, every comedy would have a tragic ending, and every tragedy would culminate in a farce. They are charmingly artificial, but they have no sense of art …
>
> "She will never come to life again now," muttered the lad, burying his face in his hands.
>
> "No, she will never come to life. She has played her last part. But you must think of that lonely death in the tawdry dressing-room simply as a strange lurid fragment from some Jacobean tragedy, as a wonderful scene from Webster, or Ford, or Cyril Tourneur. The girl never really lived, and so she has never really died. To you at least she was always a dream, a phantom that flitted through

Shakespeare's plays and left them lovelier for its presence, a reed through which Shakespeare's music sounded richer and more full of joy. The moment she touched actual life, she marred it, and it marred her, and so she passed away. Mourn for Ophelia, if you like. Put ashes on your head because Cordelia was strangled. Cry out against Heaven because the daughter of Brabantio died. But don't waste your tears over Sibyl Vane. She was less real than they are." (Chapter 8)

It surely behoves us to object to Henry's offensive nonsense, especially as it so fully accords with James Vane's misjudgement that Sibyl is a victim, albeit of a sexual rather than an aesthetic crime. We await Sibyl's posthumous contradiction of misogynistic Aesthete and sentimental Philistine alike, who agree on nothing except women's dependence on them.

Immediately after satisfying themselves that they have done Sibyl justice, Dorian and Henry attend that evening a performance by the then *prima donna assoluta* of the opera stage, Adelina Patti. "It's a Patti night," enthuses Henry. "Remember, Patti is singing," he reminds Dorian a little later. But when Basil hears that the two have thus amused themselves, he is scandalised:

"You went to the opera?" said Hallward, speaking very slowly, and with a strained touch of pain in his voice. "You went to the opera while Sibyl Vane was lying dead in some sordid lodging? You can talk to me of other women being charming, and of Patti singing divinely, before the girl you loved has even the quiet of a grave to sleep in? Why, man, there are horrors in store for that little white body of hers!" (Chapter 9)

But despite this dispute, none of the trio understands what listening to Patti at the opera must mean "while Sibyl Vane was lying dead" elsewhere. If it is a Patti night then it is no less a Sibyl night, Sibyl's performance no less sublime than Patti's, and had Patti been performing Ruggero Leoncavallo's *I Pagliacci* (1892), one could hardly have distinguished between two melodramatic masterpieces.

Once James Vane returns to London decades later, he devotes himself to stalking and murdering the man whom he and Sibyl know only as Prince Charming. Chapters 16 through 18 each conclude with Dorian's terrified recognition of his nemesis, first on the street in London's docklands, then at the window of Dorian's estate, Selby Royal, and finally, in the woods of the estate, accidentally killed by the local fox hunt's beaters. Although Dorian is thoroughly unhinged by these three shocks, he then relaxes in a false sense of security after this first embodiment of his nemesis perishes, wilfully forgetful that nemesis is inescapable and that if one of its agents fail then another will appear in its stead, almost certainly unrecognisable, as duly happens when Dorian falls in love with Hetty Merton, whom he fatuously persuades himself may serve as the medium of his redemption when he refrains at the last moment from compromising her, which fantasy Henry justly derides in Chapter 19. As Sibyl recalls the novels of Charles

Dickens, so Hetty recalls those of George Eliot, specifically Hetty Sorrel in *Adam Bede* (1859), as if Dorian will meet his nemesis or comeuppance in whichever Victorian novel he reads.

Involving Dorian in a tragedy of her devising, Sibyl is the aesthete who confers meaning on Dorian's performance, rather than the converse as Dorian and Henry think, contradicting the tendency of the "poisonous book" Dorian reads in Chapter 11 that reduces aestheticism to a drag show for beautiful men. Sibyl's history confirms women's capacity to conquer the forces of nature that they are misogynistically believed to embody, and it is important that Sibyl wields the aegis of Shakespeare, performing parts once reserved for the boys. This is the cryptic but essential burden of Wilde's dream text. If Dorian's aesthetic life does not go according to plan, it is because Sibyl's aesthetic life does. Sibyl's *coup de théâtre* mesmerises Wilde in his revisionist dream even though Wilde the conscious writer and reader may not know what Wilde the dreamer means. Wilde wrote to an admirer that "I am so glad you like that strange coloured book of mine – it contains much of me in it – Basil Hallward is what I think I am; Lord Henry what the world thinks of me; Dorian Gray what I would like to be – in other ages perhaps." He does not mention Sibyl. Wilde is as likely to misread his work sentimentally as anyone else, but Sibyl's is the dream text, which is the truthful text.

Prescribed reading for the series of lectures that included these two

Hegel, G.W.F. *Introductory Lectures on Aesthetics*. Pub. Posth. 1835. Trans. Bernard Bosanquet. 1886. Ed. Michael Inwood. London: Penguin, 1993.

James, Henry, Jr. "The Last of the Valerii." 1874. In *A Passionate Pilgrim, and Other Tales*. Boston: James R. Osgood, 1875, 125–77.

Kant, Immanuel. *Critique of the Power of Judgment*. 1790. Rev. 1793. Trans. Paul Guyer and Eric Matthews. Cambridge: Cambridge University Press, 2000.

Pater, Walter. *Studies in the History of the Renaissance*. 1873. Rev. 1877 and 1888 as *The Renaissance: Studies in Art and Poetry*. Ed. Matthew Beaumont. Oxford: Oxford University Press, 2010.

Ruskin, John. *Of Mountain Beauty*. Part 5 (in Vol. 4) of *Modern Painters*. 1856. As Vol. 6 of *The Works*. Ed. Edward Tyas Cook and Alexander Wedderburn. London: George Allen, 1904.

Wilde, Oscar. *The Picture of Dorian Gray*. 1890. Rev. 1891. Ed. Michael Patrick Gillespie. New York: Norton, 2007.

15

Luce Irigaray's *The Forgetting of Air in Martin Heidegger*

Bruce Gardiner

I taught seminars on Irigaray's *The Forgetting of Air in Martin Heidegger* (1983) from 2016 to 2020, each time following seminars on Heidegger's "Language", "The Thing" and "The Origin of the Work of Art", in a course on twentieth-century literary theory initially required for admission to English Honours. During the 2020 COVID-19 lock-out, averse to videoconferencing, I chose to conduct instead of classroom discussions an online written discussion lasting the entire semester, to which I asked students to contribute at least two critical reflections on Irigay, each of between 100 and 250 words. To prompt the discussion, I wrote two commentaries on selected chapters of Irigaray's book, and then joined the discussion by writing three compendious commentaries on students' contributions to it. I quote from the English translation of Irigaray's book by Mary Beth Mader (Austin: University of Texas Press, 1999).

Commentary on Chapters 2, 5, and 6 of *The Forgetting of Air in Martin Heidegger*

These remarks are not a general introduction to Irigaray, which many other sources reliably offer. Rather, they outline my own views of these chapters, concentrating on the passages in them that I find most intriguing or challenging. Your own views of these chapters will not be mine, and Irigaray hardly invites unanimity, which she believes mistakes the plurality of truth.

Irigaray laments, near the end of Chapter 6, that "the thinker [Heidegger], whose care it is to recollect the initial loss [of our intuition of the truth of our being] in our history, perpetuates the unthought in man's relation to his body" (102). This is the keynote of her reading of Heidegger. But is she correct? I suspect not. Irigaray alleges that Heidegger excludes all physical, physiological, biotic and biological considerations from his account of our primary and immediate intuition of the nature of our human being. I suggest instead that he takes them into account no less thoroughly than she, but in a radically different way, heeding theories of physics and biology contrary to hers.

As phenomenologists, both Heidegger and Irigaray consider not only empirical phenomena, including physical and bodily phenomena, to understand their phenomenality as such, but also whatever prior explanations, especially scientific explanations, other thinkers have advanced about them. Irigaray regards as especially suggestive two scientific theories that scientists no longer endorse: the physics of the universal ether and the biology of preformationism, specifically ovism. Heidegger regards as no less suggestive two contrary scientific theories that scientists currently do endorse: the physics of the cosmic vacuum and the biology of epigenesis.

For Irigaray, physical phenomena such as amniotic fluid, oxygen-transmitting blood (and, for that matter, chlorophyll and plant sap), the earth's water cycle, and the earth's atmosphere suggest the unbroken, unbreakable, and indeed unlimited continuity of all beings, the being of each an event or occasion in which all other beings meet with it as they impart to it and draw from it their shared substance and movement. For Irigaray, likewise, bodily phenomena such as conception, gestation, parturition, lactation, caregiving and sexual desire suggest the unbroken, unbreakable, and indeed unlimited continuity of all human beings, the being of each an event or occasion in which all other human beings meet with it as they impart to it and draw from it their common humanity, kindred embodiment, and evolving spirit.

On the contrary, for Heidegger, physical phenomena such as atomism, the cosmic vacuum, and the quantum vacuum suggest the discreteness, discontinuity, and difference of each being from all other beings. For Heidegger, likewise, bodily phenomena such as the immunological singularity of each human being, the body's characteristic physical integrity and autonomy, every person first becoming aware of its being years after birth, and the ease with which elective affinities can eclipse inherited ones suggest the finitude, discreteness, discontinuity and difference of each human being from all other human beings.

For Heidegger, finitude, nothingness, negation and death are positive, productive and necessary aspects of being, whereas for Irigaray they are part of "his" remorseless, denaturing and dehumanising war against being as she conceives it. He regards being as autogenic and autotelic, whereas she regards it as allogenic and allotelic. He believes that we receive the mortality-transcending capacities of our being immediately from the language, art, thought and statehood of the historical people of whom we are a member, whereas she believes that we receive such capacities immediately through the bodies that bear or join ours and those that ours bear or join, including the body of the earth as well as the body of every human being, whose substantial being he allegedly reduces to so much stuff that he might shape as he wishes, the stuff of himself as much as the stuff of his fellows and the stuff of the earth. For Irigaray, "he" is Heidegger, masculine and patriarchal action and reason, and the human world as he and they denature it, whereas "she" would be Irigaray only if she and the feminine, matriarchal and feminist world that beckons her could repossess their own bodies, being and language, which he has taken from them.

According to Irigaray, "he" both destroys "her" thought and language and incorporates it into "his" by means of two dialectical processes, as false and falsifying as she regards all dialectical thought: assimilation and participation; and erection and ejaculation.

First, we can see the dialectic of assimilation and participation at work in a poem by Carolyn M. Rodgers, "It Is Deep (don't never forget the bridge you crossed over on)" (1969). It is ever so much deeper than the poet suspects. To Irigaray's way of thinking, the poet completely mistakes her relation to her mother, even and especially at the end when she believes she has at long last discharged in full the debt she owes her, but also earlier when the poet insists that her mother is out of her depth when she enters her daughter's world, which she defines by way of her mother's remoteness from it.

But, according to Irigaray, the poet's mother has never disappeared from her daughter's life, and never ceased playing as central a role in it as she did when forming her daughter-to-be in her womb, although her daughter, hoodwinked by "his" thinking, epitomised by "the poster of the / grand le-roi (al) cat on the wall" that her mother "did not / recognize" (referring to Rodgers' fellow poet LeRoi Jones as the leonine head of the pride of poets to which she has decided she belongs), has expunged her mother from it and then conceded that she might reappear in it as a beloved servant and essential prop.

The umbilical cord first dwindles to a very uncertain telephone connection that the mother rather than the daughter rushes to reconnect and is then piously commemorated as a bridge, like one of Ruskin's sublime sentinels of endurance in *Modern Painters* and, like most New York City bridges, connecting one island borough with another. Likewise, the bounty and power of the mother's body, especially the placenta, supposedly discarded and superseded, have surreptitiously been denatured and reshaped into the very stuff of the world. The city's emergency services, public utilities, banks and markets, and the daughter's apartment, kitchen and refrigerator are what she and everyone else have made of her mother, the basic material substance and serviceability of their world, to which the living body of her mother has been reduced, no longer recognisable as the being with whom one's closest relation subsists without diminution or intermission. Into this world leached from her mother's being, the poet readmits her mother as a party, an autonomous participant, to play a role that she may take up or not, in this or that communal drama such as those mentioned: communism, unionism, and Black nationalism. I would contend that this is precisely how "he" in "his" language treats "her" being by means of assimilation and participation as Irigaray describes them (Chapter 2, 39ff; Chapter 5, 81ff).

The dialectic of assimilation and participation denatures our nature and the world's long before we come of age (as we say), having begun to do so long before we are born and certainly during infancy. A painting by Pablo Picasso, *First Steps* (1943; Yale University Art Gallery), reveals how. Already, in this painting, the child's body, angular and tense with effort, bursts with energy it draws from its mother, whom it treats as a battery, a reliable source of power, and as a garage, a shelter to which it can return between trips towards an autonomy that imagines it can eventually serve as its own battery and garage. The mother sags like a balloon losing air (as the child's face fills with it) and stoops as much to fit within the frame of the painting and the view of the painter as to steady the child. She is the arch (or portico, 34) through which others walk, the framework (or *Gestell*, 33) by which they orient themselves. Her left hand releases and gives up the child's left hand; her right clasps and retains its right, this final interlacing of fingers the focus of her gaze, the threshold of yet another phase of their joint being that both mistakenly sense as attenuating and finally severing it, persuaded thus by "his" thought and language, beyond which they can hardly think or speak. The umbilical cord lapses to a handshake, we suppose.

Next, we can see the dialectic of erection and ejaculation at work in a poem by Wallace Stevens, "Anecdote of the Jar", from *Harmonium* (1923). For the poet, the world is a "slovenly wilderness" only of use when it ceases to be itself, or rather, nothing until he makes something of it. The jar's power, serving its owner, to order and shape conquers nature's proclivity merely to burgeon and bewilder, if we take "wilderness" to mean a wildered as well as wild state, with the poetic imagination a kind of Cartesian engineering, fixing everything in its axes and circles like a massive magnet or seismic shock. Those who once lived in the slovenly wilderness without denaturing or renaturing it must disappear into it, their being reduced to a place name that their conqueror graciously condescends to adopt as a sign of cultural assimilation and supersession. We should understand that, in the early twentieth century, Tennessee was among the poorest states of the United States, a decade or so before the vast engineering projects of the Tennessee Valley Authority transformed it along the lines that the poet envisages. The poet's erection of his apotropaic token and its shaping so much rude stuff into surrounding ground by the ejaculation of its "dominion everywhere" closely resemble Irigaray's account of the effect of the architectonic, technocratic power of "his" thought and language on "her" being (90f).

I am led to review my conjecture that Heidegger's notion of the nearness and remoteness of things and persons depends on metonymy and prosopopoeia as the fundamental events of thought and language. From Irigaray's point of view, they may rather be the indices, either vestiges or harbingers, of yet more intimate relations within and among things and persons that we can now understand and express only in such attenuated rhetoric forms.

Commentary on Chapters 7, 9, and 10 of *The Forgetting of Air in Martin Heidegger*

In these three chapters Irigaray meditates on several more phenomena to pursue her investigation into "his" language and thought, and her work towards (re)(dis)covering "her" language and thought, which "his" has always and everywhere consigned to an oblivion of which both "he" and "she" are oblivious, the "unknown unknown" truth of their joint interbeing.

To the three phenomena that exemplify in Chapters 2, 5 and 6 the phenomenality of "his" language and thought – the bridge; the portico; and the erection – Irigaray in these later chapters adds another three – the voyage; the blinkered, segregating look; and the agricultural exploitation of the earth. To the two phenomena that could exemplify in the earlier chapters the phenomenality of "her" language and thought, were they ever to appear – the circumambient fluid medium or ether that sustains embodied beings (especially air, water and blood); and the unbroken continuities of reproductive animal biology (fertilisation, gestation, parturition, lactation, sexual attraction, and copulation, not all of them mentioned) – Irigaray in these later chapters adds – the dawn (remotest origin; reawakening; and the patient and uncoercive gaze); and the rose (the natural and indeed vegetable unfolding, flowering, and volatilising of beings). The essential phenomenological task is to tease from each phenomenon the fundamental phenomenality that makes them and all such phenomena possible or not, including these six phenomena of "his" making and four phenomena of "her" elusion of that making.

Irigaray saturates herself with Heidegger's language in the hope that she may thereby discover, from the faintest and minutest traces in it, that her language has saturated his from the beginning without his being aware or wishing or allowing himself to be aware of it. This manner of reading resembles to a degree that of Michel de Certeau and Guy Debord but certainly not that of Georges Poulet, whose insistence on the distinctness of his being from another's exemplifies the very disaster from which Irigaray hopes we may one day recover despite its as yet unbroken and unbreakable hold on us.

Chapter 7

Irigaray contends in her meditation on the voyage that we so misunderstand the otherness of others that our reaching out to them can be no more than a detour, a roundabout way back to ourselves. As Stephen Dedalus surmises in the "Scylla and Charybdis" episode of *Ulysses*, "We walk through ourselves, meeting robbers, ghosts, giants, old men, young men, wives, widows, brothers-in-love. But always meeting ourselves." Even when most "faithful to the faraway" (114) we misconceive the other by our very ascription of faraway-ness to her. We reduce the sea, the medium of our reaching out, to a void or inconvenience or danger, thinking of ourselves only as sailors, rarely as seafarers (the *Flying Dutchman*), more rarely as sea-creatures (swimmers; mermen and mermaids), more rarely yet as waves and currents of the sea itself. We distinguish ourselves from the circumambient and bodily media that sustain us. Any expectation of enjoying such fluid being we either defer until after death (as in Milton's dream of angelic sexual union, *Paradise Lost* 8.615–29), as against Lucretius' frustration with the body as a barrier (*De Rerum Natura*, 4.1101–20, translated by Dryden, "Lucretius, The Fourth Book", 67–92), or relegate to mystical and ecstatic experience that extinguishes the self. The voyage is simply a ferry or a punt, a simple transformation of the bridge, which for Irigaray is equivalent to projecting an umbilical cord from oneself hoping to discover the world as if it were one's own detached placenta, a parody of "her" forgotten gift to "him" of "his" being.

Please read the poem by Constantine Cavafy titled "Ithaka" (1911), translated from the poet's Greek by Edmund Keeley and Philip Sherrard (1972), to determine if and how it exemplifies or contradicts Irigaray's phenomenological description of the voyage.

Next, Irigaray contends in her meditation on the dawn that whereas "his" seeing is like lightning, gashing the darkness in search of what appears frozen in time and space (or in a sequence of instants by a strobe light or frames of a film reel), "her" seeing is smeared over a broader continuum of space and time so that she sees the (e)merging and (un)becoming of beings with each other, when all are equivocally distinct and yet indistinct in the dusk before sunrise, which is when we sense, through a kind of seeing indistinguishable from touching, the "ever-ajar" interbeing of everything (110). This may suggest the medium or state of being that Plato describes in *Timaeus* 51e–53d as the χώρα, chôra or khôra, receptacle, which also attracts the attention of Julia Kristeva, in *Revolution in Poetic Language* (1974).

Please read the poem by Emily Brontë [Ellis Bell], "Stars" (1846), to determine if and how it exemplifies or contradicts Irigaray's phenomenological description of "her" way of seeing as opposed to "his".

Chapter 9

Irigaray contends that agricultural practice is congruent with "his" linguistic practice, in that both subdue "her" along with the body and being of the earth, to his ends, clearing a portion of their being as if it were a blank page, scarring it with his plough and pen, sowing it with his seed and inscribing it with his significance, reducing it to so much property and produce that he designs and owns. Some early Greek inscriptions are βουστροφηδόν, boustrophedon, ox-turning, with alternate lines written in reverse. Gerard Manley Hopkins' "The Windhover" offers a vivid instance of this congruence, especially revealing in its disavowed sadomasochism:

No wonder of it: sheer plod makes plough down sillion
Shine, and blue-bleak embers, ah my dear,
Fall, gall themselves, and gash gold vermillion.

Irigaray characterises the "clearing" that "his" permanent settlement and agricultural and linguistic practice entail as confinement to a framework that does not allow "him" to think beyond it, that closes off from him most of the world, which is not (yet) his, constrained by the rule of what we might call his own *Académie ontologique*. Irigaray's implication seems twofold: first, that nomadic human beings who live by hunting and gathering are not "guilty" of destroying "her" being and have not separated themselves from the bodily being common to all animals; and second, that linguistic frameworks constrain us much as Edward Sapir and Benjamin Lee Whorf hypothesise. Donald Davidson, among others, disputes that they do so in "On the Very Idea of a Conceptual Scheme", *Proceedings and Addresses of the American Philosophical Association* 47 (1973–1974): 5–20.

In "his" language "she" can neither speak nor be heard or taken seriously. In what literary texts among those you have read does such non-communication figure prominently? In which of them do silent, silenced, or unheeded characters loom as large as those who silence, ignore or disparage them? Are there few or many such texts, and how easily can we recognise them given that we (may) have only "his" language with which to speak and think or refrain from speaking or thinking about them? Need we look for evidence of Irigaray's thesis chiefly in experimental and avant-garde literary texts or do the most traditional and unremarkable texts attest it? Are there any literary texts at all that do not? For example, James Fenimore Cooper's *The Deerslayer* (1841) is as obviously the tale of Judith Hutter's eclipse as of Natty Bumppo's apotheosis.

Next, Irigaray contends that the rose in its flowering "without a why" is congruent with what would be "her" language could she speak it, evoking a sensuous carnality of speech and thought inimical to the machinery of reason and exploitation that marks "his". Doubtless by design, Irigaray's thesis is not only provocative but also preposterous. To speak as a rose flowers, we must set aside what we know, speaking "his" language, to be the case, that any rose we so encounter "is" the product of the most concerted and sustained floriculture that we can conceive. But Irigaray thereby sets us a grand challenge, to realise, in what would be "her" language, that we have not created the rose but have recreated ourselves so that we might be the fit recipients of the rose's gift of itself to us as it has over the time of its emergence infused the bounty of its evolving being into us to render us capable of speaking of its being along with it. Irigaray's counterpointing of "her" floricultural speech against "his" agricultural writing begs the question of the relation of speech and writing in general, thereby laying itself open to Jacques Derrida's critique of this difference, as explained especially in *Of Grammatology* (1967). Irigaray then beguilingly characterises our dreams as the sole field, in the clearing of our being not so completely ruled by "his" language, in which "her" language can still flower though not flourish, like a weed. Her flowering speech also entails the transformation of the senses, so anaesthetised and set at odds by "his" language and thought to have forgotten their primordial synaesthetic community. Think of William Blake's question in *The Marriage of Heaven and Hell* (1793):

> How do you know but ev'ry Bird that cuts the airy way,
> Is an immense world of delight, clos'd by your senses five?

Irigaray might add a sixth sense, proprioception, as much the culprit as vision in "his" Cartesian excision of both from their fellow senses to distinguish the mind from the body.

Chapter 10

I call attention only to the essential project sketched in this chapter. Irigaray describes the way in which "she" might read what "he" has written:

> Language never gives back what it takes. Unless language is opened back up at great depth. Unless everything that language (re)says, veiled in death already, is gone back through? Unless a path is traced all the way to the heart of this empty clearing, where that which language has never known how to say is commemorated? (155)

She thereby hopes "To re-open the horizon, to shake the ground, to unhinge thought" (157). But what would unhinging thought and opening language back up at a great depth look and sound like? How would we recognise such unhinging, such deep mining or extreme caving? What literary texts and hermeneutics pursue these projects, and might they be pursued without an author's knowing or intending them, or might they even be pursued *only* thus? For instance, do we look for such a project in Gertrude Stein's *Three Lives* (1909) rather than in Charlotte Brontë's *Villette* (1853) or Sei Shōnagon's *Pillow Book* (1002)?

First Compendium of Comments on Discussion Contributions

Many thanks to those of you who have so far posted contributions to our discussion of Irigaray, all of them truly thoughtful and judicious. I hope those of you yet to post a contribution take heart from these initial ones and post your own contributions when you can. Every single contribution helps everyone. I will respond to some contributions singly and to others as a group and will defer commenting on others until more of you post contributions about similar topics.

I'm most intrigued that Cavafy's poem has so far attracted more comments than Brontë's. In their reflections on Cavafy's poem, **Kaitlyn**, **Charlotte**, **Yasmina** and **Sophia** each come to a different conclusion about its compatibility with Irigaray's parable of the sea voyage. **Kaitlyn** emphasises Odysseus's self-involvement (let's give Cavafy's voyager Homer's name for him), **Charlotte** emphasises Penelope's disappearance (a striking departure from Homer's story), **Yasmina** likewise emphasises the purging of all female personae from Odysseus' adventure, and **Sophia** emphasises how equivocal Cavafy's acknowledgement of others and otherness seems. The poet warns the would-be Odysseus to expel the monsters within him lest they haunt and disable him on the voyage. As they are all insuperably violent male beings, could Cavafy be warning Odysseus to abjure masculinity and virility as traits that thwart intimate and productive relations with others? Could he also be doubting the standard (masculine) account of character formation or *Bildung*, first announced by Wilhelm von Humboldt, in which one's personal growth entails the realisation of one's own inherent potential, rather than others' gracious gifts of powers one cannot presume to derive from oneself? If so, he would be questioning the mode of character development that dominates the modern European novel's account of its autonomous (male) protagonist. The poet certainly seems to absorb Penelope into Odysseus' dwelling-place, confirming Irigaray's thesis about the absorption of the feminine into the natural and the concomitant reduction of her being to a kind of amorphous stuff. But I suspect that the poet is even more radically opposed to Irigaray's way of thinking, hinting that Ithaka is Odysseus' grave, his death, and that his death, not his birth, gives him his being and gives his being its meaning, its truth. If that's so, then one's home only comes into being at the end of one's life, before which one can have no home. It isn't that one's life and death are of one's own devising, but that everything and everyone whom one meets, all going well, give one gifts that portend Death's final gift and whose worth depends on how they prepare one for Death. Heidegger believes Death is the central truth of human being, whereas Irigaray emphatically disagrees. As Wallace Stevens remarks in his poem "Sunday Morning", "Death is the mother of beauty". Stevens' poem is worth reading in its entirety. I'll say more about Cavafy's poem after more of you post your reflections on it.

Irigaray's strictures about "his" conception of the sea voyage surely apply to the classical epics that depict it, Homer's *Odyssey*, Apollonius' *Argonautica*, and Virgil's *Aeneid* (perhaps especially Virgil's treatment of Queen Dido), and to their modern progeny such as Luís Vaz de Camões' *Lusiads* and S.T. Coleridge's *Rime of the Ancient Mariner*. But do they apply to another maritime literary tradition that celebrates the abandonment of one's patriarchal responsibilities and the ecstasy of one's own shipwreck? I'm thinking of two poems by Stéphane Mallarmé and their English analogues: "Brise Marine" (Sea Breeze) and Alfred Tennyson's "Ulysses"; and "Un coup de dés jamais n'abolira le hazard" (A throw of the dice will never abolish chance) and Gerard Manley Hopkins' "The Wreck of the Deutschland". "Un coup de dés" certainly appears to have inspired the last (twelfth) chapter of Irigaray's *The Forgetting of Air*, the chapter beyond the six assigned for class that might prove the most rewarding to read. Of other modern voyages modelled on Homer, Ezra Pound's *Cantos* certainly fall foul of Irigaray's strictures, but James Joyce's *Ulysses* may elude them and even reconceive language along "her" lines, if somewhat equivocally so.

In her reflections on Brontë's poem, **Isabella** argues persuasively that the sun's rule of the day epitomises patriarchal power. Note the series of hymeneal membranes, eyelid, pillow, door and curtain that the sun tries forcibly to tear open in an unforgiving assault on the poet, which will be unsuccessful only because the sun will soon enough set, and the poet has absorbed just enough strength from the stars to resist it until it does. But I'm not so sure the moon is involved, because the sun's singularity is opposed to the stars' indiscriminate multiplicity, which is not reducible to one or oneness, thus akin to the manifold being of the feminine-maternal as Irigaray envisages it. I'll say more about Brontë's poem after more of you post your reflections on it.

Ruby's reflections on Irigaray's affinity with Laura Mulvey's "Visual Pleasure and Narrative Cinema", *Screen* 16, no.3 (1975): 6–18, available online, prompts me to think about films in which "his" lightning-like isolation of one thing from another is eluded, attenuated or subverted. What of imageless films such as Derek Jarman's *Blue* (1993), or films that use softly focused, diaphanous or superimposed images? What of representational paintings such as J.M.W. Turner's landscapes at dawn or dusk or in fog or storm, and non-representational paintings by Mark Rothko, Agnes Martin and Helen Frankenthaler of glowing and shimmering manifold washes of colour? I'll link **Alexandra**'s reflections on Conrad's *Heart of Darkness* to Ruby's on film. The episode in Conrad's novella that verges closest to Irigaray's sense of the crepuscular quality of the truth of being and (non)individuation is Marlow's stepping ashore at the Company's station and strolling into the shade of a forested ravine (in Chapter 1). Both Gayatri Spivak and Hélène Cixous, among others, associate the patriarchal with the colonial gaze and regard women as colonised subjects. See Cixous' "The Laugh of the Medusa", trans. Keith and Paula Cohen, *Signs* 1, no.4 (1976): 875–93, at 877–8, 884–5.

Maddy's reflections on matters that we can sense but not speak or think about clearly or at all strongly suggest that Irigaray may be indebted to the Romantic doctrine of ineffability, most famously formulated by Friedrich Schlegel in his essay "On Incomprehensibility" (1800).

Fiona's reflections on Maria Cimitile's article, which appears in the bibliography I've given you, about the horrifying silencing of the female voice and denaturing naturalisation of the female body, if I can put it paradoxically, reminds me of the most farcical episode in Joyce's *Ulysses*, "The Oxen of the Sun", in which a group of male doctors and medical students raucously converse in a hospital meeting room, their conversation drifting through dozens of historical English prose styles, while a woman, in protracted labour in the obstetric ward, contributes nothing to the conversation, even from a distance. Among the men, only Leopold Bloom listens for the woman's voice above the men's noise. The noisy "gestation" of the English language almost wholly stifles and muffles the Irish woman's creative, labouring cries, almost exactly as Irigaray explains.

Second Compendium of Comments on Discussion Contributions

Some of you, **Isabella**, **Alexandra**, **Sophia** and **Anthony**, ponder Irigaray's apparent, alleged, or patent essentialism, and her ideas of nature, the nature of human beings and of the world. I'd say that for Irigaray, essentialism is an instance of appropriation and social constructionism an instance of participation, neither of them escaping the prison of dialectical thinking in general, or dialectical thinking about gender in particular as a dialectical difference. For Irigaray, the idea of nature itself is an attenuation of "her" being into a question of the serviceability or recalcitrance of things as they are. **Isabella** considers "the why of the rose", which Irigaray explains as a denaturing of it in "his" non-specific scientific-technical reasoning about it, but which may be otherwise in "her" tongue, perhaps considering a particular rose's realisation and potentiation of all roses hitherto and prospectively related to it, the ontology of the rose's rose-ness, whether or not like Gertrude Stein's epigram. **Alexandra** quotes Alison Stone on the apparently "pre-given and determinant qualities of the feminine" (I hope Stone means "determinate") in Irigaray, but I'd say that it's precisely the givenness and determination of the feminine against which Irigaray protests, suspicious of anything that is already given and determined, and wanting to apply to it a solvent to render it less certain a given, and less fixedly determined. **Sophia** mentions Judith Butler's aversion to Irigaray's thinking in this regard, which we are about to encounter. But I wonder if Butler examines with due care the phenomenal, ontological dimensions of Irigaray's notion of "her" being, instead focusing solely on the social, psychological and empirical predicament of women. **Anthony** looks carefully at the phenomenality of air and of the human voice, and I'd describe Irigaray's treatment of them not so much as an abstraction as a substantialisation, more rather than less palpable and immediate. Anthony's point makes me think of the element common to all fluids Irigaray considers, oxygen, the fuel that all known living things burn to become what they are, including both plants and animals. How would Irigaray regard the Gaia Hypothesis, and how regard the great preponderance of plant life in the earth's biomass, whatever she might say about the scientific terms I am using to describe them?

Now that we have encountered Lacan's thinking about language, Irigaray's may make more sense. I'd say that Irigaray attributes to Heidegger a theory of language that closely resembles Lacan's, despite Heidegger's pre-emptive and emphatic complaint that he thinks nothing remotely of the kind, a complaint to which Irigaray deafens herself. However that may be, Irigaray is at loggerheads with Lacan, for whom Heidegger appears to serve as her proxy. I'm not sure why this is so. **Yusuf** writes most intriguingly of Irigaray's relation to Heidegger in almost psychoanalytic terms, and the stridency of her anti-Heideggerian rhetoric, her mistaking him for someone else, as if contesting another's inheritance of Heidegger's estate, is worth further reflection. **Sarah** notes a feature of Irigaray's theory of "his" language that mirrors Lacan's, that it is a system of symbolic domination that inflicts suffering on those who can never fit themselves to it, to which **Sze Pui** quite plausibly ascribes superhuman power and authority, though of an impersonal kind, as anthropologists such as Claude Lévi-Strauss would ascribe to social codes generally, an impersonal demand emanating from within each human subject as its definitive project of being among others, not unlike Althusser's theory of interpellation internalised. **Vince** emphasises language's power to bend us to its will, as if "it" is an agent rather than a medium of our or another human being's agency. In the beginning is gender, which thereupon pervades all other differences. I relished the complementary contributions by **Fiona** and **Marnie**, one sensitive to the horror of "her" predicament, the other to its humour, together suggesting the macabre farce in which "she" is trapped. **Soph** approaches this farce by way of a comment on grammatical and natural gender in the English language, especially in its pronominal system. Proposals for gender-neutral pronouns in English appear as early as the eighteenth century, if not earlier.

If I may speculate further about "her" ontological predicament in a world such as Lacan envisages, in the mirror stage she may be not so much a virtual being created by the concatenated reflections of others, but the medium of mirroring and reflecting, absorbed into his virtual being, hers thus doubly virtual. Likewise, his accession to the symbolic system to which he must submit himself in order to understand and shape himself, as he supposes, may be predicated on her absorption into the system rather than accession to it, she the symbolic medium through whom he conducts and construes his relations with his fellows.

Responding to **Zaynab** and **Viki**'s comments on Emily Brontë's "Stars", I'd say that the poet holds out no hope of reconciliation between "his" diurnal sovereignty and "her" nocturnal sovereignty, grimly hopeful of surviving the first, which rules her body and all other bodies, because the human body is mortal, whereas the human spirit is immortal, and will eventually be released from its daily bodily subjection to waking life, into an uninterrupted eternity of joy in the company of its fellow spirits. Brontë is unapologetically a visionary poet, setting no store by actuality, and feels closer to her dead mother and two dead sisters than to anyone else. For her, the "abyss" that Irigaray contends Heidegger dreads is where her true being flourishes. The sun is merely a local tyrant who rages whenever he wakes and forces all on earth to do likewise, in an inane clockwork puppet show, whereas the night sky, only temporarily obscured by the sun, never fails its denizens. Matters look hardly more hopeful for much or all of *Wuthering Heights*. The poet is shocked to discover her body is essentially a series of hymeneal barriers, unlike her spirit, which is unguardedly at one with all those whom she loves, none of them possessive or domineering in their interrelations. The poem attests to the social and sexual pressures brought to bear on the female body of a certain age, the demand to marry, manage a household, and produce children, a demand emanating from within almost as much as from without. I hear incredulity, outrage and agony throughout the poem. The simile of the "petrel on the sea" alludes to Matthew 14, to a storm at sea at night during which Peter, after whom the species of bird is named, petitions

Jesus to empower him to walk over the water to him. Let's suppose that Emily writes this poem to encourage her more diffident surviving sisters, Charlotte and Ann, not to go over to the other side, not the Dark Side but the Sunny Side.

Thinking some more about Cavafy's "Ithaca", I note we have as yet focused solely on the voyager. But isn't the poem as much about the advisor addressing the voyager? Does the advisor give his advice as a gift for which he expects no reward? Does he imagine the voyager will discover that his advice awaits him on the voyage, in one of the "numerous Egyptian cities" in which the voyager will "fill [him]self with learning from the wise"? Does the advisor thrill with vicarious pleasure at the prospect of the voyager's pleasure? Does the advisor dispense the advice we would expect from a father, an uncle, a teacher, or a besotted lover about to be left behind? Is the voyager Telemachus rather than Odysseus?

Third Compendium of Comments on Discussion Contributions

Emily Brontë's "Stars" and Reproductive Destiny

Jess is not the only one among you to long for the moon in "Stars", but Brontë refuses to exploit it in the hopeful manner Jess suggests because the fundamental distinction Brontë makes is between the complete equality of one star among many and the total subjection of bodies in the solar system, including the moon, to the sun. Planetary relations are exclusive, hierarchical and patriarchal, even among patriarchs, whereas interstellar relations are promiscuous, non-hierarchical and non-coercive, as astronomical discoveries at the time suggested. From the late 1840s, when Brontë wrote the poem, the first accurate measurements of distances between stars implied that the sun was indifferently one star among many, and the first plausible solutions to Heinrich Olbers' Paradox (why is the night sky dark?), offered by Edgar Allan Poe among others, implied a strict limit to every star's existence, it became ever easier to extricate oneself from the bonds of all kinds of heliocentric thinking, literal and figurative, notably those mentioned by **Charley** and **Reagan**. It isn't so much that Brontë describes the elopement of illicit lovers as Reagan describes them, but that our current idea of sexual relations is so atrociously degraded and degrading that we can hardly imagine alternatives to them as sexual rather as visionary, following Milton's sketch of them in *Paradise Lost*, as **Corinne** begins to explain in terms of exhilaration, comfort and bliss. Although **Ziyan** does not refer to this poem in her general comment on the patriarchal understanding of women's reproductive destiny, she echoes exactly Brontë's critique of it.

Cavafy's "Ithaca" and Travel as Tragedy

I am less certain than **Zoe** and **Tayla** that Cavafy's poem exemplifies Irigaray's thesis of inviting the other's otherness to infuse itself into one's own being and thus to other it. Irigaray derides "him" for thinking of meeting the other merely as a "detour necessary for returning more securely to oneself", as if in an episode of Channel Nine's *Travel Guides* television series. **Madeleine**'s comments lead me to wonder how Virginia Woolf eludes the dialectic of assimilation-participation in her novels about the sea and voyaging, *The Voyage Out*, *To The Lighthouse* and *The Waves*. As an example of a journey that transforms a traveller more decisively than Odysseus' journey may transform him in Cavafy's poem, I suggest Thomas Hardy's poem "When I Set Out for Lyonnesse".

In his thought-provoking characterisation of tragedy as a voyage of discovery such as Irigaray conceives it, **Vince** wonders about the difference between the tragic hero and the tragic heroine, particularly Antigone, whose portrayal by Sophocles attracts the attention of Heidegger and Lacan as well as Anne Carson, as Vince notes. What exactly do Greek tragic heroines have in common, especially the half dozen or so in Euripides' plays?

Picasso's First Steps

The patently pathetic depiction of the mother or caregiver letting go the child as it first walks on its two feet alone, analysed scrupulously by **Christie**, **Isabella** and **Alessandra**, may indicate that Picasso means us to be quite shocked by it rather than ignore it, whether he thinks her melancholy plight universal and ineluctable or merely occasional and accidental. Picasso's depiction of mother or caregiver is diametrically at odds with another celebrated painting of a child's first steps, Jean-François Millet's *First Steps* (c.1859–1866), chalk and pastel on paper (Cleveland Museum of Art), copied by Vincent Van Gogh, *First Steps, After Millet* (1890), oil on canvas (Metropolitan Museum of Art, New York City).

Millet and Van Gogh depict the newly automotive child shuttling from one parental garage to another, each of them equally energetic springs that bounce the child symmetrically between them, the mother in no sense the lesser or inferior of the two, except that the father has downed the tools of his (other) trade to join in whereas the mother's trade is the production of the child to the point of testing its ground-worthiness. Perhaps, instead, we should compare Picasso's depiction of the child's mother to a depiction of the Virgin Mary in a *pietà*.

Carolyn Rodgers' "It Is Deep" and Aesthetics

Tayla's contention that a formal and aesthetic evaluation of poetry is at odds with a thematic and ideological evaluation of it is eminently arguable, but I think the reading I offered fundamentally formal and aesthetic. The poet's aesthetic is precisely the obverse of her mother's. The poet's aesthetics involves irony (scare-quotes), identifying speech as belonging to particular people (verbatim quotations), cherishing role-models (her poster of LeRoi Jones), quickly and deftly sketching scenes (impressions) as they happen, and self-justification. The mother's aesthetic involves connection, girdling, warm wind, self-forgetfulness, intuition rather than intellection, gift-giving, and unconcern about individuality. These are all formal and aesthetic dimensions of the spoken and performance arts, and the poem debates two contrary aesthetics, one close to Irigaray, another incompatible with her views. **Madeleine**'s comments on the poem's language presuppose this and suggest that the poet's mother is essentially the wind from the south and the gregarious labour it inspires, an atmospheric, chthonic and organic continuity from which the poet imagines she has detached herself even as she insists that she is its politically most astute representative.

The Open Expanse; Nature's Physicality; the Being and Biology of Air

The "open expanse" about which **Yusuf** wonders is Heidegger's notion, closely related to his notions of clearing, dwelling, "enowning" and caring, all of which Irigaray criticises as "his" ways of obliterating "her" being. **Lucy** considers caring, **Marina** and **Corinne** consider shelter, and **Jess** considers exploitation and ownership of the earth as a resource, all aspects of this territoriality for which **Cheuk Yi** coins the wonderful term "knotwork" to suggest how it cordons off one part of the world from all others. Heidegger's thinking draws deeply on the many summers he spent in his hut writing in the Black Forest with its mosaic of agricultural clearings and forests through which he walked, the catalysts for all the agricultural and domestic notions to which Irigaray objects most strenuously in his philosophy.

For Irigaray, opening and clearing a space implies the destruction of whatever may already have subsisted in it; dwelling, including language-as-dwelling, implies a home for some rather than others; domestic economy renders whatever it excludes undomesticated and uneconomic; care renders whatever eludes it beyond caring: *tout court*, "her" being. Heidegger does not conceive of his own thought in this privative and restrictive way, but Irigaray certainly does, as do **Luke**'s astute comments about "speaking to one's self … within [one's] own territory" only.

For Heidegger, the open expanse is closely related to the idea of φύσις (physis / phusis) or nature as that which appears, exists and grows, stemming from the verb φύειν (phuein), to appear, to grow. Whereas Heidegger regards the human mind as an endowment of nature, Irigaray regards the mind as it now is as fundamentally severed from it. For Heidegger, things and world appear as they are in the mind's clearing, in its clear mindedness. **Anthony** most felicitously identifies Irigaray's parable of the rose as her clearest account of nature allegedly beyond his grasp, as **Corinne** does also. Irigaray claims that physicality as such is Heidegger's blindspot, as **Ziyan** suggests in her emphasis on the "physical link" between human beings.

For Irigaray, being is not so much a matter of opening up or out and closing off or in but of interfusion without intermission: the physics of natural things and the biology of living things are fluid rather than solid. We are not stand-alone, discrete and contiguous beings, but interdependent, conjoint, continuous and fluid beings held to a certain shape for a certain time by the material flux that forms and re-forms us within the biosphere's continuum of physical and biological exchanges. We are airy, watery and cloudy, as **Hayley** and **Marnie** note, not only metaphorically and ironically but also literally and actually. **Chloe** nicely characterises the (figurative) dynamic fluidity and (literal) fluid dynamics of Irigaray's notion of being, whereas **Sze Pui**'s thoughts on the traditional biological understanding of the female body reveal how far Irigaray is from endorsing them. Perhaps responding to mid-twentieth-century research findings that almost every atom in the human body is replaced every year, Irigaray regards the body as a kind of standing wave given to generating other standing waves.

Although Irigaray contends that air is inapprehensible, as **Katie** carefully explains, it is in fact so vividly, immediately and continuously apprehensible that we simply overlook it. During the day the colour of the sky and during the night the twinkling of the stars are in truth the air's visibility apprehended as translucency, unconscious acknowledgement that the air is the fluid lens through which we see everything. Of course, the air's weight also bears upon us. I am as much taken by **Zaynab**'s reflection that philosophy has hardly begun to understand phenomena as obvious as air and the space it pervades as I am by **Isabella**'s reflection on "the almost-ness" and "vagueness" that continues to screen "her" from herself as much as from anyone.

Essentialism and Binarism: Confirmation or Critique?

Many of you, including **Charley** and **Chloe**, express disquiet about the biological essentialism you find in Irigaray's thinking, which I attribute not to "her" but to "him" as she metabolises his binarism, dualism and essentialism through her alchemical and rhetorical retorts, as **Marina** suggests, citing Butler. "He" separates and dichotomises the male and the female, whereas she detects one always lodged non-dichotomously, cryptically and chimerically in the other, in line with Jacques Derrida's idea of "chiasmic invagination". **Sophie** sums this idea up nicely. For "him", binarism means either/or, whereas for "her", binarism is the finite code generating an infinity of sexual and gendered values, as a base-two numbering system generates all possible numbers no less reliably than a system with a higher base such as ten. The notions of opposite-sex, same-sex and trans-sex are governed by his binarism, as is the distinction between the unexceptional and the exceptional. I'd say that Irigaray is attempting to elude and transcend all such categories, about which some of you, including **Bhavani** and **Rachael**, remain puzzled, not without reason. **Luke** wonders what understanding would be like were such frameworks to fall away. **Isabella** suggests some kind of "multivocality", whereas **Christie** cites Wittgenstein on the absolute limitation that language may place on all understanding.

His and Her Language

Cheuk Yi's optimism that "language still has its potential" is not shared by Irigaray. After all, the world's languages have all undergone immense change, but how much have they changed in relation to giving "her" her own authentic speech? Is Modern English much different from Middle English or Old English in this respect? Have the languages exclusively spoken by women even done so, such as Nüshu in China's Hunan province? Have the literatures dominated by women writers done so, such as that of the Heian Court in Japan, including the astonishing work of the Lady Murasaki, the Lady Izumi, Sarashina and Sei Shōnagon? **Marina**'s examination of the characteristic absence of women from history as Herodotus and others conceive it and **Hayley**'s of their comparable absence from philosophy look like *prima facie* evidence supporting Irigaray's case. **Varsha** deftly describes the way in which "his" language digests and forgets "her" nature to sustain itself as it were self-sustaining, transforming her omnipresence into an absence.

Works Discussed

Brontë, Emily, as Ellis Bell. "Stars." 1846. In *The Complete Poems*. Ed. Janet Gezari. Harmondsworth: Penguin, 1992, 5–6.

Cavafy, Constantine. "Ithaka." 1911. Trans. Edmund Keeley and Philip Sherrard. In *Selected Poems*. Princeton, NJ: Princeton University Press, 1972. 18–9.

Irigaray, Luce. *The Forgetting of Air in Martin Heidegger*. 1983. Trans. Mary Beth Mader. Austin: University of Texas Press, 1999.

Millet, Jean-François. *First Steps*. c.1859–1866. Chalk and pastel on paper. Cleveland Museum of Art.

Picasso, Pablo. *First Steps*. 1943. Oil on canvas. Zervos XIII.36. Yale University Art Gallery.

Rodgers, Carolyn M. "It Is Deep (don't never forget the bridge you crossed over on)." 1969. In *The Norton Anthology of African American Literature*. Ed. Henry Louis Gates Jr. and Nellie Y. McCay. New York: Norton, 1997, 2009–10.

Stevens, Wallace. "Anecdote of the Jar." *Harmonium*. 1923. In *The Collected Poems*. 1954; New York: Vintage, 1982, 76.

Van Gogh, Vincent. *First Steps, After Millet*. 1890. Oil on canvas. Metropolitan Museum of Art, New York City.

Bibliography

Among the works I consulted, I found the following most helpful.

Ainley, Alison. "Luce Irigaray: At Home with Martin Heidegger?" *Angelaki* 2, no.1 (1997): 139–45.

Burke, Carolyn, Naomi Schor and Margaret Whitford, Eds. *Engaging with Irigaray*. New York: Columbia University Press. 1994.

Butler, Judith. "Bodies that Matter." In *Bodies that Matter: On the Discursive Limits of "Sex"*. New York: Routledge, 1993, 27–55, 257–65.

Butler, Judith. "Sexual Difference as a Question of Ethics: Alterities of the Flesh in Irigaray and Merleau-Ponty." In *Senses of the Subject*. New York: Fordham University Press, 2015, 149–70, 210.

Cimitile, Maria. "The Horror of Language: Irigaray and Heidegger." *Philosophy Today* 45, no.5 (2001): 66–74.

Fielding, Helen. "Questioning Nature: Irigaray, Heidegger and the Potentiality of Matter." *Continental Philosophy Review* 36, no.1 (2003): 1–26.

Froese, Katrin. "Woman's Eclipse: The Silenced Feminine in Nietzsche and Heidegger." *Philosophy and Social Criticism* 31, no.2 (2005): 165–84.

Grosz, Elizabeth. *Sexual Subversions: Three French Feminists*. Sydney: Allen & Unwin, 1989, 100–83.

Guenther, Lisa. "Being-from-Others: Reading Heidegger after Cavarero." *Hypatia* 23, no.1 (2008): 99–118.

Keltner, Stacy. "The Ethics of Air: Technology and the Question of Sexual Difference." *Philosophy Today* 45 (2001): 53–65.

Leeuwen, Anne van. "An Examination of Irigaray's Commitment to Transcendental Phenomenology in *The Forgetting of Air* and *The Way of Love*." *Hypatia* 28, no.3 (2013): 452–68.

Mader, Mary Beth. "*The Forgetting of Air in Martin Heidegger*: A Translation of and Commentary on Luce Irigaray's *L'oubli de l'air*." University of Texas at Austin: PhD dissertation, 1998.

Pinto-Correia, Clara. *The Ovary of Eve: Egg and Sperm and Preformation*. Chicago: University of Chicago Press, 1997.

Stone, Alison. *Luce Irigaray and the Philosophy of Sexual Difference*. Cambridge: Cambridge University Press, 2006.

Ziarek, Krzysztof. "Proximities: Irigaray and Heidegger on Difference." *Continental Philosophy Review* 33, no.2 (2000): 133–58.

Part IV. The Poetics of Pedagogy

16

Lyrebirds

Alexis Harley

In 2019, Sharon Edgar-Jones and Albert Burgman published their *Wanarruwa: Beginner's Guide*, a book that works with the Wanarruwa people of the so-called Hunter River region of New South Wales to "repatriate and revitalise our linguistic identity".[1] On the book's cover is a bird, luminous in purple, orange, gold and magenta. His huge tail feathers uncoil from his body, curling this way and that, wildly asymmetrical, as he fixes a gleaming orange eye on the viewer. He is what many of us know as a lyrebird.

There is no word for the lyrebird among the book's lists of words salvaged from the wreckage of over two hundred years of hostile occupation, but this painting by Wanarruwa and Anaiwan artist, Saretta Fielding, suggests how far away his Wanarruwa name might be from the prevailing English one. The figuration of lyrebirds as *lyrebirds* hinges on an ideologically freighted imagining of other-than-human and other-than-European life that is coterminous and complicit with the colonisation of Australia. It also hinges on the fact that some people came genuinely to believe that the male bird's tail (which mostly flops behind him, but in display splays wide open, inverted in a shower of feathers over his head), has the erect tight symmetry of a lyre. It seems that the first portrayal of the lyrebird in this guise, and the first discussions of the bird as a *lyre*bird, occurred on European soil, and were gradually shipped back to the places where lyrebirds were being hunted down, first as ornithological curiosities and later to use their tail feathers as adornments for hats. By the late 1840s, the belief that this bird possesses a lyre-like tail had pervaded settler Australian culture and continues to, but Fielding's painting shows how differently an eye schooled in more than European cultural reference points might see this bird.

---

1   As Callum Clayton-Dixon writes of the comparable Anaiwan Language Revival Program, of which he is a co-founder (see Clayton-Dixon, "In reclaiming our history of resistance, we can also revitalise decimated languages", *The Guardian*, 17 January 2018).

How the fable of a bird with the tail of a lyre could arise and be replicated is a story that itself might seem to find parallels in the lyrebird's own practice of replication and repetition, or vocal mimicry, a practice into which commentators have knitted their worries about imitation more generally. Britain's establishment of the prison camps of New South Wales coincided in England with a poetic culture that worried at the Enlightenment's trenchant division between human and nonhuman/more-than-human semiosis, and that in turn attracted ongoing worry about the semantic emptiness of mimetic representations of "nature" and other imitative practices. Critiques of Romantic culture from the early nineteenth century, and well into the twentieth, treat mimetic modes as a kind of shibboleth for sorting rational, meaningful, human song from irrational, mechanistic or organic nonhuman sound-making. Subscribers to this binary deplore a Romantic poetry that conjures affective experience seemingly resistant to paraphrase. Yvor Winters, for instance, criticises "Romantic nature poetry", Percy Bysshe Shelley's in particular, for its "implicit reference to a non-existent symbolic value". Poetic language that is used "to embody a feeling", but that can't be paraphrased, he writes, is meaningless.[2] Although F.R. Leavis does not articulate quite so clearly his objections to mimetic poetry, his description of Shelley's writing as "repetitive, vaporous, monotonously self-regarding and often emotionally cheap"[3] smacks of a similar objection to the mimetic mode: Shelley's poetry is "repetitive" of its subject, re-enacting it rather than describing it. And it reproduces feeling rather than meaning; this, at least, is how I parse the words "emotionally cheap", although they more obviously suggest that Shelley's performance of emotion does not correlate with his real emotion (in this one might detect an echo of Plato, for whom all representational art is a form of "mimesis" that actively scrambles viewers' access to truth by taking them further from the reality of things).[4]

In suggesting that the mimesis of Yvor Winters' phrase "mimetic fallacy" (let alone "mimesis" as Plato uses it) has anything to do with the mimetic behaviour of lyrebirds, I might seem to be collapsing and confusing two senses of the word. One kind of mimesis might be supposed to be a matter of literary style, a deliberate disposition of form in relation to content, commonly opposed as a discursive mode to "diegesis"; the other is supposedly an instinctive copying, the programmatic work of a duplicating organism. But I both want to trouble this distinction and note that it has been troubled since long before I got here. When lyrebirds sing the song of another bird species, they are showing or enacting the story of that bird (as in mimetic narrative), rather than recounting it (as in diegetic narrative). Literary mimesis refers to the world it represents by copying it rather than "telling" it. Earl Miner has claimed, in a cross-cultural discussion of lyric modes, that "The first

---

2   Yvor Winters, *In Defence of Reason* (Denver, CO: University of Denver Press, 1947), 50.

3   F.R. Leavis, "Literary Criticism and Philosophy: A Reply", *Scrutiny* 6 (1937): 69.

4   See, for instance, Plato, "Theory of Art", *The Republic*, trans. H.D.P. Lee (London: Penguin, 1955), 231–45.

thing to be said about lyric poetry systems is that they are not mimetic".[5] But why not? It is no coincidence that Shelley describes another mimicking bird, *Alauda arvensis*, as a poet pouring her "full heart / In profuse strains of unpremeditated art".[6] His representation of the mimicking skylark as a lyrical poet deliberately marries the idea of lyricism and re-presenting (that is, copying) sense impressions from the material world. He in turn imagines the affective materiality of (his) poetry as an attribute of the more-than-human world. In this he reproduces a tendency of Romantic lyrics to trouble the distinction between (human) mind and (nonhuman) organicism by representing the felt dimensions of the more-than-human world.

In the poetic traditions of white Australia, the figure of the lyre has vied with the lyrebird's imitativeness, making the bird a more or less fit avatar for the poet. For settler Australian poets, the lyrebird facilitates a discussion about whether Australian avifauna provide the kinds of poetic inspiration that the songbirds of Europe do, whether white Australian poets are working at a disadvantage that can be blamed on the prevalence of, say, rowdy parrots and the absence of nightingales – whether Australian birds are as lyrical and inspiring as the songbirds of England. Ultimately, they are asking if white Australian poetry is possible. In an essay of 1965, Judith Wright argues that a fully-fledged (white) Australian poetry would indeed be possible, if only settler poets could arrive at an accommodation with what she calls Australia's "landscape". Before "one's country can become an accepted background against which the poet's imagination can move unhindered," she writes, "it must first be observed, understood, described, and as it were absorbed. The writer must be at peace with the landscape before he can turn to its human figures." This peace, she suggests, is far from having been achieved: "in Australian writing, the landscape has, it almost seems, its own life, hostile to its human inhabitants."[7] Almost sixty years later, the settler trope of a hostile and inhuman landscape persists in Australian literature.

Judith Wright's vision for an Australian literature that works with Australian landscape is at work in her poem "Lyrebirds", first published in 1962. She makes no explicit reference to the lyrebirds' imitativeness and instead focuses on their association with lyricism. She describes them as "the few, the shy, the fabulous, / the dying poets". One bird bears "like a crest the symbol of his art, / the high symmetrical shape of the perfect lyre".[8] While Les Murray's relationship to the

---

5   Earl Miner, "Comparative Lyric", in *The Lyric Theory Reader: A Critical Anthology*, ed. Virginia Jackson and Yopie Prins (Baltimore, MD: Johns Hopkins University Press, 2014), 579.

6   Shelley further complicates the dynamics of originality and imitation and lyricism (and songbirds), writing: "Virgil … had affected the fame of an imitator, even whilst he created anew all that he copied; and none among the flock of mock-birds, though their notes were sweet … have sought even to fulfil a single condition of epic truth". In Percy Bysshe Shelley, *The Defence of Poetry Fair Copies: A Facsimile of the Fair Copy Transcript by Mary W. Shelley*, ed. Michael O'Neill (New York and London: Garland Publishing, 1994), 63.

7   Judith Wright, *Preoccupations in Australian Poetry* (Oxford: Oxford University Press, 1965), ix.

8   Judith Wright, *Birds* (Canberra: National Library of Australia, 2003), 54.

landscape cannot be exactly opposed to Wright's, it is a more fraught one: he oscillates, as Bruce Clunies Ross has claimed, from feeling the "difficulty" of the Australian environment, reckoning with "the way it drives some to despair and anger", and "a deep love of the land".[9] Wright's lyrebird poem works to establish a sympathy between lyrebirds and poets (a work still informed, I think, by a colonising impulse, despite Wright's effort to recognise the violence of colonisation). Les Murray's "Lyre Bird", on the other hand, stresses the lyrebird's role as a mimic. Murray deflates the association of the lyrebird with the lyre in the poem's first word, "Liar". The bird's tail is, for Murray, mere "froufrou" (a reduplicative that perhaps reprises the bird's duplication of song), and "a quiff", both terms that indicate a frivolous and ornamental excess.[10] This characterisation of ornament suggests the lyrebird's feminised ditziness, and Murray's lyrebird, apparently the poem's narrator, engages in a kind of garbled prattle to match: his always rather opaque narration disintegrates into a series of near-homophones ("cattlebell" meets "kettle-boil" and the like). He cannot render a meaning that survives his obsession with sonic form. If this is Murray's point, it is one he – ironically? – makes through his own adroit manipulation of sonic form.

That there is a tension between the lyrical and the mimetic perhaps seems obvious: one is associated with originating genius, the other with the opposite. The university (which like the penal colony of New South Wales is fundamentally an institution of the Enlightenment) derides what it understands to be imitation and celebrates what it understands to be originality. Breaches of "academic integrity", a term that could refer to so many of the politically and ethically charged dimensions of students' learning, in university policy documents denote variations on the theme of plagiarism. Concomitantly, the supposed originality of a supposedly original contribution to knowledge is regularly framed as more important than the beauty or utility of what is known, or its capacity to move. The reasoning mind analyses and describes; it does not re-present. But alongside the Enlightenment enthusiasm for the idea of the rational human as an originating genius, anti-rationalist poetics produced understandings of a poetry that could take dictation from nature. In this, European Romanticism anticipated some of the themes of the materialist relational ontology that has been more recently articulated and popularised by feminist theorists and process philosophers Jane Bennett, Vicki Kirby, Elizabeth Grosz, Bruno Latour, Donna Haraway and Karen Barad.

How much these vitalist poetics registered in the coastal prison camps of early nineteenth-century Australia is another question. Many scholars have noted the remarkable lack of a Romantic literary tradition in early colonial Australia. Paul Kane, for one, begins his *Australian Poetry: Romanticism and Negativity* with the

---

9   Bruce A. Clunies Ross, "Landscape and the Australian Imagination", in *Mapped But Not Known: The Australian Landscape of the Imagination*, ed. Philippa Robin Eaden and Francis Hugh Mares (Adelaide, SA: Wakefield Press, 1986), 240–41.

10   Les Murray, *Translations from the Natural World* (Manchester: Carcarnet Press, 1993), ch. 18.

idea that "romanticism has had a profound impact on Australian poetry by way of an absence".[11] But that absence overlaps with the vital presence of an Australian indigenous philosophy that elaborates the intra-active agency of the more-than-human world. As Alison Ravenscroft has written, "In Australian Indigenous materialisms – at least to my stranger's eyes – 'human' and 'inhuman' are so extensively, elaborately, and constitutively entangled that the very terms *human* and *inhuman*, *culture* and *nature*, *body* and *ground* as conceived within a Western-oriented epistemology start to tremble, if not fall".[12] To ignore Indigenous materialisms in any origin story of "new" materialist philosophies, is, as Ravenscroft argues, another act of colonial erasure. She quotes Amiskwaciwâskahikan scholar Zoe Todd's frustrated recollection of waiting through a lecture by Latour for him to "credit Indigenous thinkers for their millennia of engagement with sentient environments, with cosmologies that enmesh people into complex relationships between themselves and *all* relations, and with climates and atmospheres as important points of organisation and action. I waited. I waited. … It never came. He did not mention Inuit. Or Anishinaabeg. Or Nehiyawak. Or any Indigenous thinkers at all."[13] There have been many attempts to explain the belatedness of the emergence of anything resembling a Romantic literary movement in Australia, the better part of a century after its high moment in England. The echoes of local indigenous ontology in Romanticism's anti-rationalist vitalism may have been enough for the colonists of the early nineteenth century to reject Romanticism's modes of thought and expression in decades where their dominion was far from assured. The prevalence of Romantic culture in Europe and its relative absence in the colonial population of Australia may explain how the lyrebird came to be a *lyrebird* in Europe while early colonists continued to refer predominantly to the more prosaic "native pheasant".

It is unclear exactly who or what inaugurates the tradition of the *lyre*bird. In Penny Olsen's inimitable compendium of early lyrebird portraiture, the earliest depiction of a lyrelike tail occurs in Pauline Knip's *Oiseau-lyre* of 1812.[14] The first instance in print of the bird as "lyrebird" that I have found is by a French critic of Knip's painting, who notes in 1812 that Knip's work, hung in the Galerie des Peintres Français and titled there *Manoura Magnificat*, is of a "*oiseau-lyre*" (this review may be the origin of Olsen's caption for Knip's painting, as *Oiseau-lyre* does not seem to be Knip's own title, although the conceit of the tail as lyre clearly informs her painting). For this critic, Knip's bird spreads his tail like a peacock

---

11   Paul Kane, *Australian Poetry: Romanticism and Negativity* (Cambridge: Cambridge University Press, 1996), 8.

12   Alison Ravenscroft, "Strange Weather: Indigenous Materialisms, New Materialism, and Colonialism", *Cambridge Journal of Postcolonial Literary Inquiry* 5, no. 3 (2018): 357.

13   Zoe Todd, "An Indigenous Feminist's Take on the Ontological Turn: 'Ontology' Is Just Another Word for Colonialism", *Journal of Historical Sociology* 29, no. 1 (2016): 6–7.

14   Penny Olsen, *Upside Down World: Early European Impressions of Australia's Curious Animals* (Canberra: National Library of Australia, 2010), 181.

and bears "la plus exacte resemblance avec une lyre".[15] Knip's lyrebird is eroticised (well before Darwin clarified the idea that extravagant, ornamental features in the bodies and voices of birds had been drawn out by the erotic preferences of their foremothers).[16] We see Knip's bird from behind, his round downy rump at the fore of his portrait. His outer-tail feathers (the so-called lyrates) project, lyrelike indeed, up from this rump, and he looks back at us – as it were over his shoulder – so that his eye meets ours through the gauzy fan of his filamentary feathers.

Knip was likely working from a specimen in Paris (the first lyrebird corpses reached England in 1799; by 1803, there seem to have been several specimens in London, and at least two in Paris). Major Thomas Davies, writing to the Linnaean Society in 1801, named the bird *Menura superba* ("menoura", literally "moon-tail" in Greek, might refer to the arguably crescent-moon shaped markings on the lyrates).[17] As is common in early nineteenth-century ornithology, the man who named the bird had never actually seen one alive. Rather he happened to find a dead one in the possession of Mary Howe, the daughter of Admiral Lord Howe, and got further information from correspondence with Major John Hunter, who in turn, being too old for forays into the forests of New South Wales, was depending on the information of an unnamed informant, or possibly two informants – who called it a pheasant. Although the conceit of the lyre came to circulate soon afterwards, as we can see from the review of Knip's *Manoura Magnificat*, it does not seem to have caught on so soon in the lyrebird's own country. The 1813 Thomas Skottowe manuscript, held in the Mitchell Library, includes a portrayal by convict T.R. Browne of a lyrebird with the caption *Mamura superba*. Skottowe notes that it is "commonly called the mountain pheasant", "remarkable for the beautiful plumage of its tail". "It is said … to possess a sweet note by those who have had the pleasure of hearing it", Skottowe writes, suggesting no insight into the bird's repertoire of imitations. He concludes his account with the words: "Native Name Golgol".[18]

In 1834, a thirty-year-old physician and fellow of the Linnean Society, George Bennett, would introduce his discussion of the lyrebird in his travelogue, *Wanderings in New South Wales*, with a short catalogue of names ascribed to the lyrebird: "The 'Native or Wood-pheasant,' or 'Lyre bird' of the colonists, the '*Menura superba*' of naturalists, and the 'Béleck, béleck,' and 'Balangara' of the aboriginal tribes".[19] Bennett goes on to explain that "the tail of the bird bears a striking

15 Anon., *Journal des Arts, des Sciences et de la Littérature* (Paris: Porthmann, 1812), 353.

16 This idea is elaborated throughout *Descent of Man*, but see especially Charles Darwin, *Descent of Man, and Selection in Relation to Sex*, vol. 2 (London: John Murray, 1871), 99–101.

17 Thomas Davies, "Description of *Menura superba*, a Bird of New South Wales", *Transactions of the Linnean Society* 6, no. 1 (1802), 207–10.

18 Thomas Skottowe, *The Skottowe Manuscript: Thomas Skottowe's select specimens from nature of the birds, animals, &c. &c. of New South Wales*, ed. T. Bonyhady and J. Calaby (Sydney: Hordern House, 1988), 34.

19 George Bennett, *Wanderings in New South Wales: Batavia, Pedir Coast, Singapore and China; Being the Journal of a Naturalist in Those Countries During 1832, 1833, and 1834*, vol. 1 (London: Richard Bentley, 1834), 277.

resemblance, in its graceful form, to the famous lyre of the Greeks, from which circumstance it has received the name of the 'lyre bird' of Australia".[20] Bennett is mistaken on a number of fronts in his discussion of the lyrebird: he is mistaken in believing that the birds lay their eggs in tree hollows, and also about the colour and number of their eggs. His two "aboriginal" names for the bird are a frustratingly inadequate sample from among the languages he must have overheard. But about the tail's resembling a lyre? By now, this was clearly established as a matter of fact.

Anyone versed or immersed in Australiana will know this fact. The lyrebird with tail-as-lyre appears everywhere, even on many of the fibrous plaster ceilings surviving in Sydney from the early 1900s (complete, strangely, with peacock crest feathers).[21] Such representations, minus the crest feathers, are almost certainly copies of what is probably Elizabeth Gould's illustration of the lyrebird for John Gould's *The Birds of Australia*, published in seven volumes between 1840–48. The male bird's tail projects straight upwards from his body; the lyrates curve symmetrically, meeting at their tips to then curl a little outwards, and the finer filamentary feathers seem to suggest the parallel strings of the lyre. Gould claimed the lyrebird as *the* emblem for Australian birdlife, as Jonathan Smith notes, and it appeared on the cover of each of the seven volumes and of supplement volumes of *Birds of Australia*.[22] Gould's depiction was almost certainly taking dictation from the work of a taxidermist who was in turn influenced by another commentator or specimen arranger. In *its* turn, published in perhaps the most culturally significant work of nineteenth-century colonial Australian natural history, Gould's lyrebird was immensely influential on subsequent lyrebird depictions. Jonathan Smith discusses Gould's identification of the lyrebirds with Queen Victoria and Albert, after whom John Gould named a species of lyrebird – the *Menura alberti* which still bears that name and the *Menura novaehollandiae* (at that point called the *Menura superba* and renamed *Menura novaehollandiae victoriae* by Gould). Smith argues that in producing the lyrebirds as fitting avian representatives for a royal couple who strove to project an image of "exemplary married domesticity", his representations of the birds "depended on suppression, reconfiguration, and even invention of evidence".[23] Although Smith mentions that the Goulds' lyrebird tail is figured "with rigorous bilateral symmetry", he doesn't cite this as a particular example of the Goulds' reconfiguration or invention of evidence (he is more interested in the contrivance involved in producing the "informal, unsymmetrical domestic pose" of the male and female that stand and sit side by side as if in a Victorian family portrait).[24] But the position of the displayed tail in Gould's

---

20   Bennett, *Wanderings in New South Wales*, 278.
21   See "George Taylor's Improved Fibrous Plaster", *Sydney Living Museums*, accessed 26 May 2023. https://sydneylivingmuseums.com.au/stories/george-taylors-improved-fibrous-plaster.
22   Jonathan Smith, "Gender, Royalty, and Sexuality in John Gould's *Birds of Australia*", *Victorian Literature and Culture* 35, no. 2 (2007): 569.
23   Smith, "Gender, Royalty, and Sexuality", 569.
24   Smith, "Gender, Royalty, and Sexuality", 580.

drawing, as ornithologist A.H. Chisholm points out, is not in a living lyrebird's usual display position.[25] One or both of the Goulds, Chisholm suggests, worked from a British museum display undoubtedly prepared by a taxidermist of the early 1800s who had never seen a living lyrebird and was swept up in a tradition of conflating male lyrebird display with the shape of the lyre.

The history of the European and colonial representation of lyrebirds is a history of copying. Figurations of the birds hop ekphrastically across media, between paintings and etchings, travel narratives and ornithological literature, between the arrangement of the dead birds' bodies and the very naming of the birds. Somewhere in this process, the conceit of the lyre inserted itself, a conceit that depended on the misapprehension that the bird held his tail upright with its thickest feathers in the configuration of the arms of a lyre, connecting at the top to form the semblance of a lyre's crossbar. Having inserted itself, this conceit was copied.

What, if anything, does this copying have in common with the lyrebird's copying? Lyrebirds are accomplished samplers and reproducers of the sounds of their auditory environment, in ways that both resemble and at times interact with and reproduce human cultures of transmission. Alec Chisholm recorded in 1960 "some queer consequences of the bird's mimicry. One example relates to the interruption of the timber-men's activities because a Lyrebird imitated the mill whistle. In another instance an enterprising bird threw a group of survey workers into confusion through imitating (at the wrong time) the code of shrill signals issued by the foreman."[26] David Attenborough's documentary of 1998, *The Life of Birds*, includes footage of lyrebirds performing the sounds of camera shutters and chainsaws, besides a suite of other bird songs, suggesting that even if the lyrebirds' impulse to reproduce sounds might be relatively static, individuals are highly responsive to changes in their acoustic environments. Alongside this capacity for rapid musical adaptation is evidence for the persistence of lyrebird song culture. In 1934, twenty-one lyrebirds from mainland Australia were released in Tasmania's Mount Field National Park, which was designated a settler sanctuary for the species, understood to be endangered by the galloping destruction of mainland forests. Thirty years later, Tasmanian-born descendants of this settler population were heard singing a song associated with the whipbird, a species unknown on the island.

In late August 2021, three months into Sydney's COVID-19 delta-variant lockdown, a lyrebird captive in Taronga Zoo was recorded in a song that, as one journalist reported, "perfectly mimics the ear-splitting wail of a crying baby". Echo, as this bird is named, was also reported as having "mastered a rendition of the Sydney zoo's fire alarm, complete with the 'evacuate now' announcement".[27] The zookeeper's recording of Echo's uncannily evocative rendition of a baby's cry made

---

25   Alec H. Chisholm, *The Romance of the Lyrebird* (Sydney: Angus & Robinson, 1960), 38–43.
26   Chisholm, *The Romance of the Lyrebird*, 111.
27   Donna Lu, "Taronga zoo lyrebird perfectly mimics the ear-splitting wail of a crying baby", *The Guardian*, accessed 26 May 2023. https://tinyurl.com/46ypsp62.

its way online. In the relative hush of a zoo evacuated of its normal human babble, Echo had been, it seems, remembering, rehearsing and honing his quotation of preverbal human emotion. His recollection in tranquillity, if that is what it was, made for just the kind of footage calculated to go viral on sites where it provided a wondrous distraction from endlessly refracting reportage on the theme of an actual virus. Within the week, the human recording of this lyrebird's anthropophonic recitation had been shared and replayed hundreds of thousands of times on social media.

Echo's name recalls another Echo, the tragic figure of Ovid's *Metamorphoses*, the nymph who is cursed by the goddess Juno "to sport with ev'ry sentence in the close", to say nothing that is not a repetition of the closing word or phrase of what someone else has said. Despite this formidable restriction, Ovidian Echo's utterances are remarkably salient to the situations in which she finds herself. She falls in love with the young Narcissus, who is in turn besotted with his own reflection, heartbroken that its replies to his claims of love are inaudible, and disgusted at Echo's interest in him. When Narcissus cries to his reflection, "Ah youth! Beloved in vain!", Echo responds (aptly) with the same words. As Narcissus dies, lovelorn, sighing "Farewel" to his reflection, Echo sighs back, "Farewel", as she might be expected to.[28] In Ovid's and his translators' handling, Echo's echolalia generates sounds that denote something often very like what she might actually want to say. Her compulsive vocal imitation, coupled with the conditions in which she speaks, means that what she does say might seem either semantically void or expressive of what a sympathetic listener would imagine her meaning to express. It creates an epistemological problem for the listener: how can we know how meaningful her speech is? Can her compelled copying also constitute an intentional engagement with the sounds made available to her in her environment?

Is there perhaps even a sense in which Echo may have participated in shaping the sonic field from which she will excerpt her sounds? In her 2019 study of sex, mate choice and cognition in Australian native birds, Gisela Kaplan tells the story of a co-evolutionary partnership between the superb lyrebird and the Antarctic beech forest of the so-called New England National Park. The lyrebirds have grown the forest into what it is through their constant interference with the forest floor, Kaplan shows; in turn, the shape of the forest contributes to the lyrebird's success in his erotic performance art. The absence of undergrowth means that "a displaying male lyrebird would be visible from some distance, having no shortage of suitable display areas".[29] "The forest also produces," Kaplan writes:

---

28 G. Sewell, ed., *Ovid's Metamorphoses, In Fifteen Books, Made English by Several Hands, Adorn'd with Cuts*, vol. 1 (London: S. Palmer et al, 1724), 82.

29 Gisela Kaplan, *Bird Bonds: Sex, Mate-choice and Cognition in Australian Native Birds* (Sydney: Pan Macmillan, 2019), 22.

an undeniable echo and when a displaying lyrebird male begins to sing during his mating display, the sound is enhanced and bounces back between the trees. The forest becomes a singing forest – by its structure and by having forced out any understorey via its extensive and surface-producing root system, making it seem almost an active participant in the effect of the song.[30]

Kaplan's account of literal echoes of course itself echoes the lyrebird's own echoing, his vocal mimicry of the sounds he has selected from the forest. Kaplan's rendering of the co-evolutionary temporal loop here, the back-and-forth through evolutionary time between a bird and a forest, recalls, too, the complex looping chatter of sexual selection, a co-evolutionary relationship negotiated around aesthetic and erotic desire, occurring between lyrebirds, or proto-lyrebirds, even as the lyrebirds themselves evolve with the forest. The phenomenon of sexual selection also raises questions about the quality of intentionality in biological processes. On the one hand, it offers a radical account of animals' agency in shaping their species, a radical account of animals practising what we might think of as "culture", expressing their preferences for certain songs, colours and shapes. On the other hand, their preferences are structured by the interplay of their bodies and constrained by the array of options presented to them. Then again, whose preferences are not?[31]

The lyrebird's song brings together the deep time of lyrebird evolution and the immediate present tense of a bird's individual life and acoustic experience. In her essay "On Writing *Carpentaria*", Alexis Wright discusses the complexity of that staggering novel's effort both to "understand the idea of Indigenous people living with the stories of all the times of this country" and then to embrace all these times within the singularity of a novel.[32] *Carpentaria*, as a result, is:

> a spinning multi-stranded helix of stories. This is the condition of contemporary Indigenous storytelling that I believe is a consequence of our racial diaspora in Australia. The helix of divided strands is forever moving, entwining all stories together, just like a lyrebird is capable of singing several tunes at once. These stories relate to all the leavings and returnings to ancient territory, while carrying the whole human endeavour in search of new dreams.

Alexis Wright is like so many writers on this continent in reaching for the lyrebird in her discussion of her own writing. But unlike in the many lyrebird poems of white Australian poets, the lyrebird attribute for which Wright reaches here escapes the conventional European figurings. This lyrebird is neither a mere mimic nor a

---

30   Kaplan, *Bird Bonds*, 22.
31   Darwin suggests that human speech has evolved in ways similar to birds' courtship songs. See *Descent of Man*, vol. 1, 56.
32   Alexis Wright, "On Writing *Carpentaria*", *HEAT* 13 (2007), accessed 26 May 2023. https://giramondopublishing.com/heat/archive/alexis-wright-on-writing-carpentaria/.

poet because his tail is seen to look a bit like an ancient Greek stringed instrument. His capacity to sing several tunes at once, brought into comparison with Wright's project of rendering all times simultaneously, exults the complexity of lyrebird song and suggests the ways in which his bringing together of songs past is also a renewing.

* * *

One late twentieth-century morning, as we staggered out of one of Bruce Gardiner's lectures, my friend proposed a computer program into which one would be able to input a poem and then print out a fully-formed Gardinerian textual analysis. It was a joke, of course. For one thing, neither of us had used a computer for anything more sophisticated than typing up our handwritten essays and playing Tetris. But also – and this was the point of the joke – Bruce Gardiner's readings were inimitable, irreducible treatments of language and culture. Irreducible, even, in some crucial way, to the page. They took place in time and space, in Bruce's famously on-theme clothing, in the ear and eye and then the mouth of his students. The lecture we had just witnessed had culminated in Bruce's suggestion that the assonance in a poem by Yeats evokes the throbbing of a contracting uterine sphincter. Unbidden, fifty students had begun quietly, then noisily, imitating Yeats', that is to say, Gardiner's, syllables, testing out the feeling of "oo", "oo" made strange in their own mouths.

I was an undergraduate student who had clung grimly to the practical criticism and literary canon of my high school English teachers when I stumbled into Bruce's subject, *American Claims: Indian, Settler, Slave* in 1998. By the end of term we had read Toni Morrison's *Sula*, Harriet Jacobs' *Incidents in the Life of a Slave Girl*, Iroquois and Nabajo song cycles, *Leaves of Grass*, Jean Toomer's *Cane*: this subject would take us, in other words, deep into the trouble of Americanness. But we began – and this was Bruce telling the truth of that trouble, but telling it slant – with poems about hummingbirds that he had anthologised, a collection that we read like we would read the specimen case of jewel-bright formaldehyded birds he had procured from somewhere (the Zoology department, his personal archive?) and brought to class. We watched a fragment of a brand new David Attenborough documentary on VHS, footage of tiny bright birds fibrillating around the flowers they suck from, and Bruce told us that the voice-over of Attenborough was the disembodied voice of the Angel Gabriel, whose job it is to justify the ways of God to Man (a characterisation of Attenborough that's been waking me up at night now for a quarter of a century).

This year I am teaching a subject that reckons, a bit, with the trouble of Australianness, with (to borrow from Bruce's description of *American Claims*) the genres and themes through which peoples lay claim to lands or declare themselves (or refuse to declare themselves) "Australian". We begin with the so-called "lyrebirds". Students are given many of the objects discussed in this essay: late eighteenth- and early nineteenth-century colonists' accounts of the *Menura superba*; twentieth-century settler-colonists' poems in which either lyrebirds are romanticised as poets or poets are chastised for romanticising lyrebirds as poets; recordings of the birds' song repertoire (one narrated by the Angel Gabriel himself); visual materials ranging from a Gadigal engraver's pre-colonial depiction to the impress on a now seldom-seen ten cent Australian coin. I don't replicate for my students Bruce's rhetorical splendour, or his agile chasing of theme and form across genres, or the careful excavation of identity-making and claim-laying work that his hummingbird seminars offered, but it's not for want of trying.

Bibliography

Barad, Karen. *Meeting the Universe Halfway*. Durham, NC: Duke University Press, 2007.

Bennett, George. *Wanderings in New South Wales: Batavia, Pedir Coast, Singapore and China; Being the Journal of a Naturalist in Those Countries During 1832, 1833, and 1834*, 1. London: Richard Bentley, 1834.

Bennett, Jane. *Vibrant Matter: A Political Ecology of Things*. Durham, NC: Duke University Press, 2010.

Clayton-Dixon, Callum. "In Reclaiming Our History of Resistance, We Can Also Revitalise Decimated Languages". *The Guardian*. Accessed 26 May 2023. https://tinyurl.com/2afda5zk).

Bierhorst, John, ed. *Four Masterworks of American Indian Literature: Quetzalcoatl, the Ritual of Condoldence, Cuceb, the Night Chant*. Tucson: University of Arizona Press, 1984.

Chisholm, Alec. *The Romance of the Lyrebird*. Sydney: Angus & Robinson, 1960.

Clunies Ross, Bruce A. "Landscape and the Australian Imagination". In *Mapped But Not Known: The Australian Landscape of the Imagination*. Edited by Philippa Robin Eaden and Francis Hugh Mares, 224–43. South Australia: Wakefield Press, 1986.

Darwin, Charles. *Descent of Man, and Selection in Relation to Sex*, 2 vols. London: John Murray, 1871.

Davies, Thomas. "Description of *Menura superba*, A Bird of New South Wales". *Transactions of the Linnean Society* 6, no. 1 (1802): 207–10.

Gardiner, Bruce. *American Claims: Indian, Settler, Slave*, seminar series. Sydney: The University of Sydney, 1998.

Edgar-Jones, Sharon and Albert Burgman. *Wanarruwa Beginner's Guide*. Nambucca Heads: Muurrbay Aboriginal Language and Culture Co-operative, 2019.

Fielding, Saretta. *Kulkal-Lyrebird*. 2018. Mixed medium on canvas. 500–400 mm. Saretta Art & Design, Toronto, NSW. https://www.saretta.com.au/products/kulkal-lyrebird.

"George Taylor's Improved Fibrous Plaster". *Sydney Living Museums*. Accessed 26 May 2023. https://sydneylivingmuseums.com.au/stories/george-taylors-improved-fibrous-plaster.

Gould, John. *The Birds of Australia*, 7 vols. London: John Gould, 1840–1848.

Grosz, Elizabeth. *The Incorporeal: Ontology, Ethics, and the Limits of Materialism*. New York: Columbia University Press, 2017.

Haraway, Donna. *The Companion Species Manifesto: Dogs, People, and Significant Otherness*. Chicago, IL: Prickly Paradigm Press, 2002.

Jacobs, Harriet. *Incidents in the Life of a Slave Girl*. Rev. ed. Peterborough, Ontario: Broadview Press, 2023.

Knip, Pauline. *Oiseau-Lyre*. 1812. Watercolour. Château Fontainebleau, Fontainebleau.

Kane, Paul. *Australian Poetry: Romanticism and Negativity*. Cambridge University Press, 1996.

Kaplan, Giselle. *Bird Bonds: Sex, Mate-Choice and Cognition in Australian Native Birds*. Sydney: Pan Macmillan, 2019.

Kirby, Vicki. *Quantum Anthropologies: Life at Large*. Durham, NC: Duke University Press, 2011.

Latour, Bruno. *An Inquiry into Modes of Existence: An Anthopology of the Moderns*. Trans. Catherine Porter. Cambridge, MA: Harvard University Press, 2013.

Leavis, F.R. "Literary Criticism and Philosophy: A Reply", *Scrutiny* 6 (1937): 59–70.

Lu, Donna. "'Taronga zoo lyrebird perfectly mimics the ear-splitting wail of a crying baby". *The Guardian*. 2 September 2021. https://tinyurl.com/mt2thb6e.

Miner, Earl. "Comparative Lyric". In *The Lyric Theory Reader: A Critical Anthology*. Ed. Virginia Jackson and Yopie Prins, 577–88. Baltimore, MD: Johns Hopkins University Press, 2014.

Morrison, Toni. *Sula*. New York: Knopf, 1973.

Murray, Les. *Translations from the Natural World*. Manchester: Carcarnet Press, 1993.

Olsen, Penny. *Upside Down World: Early European Impressions of Australia's Curious Animals*. Canberra: National Library of Australia, 2010.

Ovid. *Ovid's Metamorphoses, In Fifteen Books, Made English by Several Hands, Adorn'd with Cuts*, 1. Ed. G. Sewell. London: S. Palmer et al., 1724.

Plato. *The Republic*. Trans. H.D.P. Lee. London: Penguin, 1955.

Ravenscroft, Alison. "Strange Weather: Indigenous Materialisms, New Materialism, and Colonialism". *Cambridge Journal of Postcolonial Literary Inquiry* 5, no. 3 (2018): 353–70.

Shelley, Percy Bysshe. *The* Defence of Poetry *Fair Copies: A Facsimile of the Fair Copy Transcript by Mary W. Shelley*. Ed. Michael O'Neill. New York and London: Garland Publishing, 1994.

Shelley, Percy Bysshe. *Shelley's Poetry and Prose*, Donald. H. Reiman and Neil Fraistat, eds. New York: W. W. Norton, 2002.

Skottowe, Thomas. *The Skottowe Manuscript: Thomas Skottowe's Select Specimens from Nature of the Birds, Animals, &c., &c., of New South Wales*. Ed. T. Bonyhady and J. Calaby. Sydney: Hordern House, 1988.

Todd, Zoe. "An Indigenous Feminist's Take on the Ontological Turn: 'Ontology' Is Just Another Word for Colonialism". *Journal of Historical Sociology* 29, no. 1 (2016): 4–22.

Smith, Jonathan. "Gender, Royalty, and Sexuality in John Gould's *Birds of Australia*". *Victorian Literature and Culture* 35, no. 2 (2007): 569–87.

Toomer, Jean. *Cane*. Rev. ed. London: Penguin, 2019.

Whitman, Walt. *Leaves of Grass*. Ed. Michael Moon. New York: W.W. Norton, 2002.

Winters, Yvor, *In Defence of Reason*. Denver, CO: University of Denver Press, 1947.

White, Brock, director. *The Life of Birds: David Attenborough*. BBC, 1998: 10 episodes.

Wright, Alexis. "On Writing *Carpentaria*", *HEAT* 13 (2007). Accessed May 26 2023. https://giramondopublishing.com/heat/archive/alexis-wright-on-writing-carpentaria/.

Wright, Judith. *Preoccupations in Australian Poetry*. Oxford: Oxford University Press, 1965.

Wright, Judith. *Birds*. Canberra: National Library of Australia, 2003.

17

The Queer Optimism of Ginsberg's "Kaddish" (for Bruce Gardiner)

Kate Lilley

1.

> Not only is the literary thing produced, but we must also say that it produces, that it is productive, that is, that it has a fecundity proper to it that is ultimately inexhaustible, to which the interminable cycle of its reproductions bears witness, a cycle to which no explication, no exegesis, can come to put a final stop: because without this, it would not be worth one hour of trouble.
> Pierre Macherey and Audrey Wasser[1]

I first encountered Bruce Gardiner in the last year of my undergraduate degree in 1982 as one of the teachers of the year-long Twentieth Century Literature Honours Seminar. A new appointment to the English department at the University of Sydney, fresh from his PhD at Princeton, he was young, full of personality and clearly delighted to be teaching. I was so struck by Bruce himself that I do not remember the subject of that first seminar. Rather, what has stayed with me is an elegant, allegorical anecdote involving the Empire State Building, and the surprise it engendered. More than forty years since my first exposure to his unexpected way of approaching the singular mystery of texts and persons alike, that sense of surprise and interest has never left me. I did not know then that we would be friends and colleagues for the rest of our lives. After I returned from doctoral and postdoctoral study in the UK to teach in the department in 1990, Bruce and I shared a course on nineteenth- and twentieth-century women's writing. I also sat in on Bruce's American literature courses for the sheer enjoyment of it, learning a lot about how to read inexhaustibly, and how to combine scholarship and teaching in a way that was energised but not overwhelmed by its personal stakes. For the first twenty years

---

1   Macherey, Pierre and Audrey Wasser, "The Literary Thing". *Diacritics* 37, no.4 (Winter 2007): 30.

or so of my working life as an academic, there was plenty of passionate argument and disagreement (to put it politely) about what and how to teach, but for the most part live-and-let-live pluralism reigned. A large, traditional literary-historical department with many and varied electives reflecting the wide-ranging interests of staff, each one a world unto itself, both teachers and students were involved in continuously assembling their own bespoke, mosaic curriculum. That live process of choice and negotiation, from semester to semester, year to year, first as a student and later as a teacher, was at the core of my ongoing sense of discipline, vocation and agency.

Over the thirty-five years in which Bruce and I worked as allies and collaborators, the rise of neoliberal, commercial imperatives and bureaucratised management have decimated most humanities departments and changed academic culture almost beyond recognition. In the highly surveilled, notionally "efficient" contemporary university, academic personality and independence – not so long ago *de rigueur* – is often reframed as a mini-cult of personality. As a specialist in the intricacies and coteries of queer decadence, Bruce's training helped him to double down and regroup in defence of the chiastic relation between queer scholarly personality and personal scholarship. His legacy exemplifies what Michael Snediker has called "queer optimism".[2] Of course, no one in their queer right mind would resile from the generative, negative side of this formulation. Indeed, the reparative emphasis of "queer optimism" and "its particular *élan*" *requires* the counterweight of Edelman's "queer pessimism", Berlant's "cruel optimism" and Sedgwick's "paranoid and reparative reading".[3] Snediker argues that:

> In current critical thought, optimism's very sanguinity implies an epistemological deficit. This ostensibly definitional antagonistic relation to knowledge has had the perhaps unsurprising effect of taking optimism out of critical circulation. Queer optimism, oppositely, is not promissory. It doesn't ask that some future time make good on its own hopes. Rather, queer optimism asks that optimism, embedded in its own immanent present, be *interesting*. Queer optimism's interest – its capacity to be interesting, to hold our attention – depends on its emphatic responsiveness to and solicitation of rigorous thinking.

Walking around the University of Sydney, official posters exhort its denizens to "Unlearn". Another cutesy administrative adage in circulation counsels us to "fail faster" and cut our losses. These cruelly optimistic, counterintuitive commands implicitly promise a pay-off – time saved, quick breakthroughs, change-management

---

2   Michael Snediker, "Queer Optimism", *Postmodern Culture* 16, no.3 (2006).

3   Lee Edelman, *No Future: Queer Theory and the Death Drive* (Durham, NC: Duke University Press, 2004). Lauren Berlant, *Cruel Optimism* (Durham, NC: Duke University Press, 2011); Eve Kosofsky Sedgwick, "Paranoid Reading and Reparative Reading, Or, You're So Paranoid, You Probably Think This Introduction is About You", in *Touching Feeling: Affect, Pedagogy, Performativity* (Durham, NC: Duke University Press, 2003).

for the greater good – but as all the worker bees know, good cheer is hard to find on campus these days. It is now a commonplace, taken as read, that the university is no longer a place conducive to what Snediker suggestively calls "lyric personhood".[4] This is where queer optimism comes in. As Snediker argues, it is not that "if one were more queerly optimistic, one would feel happier. *Rather, queer optimism can be considered as a form of meta-optimism*: it wants to *think* about feeling good, to make disparate aspects of feeling good *thinkable*."[5] English department life has not always been happy or even optimistic in the ordinary sense: at times, far from it. It has, however, never been less than "interesting" in a "meta-optimistic" way. In fact, its very existence is predicated on the "immanent value" of literary studies as a disciplinary field and the pleasure of "rigorous thinking" about its methods and objects *in the present*. Over many years, Bruce's contribution to this project has been indefatigable, inimitable, personal, lyrical. From my first encounter with him in that Honours seminar in 1982 I had an inkling that this was a lucky chance.

2.

America I'm putting my queer shoulder to the wheel.
Allen Ginsberg, "America"[6]

In what follows I turn my attention to Allen Ginsberg. His life and oeuvre, often thought to exemplify "the utopic energy that motivates counterpublics", can helpfully be understood as "queerly optimistic" in Snediker's terms: that is, "immanently rather than futurally oriented".[7] The immediate and exponential notoriety of "Howl" from the time of its first public reading and publication in San Francisco in 1955–1956 established the formerly obscure, thirty-year-old Ginsberg as an activist-celebrity poet on the world stage, but it was his queer "lyric personhood" and the voluminously consistent writing and teaching performed under its aegis over many decades that established his enduring presence as a literary lion.[8] My focus here is on Ginsberg as elegist and the copresence of praise

---

4   Michael Snediker, *Queer Optimism: Lyric Personhood and Other Felicitous Persuasions* (Minneapolis: University of Minnesota Press, 2008), the book, which developed from the 2006 article "queer optimism", is coupled with "lyric personhood". Snediker asks, "What would it mean to imagine onself as a figure, granted figuration's various capacities?", 32.

5   Snediker, "Queer Optimism", para 4, emphasis in original.

6   This is the last line of "America". Allen Ginsberg, *Howl And Other Poems* (San Francisco: City Lights Books, 1956), 34. All subsequent quotations from *Howl* will be from this edition.

7   Snediker, "Queer Optimism", paras 3–4. Anne Hartman makes a compelling argument in favour of "unsettling" the category of "confessional poetry" by including O'Hara and Ginsberg, reading their actual and figurative deployment of queer community as "interpellat[ing] a homosexual counter-public, while exploiting confession's ability to unsettle normative categories". "Confessional Counterpublics in Frank O'Hara and Allen Ginsberg", *JML* 28, no.4 (2005): 41.

8   For a respectful and perceptive account of Ginsberg's sustained poetic career and its divided reception, see Marjorie Perloff, "A Lion in Our Living Room: Reading Allen Ginsberg in the

and blame, joy and melancholy, optimism and pessimism (elegy's signature) in Ginsberg's most famous poems, "Howl" ("for Carl Solomon", 1956) and "Kaddish" ("for Naomi Ginsberg", 1961). I first worked on "Kaddish" as a PhD student in the 1980s and have since enjoyed teaching both "Howl" and "Kaddish" many times. This volume seems an appropriate occasion to think again about Ginsberg in relation to affect, genre and taxonomy, personality and coteries, families and institutions, returning to these galvanising companion poems, particularly in light of the psychiatrist Stevan M. Weine's significant recent book, *Best Minds: How Allen Ginsberg Made Revolutionary Poetry from Madness*.[9] Through Weine's research in hospital records, the Ginsberg papers at Columbia and Stanford, and his account of his interactions with Ginsberg himself along the way, we have a newly detailed, multi-layered, psychiatrically informed sense of the inextricably entwined experiences of Allen and his mother, Naomi Levi Ginsberg (1894–1956), in and out of the American mental health system. Weine provides a substantively different understanding of the chronology and meaning of key events and texts, which, in turn, have implications for the reading of Ginsberg's poetry.

As Weine shows, Ginsberg received a letter from Pilgrim State Hospital, where Naomi had most recently been incarcerated since April 1947, recommending her as an appropriate candidate for a prefrontal lobotomy, at that time regarded as an extremely promising new treatment for intractably psychotic patients. Allen's early life had been dominated by Naomi's increasingly frequent psychotic episodes (she was first hospitalised at eighteen). Naomi had been hospitalised for two years prior to Allen's commencement at Columbia in September 1943, following the harrowing Lakewood incident memorably narrated in "Kaddish II". Over the next few years Ginsberg established the core of his "angelic" literary friendship circle, including William Burroughs, Jack Kerouac and Neil Cassady, the dedicatees of *Howl And Other Poems*. Allen tried to distance himself somewhat from his family and establish an independent life as a queer poet at large in New York but, after his parents separated, he was directly responsible for Naomi's treatment. On 16 November 1947, aged twenty-one, Allen provided written consent for the lobotomy, performed on 13 January 1948 (Naomi was then aged fifty-three). Despite several "attacks of disturbance" in the following months, Naomi's lobotomy was deemed to have been a success and she was released into the care of her sister, Elinor, on 1 May 1949.[10] Thirteen months later, in February 1951, after assaulting

---

Eighties", in *Poetic License. Essays on Modernist and Postmodernist Lyric* (Evanston, IL: Northwestern University Press, 1990), 199–230. Like Perloff, I regard Ginsberg as a dedicated formalist.

9   Stevan M. Weine, *Best Minds: How Allen Ginsberg Made Revolutionary Poetry from Madness* (New York: Fordham University Press, 2023). All further quotations are from this edition.

10   In October 1943, Naomi had been discharged from New Jersey State Hospital at Greystone, and divorced Allen's father, the poet and teacher Louis Ginsberg, her husband of many years. She had gone to live with her sister in New York and soon after taken up with a communist physician, Dr Leon Luria, with whom she lived until 1946. After sharing a room with Allen's older brother, Eugene, for a while, Naomi again moved in with her sister but was soon

Elinor, she was involuntarily readmitted to Pilgrim State (again, Allen signed the papers) where she remained until her death on 9 June 1956.

In a telling criss-cross, Allen, then a student at Columbia University, had been arrested one month before Naomi's post-lobotomy discharge, on 1 April 1949, and charged in connection with possession of goods stolen by his drug-addicted friends. In June 1949, a year after having authorised Naomi's lobotomy, Ginsberg was admitted to the Psychiatric Institute of Columbia Presbyterian Hospital (PI), in accordance with the terms of a plea deal brokered with the help of Ginsberg's eminent literature professors at Columbia, Lionel Trilling and Mark Van Doren. He spent the next eight months at PI in psychoanalytic psychotherapy designed to diagnose his mental state and correct antisocial, homosexual tendencies. Working in succession with three young residents in psychiatry, the last of whom he continued to see in private practice for two years after being released from hospital, this enforced stay at PI was highly significant for Ginsberg. He was relieved to have been spared any more dire criminal consequences and regarded this period of sequestration as an opportunity to reset his life and writing, still broadly under the umbrella of Columbia. Allen had wanted to be in therapy for years, especially since being experimentally "analysed" in 1945–1946, according to Reichian principles, by his friend and mentor, William Burroughs.[11] While at PI, Allen became close friends with fellow patient Carl Solomon, later the dedicatee of "Howl". In his second resident doctor at PI, a woman whom Weine does not identify, Allen also found an important ally in negotiating his homosexuality and standing up to his father's homophobia. Allen had come out to his father Louis in November 1947, in the same month that he had given permission for his mother's lobotomy. It had not gone well. Now, in a meeting with both father and son, the doctor advised Louis to accept Allen's sexuality if he wanted to have a relationship with his son. Louis responded by successfully demanding that the woman be removed from Allen's case, but it did force an uneasy truce.[12]

After finding the relevant original documents in the Ginsberg archive and studying the hospital files, Weine was able to show Allen conclusive proof that he had authorised his mother's lobotomy in 1947 and not, as he had long thought, in the early 1950s: that is, *before* the events that led to his own arrest and psychiatric admission.[13] Weine also reveals that, although Allen's extensive clinical case file at PI noted Naomi's lobotomy and recent discharge from hospital, the undoubtedly traumatic fact of Allen's authorisation of the operation is nowhere mentioned in the record of his psychotherapy.[14] This startling omission, along with the absence

---

readmitted to Pilgrim State. Barry Miles, *Ginsberg: A Biography* (New York: Simon and Schuster, 1989), 39, 76.

11 Weine, *Best Minds*, 50.

12 Weine, *Best Minds*, ch. 5.

13 Weine, *Best Minds*, 73–9.

14 Weine offers much disturbing detail about the clinical context of Naomi's treatment at Pilgrim State Hospital, where lobotomies were regarded as offering an exciting breakthrough in the

of any explicit narrative in Allen's contemporaneous journals and his conscious or unconscious revision of the timeline, suggests Allen's drive to conceal its significance not only from his psychiatrists but also from himself/his writing. The timeline established by Weine does not so much *clear up* confusion or *correct* error as confirm its personal and poetic generativity. When Ginsberg gave Weine permission to access the hospital files he himself had never seen, he opened the queerly optimistic possibility of increase and poesis: more knowledge, complexity, interest, more thought and writing, more misprision, in the spirit of Edelman's "*jouissance* that at once defines us and negates us".[15]

It had been Allen's practice, from age eleven, to keep a journal. At first the entries are brief, intermittent, and almost exclusively concerned with Naomi's illness, newspaper headlines and movies. Over time they become more expansive, literary and erotic, including transcriptions of dreams, sexual fantasies and experiences; dialogues and letters; lists of books and vocabulary; and drafts and excerpts from his own and others' literary and philosophical writings.[16] With the encouragement of William Carlos Williams, who did not approve of the rhyming lyrics Ginsberg first sent him in 1950, these prose journals provided the basis for the new compositional method and aleatory poetic which led to the poems of *Empty Mirror* and, especially, *Howl And Other Poems*.[17] "Kaddish" continues what Ginsberg described in his liner essay for the LP "Notes for *Howl And Other Poems*" (1959) as "experiments with the formal organization of the long line … to *build up* large organic structures".[18] These "rhapsodic" (320), procedural experiments in "romantic inspiration – Hebraic-Melvillian bardic breath" (318), involved reactivating and redisposing an archive of texts and memories in conjunction with prolonged, drug-enhanced spontaneous composition designed to "open secrecy" (318) and produce "strange writing which passes from prose to poetry & back, like

---

management of chronically psychotic patients like Naomi, who had been in and out of mental wards since she was eighteen (Weine, *Best Minds*, 40). Weine notes that, in line with the legal circumstances of Ginsberg's admission, his anamnesis is less concerned with his family of origin and focused on the influence of unsavoury associates who have preyed on Allen's vulnerability, drawing him into drug use, homosexuality and criminal activity (Weine, *Best Minds*, 95–6).

15　Snediker identifies "interest" as central to queer optimism: "Queer optimism, oppositely, is not promissory. It doesn't ask that some future time make good on its own hopes. Rather, queer optimism asks that optimism, embedded in its own immanent present, be *interesting*. Queer optimism's interest – its capacity to be interesting, to hold our attention – depends on its emphatic responsiveness to and solicitation of rigorous thinking" ("Queer Optimism", para 3). The citation from Edelman's *No Future* (5) is Snediker's.

16　Allen Ginsberg, *The Book of Martyrdom and Artifice: First Journals and Poems,1937–1952*, ed. Juanita Liebermann-Plimpton and Bill Morgan (Cambridge, MA: Da Capo, 2006).

17　Between them, Ginsberg's biographers, Gordon Ball, Bill Morgan and Michael Schumacher, have edited six volumes of Ginsberg's journals to date, focused on the 1930s to the 1960s. By his own account, Morgan's selection of Ginsberg's letters presents 165 examples from an archive of about 3,700. Given its sheer magnitude, much of Ginsberg's personal, "informal" writing is unpublished and is likely to remain so.

18　"Notes for *Howl and Other Poems*" [1959] in *The Poetics of the New American Poetry*, ed. Donald M. Allen and Warren Tallman (New York: Grove Press, 1973), 319.

the mind" (320). The ways in which both journal entries and the poems developed from them combine transcription and alteration, disclosure and omission are central to the question of their presence and imminence. As Rachel Blau DuPlessis has argued in relation to "Howl": "The work is post-apocalyptic act, assuming that we are living beyond end time – a moral, political, sexual afterwards that is not simply aftermath, but defines a totally 'new time'".[19] Framed as a three-year anniversary memorial, belated but nonetheless timely, "Kaddish" engages the familiar problematic of masculine elegy as genealogical (political, sexual, ethical, poetic) crisis and revelation, in a highly unusual way, as maternal *agon*. With its epigraph from "Adonais", Shelley's elegy for Keats, "Die, / If thou wouldst be with that which thou dost seek!", "Kaddish" seals Naomi in the monumental body of Allen's "great formal elegy for [his] mother".[20]

William Carlos Williams, in his surprising "Introduction" to "Howl for Carl Solomon" (published as a foreword to *Howl And Other Poems*), had praised Ginsberg and his title poem "to the hilt" as a radical, heroically manly and "well made" love poem in both homoerotic and homosocial senses:

> Everyone in this life is defeated but a man, if he be a man, is not defeated.... This poet sees through and all around the horrors he partakes of in the very intimate details of his poem. He avoids nothing but experiences it to the hilt. He contains it. Claims it as his own – and, we believe, laughs at it and has the time and affrontery to love a fellow of his choice and record that love in a well-made poem.[21]

Williams' final line, "Hold back the edges of your gowns, Ladies, we are going through hell", strategically imputes fastidious, homophobic distaste to "Ladies", aligning enjoyment and approval of this queerly "contained" explosion of a "well-made poem" with real, right-thinking men who do not "look aside". The subsequent obscenity trial, *The People of the State of California v. Lawrence Ferlinghetti*, in which the powerhouse team of J.W.K. (Jake) Ehrlich, Lawrence Speiser and Albert Bendich, funded by the American Civil Liberties Union, successfully defended the owner of City Lights Books and publisher of The Pocket Poets Series, conferred on both Ginsberg and his book enduring significance and celebrity. Ferlinghetti described the outsize significance of Pocket Poets #4 as "the catalyst in a paradigm shift in American poetry and consciousness".[22] In his "not guilty" ruling (3 October 1957), the presiding judge, W.J. Clayton Horn, affirmed *Howl*'s "redeeming social importance" as individual, literary expression and thus its

---

19 Rachel Blau DuPlessis, "Manhood and its Poetic Projects", *Jacket* 31 (October 2006), para 20.
20 Allen Ginsberg to Jack Kerouac, 13 November 1957. Cited in Barry Miles, *The Beat Hotel: Ginsberg, Burroughs, and Corso in Paris, 1957–1963* (New York: Grove Press, 2000), 50. Ginsberg had recently visited the graves of Keats and Shelley in Rome.
21 William Carlos Williams, "Howl for Carl Solomon: Introduction", in *Howl*, 8.
22 Lawrence Ferlinghetti, "Introduction", in *Howl on Trial: The Battle For Free Expression* (San Francisco: City Lights Books, 2006).

protected commercial status, according to the First Amendment obscenity test.[23] The book could be freely sold; and sell it did. The original print run was one thousand copies. By the time Allen returned to New York in 1959 and finished "Kaddish", twenty thousand copies of *Howl* were in circulation, and he was one of the most famous queers in America, if not the world.[24]

The forty-three page, ten-poem manuscript of *Howl And Other Poems* was in press when Naomi died but Allen had sent a mimeographed preprint to her and other family and friends in May 1956. Louis, who had been privy to the book's genesis, responded promptly with his characteristically ambivalent combination of criticism and support, calling it "a weird, volcanic, troubled, extravagant, turbulent, boisterous, unbridled outpouring, intermingling genius and flashes of picturesque insight with slag and debris of scoraic matter". Presciently, he added: "The poem should attract attention and perhaps be a sensation; one will hear defenders and detractors. But it should give you a name."[25] Naomi's reply bore no date but was, eerily, postmarked 11 June 1956, two days after her death, the day of her funeral. Allen learned of his mother's death on 9 June. He was due to ship out for three months on the USNS *Pendleton* on 15 June and did not make the trip from San Francisco to the cemetery in Long Island, New York.[26] Following her last involuntary admission on 2 February 1951, he had visited her in Pilgrim State every few months up until July 1953.[27] These visits, later represented in "Kaddish", were harrowing and he had not seen her for the last three years. A few weeks before her death, he had written to his brother Eugene that "nobody wants or can help her, really" but he still hoped that she might "be well enough to get along one way or other on the outside".[28] Instead, Naomi died and her last words found him posthumously in mid-July when the ship made a stop in Tacoma.[29] Naomi's letter repeatedly enjoins Allen to "get a good job so you can get a girl to get married" and "behave well", closing: "Don't go in for too much drink and other things that are not good for you. ... I hope you are not taking any drugs as suggested by your poetry. That would hurt me. Don't go in for ridiculous things. / With love & good news, / (mother) Naomi."[30] The "good news" adverted to here seems to be Naomi's queerly optimistic desire to be "out of here and home at the time you were young; then I would be young. I'm in the prime of life now – / Did you read about the two

---

23 Joel E. Black, "Ferlinghetti on Trial: The Howl Court Case and Juvenile Delinquency", *Boom* 27 (2012), 39.

24 Michael Schumacher, *Dharma Lion: A Biography of Allen Ginsberg* (Minneapolis: University of Minnesota Press, 2016), 291.

25 Louis Ginsberg to Allen Ginsberg, 27 May 1956, *Family Business: Selected Letters between a Father and Son*, ed. Michael Schumacher (New York: Bloomsbury, 2002), 46.

26 Weine, *Best Minds*, 164.

27 Weine, *Best Minds*, 148.

28 Schumacher, ed., *Family Business*, 44.

29 Weine, *Best Minds*, 165; Schumacher, ed., *Family Business*, 50.

30 Naomi Ginsberg to Allen Ginsberg (n.d.), postmarked 11 June 1956; Schumacher, ed., *Family Business*, 50–51.

men who died at 139 & 149 yrs. of age? I wonder how they lived. / I'm looking for a good time."[31] The poetic properties of this letter are both internal and external: received after its author's death, at a poste restante, its contents produce "good news" by containing past and future in the textual present: "I'm in the prime of life now … I'm looking for a good time". As Weine shows, the letter incorporated into "Kaddish II" as Naomi's last is, in fact, a mash-up of this one and another letter sent to Eugene, and sent on by him to Allen: "God's informers came to my bed, and God, himself, he saw it in the sky – it was after Jan 1, 1956. The sunshine showed it too, a key on the side of the window for me to get out. The yellow of the sunshine, also showed me the key on the side of the window. I'm begging you to take me out of here."[32]

Naomi's radiant vision of the key in the window in the sunshine, sent to Eugene and then to him, becomes the central figure of Ginsberg's "Kaddish", stretching across all time and space: "Sun of all sunflowers and days on bright iron bridges – what shines on old hospitals – as on my yard" ("Kaddish II"). In "Kaddish I", Ginsberg traces his own returning path to the present of the poem, "thru Paterson, and the West, and Europe and here again", as he inscribes their meeting in the space of the immemorial memorial poem – Manhattan, "a single vast beam", "beginningless, endless". The poem contrives the crossing of Naomi's immigrant life and death, the "little girl – from Russia" on the Lower East Side – "Toward education marriage nervous breakdown, operation, teaching school, and learning to be mad, in a dream" – and her son's nomadic itinerary, both moving "Toward the Key in the window", "mortal changed" ("Kaddish I"). In "Kaddish II", the detailed narration of their life together ends with news of Naomi's death reaching Allen in Berkeley and the poetic incorporation of the reprocessed and altered mash-up of the two letters into a single, phantom text that exists only in this form:

> Strange prophecies anew! She wrote – "The key is in the window, the key is in the sunlight at the window – I have the key – Get married Allen don't take drugs – the key is in the bars, in the sunlight in the window.
>
>   Love,
>   your mother"
>   which is Naomi –

---

31 Naomi Ginsberg to Allen Ginsberg (n.d.), postmarked 11 June 1956; Schumacher, ed., *Family Business*, 50.

32 Naomi Ginsberg to Eugene Ginsberg, 1956. Allen Ginsberg Papers, Columbia University. Cited in Weine, *Best Minds*, 10. A letter dated the same day from his brother, Eugene, called it "the smallest funeral on record": "After a brief prayer by the functionary, who could not give 'Kaddish' because a quorum of ten males was not present (a 'minyan') … the casket was lowered, and as Lou said, Naomi (mother) was 'let down' for the last time. So ended a somewhat pathetic life" (11 June 1956, Schumacher, ed., *Family Business*, 51). Had Allen attended there would still not have been the requisite number for Kaddish.

Determined by maternal, Jewish, communist history and origin in the time of the Holocaust and of Stalin, "Kaddish" continued the project of "Howl", staging a homecoming from a distance, the angelic, queer poet-son's reverse-annunciation.[33] The poem's dateline is "Paris, December 1957–New York, 1959". Taking its place at the centre of Ginsberg's oeuvre, "Kaddish" is chief among the formal elegies and elegiac poems through which he asserted his place in the homographic "fold of the universe where Whitman was / and Blake and Shelley saw Milton dwelling as in a starry temple", "fellow travellers" and "beloved brothers of an unknown moon": "My immortality".[34] The son-elegist of "Kaddish" is a flâneur in the ruins, post-"Howl" and motherless:

> Dreaming back thru life, Your time – and mine accelerating toward Apocalypse,
>
> the final moment – the flower burning in the Day – and what comes after,
>
> looking back on the mind itself that saw an American city
>
> a flash away, and the great dream of Me or China, or you and a phantom
>
>   Russia, or a crumpled bed that never existed –
>
> like a poem in the dark – escaped back to Oblivion –
>
> No more to say, and nothing to weep for but the Beings in the Dream,
>
> trapped in its disappearance,[35]

In the opening lines of "Kaddish", Ginsberg exchanges the cascading "I saw" of "Howl" for the continuous epic present in which apocalypse as event and atmosphere encompassing all human and cosmic time coincides with processual *poesis*:

> Strange now to think of you, gone without corsets & eyes, while I walk on
>
> the sunny pavement of Greenwich Village.
>
> Downtown Manhattan, clear winter noon, and I've been up all night, talking,
>
> Talking, reading the Kaddish aloud [...][36]

---

33 For an illuminating reading of the "omnipresen[ce]" of the Holocaust in both Naomi's terrors and Ginsberg's elegy, see Scott Herring, "'Her Brothers Dead in Riverside or Russia': 'Kaddish' and the Holocaust", *Contemporary Literature* 42 (2001), 535–56. Weine, *Best Minds*, ch. 7, writes interestingly about Ginsberg's intense interest in Fra Angelico's "Annunciation" in the period leading up to the writing of "Kaddish".

34 Allen Ginsberg, "POEM Rocket" [1957], *Collected Poems 1947–1980* (New York: Harper & Row, 1984), 164.

35 Ginsberg, "Kaddish I", *Collected Poems*, 209.

36 "Kaddish I", *Collected Poems*, 209.

Ginsberg summons the poetics of maternal orientation and disorientation as hauntology: "I go out and walk the street, look back over my shoulder [...]". The visionary, orphic child assumes his mother's paranoid orientation, imagining Naomi in his poetic power – here and gone – *fort/da*. After the anarchic trip of "Howl", "waving genitals and manuscripts", Ginsberg returns from Europe a figure of Benjaminian "melancholic progress", as Ben Lee memorably puts it, with Naomi and her son, in succession, enrolled as angels of history, "moving forward while gazing backward".[37]

Written over three years in the aftermath of Naomi's death and completed in 1959, Ginsberg's anniversary poem is framed, in part, as a fantasmatic, postponed, graveside "Kaddish"-elegy: a minionless kaddish, the work of Allen alone. As transcultural and transcontinental communion/excommunication, "Kaddish" sublimes the literal absence of the kaddish, and Allen himself, from Naomi's funeral, in the process becoming the most celebrated maternal elegy in the English language and one of the most noted elegies of the twentieth century. "Kaddish" staged a return to New York as a scene of diasporic mourning, at once apocalyptic and everyday. In the aftermath of his mother's death and the *succès de scandale* of *Howl And Other Poems* (1956), Ginsberg retraced his own and Naomi's inextricable histories with Shelley's "Adonais", the Hebrew kaddish, his own lifelong journals and the body of his errant, incarcerated mother as guides. What emerged is a transnational *visio*: a prophetic dreaming of the aftermath of the Holocaust, the Bomb, and what Ginsberg later called the "Fall of America", through the eyes of Naomi and, at second distance, her scribe, true heir, and youngest son.

Howl And Other Poems had staged what proved to be a spectacular coming out in which the radical potential of queer dissidence is broadly conceived. As DuPlessis argues, Ginsberg aligned himself with the community of "deviant Others – people in minority cultures, internal exiles for political reasons (communists, anarchists, anti-Bomb radicals), exiles for psychological reasons (the dissident/odd, psychotic, crazy or driven mad) as well as the sexual exiles and outcasts (mainly male homosexuals, also the sexually promiscuous, and others who do not enter the family economy)".[38] "Kaddish", "Howl"'s sequel and companion text, revisits this territory precisely as Gothic family romance and schizo-analysis, to tell the story of his own queer invention. If "Howl" was Ginsberg's spectacular poetic coming out, "Kaddish" narrates a crisis of *coming after* and trying not to go under: the etiology of the queer poet-heir. Ginsberg sources his own inalienable queer dissidence in what he called Naomi's "unnamed wildness", foregrounding and preserving Naomi's incurable, unbearable alterity as his true inheritance.[39] Ginsberg's iconoclastic free

---

37   Ben Lee, "'Howl' and Other Poems: Is There Old Left in These New Beats?", *American Literature* 76 (2004), 370.
38   DuPlessis, "Manhood", para 3.
39   In a letter to his father, 25 October 1957, Allen wrote: "I'm not really a Jew anymore than I am a Poet. Sure I'm both. But there is a nameless wildness – life itself – which is deeper." Cited in Barry Miles, *The Beat Hotel*, 47.

translation and appropriation of the structure and text of the mourner's kaddish, in memory of his bible-reading, Yiddish-speaking, non-conforming, incarcerated, Russian-American communist mother, angered some of the poem's early Jewish critics. Mortimer J. Cohen, in the *Jewish Exponent* for 10 November 1961, for instance, complained: "There is a kind of illegitimate use of Jewish Tradition that is exceedingly exasperating … a total absence of any spiritual quality that in the slightest way warrants the use of the word Kaddish".[40] The transvaluation of the proper meaning and use of words and cultural practices is, of course, a vital tactic of queer signification. Ginsberg's syncretic, reprocessed, durational kaddish-elegy is part of a left modern reckoning in which, as Amelia Glaser argues, "the distinctly Jewish password was passing, in a non-Jewish language, to a secular, multicultural audience".[41]

In "How *Kaddish* Happened" (1972), Ginsberg described his intention to tell "the whole secret family-self tale … in all its eccentric detail. I realised that it would seem odd to others, but family odd, that is to say, familiar."[42] Ginsberg naturalises what would seem "odd to others" as an eccentricity nonetheless proper to the family and to poetry. To himself he assigns the virtue of telling what should (not) be told, and what we now know he did not tell in his psychotherapy at the Columbia Psychiatric Institute. Naomi had died on 9 June 1956, a few days after Allen's thirtieth birthday, and just a couple of months before Ginsberg's scandalous, wildly successful career as a published poet was fully launched by Ferlinghetti's publication of *Howl And Other Poems* as number four in The Pocket Poets Series. The sensational obscenity trial which followed in 1957, and Judge Horn's favourable ruling, made Ginsberg an instant celebrity and iconic counter-cultural figure. Donald Allen's canon-making 1960 anthology, *The New American Poetry*, included both "Howl" Parts 1 and 2 and "Kaddish" I, III, IV, V. Allen's anthology notably excluded "Kaddish II", the detailed central narration of Allen's life in the vortex of Naomi's psychosis and hospitalisations, with its brief embedded tale of his first big crush on another schoolboy and, "Later a mortal avalanche, whole mountains of homosexuality, Matterhorns of cock, Grand Canyons of asshole – weight on my melancholy head –." At twelve dense pages, Part 2 is twice as long as the other five sections of the poem put together. Only nominally contained by the ritual structure of the kaddish, the copia of Part 2 forms the traumatised body of the elegy. In it the attempt to access homosexual desire and compulsion as a positive source of sublimity always returns to the inescapable phallic mother. At the level of narrative, "Kaddish II" unsparingly recalls how Allen as a child (the poem twice records his age as twelve but he was in fact fifteen, as Weine shows) tries and fails to save

---

40   Reprinted with other reviews in *The Poetry of Allen Ginsberg*, ed. Lewis Hyde (Ann Arbor: University of Michigan Press, 1984), 101.

41   Amelia M. Glaser, *Songs in Dark Times: Yiddish Poetry of Struggle from Scottsboro to Palestine* (Cambridge, MA: Harvard University Press, 2020), 248.

42   Allen and Tallman, ed., *Poetics of the New American Poetry*, 345.

Naomi, by doing her (psychotic) bidding, and then himself.[43] The poem's "release of particulars" is evidentiary and apotropaic, an epideictic catalogue of praise and blame. A pastoral tableau of the young Naomi as "holy mother", "crowned with flowers" – "O glorious muse that bore me", "O beautiful Garbo of my Karma" – finds its apotheosis in a monstrous counter-image of Naomi cursed, denatured, lobotomised: "Back! You! Naomi! Skull on you!" As "Kaddish II" draws to a close, the poem moves from "All the Horror!" of the poet's last sight of Naomi, in which both son and mother are annihilated – "'You're not Allen –' I watched her face – but she passed by me, not looking – / Opened the door to the ward, – she went thru without a glance back" – to news of her death and the arrival of her last letter: a poetically orchestrated benediction clearing the way for "Svul Avrum – Israel Abraham – myself – to sing in the wilderness toward God".[44]

In his "Note" on composition, first published as the liner notes for a 1959 Fantasy album of Ginsberg reading from "Howl" and "Kaddish", Ginsberg described his desire to

> write what I wanted to without fear, let my imagination go, open secrecy, and scribble magic lines from my real mind – sum up my life – something I wouldn't be able to show anybody, write for my own soul's ear and a few other golden ears. … Mind is shapely, Art is shapely. Meaning Mind practiced in spontaneity invents forms in its own image & gets to Last Thoughts. Loose ghosts wailing for body try to invade the bodies of living men. I hear ghostly Academics in Limbo screeching about form.[45]

We hear the echo of Whitman's homoerotic *enargia* and his claim in *Leaves of Grass* – "What I experience or portray shall go from my composition without a shred of my composition". But Ginsberg's grammatically ambiguous phrase, "open secrecy", and his intimation of the mirroring pleasures of coterie manuscript circulation – "my own soul's ear and a few other golden ears" – cannot ward off the "loose ghosts" seeking "to invade the bodies of living men". (*The Invasion of the Bodysnatchers* was released in 1956, the year of Naomi's death and of the publication of "Howl".) Ginsberg immediately associates the colonisation threatened by these ungendered, inhuman bodysnatchers with "academics in limbo" – disapproving authority figures like Ginsberg's Columbia professor, Lionel Trilling and, to some extent, Ginsberg's own father, Louis, a modestly successful lyric poet, Columbia graduate and homophobe. Ginsberg's fantasy of revenge on these predatory paternal ghosts – "creeps [who] wouldn't know Poetry if it came up and buggered them in broad daylight" – is offered as the corollary of his "scared love" of feminised "forms in

---

43   Weine, *Best Minds*, 43.
44   This line is glossed in Ginsberg's *Collected Poems*, 766: "Israel Abraham, equivalent to Irwin Allen, names on the author's birth certificate."
45   Allen Ginsberg, "Notes for *Howl and Other Poems*", in *Postmodern American Poetry*, ed. Paul Hoover (New York: Norton, 1994), 635.

[his] own image" pointing back to the engulfing creator-mother, "a poem in the dark – escaped back to Oblivion".[46]

As the ambivalent inheritor of his schizophrenic mother ("you knew, and I know" [Kaddish I]), Ginsberg swerves away from the rhymed lyrics of his father towards more anarchic and expansive versions of experimental masculine/queer textuality – Whitman, Blake, Shelley. But even so, Louis had instilled in both his sons a love of poetry and a desire to write it. Louis' own poetry, though cast in conventional rhyming quatrains, clearly left its mark on Allen. Take these apostrophic lines from "Special Delivery Letter to Shelley", from Louis' first book *The Everlasting Minute and Other Lyrics*:

> Walk swiftly on our greed and plunder. Heal
>> With benison of your compassion and pity
> Our malady erupting stone and steel:
>> Capsize your crystal wonder on the city!...
>
> Unleash a hurricane and send it sweeping
>> On bombers that in fens of man's soul hide
> With poison-gases. Shelley, help in keeping
>> Our century from committing suicide.
>
> Call the tornado; call the tempest! Hurl them
>> On howitzers, on tanks, on cannon all! –
> Ambush all massed artillery and whirl them,
>> Like panicky leaves, in ruin beyond recall!
>
> O Shelley, call the tempest; call the lightning;
>> O Shelley, Shelley, unkennel now the thunder
> To leap upon the menaces of frightening
>> Munition factories and plow them under![47]

Like the poetically altered, special-delivery, posthumous letter from Naomi to Allen which ends "Kaddish II", Louis' 1937 poem seems to prophesy his queer son's mainlining of Shelley's "Adonais" a generation later.[48]

---

46   Hoover, ed., *Postmodern American Poetry*, 637.

47   Louis Ginsberg, *The Everlasting Minute* (New York: Liveright, 1937), ll.21–36.

48   On 4 September 1957, Allen sent Louis a clover picked from Shelley's grave in Rome. Barry Miles, *The Beat Hotel*, 46.

3.

> Make a joy out of everything you do –
>> Naomi Ginsberg to Allen Ginsberg, 1947[49]
> I inseminate thee Universe in thine own sweet
>> asshole: Death.
>>> That's why I'm Queer
> to make Birth obsolete
>> Allen Ginsberg[50]

Like the cascading "who" of "Howl I", the six sections of "Kaddish" ("Proem", "Narrative", "Hymmnn & Lament", "Litany & Fugue") stage an allegory of the fraught, intimate mother–son relation through the grammar and rhetoric of anaphora and deixis; orientation and relation: "toward", "done with", "no more" ("Kaddish I"), "by" ("Kaddish II"), "in the [x] blessed be" ("Hymmnn"), "only to have" ("Kaddish III"), "O mother / farewell / with your …", ("Kaddish IV") and "Caw caw", "Lord Lord" ("Kaddish V"). The poem's maternal tropism – "I walk toward the Lower East Side / – where you walked fifty years ago, little girl – from Russia, eating the / first poisonous tomatoes of America" – is concentrated in Allen's repurposing of Naomi's figuration of the key in the window. In the coda of "Kaddish II", with news of Naomi's death and the arrival of her posthumous letter of maternal advice, Ginsberg lays Naomi's ghost, figuratively reburying his mother in the belated, immemorial present tense of "Kaddish". The poetically altered posthumous maternal intertext reaches its destination as twice-mediated, co-authored inclusion at the centre of the son's crypt-elegy, "my own as hers" ("Kaddish V"):

> Strange prophecies anew! She wrote – "The key is in the window, the key is in the sunlight at the window – I have the key – Get married Allen don't take drugs – the key is in the bars, in the sunlight in the window.
>> Love,
>>> your mother"
>>> which is Naomi – [51]

Replacing her, the embedded, rescripted letter, foreshadowed in "Kaddish I" ("Toward the Key in the window") and appearing in both "Kaddish II" and "Kaddish III", offers an affective and aesthetic condensation of the work of

---

49   Naomi Ginsberg to Allen Ginsberg, [Fall] 1947, Allen Ginsberg Papers, Columbia University. Cited in Weine, *Best Minds*, 55.
50   Allen Ginsberg. *Journals. Early Fifties Early Sixties*, ed. Gordon Ball (New York: Grove Press, 1977), 145.
51   "Kaddish II", *Collected Poems*, 224.

mourning and the work of poetry, secreted within the son's elegy as radiant open secret.

Ginsberg's incantation of Naomi's life as communist activist and incarcerated, lobotomised madwoman, forms the ground of "Kaddish" as cyclical, melancholic perseveration. Naomi is before and after "the flash of existence", "beginningless and endless": "Forever. And we're bound for that, Forever – like Emily Dickinson's horses – headed to the End".[52] The erotic, cosmopolitan camaraderie of angel-headed hipsters that suffused "Howl" may seem all but extinguished in "Kaddish" by the spectre of "the Naomi" as another zombified, child-eating Moloch, at once dead and alive: "Naomi underneath this grass my halflife and my own as hers caw caw my eye be buried in the same Ground where I stand".[53] In the final graveside section of the poem, however, the return to Whitman and *Leaves of Grass*, although buried, is unmistakeable. Ginsberg consigns his own backward glance – the panoptic, maternised eye of "Kaddish" – to the grave, along with Naomi's remains, conjuring in its place an unstable queer echo on the border of the inhuman: "Lord Lord Lord caw caw caw Lord Lord Lord caw caw caw Lord".[54] Naomi laid, inlaid: half-life, half-rhyme; Mother as poisoned and life-giving pharmakon; the poem as part-object, half-mad; the poet-son as "fag attendant".[55] Ginsberg brings his queerly optimistic kaddish-elegy – singular work-product, magnificent workaround – "home", graveside, on Long Island: Whitman's birthplace.

Bibliography

Berlant, Lauren. *Cruel Optimism*. Durham, NC: Duke University Press, 2011.

Black, Joel E. "Ferlinghetti on Trial: The Howl Court Case and Juvenile Delinquency." *Boom* 27, no.4 (2012): 27–42.

DuPlessis, Rachel Blau. "Manhood and its Poetic Projects." *Jacket* 31 (October 2006), para 20. Online, http://jacketmagazine.com/31/duplessis-manhood.html.

Edelman, Lee. *No Future: Queer Theory and the Death Drive*. Durham, NC: Duke University Press, 2004.

Ferlinghetti, Lawrence. "Introduction: 'Howl' at the frontiers", in *Howl on Trial: the Battle For Free Expression*, xi– xiv. San Francisco: City Lights Books, 2006.

Hartman, Anne. "Confessional Counterpublics in Frank O'Hara and Allen Ginsberg." *JML* 28, no.4 (2005): 41.

Ginsberg, Allen. *The Book of Martyrdom and Artifice: First Journals and Poems,1937–1952*. Eds. Juanita Liebermann-Plimpton and Bill Morgan. Cambridge, MA: Da Capo, 2006.

Ginsberg, Allen. *Collected Poems 1947–1980*. New York: Harper & Row, 1984.

Ginsberg, Allen. *Journals. Early Fifties Early Sixties*. Ed. Gordon Ball. New York: Grove Press, 1977.

---

52   "Kaddish I", *Collected Poems*, 211.
53   "Kaddish II", *Collected Poems* 224; "Kaddish V", *Collected Poems*, 227.
54   "Kaddish V", *Collected Poems*, 227.
55   "Kaddish II", *Collected Poems*, 215.

Ginsberg, Louis. *The Everlasting Minute*. New York: Liveright, 1937.

Ginsberg, Allen, and Louis Ginsberg, *Family Business: Selected Letters between a Father and Son*. Ed. Michael Schumacher. New York: Bloomsbury, 2002.

Ginsberg, Allen. *Howl And Other Poems*. San Francisco: City Lights Books, 1956.

Ginsberg, Allen. "Notes for Howl and Other Poems". In *Postmodern American Poetry*. Ed. Paul Hoover. New York: Norton, 1994, 635–7.

Ginsberg, Allen. "Notes for *Howl And Other Poems*" [1959]. In *The Poetics of the New American Poetry* Ed. Donald M. Allen and Warren Tallman. New York: Grove Press, 1973, 318–21.

Glaser, Amelia M. *Songs in Dark Times: Yiddish Poetry of Struggle from Scottsboro to Palestine*. Cambridge, MA: Harvard University Press, 2020.

Herring, Scott. "'Her Brothers Dead in Riverside or Russia': 'Kaddish' and the Holocaust". *Contemporary Literature* 42 (2001): 535–56.

Hyde, Lewis, ed. *The Poetry of Allen Ginsberg*. University of Michigan Press, 1984.

Lee, Ben. "'Howl' and Other Poems: Is There Old Left in These New Beats?" *American Literature* 76, no.2 (2004): 367–89.

Macherey, Pierre, and Audrey Wasser. "The Literary Thing". *Diacritics* 37, no.4 (Winter 2007): 21–31.

Miles, Barry. *The Beat Hotel: Ginsberg, Burroughs, and Corso in Paris, 1957–1963*. New York: Grove Press, 2000.

Perloff, Marjorie. "A Lion in Our Living Room: Reading Allen Ginsberg in the Eighties." In *Poetic License. Essays on Modernist and Postmodernist Lyric*. Evanston, IL: Northwestern University Press, 1990, 199–230.

Schumacher, Michael. *Dharma Lion: A Biography of Allen Ginsberg*. Minneapolis: University of Minnesota Press, 2016.

Sedgwick, Eve Kosofsky. "Paranoid Reading and Reparative Reading, Or, You're So Paranoid, You Probably Think This Introduction is About You." In *Touching Feeling: Affect, Pedagogy, Performativity*. Durham, NC: Duke University Press, 2003, 123–51.

Snediker, Michael. "Queer Optimism." *Postmodern Culture* 16, no.3 (2006): 1–48.

Snediker, Michael. *Queer Optimism: Lyric Personhood and Other Felicitous Persuasions*. Minneapolis: University of Minnesota Press, 2008.

Weine, Stevan M. *Best Minds: How Allen Ginsberg Made Revolutionary Poetry from Madness*. New York: Fordham University Press, 2023.

18

Teaching Interpretation: The "Genuine Sense" in Bruce Gardiner's Lectures

Marc Mierowsky

In a lecture titled "What is Interpretation?", Bruce begins with "Religio Laici" (1682) and "The Hind and the Panther" (1687), a pair of John Dryden's poems that to his mind best disclose what is at stake in this question.[1] "Religio Laici" was Dryden's first attempt in verse to define interpretation. The poem's task was set in motion by Richard Simon, whose work tracing the corruptions that entered the Old Testament during its transmission and translation prompted Dryden to find a way of reading that acknowledged these corruptions but read across and above them. Behind Dryden's method was a confidence that "truth by its own sinews will prevail".[2] Following his conversion to Catholicism in 1685, Dryden was forced to revise this method radically, which he did in "The Hind and the Panther". With characteristic range, Bruce draws from Dryden's awareness of the textual variations, revisions, redactions and gaps in the transmission of the Bible – not least the poet's change in relation to this transmission pre- and post his conversion – a mode of reading that is appreciative of the chaos of a text's composition, decomposition and afterlife.

My initial aim for this chapter was to respond to the critical history Bruce sets out in "What is Interpretation?". I struggled to navigate the breadth and concentration Bruce balances. And so instead I offer a partial response. My hope is that it nonetheless captures in some small way what it was like to be taught by Bruce: the intimidation that comes from exposure to the chaos of the text and its endless expanse of intertextual connections, but also the excitement and energy produced as Bruce guides us through the chaos, giving students the vantage to see where a text's part might fit into wider literary, intellectual and social wholes.

---

1 Bruce Gardiner, "What is Interpretation?" Lecture notes supplied by the author. Future page references are to this lecture, and will be cited parenthetically by page number.

2 John Dryden, "Religio Laici", in *Dryden: Selected Poems*, ed. Paul Hammond and David Hopkins (Abingdon: Routledge, 2012), 253. All subsequent references are to this edition and cited in parentheses in the text by page number or poem line number.

Bruce begins the lecture when Dryden, still an Anglican, is seeking out a way that he and other English gentlemen might read the Bible for themselves. To Catholics who assert that the "right to interpret" lies with their Church alone, the poet answers:

The book's a common largess to mankind,

Not more for them than every man designed;

The welcome news is in the letter found;

The carrier's not commissioned to expound.

It speaks itself, and what it does contain,

In all things needful to be known is plain. (II.364–69)

Dryden's vision of the Bible does not only reject Catholicism, which requires its adherents to submit to the absolute authority of the priestly interpreter. It also rejects non-conforming varieties of Protestantism, in which unchecked personal interpretations flaunt the suggestion of external authority by their very nature. In Dryden's mind, extending latitude to this extent cannot help but foment political upheaval. "Needful" sets the limits to Dryden's middle way. The Bible makes plain what its readers *need* to know and leaves obscure those aspects of revelation beyond earthly requirement or comprehension at the moment of reading. For Dryden, the Bible is "Neither so rich a treasure to forgo", nor do its proper readers "proudly seek beyond our power to know" (II.429–30). He does not resign the text to the hands of the priests, but nor does he allow its largesse to be spread equally.

In place of the absolutism of Catholic interpretive doctrine or the radically democratic reading practice of Nonconformists, Dryden seeks a hierarchy of readerly merit. Those like the learned friend to whom he showed "Religio Laici" before publishing it know more and so interpret better. These men – and for Dryden they are all men – are fashioned by nature as teachers:

The few by nature formed, with learning fraught,

Born to instruct, as others to be taught

Must study well the sacred page, and see

Which doctrine, this, or that, does best agree

With the whole tenor of the work divine,

And plainliest points to heaven's revealed design;

Which exposition flows from genuine sense,

And which is forced by wit and eloquence. (II.326–33)

The learning these elite readers carry gives them the scope to see where the part touches the whole. They can find the plainest path to this point by cutting away interpretations based on "genuine sense" from those adulterated by self-satisfied verbal and intellectual display.

Dryden's emphasis on textual criticism as a means to find the truth marks a shift away from sacerdotal authority and towards the kind of authority established by the humanist teacher. By distilling centuries-long hermeneutic battles into sets of heroic couplets, Dryden holds them up as sententiae. The simultaneous reach and compactness of the couplets displays his learning, brandishing his pedagogic authority. In the tradition of humanist education, sententiae are also the basis for further thought and instruction. At once plain and gnomic, they convey a lesson but also stimulate further discussion and debate.[3] With them, the poem becomes by its own criteria a suitable vehicle to interpret and teach Biblical interpretation.

It is in the poet's approach to the nature of sense that his humanism meets the intellectual method proffered by the New Science. As an early, if inactive, member of the Royal Society, Dryden would have understood "sense" as both the means and product of perception; the sensed data upon which one reasons and the resulting sense of the object perceived.[4] But the poem keys into a further sense of sense. In "Religio Laici", the term appears six times, three of them modified (as "human sense" in two cases or "genuine sense" here). As Dryden uses and repeats these collocations, "sense" comes to invoke that smoke of the Godhead that is given off by the text of the Bible; that stokes reasoning but cannot be contained by it; the full heat of which the reader intuits but understands only partially.

The modification that "human" performs keeps the Promethean promise of this sense in check. We can only grasp God in the world and the word by invoking the "Infinite", a term that Dryden concedes acknowledges one's inability to fully comprehend God's magnificence. Putting "genuine" before sense registers its limits and requirements and transmutes them so that they set the standard for textual interpretation. As such, a "genuine sense" possesses empirical protocols and rests on a body of established learning. Above all it is aware that fidelity to the text and a clear reckoning of the outer limits of human reach mark the point, in Alexander Pope's phrase, "where sense and dullness meet".[5]

Dryden's "genuine sense" is a good starting point for describing the experience of being taught by Bruce. In the lecture and in the way Bruce models and teaches criticism, the genuine comes to define a habit of noticing that is precisely attuned to the poem, aware of the history of its composition and transmission, and alert to all manner of possible precursors and intertextual interlocutors. In a lecture that shows a poet thinking through how the limits to this sense might be reached and pushed and then revising them in precisely the way he first thought they could not

---

3   My account of humanist teaching follows Jeff Dolven, *Scenes of Instruction in Renaissance Romance* (Chicago, IL: Chicago University Press, 2007).

4   James Anderson Winn, *John Dryden and His World* (New Haven, CT: Yale University Press, 1987), 129.

5   Alexander Pope, "Essay on Criticism", in *The Poems of Alexander Pope: A One Volume Edition of the Twickenham Pope*, ed. John Butt (Abingdon: Routledge, 1996), I.51.

be revised, Bruce leaves his students forever changed by their awareness that the text before us might not be fully comprehensible at that moment, if ever. Despite this there is no doubt in the manner Bruce teaches that our interpretations remain important. In Bruce's care and precision we find that there are ways to touch the intellectual, aesthetic and social firmament of the text that can radically shift and expand our sense of our sense.

There is a communitarian aspect to this approach, an acknowledgement that interpretation is a transhistorical enterprise, and, as such, no one interpreter or interpretation can be all encompassing. As the lecture unfolds, it becomes clear that each interpretive effort should be approached with even-handedness and judged on how well the terms it sets meet and amplify the terms of the text. We see this principle put into practice in the rare respect Bruce shows student essays. He treats our enthusiasms, our leaps of fancy – however sophomoric – our missteps and misreading with seriousness. Anyone who has been taught by Bruce immediately recognises the letters he wrote in response to our work, his refined hand drawing us into the community of interpreters by engaging us as if we were part of it already – and thanking us, sincerely, for our attempts. The interpretive habit imparted in these letters, as in Bruce's lectures, is formed from the kind of concentrated attention that can only be sustained if one reads and cites ecumenically – catholically, not as Dryden at first would have it, but in its original inclusive sense.

I hope this accounts for why I had such difficulty responding to the critical history Bruce's lecture traces. From Dryden, Bruce moves to Jonathan Edwards and Friedrich Schleiermacher, covering Heidegger, Hobbes, Bishop Lowth, Richard Hooker, Kant, Darwin, Freud, Walter Benjamin, Trotsky, W.E.B. Du Bois, Derrida and others along the way, stopping briefly to rout Stephen Greenblatt and the narrowness of an archaeo-historicist criticism, which seems narrower still when set against the expansive terrain Bruce traverses.

As I chafed against the edges of my reading and understanding, I found some comfort in Bruce's invocation of Jonathan Edwards' *A Divine and Supernatural Light* (1733). Pushing against his Puritan background and its emphasis on the gradual preparation for conversion, Edwards makes a claim for the immediacy with which God imparts spiritual knowledge. For Edwards, this knowledge is so present in the text that "persons with an ordinary degree of knowledge are capable" of being "taught by the Spirit of God, as well as learned men". The distinction Dryden insisted upon between those "Born to instruct" and those to be "taught" collapses in Edwards' sermon. In Bruce's account, this parity points to a theory of reading that "lifts us beyond our peculiar limitations into an intersubjective, supra-subjective realm in which language releases us from our selves" (2).

The notion that reading offers a sense of communion clarifies why so much anxiety has surrounded the act. Historically, interpretation was not simply the basis for confessional politics but civic life. Those who controlled access to the world of the text and its hermeneutic processes exerted a clear influence on how societies were organised, how communities were formed, how hierarchies were assembled or challenged. I was introduced to this idea in Bruce's lectures and it has shaped my work on the literary histories of sovereignty, immigration and statecraft ever since. As with all of Bruce's lectures – at least as I experienced them – the idea that interpretation has civic and spiritual aspects closely linked to its critical methods worked its way on me over time.

The point where interpretation meets the world beyond the page, like the perdurable effects of Bruce's pedagogy, is captured by the way reading moves us beyond ourselves in Edwards' interpretive theology. At the moment of release we gain perspective, clocking both the potential range and exacting demands of the task, its importance and the modest part we play. We thrill to the smallest details and the connections such details open up. These connections take in the non-literary aspects of language, its communicative and organisational functions. (A.E. Housman reminds us that "Poems very seldom consist of poetry and nothing else".[6]) They also span outwards to a textual world not limited by known channels of influence or scholarship.

As a guide Bruce offers a mode of literary interpretation that echoes both Richard Simon's interpretation of the Bible and Darwin's interpretation of the book of nature. Bruce urges us to interpret literary texts as a "radically confused and partial stratigraphy, a writing in layers, each of which, extant and lost, reaches beyond itself into other texts in which it is subject to very different confusions and metamorphoses" (5–6). In seminars Bruce carried a stratigraphic map on A3 paper, held down by a can of Diet Coke. He showed us that the good interpreter is a geologist not a miner, an observer of the layers, not one who bores through them looking for that single vein of ore.

Since graduating, my discussions with Bruce have often circled back to the point of origin for his history of interpretation, Biblical hermeneutics. And so here I want to return to one of the central ideas traced through his lecture: that, from the Enlightenment onwards, "the resemblance of human and divine authorship grows ever variously closer" (2). "Variously" does some heavy lifting in this maxim, hinting at the radical upheaval of thought required to apply the methods for reading the Bible to literary works. For Bruce, Dryden provides a good starting point for this history because he can be thought of as "an early English harbinger" (2) of Schleiermacher, the German theologian and textual scholar who founded the modern discipline of hermeneutics by turning its Biblical focus to all texts and modes of communication.

The sacred origins of interpretation continue to shape perceptions of literature and its status, as they do the authority of the critic and her task. In this essay I want to look at two moments in the history of interpretation, united as much by my interest as anything else, where the sacred vestiges of textual scholarship confront readers trying to negotiate the value of literature and its relation to their religious

---

6   A.E. Housman, *The Name and Nature of Poetry* (Cambridge: Cambridge University Press, 1933), 55.

identity. The first occurs after Dryden's conversion when his search for the original text leads him and other Christian Hebraists to confront a Hebrew-speaking God, whose Rabbinic interpreters they attempt to supplant. The second occurs when an early generation of Jewish critics naturalised to the republic of American letters began to reclaim the value of this Rabbinic gestalt for the discipline of English literary studies. I have none of Bruce's range, but these two layers raise interesting questions about transmission and tradition, the ethos of the critic, and the social place of interpretation. My intent in considering them is to find by Bruce's light a way to read that resists the neatness of any one system, the limits of a single context, and (not so implicitly) the drive to specialisation that marks the teaching and practice of interpretation today.

Literature and the Layman's Faith

Canvassing the errors made "Both in the copier's and translator's trade" (I.249), Dryden cannot see how any religion can stake its authority on a unique capacity to possess and interpret the original Biblical text. In "Religio Laici", this misguided belief in textual fidelity applies equally to "Jewish" and "Popish" interests, to the "rabbins' old sophisticated ware" – the arcane rigours of Talmudic exegesis that "make algebra a sport" – and to the "country curates" who without any knowledge of Hebrew "make most learn'd quotations" (ll.237–43). Any interest in the purity of text is folly; and a disturbing folly at that, because this interest sets itself against the central insight of Dryden's Anglicanism: that each person's interpretive ability is sufficient for their salvation. Dryden is confident that it is both "safe" and "modest" to say

God would not leave mankind without a way,

And that the scriptures, though not everywhere

Free from corruption, or entire, or clear,

Are uncorrupt, sufficient, clear, entire

In all things which our needful faith require.

If others in the same glass better see,

'Tis for themselves they look, but not for me:

For my salvation must its doom receive

Not from what others, but what I believe. (II.296–304)

For Simon the corruptions found in the Biblical text are unmistakeable evidence that readers should seek guidance in "Tradition". Dryden takes the opposing position. Following Tillotson, he maintains that the Scriptures, though in parts corrupted, are sufficiently whole and plain. Dryden introduces "needful" not simply as the limit point of an Anglican *via media* but to convey the idea that this middle way is individuated. There is enough clarity in the Bible to give lay interpreters what they need according to their ability to interpret it. Each reader has enough to sustain their faith. At this stage in his thinking, Dryden holds that tradition should work to confirm individual belief and judgement, rather than determining them *a priori*.

Dryden's poem does not deny the importance of tradition. Rather, it urges readers to seek it for themselves, a process that involves cultivating communities of other readers (in person, through the national church and in print) against whose interpretations they can temper their own. The ideas of other readers do not impinge on one's faith, but form a communion encompassed by the national church. "Religio Laici" is in and of itself a community-building exercise, giving Dryden's extensive lay readership a shared point of interpretive contact. Access is crucial. It is the reason for translating the Bible into English, a justification for interpreting the Bible in verse, both of which strengthen the ties of national communion.

Poetry's immediacy and reach present a problem after Dryden's conversion to Catholicism. To Catholics the arcana of the original text are a source of clerical authority. And the poet himself questions the reverence of directly interpreting the Bible in verse. In the preface to "The Hind and the Panther", Dryden cites intense partisanship as the reason for why his earlier idea of a community of readers cannot work in practice:

> All men are engaged either on this side or that, and though conscience is the common work which is given by both, yet if a writer fall among enemies, and cannot give the marks of *their* conscience, he is knocked down before the reasons of his own are heard. (380)

Six years earlier, in the preface to "Absalom and Achitophel" (1681), Dryden vaunted the ability of verse satire to win over opponents, however gradually: "There is a sweetness in good verse that tickles while it hurts; and no man can be heartily angry with him who pleases him against his will" (156). Read against this, the preface to "The Hind and the Panther" shows Dryden's loss of confidence in the suasive capacity of verse. In the account of the poem that follows, this loss of confidence leads Dryden to separate the poem's aesthetic and argumentative aspects. Because the first part of "The Hind and the Panther" consists in "general characters and narration" the poet feels comfortable giving it "the turn of heroic poesy". Because the second part "concerns church authority" Dryden is obliged to make it "as plain and perspicuous" as possible, subordinating aesthetic considerations to argumentative clarity. The third part is a familiar "conversation". It works on a personal level at justifying and so encouraging a conversion to Catholicism, a task that transcends the heroic and the poetic. In concert the poem's three parts stage and vindicate a reversal in the poet's interpretive practices –

one that requires Dryden maintain more separation between poetic beauty and religious polemic than he had in "Religio Laici".

The poem takes the form of a beast fable, with the Panther standing for the Anglican Church, the Hind the Catholic Church, and the varieties of non-conforming Protestantisms represented by a host of other animals. When the Hind and the Panther speak to each other in the poem's final part they also speak in fables: the Panther uses the fable of the Swallows to depict the internecine squabbles of English Catholics (though she does so in a way that ends up representing English Catholicism more positively than she would like). The Hind responds with the fable of the Pigeons and the Buzzard (Anglican cleric Gilbert Burnet), which depicts the dangers of the clergy opposing the authority of the Catholic King James II. The embedding of fables within fables gives the poem a Midrashic tenor. The tales encode their own interpretation, as does the poem. Contra "Religio Laici", it is less a vehicle for a particular reading of the Bible than an allegorised depiction of reading itself. The figure of the Hind renders simplicity, humility and grace the virtues of a particularly Catholic mode of interpretation. These values are absent in the Panther who, at the poem's close, shows that those who claim they are most open – most susceptible to reason and good sense – are in fact the least receptive of readers. Hearing the Hind's tale, the Panther sighs into "affected yawnings" (III.1291) before settling herself into the complacent sleep of the satisfied status quo.

The interpretive virtues of the Hind are a product of her faith in tradition. No longer a body against which to confirm individual sense, the idea of tradition revised in the poem is one transmitted via the hierarchy of the Church to the lay reader. The Panther acknowledges apostolic tradition but tests it against scripture. The Hind, on the other hand, interprets scripture according to tradition, stressing that the lack of an external point of authority is not simply the source for sectarian disputes within Protestantism but the source of England's political and civic divisions.

In "Religio Laici", such slavish adherence to tradition smacks of a "Popish" or even "Jewish" obsession with originality. In "The Hind and the Panther", Dryden had to untie this knot. He had to find a way to endorse a tradition authorised by its primacy – its claim to possess the original interpretation of the text – when doing so meant invoking the spectre of a Hebrew-speaking God and the Hebrew readers of his first books. To an extent this question is glossed over as the poem conveys an uncontroversial supercessionist view of the Testaments. "The Hind and the Panther" skirts the fact that in conversion Dryden embraced a more expansive Hebrew Bible, one that included the so-called apocryphal or deuterocanonical books. The poem is able to do so because the idea of tradition to emerge from the Hind's appeal is something akin to common law, but with a selective view of common law's capacity for additions and revision. The poem presents an unwavering belief in the security offered by a body of interpretation that is complete and stretches further back than any (Christian) body. This body can compensate for any gaps, corruptions or difficulties that arise with the translation of the original Biblical text. For Dryden and his new-found co-religionists there is divinity in the passing on of tradition. To challenge its authority (or even to subordinate it to individual judgement) is to make a rival claim upon that divinity and so raise man to the level of God.

Dryden may have abrogated the poet's ultimate authority as an interpreter. Yet in order to justify his conversion (in verse) he had to return to, and offer new definitions for, two crucial terms: "sense" and "needful". As we saw, the first established the value of poetry as a medium for practising and disseminating Biblical hermeneutics by virtue of its capacity to bring the full range of man's ken and experience to the text. The second set the individuated limits to that range. In "The Hind and the Panther", human sense is "imperfect" (I.ll.83), more likely to lead to doubt than knowledge. In a series of triplets Dryden yokes together the reliance on individual sense in interpretation with the indulgence of the senses, positioning both as the root cause for England's moral decline:

Confessions, fasts, and penance set aside:

Oh with what ease we follow such a guide,

Where souls are starved, and senses gratified!

Where marriage pleasures midnight prayer supply,

And matin bells (a melancholy cry)

Are tuned to merrier notes: "increase and multiply".

Religion shows a rosy-coloured face,

Not hattered out with drudging works of grace;

A downhill reformation rolls apace. (I.II.364–72)

The personal preference guided by individual sense (to say nothing of sensuality or sensuousness) eases traditional moral strictures, setting aside clerical celibacy, confession, fasting and penance. In the end, works of grace are themselves set aside, as more and more people follow the Calvinistic tenet that salvation is bestowed by God and cannot be altered by man's actions to its logical but heretical conclusion that one need not do good works at all.

When the poet reaches the predetermined point where the argumentative style supplants the poetic, he finds himself less and less able to contain his argument within the bounds of the heroic couplet. Having signalled in the preface that poetry is an imperfect medium for debating the nature of Church authority because it is too concerned with beauty and the gratification of the senses, Part II renders such excess and incapacity at the level of the line. In this part Dryden increasingly relies on triplets. According to Christopher Ricks, Dryden's triplets act as formal breaking points.[7] When the verse spills into a third line in "The Hind and the Panther" it

---

7   Christopher Ricks, "Dryden's Triplets", in *The Cambridge Companion to John Dryden*, ed. Steven N. Zwicker (Cambridge: Cambridge University Press, 2004), 92–110.

constitutes both a break and a reformation (or counter reformation). Each triplet girds the poem against the weakening of the consubstantial trinity at the same time as it exposes the sensual excesses and formal weakness of heroic poetry.

Dryden is, however, unable to dismiss sense entirely. The previous range he accorded the concept meant that doing so would be to deny something at the core of humanity. Instead, he reworks sense (not entirely convincingly), giving it a new adjective that contains it within the bounds of apostolic tradition:

But what th' apostles their successors taught,

They to the next, from them to us is brought,

Th' undoubted sense which is in scripture sought. (II.II.361–3)

In "Religio Laici", the natural teachers are those gifted with insight and dedicated to reading as widely as possible. In "The Hind and the Panther", the role of teaching is itself transmitted. The "sense" of the best readers (and by this virtue, teachers) is no longer preternaturally heightened, but simply received. It is this notion of transmission that the poem conveys in its allegory of reading: demonstrating and so passing to the next generation of readers what it is to be guided by a body of received wisdom, arbitrated by the Catholic Church. To inculcate this habit Dryden has to undo the idea of "needful" that previously gave lay readers their interpretive purview. Again, he does so through a triplet, showing that any Church that authorises the error-prone work of lay interpreters in effect sacralises common man to the point of heresy:

All who err are justly laid aside:

Because a trust so sacred to confer

Shows want of such a sure interpreter

And how can he be needful who can err? (II.II.475–8)

The view of interpretive tradition is one that brooks no challenge. This is not the dissensus and argument by which Rabbinic law is conveyed, where interpretation and counterinterpretation build to form a body of oral law accessible to all who are literate. It is a view that denies the lay interpreter, and sees the pleasure of poetry as a liability, not something that can tap into parts of the world, mind and soul that cannot be broached by reason alone.

The cleverness and the paradox of "The Hind and the Panther" is that the allegorical and metaphorical aspects of verse – those that rely on something beyond Dryden's understanding of the rational – inculcate a mode of reading that is in the first place deeply uncomfortable with the pleasure poetry produces and in the second remains sceptical whether this pleasure can play a productive role in interpretive disputes. Dryden's efforts to separate poetic and religious authority show a poet trying to arrest a process he helped set in motion: one where the interpretations of laymen issue in works that bring human and divine authorship dangerously close together.

Anglican Bishop and Oxford Professor of Poetry Robert Lowth (1710–1787) was similarly exercised by the potential conflation of divine works and human analysis. His particular concern was with the poetry of the Hebrew Bible. We saw that as an Anglican, Dryden dismissed the search for Hebrew originality as a form of primitivism; and as a Catholic, he unquestioningly accepted the interpretation of sacred Hebrew verse provided by the Church Fathers. This is perhaps why he was increasingly discomfited by poetry's capacity to speak to the senses and ignite the passions that inflamed them. An inflammatory satirist for most of his career, he had formerly drawn on this capacity to alter the consciences of his readers.

Lowth's *Lectures on the Sacred Poetry of the Hebrews* (1753) offer a way to interpret the constitutionally transformative aspect of poetry by seeking a form of analysis that allows precisely what the later Dryden sought to prevent: the application of humane literary analysis to works of divine authorship. In this pursuit Lowth reads Hebrew poetry as the Biblical Hebrews had – in the original – while subjecting it to methods derived from the analysis of Greek and Roman poetry. This has the effect of acknowledging the divine authorship of Biblical Hebrew verse while wresting the tools for understanding it from the hands of Rabbinic interpreters.

Lowth's lectures are too extensive to cover in any detail here. There is, however, a moment in lecture fourteen that speaks directly to Dryden's anxieties. Throughout the lectures, Lowth characterises Hebrew verse style as "parabolic", a word he derives from the Hebrew *mashal* [משל], to mean a combination of aphoristic, metaphorical and sublime. In lecture fourteen, when discussing the sublime, Lowth makes an indirect case for why poetry can convey divine authority:

> The language of reason is cool, temperate, rather humble than elevated, well arranged and perspicuous, with an evident care and anxiety lest any thing should escape which might appear perplexed or obscure. The language of the passions is totally different: the conceptions burst out in a turbid stream, expressive in a manner of the internal conflict; the more vehement break out in hasty confusion; they catch (without search or study) whatever is impetuous, vivid, or energetic. In a word, reason speaks literally, the passions poetically.

That poetic expression is driven by the passions is not necessarily a bad thing, for

> [t]he mind, with whatever passion it be agitated, remains fixed upon the object that excited it; and while it is earnest to display it, is not satisfied with a plain and exact description, but adopts one agreeable to its own sensations, splendid or gloomy, jocund or unpleasant. For the passions are naturally inclined to amplification; they wonderfully magnify and exaggerate whatever dwells upon the mind, and labour

to express it in animated, bold, and magnificent terms. This they commonly effect by two different methods; partly by illustrating the subject with splendid imagery, and partly by employing new and extraordinary forms of expression which are indeed possessed of great force and efficacy in this respect especially, that they in some degree imitate or represent the present habit and state of the soul.[8]

Hebrew poetry is at once aphoristic and exhibits, according to Lowth, a mimetic tendency, deploying imagery of the natural world and life of the common folk that though splendid is also accessible and routine. Its power derives from the force by which it simultaneously draws one's internal life out and the external world in – the point where the two rays meet lights the habit of perception and thereby illuminates the state of the perceiving soul. Poetry's clarity is supra-rational; it is perspicuous by other means than prose. It offers images, fables, and metaphors that encourage the kind of interpretation able to reveal aspects of the divine author and human reader that the language of reason cannot reach.

By aestheticising and Hellenising Hebrew verse according to Longinian standards, Lowth cannot help but raise the idea that human poetry, even that written by pagans, might possess a similar power and efficacy to that written by God. For the Catholic Dryden, human writing that marshals such techniques to interpret God's way in the world impinges on God's role. This poetry is a power without authority, an indulgence of the senses dangerously free of the "undoubt'd sense" of doctrine. In Lowth's view, basic literacy should prevent any categorical errors that might be caused by a literary analysis of the Bible. Even the simplest reader has to see that sacred and profane poetry are separated by style as well as substance. In the hands of this Anglican bishop, the force of verse reverts back to the "needful": sacred poetry animates the object it represents just as it does the reader – according to the amplitude of their feeling as well as the depth of their understanding.

Naturalised Citizens

Looking back on her reading life, Vivian Gornick reflects on her changing view of poet and short story writer Delmore Schwartz. Where once she admired him, on re-reading she finds his work more significant for what it stands for in the history of American Jewish literature than what it does. In Gornick's revised reading, Schwartz was only ever able to mix the "high-minded" and "vernacular in private". In the idiom of evolutionary archaeology, he is a transitional form: an intermediary step before the vernacular and high-minded developed to the point of public emergence in the novels of Saul Bellow. By Gornick's account, Schwartz was

---

8   Robert Lowth, *Lectures on the Sacred Poetry of the Hebrews*, trans. G. Gregory (London: J. Johnson, 1787), 2 vols, 1.308–9.

"hobbled by the tenderness he could neither honour nor abandon, forever unable to decide how much of his people he was willing to let the world pass judgement on". Bellow, on the other hand, wanted "neither to serve high culture nor to save the Jews from embarrassment". His driving intent was "to make the page explode with the taste of his own life: a taste that could never have made itself felt through the King's English, it required a language all its own".[9]

Gornick counts herself among the last generation of American children born to the European Jews who arrived at the turn of the twentieth century. Bellow and Schwartz come from the generation before but bear the same embarrassed angst, the same guilt produced by the same cultural dislocation that occurs when American children face their Yiddish-speaking parents. It is from this intimate perspective that Gornick distinguishes Bellow from his compatriots. Able to set aside filial pieties, he is fully naturalised without being entirely assimilated. This marks the quality of his art. Shaped by the world of his fathers, he expands the language of the new world to bring the two into relation.

The conceptual frame imposed by immigration and naturalisation captures some critical developments too. Lionel Trilling was so possessed of the King's English that he was able to make it seem natural to him. In his essays, the urbane meets the urban as he expands the social world of interpretation beyond the country club hermeticism of New Criticism. Alfred Kazin's criticism displays the same exuberant force and exhilarating release as Augie March's monologing. In the contrapuntal rhythms of Trilling and Kazin beats the same base note of insistence. These are critics, like Bellow is a novelist, "born Jewish" and "awakened into America" – an awakening that Cynthia Ozick defines by the fact that they "refuse to be refused by Western history".[10] In Ozick's account, the classic expression of this refusal comes in Bellow's eulogy for Bernard Malamud, another refusenik. Discussing the weight of a largely Protestant canon, Bellow resists its pressure:

> My own view was that in religion the Christians had lived with us, had lived in the Bible of the Jews, but when the Jews wished to live in Western history with them they were refused. As if that history was not, by now, also ours.[11]

In the generation of critics and writers who followed Trilling and Bellow, the Hebrew Bible became the basis for claiming a Jewish place in Western history. Robert Alter, Geoffrey Hartman, Harold Bloom and Cynthia Ozick were foremost among the claimants. My focus here, though, is on Ozick, who has produced a body of interpretation exquisitely sensitive to its own place because it is attuned to the

---

9   Vivian Gornick, *Unfinished Business: Notes of a Chronic Re-Reader* (Melbourne: Black Inc., 2020), 85–7.

10   Cynthia Ozick, "The Lastingness of Saul Bellow", in Cynthia Ozick, *Letters of Intent: Selected Essays*, ed. David Miller (London: Atlantic Books, 2017), 346.

11   Saul Bellow, in *Saul Bellow: Letters*, ed. Benjamin Taylor (New York: Viking Books, 2010); Ozick, "Lastingness", 346.

social and literary significance of multiple intellectual and interpretive traditions. Ozick's efforts to forge a Jewish hermeneutics for literature provide some answers to the problems raised by Dryden and raise her as his unlikely heir.

The story behind the production of the Septuagint (the Greek translation of the Hebrew Bible), first recorded in the *Letter of Aristeas to Philocrates*, is as follows. Ptolemy II, the ruler of Alexandria, decided that the Torah should be included in the collection of the city's famed library. He sent gifts to the High Priest at Jerusalem who, in exchange, sent the Pharaoh seventy-two scholars: six from each of the twelve tribes of Israel. Each scholar was locked in his own room in Alexandria and set to the task of translation. In the end, all seventy-two produced identical translations.[12] The sinews of truth prevail, but so do the bones, the flesh and all its clothes. The story accords with Dryden's initial thought that transmission and translation will not diminish the Bible's essential truth. However, contra Dryden's Anglican view, the emphasis on this improbable consistency conveys the anxiety that even minor variations in translation might affect that essential truth.

Ozick argues that if we strip this story of the sacral "it encapsulates the most up-to-date thesis concerning the nature of the Hebrew Bible: that it can, after all, be read as a unity, indivisibly, like any literary work".[13] The disputes over authorship and provenance of the various books and parts of the Bible give way in the literary approach to what Robert Alter speaks of as their "moral, psychological, political and spiritual realism". If we direct our attention to the literariness of these books, Alter writes, we open ourselves "to something that deserves to be called their authority, whether we attribute that authority solely to the power of human imagination or to a transcendent source of illumination that kindled the imagination of the writers to express itself through these particular literary means".[14] The Anglican Dryden would not have countenanced – let alone endorsed – what in Alter's hands is the endpoint of raising poetry as a venue for Biblical hermeneutics: the application of literary analysis to the Biblical text. Even Lowth, who was the first to defend a literary analysis of the Bible, was strident in his belief that the ultimate author, the mover of its literary brilliance and technical skill, was unmistakeably divine. According to Alter's argument, the confusion of man and God is justified for, regardless of its source, authority manifests in the same way. There is no difference between how human and divine authorship mark the page.

This apparent lack of difference – part of the Enlightenment's legacy as Bruce lays it out – forces a choice upon Ozick. Born long after Heine's poetry carried the Haskalah through the shtetls of Eastern Europe, Ozick and her generation did not have to choose "whether to accept cultural liberation and variety", this much is given, "but whether to fuse that freedom with the Sinaitic challenge of

---

12   *Letter of Aristeas to Philocrates*, ed. and trans. Moses Hadas (New York: Harper & Brothers, 1951).
13   Ozick, "Robert Alter's Version", in *Letters of Intent*, 271–84 (271).
14   Robert Alter, *The World of Biblical Literature* (New York: Basic Books, 1992), 204.

distinctive restraint and responsibility that the rabbis laid out".[15] At the core of this "distinctive restraint" is an insistence on distinction-making, a maintenance of the line between God and idol, lest the creator and created become confused. In Ozick's work this restraint guards against the reflux that occurs as the same modern exegetical tools that originated in the study of the Bible wash back over the Bible as if it were any other literary text. This lack of distinction is the source of Ozick's famed disagreement with Harold Bloom, and the basis for her theory of interpretation.

In 1978 Bloom and Ozick were invited to take part in "an amiable discussion of the rival claims of Judaism and the aesthetic". Bloom agreed on the condition that neither one would read from a prepared text. Bloom arrived to find that Ozick carried a hefty script that detailed the contradictions in his *The Anxiety of Influence* (1973), *Kabbalah and Criticism* (1975) and *A Map of Misreading* (1975). When asked about the evening, Bloom's response was "This splendid lady sandbagged me".[16] That evening and in print, Ozick took aim at Bloom's confusion of categories. In *A Map of Misreading* he identified himself "as a teacher of literature who prefers the morality of the Hebrew Bible to that of Homer, indeed who prefers the Bible aesthetically to Homer".[17] For Ozick, this is a false dichotomy: "there is no morality, of the kind Bloom means, in Homer. And simply to speculate whether one might prefer the Bible 'aesthetically' to Homer is itself, of course, already to have chosen the Greek way: the Jewish way, confronting Torah, does not offer such a choice."[18] To consider the Bible aesthetically is to side with Athens over Jerusalem. It is to continue the decontextualising process that Lowth initiated when he considered Hebrew verse in Greek aesthetic terms.

And so despite Bloom's professed affiliation with the Hebrew Bible, Ozick finds him standing against it. This opposition extends to the idea of transmission. The kernel of Bloom's aesthetics is the recognition that we are all "disconsolate latecomers", "envious and frustrated inheritors". In Bloom's system poets have to undo their precursor's strength. The idea of tradition that emerges is one of productive misreading, in which poets foster modes of discontinuity that allow them to confront the brilliance of previous generations. The poet as interpreter does not so much break idols as reform them in new vessels. In contrast, Jewish liturgy, as Ozick outlines, "affirms recapturing without revision the precursor's stance and strength". Indeed "'Torah' includes the meaning of *tradition* and *transmittal* together." Once mainstream Judaism rejected the Karaitic claim that the only source of law was the written and not oral, the modes of interpretation applied to the Hebrew Bible gained new freedom. Yet:

---

15 Cynthia Ozick, "Bialik's Hint", in Ozick, *Metaphor and Memory* (London: Vintage, 1991), 227.
16 Giles Harvey, "Cynthia Ozick's Long Crusade", *New York Times*, 23 June 2016.
17 Harold Bloom, *A Map of Misreading* (Oxford: Oxford University Press, 2003), 33.
18 Ozick, "Judaism and Harold Bloom", *Commentary*, 1 January 1979, 9.

interpretation never came to stand for disjunction, displacement, ebbing-out, isolation, swerving, deviation, substitution, revisionism. Transmittal signifies the carrying-over of the original strength, the primal monotheistic insight, the force of which drowns out competing power-systems. That is what is meant by the recital in the Passover Haggadah, "We ourselves went out from Egypt, and not only our ancestors," and that is what is meant by the Midrash which declares, "All generations stood together at Sinai," including present and future generations. In Jewish thought there are no latecomers.[19]

Every move that brings human and divine authorship closer together violates the Sinaitic pact. So where does this leave Ozick, who is a novelist as well as a critic? Can there be a Jewish aesthetic, a way to read the Hebrew Bible that affirms its literariness without subjecting it to the Hellenising imperative of aesthetic judgement? At stake in any answer to these questions is the project of refusal that drove critics of Ozick's generation and the one before. To put it another way, the efforts of Jewish critics to become naturalised citizens of the American republic of letters without assimilating to its predominating culture hinge on presence and presentness: to live in Western culture as Christians lived in the Hebrew Bible without forgetting that these Jewish critics stood at the foot of Sinai with all other generations before and after.

Ozick's essay on *The Book of Job* sketches an interpretive method that might fuse the Enlightenment legacy of "cultural liberation" with the call of the Rabbis for "restraint" and "responsibility". Ozick's fundamental premise is that *Job* is "timeless because its author intended it so"; "timeless the way Lear on the heath is timeless (and Lear may owe much to Job)". The author, an anonymous Hebrew poet, renders an old folktale so sublimely universal by ensuring that Job himself lacks identification. He speaks beautiful Hebrew, yet is not a Hebrew. His customs are unfamiliar and yet he is not Pagan, for the story is governed by the actions of a monotheistic God. And it is the challenge to retain belief in this God's omnibenevolence in the face of unjustifiable suffering that gives the story the aspect of universality, calling forth "a questioning so organic to our nature that no creed or philosophy can elude it".[20]

The comprehensiveness of the story allows Ozick to suggest that it possesses a kind of supervening influence over the Western literary tradition. (In Ozick's argumentative shorthand this tradition is represented by Greek and Shakespearean tragedy.) In the process of establishing *Job*'s universality or eternal presentness Ozick comes up against the same interpretive crux that faced Dryden in "Religio Laici". That is, the story does not come to us bare. The history of its composition, transmission, redaction and translation, how it came to be included in the Hebrew Bible all intrude, as do the commentaries of theologians both Jewish and Christian:

---

19 Ozick, "Judaism and Harold Bloom", 17.
20 Ozick, "The Impious Impatience of Job", in *Letters of Intent*, 237–46 (237).

Rashi, Maimonides, Saadia Gaon, Gregory, Aquinas, Calvin. There is in the third place a mass of "philological evidence" that places the story in a particular time and place, showing "intrusions from surrounding ancient cultures" that shaped it. All of this seems to militate against the book's "common largesse", requiring readers to possess specialist knowledge. Suddenly *Job* seems neither comprehensive nor easily comprehensible – the meaning of the two interlinked. The long histories of philological and theological knowledge that form the basis for any interpretation of *The Book of Job* distance the text, removing it so that it becomes "triumphantly intolerant", the rightful attitude of High Culture according to art historian Jed Perl.[21]

Ozick insists that the complex and recondite histories of translation, transmission and interpretation "will not deeply unsettle the common reader" of *Job*. To justify this position and with it the "common largesse" of the Book, she proves herself a deeply uncommon reader. Ozick canvasses the names for God used in *Job*, showing its author's preference for Pre-Israelite names over the Tetragrammaton, an observation that is "veiled" by translation. She shows how the depiction of Satan as an adversary bears Persian and Zoroastrian influences. She notes that the Book's focus on personal over collective conduct draws parts of *Job* closer to Near Eastern Wisdom literature and folk philosophy than to the other books that make up the Hebrew Bible. Such knowledge, however, proves itself somewhat superfluous when Ozick finds herself seized by precisely those "passages that violently contradict what all the world, yesterday and today, takes for ordinary wisdom".[22] The common reader, who Ozick also calls the naked reader or novice reader, might have the advantage in this regard. For it is the novice readers who "come to Job's demands and plaints unaccoutered", who "perceive God's world exactly as Job perceives it". Ozick does not so much do away with Dryden's readerly hierarchy as attempt to conflate it. Contorting herself into naivety, Ozick claims with the novices that "Job's bewilderment will be ours, and our kinship to his travail fully unveiled, only if we are willing to absent ourselves from the accretion of centuries of metaphysics, exegesis, theological polemics".[23]

Ozick's self-levelling is at first glance a fiction – like the physicist's frictionless plane. She cannot unlearn what she knows, but she can imagine what it might be to slough it off momentarily in order to perceive, with Job, the central insight of his experience. The question Job asks God: how can the deity permit injustice? and God's non answer sparks Job's realisation: "'I have uttered what I did not understand,' he acknowledges, 'things too wonderful for me, which I did not know'". His new knowledge, according to Ozick, is this: "that a transcendent God denies us a god of our own devising, a god that we would create out of our own malaise, or complaint, or desire, or hope, or imagining".[24] The voice out of the whirlwind calls

---

21   Jed Perl, *Authority and Freedom: A Defence of the Arts* (New York: Knopf, 2022), 127.
22   Ozick, "The Impious Impatience of Job", 238–9.
23   Ozick, "The Impious Impatience of Job", 240.
24   Ozick, "The Impious Impatience of Job", 246.

all readers of the Book that purports to contain this voice to remain to some degree naive, humbling themselves before the text.

The humbling that Ozick endorses and practises is a vital precondition to her interpretation. It allows her to maintain the distinction Lowth insisted upon, approaching the sacred by finding in Hebrew scripture a literary artistry equal to its divine source. Where Alter sees the words on the page to be the same, regardless of their origin, Ozick finds a grain of difference. To her the ideas expressed in *Job*:

> are inseparable from an artistry so far beyond the grasp of mind and tongue that one can hardly imagine their origin. We think of the Greek plays; we think of Shakespeare; and still that is not marvel enough. Is it that the poet is permitted to sojourn, for the poem's brief life, in the magisterial Eye of God? Or is it God who allows Himself to peer through the poet's glass, as through a gorgeously crafted kaleidoscope? The words of the poem are preternatural, unearthly. They may belong to a rhapsodic endowment so rare as to appear among mortals only once in three thousand years. Or they may belong to the Voice that hurls itself from the whirlwind.

The question suggests its answer. The tools Ozick uses to separate God and idol, the Bible and literature are literary critical. Her method is comprehensive. She is acculturated to the forms and techniques of Rabbinic knowledge, has read the works of the Church Fathers alongside Greek and Shakespearean tragedy. Above all, she takes from Torah a view in which transmission and tradition are one and the same. As with *Job*'s first readers we need comfort in the face of a comfortless book. For Ozick the mode of its transmission and history of its interpretation coalesce to place us on the plane of an eternal present, along with all readers before and after us. She concludes her essay with a declamation: "how astoundingly up-to-date they are, those ancient sages – redactors and compilers – who opened even the sacred gates of Scripture to philosophic doubt!"[25] The closest thing to shedding the centuries of interpretation and textual criticism is to have a tradition that allows for the entrance of textual and philosophic doubt. It is tradition that leaves one naked. With Job we question. Like him, we are given no clear answer from his Book save for that "primal monotheistic insight": that God is not a god of our devising.

The desire to return to a naive or naked form is in itself a quest for origins. To Ozick, this does not imply a Gnostic or Kabbalistic imperative, in which to search for origins is to establish a rival claim upon them and thus issue an antinomian challenge to the Church Fathers or the Rabbis. It is more earthly than that. It is also speculative: so much so, that Ozick offers it to us not as an essay but an "Inkling", "a First Inkling":

---

25   Ozick, "The Impious Impatience of Job", 246.

> If I were to go back – really back, to earliest consciousness – I think it would be mica. Not the prophet Micah, who tells us that our human task is to do justly, and to love mercy, and to walk humbly with our God; but that other still more humble mica – those tiny glints of isinglass that catch the sun and prickle upward from the pavement like shards of star-stuff.[26]

Mica is embedded in geologic history as well as in the pavement fashioned out of the earth. It also has, quite literally, an enlightened character; it seems lit from above. Its name is one shift of stress away from the later prophet, one whom Ozick associates with Job.

The shards spark Ozick's early memory of her childhood during the Depression, of how she wondered what it was like to be a baby, to embody the perspective of each and every animal, to speak every language on earth. It is the play of light, and sky and earth that sets her wondering: "I wondered why my shadow had a shape that was me, but nothing else; why my shadow, which was almost like a mirror, was not a mirror". She wonders why she thinks these things, feels in the sense of wonder something akin to but separate from love as she has experienced it. It is only decades later that she realises what "shone up out of the mica-eyes" when she read Wordsworth's "Prelude":

> *... those hallowed and pure motions of the sense*
> *Which seem, in their simplicity to own*
> *An intellectual charm;*
> *... those first-born affinities that fit*
> *Our new existence to existing things.*

In Ozick's mind:

> those existing things are all things, everything the mammal senses know, everything the human mind constructs (temples or equations), the unheard poetry on the hidden side of the round earth, the great thirsts where, the wanderings past wonderings.

The inkling then becomes a question:

> First inkling, bridging our new existence to existing things. Can one begin with mica in the pavement and learn the prophet Micah's meaning?[27]

---

26 Ozick, "Existing Things", in *Letters of Intent*, 247–9 (247).
27 Ozick, "Existing Things", 248.

The image of the mica is a nice complement to Bruce's view of literary texts as "a radically confused and partial stratigraphy". The glints of mica – individual, particular – shine out, revealing the layers around them. In the process they show how the layers reach into each other. As the mica is absorbed and moved it becomes, to adapt Bruce's words, "subject to very different confusions and metamorphoses". Ozick's preoccupation is with the moral force behind such metamorphoses. Her essays and inklings offer an expanded idea of interpretive origins. Not as piously circumscribed as "The Hind and the Panther", the sense she intuits is deeper than the human sense of "Religio Laici". It is mammalian. Yet she faces the same conundrum that the form and message of "Religio Laici" unwittingly set forth. As divine and human authorship move closer together, literature becomes something of a rival faith. Ozick's particular solution to the idolatrous potential of literature is a view of interpretation as a distinguishing power. This view guides her as novelist as well as critic, underwriting her belief that literature must have a redemptive power, what she calls a moral corona. To the critic this corona provides "that steady interpretive light" that allows one to make distinctions, to find where creation has purpose and where it flexes its might to the point of idolatry.

Regardless of one's moral convictions or religious creed, Ozick's work illumines what is at stake in the process of interpretation, and why it is so hard to teach. At its best it is simultaneously rigorous and wonderful. It is comprehensive and yet discriminating. It can draw out the universal and yet it is doggedly and uncompromisingly particular. The negotiation of these competing forces is, for me, where the "genuine" in Dryden's formulation meets and morphs into the generous in Bruce's teaching. As with mica and Micah, the words themselves catch the light of the eye in similar ways. Seek out their origins and both genuine and generous find root in the Latin *gignere* "to beget, produce". There is a moral scrupulousness in the detail of Bruce's lectures. But it is his willingness to engage us, the particular and individual interest he has shown our interpretations, that has shaped more than how we read. Bruce's productive generosity has shaped how many of us think. The expanded sense of interpretation traced here – one that reaches across perception, intuition, wonder, delight, doubt, submission and recognition so that it fundamentally orients our existence "to things existing" – cannot be contained by a modern university classroom. To teach it is a burden greater than the one Dryden acknowledged. Bruce has borne it and all of us collected in this volume – and countless others – are its grateful beneficiaries.

Bibliography

Alter, Robert. *The World of Biblical Literature*. New York: Basic Books, 1992.
Aristeas to Philocrates. Translated by Moses Hadas. New York: Harper and Brothers, 1951.
Bloom, Harold. *A Map of Misreading*. Oxford: Oxford University Press, 2003.
Butt, John, ed. *The Poems of Alexander Pope: A One Volume Edition of the Twickenham Pope*. Abingdon: Routledge, 1996.

Dolven, Jeff. *Scenes of Instruction in Renaissance Romance*. Chicago: Chicago University Press, 2007.

Gardiner, Bruce, *What is Interpretation?* Supplied by Author.

Gornick, Vivian. *Unfinished Business: Notes of a Chronic Re-Reader*. Melbourne: Black Inc, 2020.

Hammond, Paul, and David Hopkins, eds. *Dryden: Selected Poems*. Abingdon: Routledge, 2012.

Harvey, Giles. "Cynthia Ozick's Long Crusade," *New York Times*, 23 June 2016.

Houseman, A.E. *The Name and Nature of Poetry*. Cambridge: Cambridge University Press, 1933.

Lowth, Robert. *Lectures on the Sacred Poetry of the Hebrews*. Trans. G. Gregory. London: J. Johnson, 1787.

Ozick, Cynthia. "Judaism and Harold Bloom," *Commentary*, 1 January 1979.

Ozick, Cynthia. "The Impious Impatience of Job," in *Letters of Intent: Selected Essays*, 337–52. Ed. David Miller. London: Atlantic Books, 2017.

Ozick, Cynthia. "Bialik's Hint", in *Metaphor and Memory*, 223–39. London: Vintage, 1991.

Perl, Jed. *Authority and Freedom: A Defence of the Arts*. New York: Knopf, 2022.

Ricks, Christopher. "Dryden's Triplets". In *The Cambridge Companion to John Dryden*. Ed. Steven N. Zwicker, 92–110. Cambridge: Cambridge University Press, 2004.

Taylor, Benjamin, ed. *Saul Bellow: Letters*. New York: Viking Books, 2010.

19

The Nonsense of Knowledge: A Reading of George MacDonald's *At the Back of the North Wind*

Jessica Lim

How can we know what we have not experienced? What compels us to act on that knowledge? And what implications might those actions have? These questions of epistemology underpin the pedagogical process. It is perhaps unsurprising that there are so many approaches to the nature of pedagogy, since it encompasses questions about the nature of knowledge and the nature of humanity. Amidst such confusion of definitions – is education something given *to* a student; something a student creates; something more social than individual?[1] – it is refreshing to explore George MacDonald's visions of knowledge and pedagogy in his 1871 novel, *At the Back of the North Wind*.

In some ways it is uncontentious to search for epistemological theories in a George MacDonald novel, although it is less common to culminate such searches with an analysis of the two-hundred-and-seven-line poem in the thirteenth chapter of his first novel-length children's fairy-tale-realist narrative, as this essay will. The poem is divisive: Bruce Gardiner, as my Honours undergraduate supervisor, called it "the most marvellous nonsense poem", while Roderick McGillis, despite exploring its thematic significance, has labelled it "interminable!" and "doggerel".[2] Some critics avoid it – Melody Green, in an article on death, nonsense and poetry in *At the Back of the North Wind* and Carroll's *Alice* books, omits discussion of the poem entirely.[3] And yet the context in which the poem addresses itself to readers, its themes and its narrative significance, embody MacDonald's vision

---

1   The schools of thought referenced include behaviourism and educational constructivism, with reference to social models of development, for example, Urie Bronfenbrenner's model of human development. See "Toward an experimental ecology of human development", *American Psychologist* 32, no. 7 (July 1977): 513–31.

2   Roderick McGillis, "Language and Secret Knowledge in *At the Back of the North Wind*", Proceedings of the Seventh Annual Conference of the Children's Literature Association, ed. Priscilla Ord (1982), 120–7.

3   Melody Green, "Death and Nonsense in the Poetry of George MacDonald's *At the Back of the North Wind* and Lewis Carroll's *Alice* Books", *North Wind: A Journal of George MacDonald Studies* 30 (2011), 38–49.

of the individual and social transformation that is possible when knowledge is understood as a relational act, steeped in trust and redolent with doubts. This relational concept of knowledge underpins a nonsensical mode of pedagogy that produces and anticipates what Makoto Fujimura calls "generative thinking" – thinking that enables creativity, enables the performance of and expectation of generosity, and has impacts that extend beyond one's immediate generation.[4] In order to establish what this nonsense mode consists of, this essay examines MacDonald's sense of the fluid boundaries between knowledge, testimony and gossip, turning to ways in which MacDonald's alternative vision of pedagogy challenges the scarcity models that so often threaten our ability to think generatively.

It is evident from the beginning of *At the Back of the North Wind* that MacDonald is interested in types of knowledge and ways of knowing. The novel depicts the adventures of a young boy, Diamond, with the mysterious and supernatural North Wind. These encounters are intimately linked with Diamond's frail health, and the novel ends with his eventual death. The novel thus invokes questions of faith: are Diamond's encounters real, or are they the product of a dying boy's imagination? MacDonald therefore displaces attention from Diamond as a character to foreground the question of knowledge. In his opening paragraph the narrator declares:

> I have been asked to tell you about the back of the North Wind. An old Greek writer mentions a people who lived there, and were so comfortable that they could not bear it any longer, and drowned themselves. My story is not the same as his. I do not think Herodotus had got the right account of the place. I am going to tell you how it fared with a boy who went there.[5]

As McGillis has noted, this narrative framework is destabilising. Who has asked the narrator to tell us this story, and who *is* this narrator? McGillis concludes that the narrator has been asked "To share the secret of poetry; to experience language as creativity; to know the certainty of uncertainties",[6] and while these are compelling insights I wish here to focus on the way that MacDonald highlights the interactions between personal story, testimony and second-hand testimony (or gossip) to suggest the relational basis for much of what we consider knowledge. The narrator is seemingly, at this point, an omniscient stand-in for MacDonald himself – the author and editor of *Good Words for the Young*, the magazine in which this book was first serialised. The conversational tone implies a personal relationship, but this sentence existed in two contexts: a widely-read serialised

---

4   Makoto Fujimura, *Culture Care: Reconnecting With Beauty for our Common Life* (Lisle, IL: InterVarsity Press, 2017), 17–21.

5   George MacDonald, *At the Back of the North Wind*, ed. Roderick McGillis and John Pennington (Ontario: Broadview, 2011), 45.

6   McGillis, "Language and Secret Knowledge", 125, 127.

magazine, and a publicly printed novel. "You" is plural, addressed to a multitude. John Durham Peters' description of Christ "broadcasting" his parables seems to describe MacDonald's narrator's act; the image of the narrator sharing their story with a large group of strangers mimics Christ's decision to allow recipients of his words to become self-selecting participants in an act of interpreting testimony.[7] Of course, there is a sense in which readers (or at least, subscribers and purchasers) of *Good Words for the Young* were already self-selecting readers who valued the moral strain for which the magazine was occasionally satirised,[8] but the nature of public print as a medium suggests a casting out of words without a guarantee of being able to control the responses of every single recipient. The story proceeds, then, based on readers' responses – if we trust the narrator's integrity and intention, we will read the story as one containing truth; if we distrust the narrator for whatever reason, we will be sceptical of the story that follows. As Elizabeth Fricker has discussed, whether recipients believe second-hand information depends on how trustworthy they consider the teller to be.[9] The risk of the narrator's stance is implicitly the risk that underlies the act of sharing any testimony – knowledge can only be received as such if it is received in trust.

MacDonald is not content to leave his readers to sift through his words to determine what is wisdom and what is drivel: the narrator further destabilises the situation by revealing that this story is not even his. He forces us to consider that second-hand knowledge – that is, knowledge gained through any means other than personal experience – is necessarily based on subjective means of trust. In that opening paragraph he dismisses Herodotus and, by implication, institutions of learning that codify knowledge as objective observations and facts, as subjective anecdotes: Herodotus "mentioned" a land and did not "g[e]t the right account".[10] A more reliable source of information, the narrator suggests, is a story received from a third party: "a boy who went there". For reasons that become apparent by the end of the novel (Diamond is no longer alive to share his story), Diamond's testimony can only flourish among listeners with no connection to Diamond by the "grace of gossip".[11] That is, using Bruce Gardiner's differentiation between gossip and testimony based on the importance of the sender, readers only receive Diamond's

---

7   John Durham Peters, *Speaking into the Air: A History of the Idea of Communication* (Chicago, IL: University of Chicago Press, 1999), 52–5; Bruce Gardiner, "Christ's Parable of the Sower: Intellectual Property Rights in Gossip and Testimony", *Literature and Aesthetics* 28 (2018), 193–221.

8   See the cartoon of MacDonald as "Goody Goody" in *Once a Week*, 2 November 1872, in *North Wind*, ed. McGillis and Pennington, 329.

9   Elizabeth Fricker, "Second-Hand Knowledge", *Philosophy and Phenomenological Research* 73, no. 3 (2006): 592–618.

10   In fact, it is not even Herodotus who wrote of this account of Hyperborean suicides but Pliny the Elder, further complicating the reliability of the narrator's sources. See Pliny the Elder, *Natural History* vol. 4 of 10, trans. H. Rackham, (Cambridge, MA: Harvard University Press and London: William Heineman Ltd, 1938), section 88.

11   Gardiner, "Gossip and Testimony", 196, 218.

story from an (interchangeable) sender: we must evaluate the message and the sender, who is not the origin of the message.

Although the narrator initially seems trustworthy, he invites readers to question his claim to knowledge by revealing that he is a diegetic character in the novel. At first, the narrator seems to be a mouthpiece for MacDonald – the narrator muses that he has not yet seen Fairyland at its best and is "*going*" to see it, and he later critiques the ineffectiveness of the temperance movement in passages that clearly reflect MacDonald's attitudes.[12] Yet three chapters from the end, the narrator reveals he came to know Diamond in the last months of Diamond's life, making the narrator a figure who bridges the world of the novel and the world of the readers. In doing so, MacDonald employs a narrative technique associated with female anti-Jacobin authors from the early nineteenth century.[13] Like the women writers in Lisa Wood's study, MacDonald's narratorial "self" attempts to replicate "an instructional situation in the didactic relationship between narrator and reader".[14] But this instructional situation is fundamentally unstable: in addition to the tenuous nature of testimony-presented-as-gossip, the narrator's personal association with Diamond transforms the novel into a case of "imitation and commemoration".[15] The idea that knowledge can be a form of personal memory emphasises the affective qualities of knowing. This implicitly asserts the personal and subjective nature of knowledge.

Moreover, the narrator indicates that he has pieced his story together using the testimony of yet another one of Diamond's confidants, which suggests that knowledge is always partial and incomplete. This unseen third figure is someone with whom Diamond and the narrator have spoken, but we as readers have no contact with this third figure. When recounting Diamond's time at the back of the North Wind – the very story for which the reader has been primed – the narrator bemoans, "I have now come to the most difficult part of my story. And why? Because I do not know enough about it. […] I could know nothing about the story except Diamond had told it." He goes on to reveal that "Diamond never told these things to any one but – no, I had better not say who it was; but whoever it was told me".[16] This could be mere posturing, but in Chapter 16, the narrator again comments, "[Diamond] said this much, though not to me."[17] The narrator's apparent insistence on a mysterious third source emphasises the fact that we as readers cannot verify the identity of this third figure. We must read the account in

---

12 MacDonald, *North Wind*, 56, 167. The narrator's focus on what is ahead and unknown chime with MacDonald's insistence, "The greatest forces lie in the region of the uncomprehended" in "The Fantastic Imagination", *A Dish of Orts: Chiefly Papers on the Imagination, and on Shakespeare* (Hamburg: Tredition Classics, 1893), 226.

13 Lisa Wood, *Modes of Discipline: Women, Conservatism, and the Novel After the French Revolution* (Lewisburg, PA: Bucknell University Press, 2003), 111–14.

14 Wood, *Modes of Discipline*, 114.

15 Gardiner, "Gossip and Testimony", 218.

16 MacDonald, *North Wind*, 122, 124.

17 MacDonald, *North Wind*, 150.

trust: trusting the reliability and integrity of the narrator, whom we may already be inclined to distrust, as his omniscience has been revealed as partial knowledge based on short conversations with Diamond and an unknown speaker. We must also trust the veracity of this unidentifiable third figure, whom we may presume to be a named figure in the story, though we cannot verify this. Colin Manlove has compellingly discussed the way that doubt is embedded in the concept of faith in the novel, suggesting that Diamond's very reality depends on his trust in North Wind as a real figure and not a consequence of his illness-related dreams.[18] In addition to this, MacDonald indicates that doubt and uncertainty reside within knowledge, as what we know is communicated to us by individuals whom we can never fully know and whom we must respond to with openness and trust. In fact, North Wind explicitly comments so: when Diamond presses her to prove that she is real and not a dream, the only reasoning she can give is that Diamond loves even when she is absent, suggesting that enduring love signals what is real. When he is still uncertain as to the strength of this logic, North Wind replies, "you may be hopeful, and content not to be quite sure."[19] The instability of knowing is left unresolved as something that must be nurtured by those who choose to respond to the teller in trust.

MacDonald's visions of the instructional relationship – between narrator and reader; between Diamond and the narrator; between Diamond and North Wind herself – build on a non-rational vision of education in which the process of education, that is, pedagogy, is fundamentally relational rather than rational. This is remarkable for its time, as concepts of pedagogy in the children's literature tradition into which MacDonald published his novel frequently addressed the learners' rationality. This often involved an element of *condescension* where the knowledgeable teacher voluntarily descended to nurture inherent qualities within the learner and close the gap of experience and learning. One of the bestsellers of late-eighteenth and early nineteenth-century children's literature, Anna Letitia Barbauld was praised for "condescending" to the language and cognitive abilities of a young child.[20] Barbauld does indicate that knowledge is gained in relational contexts – the opening image of *Lessons for Children Aged Two to Three Years* (1778) places Charles on Mamma's lap – but she also insists that rationality is crucial to enable individuals to become wondering, sociable beings.[21] Meanwhile, Thomas Hughes, one of MacDonald's contemporaries, elaborated on the concept

---

18   Colin Manlove, "A Reading of *At the Back of the North Wind*", *North Wind: A Journal of George MacDonald Studies* 27 (2008): 51–78.

19   MacDonald, *North Wind*, 289–90.

20   Lady Ellenor Fenn, "Preface", *Cobwebs to Catch Flies: Or, Dialogues in Short Sentences, Adapted for Children from the Age of Three to Eight Years. In Two Volumes* (London: Printed by John Marshall, 1783), *Eighteenth Century Collections Online*, Gale Document Number CW3317078925, 1: vi.

21   Anna Letitia Barbauld, *Lessons for Children Aged Two to Three Years* (London: Printed for J. Johnson, 1778), 1; Anna Letitia Barbauld, "Hymn I", *Hymns in Prose for Children* (London: Printed for J. Johnson, 1781), 4.

of muscular Christianity, asserting, "a man's body is given him to be trained and brought into subjection and then used for the protection of the weak, the advancement of all righteous causes".[22] Hughes' focus concerns mastery over the body and the rational application of physical strength in the act of Christian service. By contrast, MacDonald establishes an instructional relationship between North Wind and Diamond that parallels the uncertainty and requirement of trust that underpins the relationship between the reader and the narrator. From their first meeting, North Wind refuses to condescend to Diamond's levels of experience and cognition (neither of which are particularly developed as Diamond is young and physically frail). She almost antagonistically berates Diamond for "closing up my window" and mocks his name as "a useless thing" without ensuring that Diamond knows that most people understand diamonds as precious stones, and few would know that Diamond is the name of his father's horse.[23] Moreover, she explicitly tells him to distrust his rational interpretation of sensory perceptions. She says Diamond must hold her hand "even when you look at me and can't see me the least like the North Wind".[24] If we relate this to principles of pragmatics, North Wind is not employing either the Cooperative Principle or even the Politeness Principle; she does not make sure her conversation is relevant and instead allows Diamond to be confused by ambiguities of words. During another encounter, she does not clarify his confusion about the difference between a boat and a poet and simply concludes, "I see it is no use. I wasn't sent to tell you, and so I can't tell you."[25] If conversational principles of cooperation and politeness are "regulative factors which ensure that once conversation is underway, it will not follow a fruitless or disruptive path",[26] one can only conclude that North Wind is comfortable with fruitlessness and disruption. To this extent, the conversations reflect the antagonistic word-play conversations that characterise Lewis Carroll's *Through the Looking-Glass*.[27] Yet, after their first encounter, and in subsequent chapters, Diamond follows, trusts and loves "My own dear North Wind".[28]

What enables the relationship between Diamond and North Wind to flourish is Diamond's obedience, borne out of his irrational, intuitive love for her. As Diamond's relationship with North Wind indicates, the deepest trust is shown when one is willing to obey another, for that means surrendering one's rational interpretation of a situation and trusting another's perception and insights. Such themes are common in MacDonald's wider oeuvre which features remarks like,

---

22 Thomas Hughes, *Tom Brown at Oxford* [1861] (London: Macmillan, 1889), 99.
23 MacDonald, *North Wind*, 48, 50–1.
24 MacDonald, *North Wind*, 54.
25 MacDonald, *North Wind*, 87.
26 Geoffrey Leech, *Principles of Pragmatics* (London and New York: Longman, 1983), 17.
27 For instance the "bough/bow" discussions or Alice and the sheep talking about different kinds of crabs/crabbing: Lewis Carroll, *Through the Looking-Glass, and What Alice Found There* (London: Macmillan, 1872), 30, 109.
28 MacDonald, *North Wind*, 290.

"Love aright, and you will come to think aright", and "Obedience is the grandest thing in the world to begin with".[29] This trust, which facilitates the gaining of non-experiential knowledge, is intuitive and non-rational since it is not based on logical reasoning or causal connections. This is a theme multiple MacDonald scholars discuss: Rebecca Thomas Ankeny explores the role of feeling in knowledge and suggests that meaning in language in MacDonald's novels is inextricably linked with the dignity of its speakers,[30] and Kirstin Jeffrey Johnson suggests that in MacDonald's novels, "academic education means little [...] unless this relational truth is apprehended".[31] Notably, such insights correspond with twenty-first century moral psychological studies: Jonathan Haidt, for instance, describes the human inclination to agree or disagree with moral propositions in terms of intuition, suggesting that logical reasoning is largely the handmaiden of affect and emotion.[32] If affect and emotion are the seat from which cognition is nurtured, then relationship is the structure enabling education. Pedagogy, in this light, becomes a reclamation of the origin of the *paedagogium* as a place of hospitality, rather than a place of theoretical knowledge-transfer or skill-training.[33]

Subsequently, MacDonald's vision of education and pedagogy explicitly challenges models of knowledge transference or skill-training. His essay "The Imagination: Its Functions and Its Culture" insists that the purpose of education is more than "the development of this and that faculty, and the depression, if not eradication, of this and that other faculty" and is instead "a noble quest [...] a ceaseless questioning of the past for the interpretation of the future, an urging on of the motions of life".[34] More than this, the *delivery* of MacDonald's vision of education is insistently relational; as Jeffrey Johnson notes, MacDonald's works share two "inextricable" threads: the insistence that identity is formed in relationship, and that individual transformation occurs as a result of relationship.[35] At the heart of education, thus, is the question of how communication in hospitable relationships can support such "ceaseless questioning". As John Durham Peters notes, communication in at least one sense concerns "imparting or partaking" and can be defined as "the project of reconciling self and other", working concurrently

---

29 MacDonald, "A Sermon" and "True Christian Ministering", *A Dish of Orts*, 210, 219.
30 Rebecca Thomas Ankeny, "Teacher and Pupil: Reading, Ethics, and Human Dignity in George MacDonald's *Mary Marston*", *Studies in Scottish Literature* 29 (1996): 227–37; Rebecca Thomas Ankeny, "The Mother Tongue: Acquiring Language and Being Human", in *Truth's Bright Embrace: Essays and Poems in Honor of Arthur O. Roberts* (Newberg, OR: George Fox University Press, 1996), 223–37.
31 Kirstin Jeffrey Johnson, "Rooted in All Its Story, More is Meant Than Meets the Ear: A Study of the Relational and Revelational Nature of George MacDonald's Mythopoeic Art" (unpublished PhD dissertation, University of St Andrews, 2011), 48.
32 Jonathan Haidt, *The Righteous Mind: Why Good People are Divided by Politics and Religion* (London: Penguin, 2013), 71–80.
33 David I. Smith, *On Christian Teaching: Practicing Faith in the Classroom* (Grand Rapids, MI: William B. Eerdmans, 2018).
34 MacDonald, *Dish of Orts*, 8.
35 Jeffrey Johnson, "Rooted in All Its Story", xxi.

with the truth that "we can never be each other".[36] In this view, communication, the mode by which education occurs, is always incomplete. This incompleteness propels continued communication, humility and unsettledness, and is inherent in a relational pedagogy. David I. Smith, in his exploration of implications of the *paedagogium* as a place of hospitality, notes that hospitality requires the host to be mindful of their own strangeness in relation to their guests. This stance enables the host to recognise that they require their guests' hospitality, too.[37] In other words, abiding together in a shared space requires a constant interplay of simultaneous, multiple identities. This dynamic model of discernment and being resists trajectories that stultify communication and relationship between individuals, for example locking a student and teacher into fixed identities.

Crucially, the basis for and nature of relationship is non-rational: Diamond trusts North Wind despite her obstructive conversations and her propensity to do things that seem cruel, like sinking a ship, suggesting the pervasiveness of nonsensical paradigms in that inescapable aspect of our lives – relationships.[38] This nonsensical paradigm differs from concepts of nonsense-as-genre, in which discussions focus on logic, language and power, and studies cluster around Lear and Carroll.[39] Although I do not share the assumption that nonsense (at least in MacDonald's hands) works quite so straightforwardly as a "mirror that inverts and reverses to subvert the 'fallen mode of thinking'",[40] critics like Adam Walker rightly note that nonsense as a mode, in the hands of writers who engage with metaphysics, is more about a way of seeing than a framework for highlighting arbitrariness in linguistic or cultural norms. For instance, *The Princess and the Goblin* lacks the puns which characterise Lewis Carroll's *Alice* books; the nonsense lies in the vindication of Princess Irene's non-rational trust in her great-great-grandmother, a woman invisible to and unknown by nearly every other character in the novel.[41] In that novel, as in *At the Back of the North Wind*, the nonsense lies in the nonsensical nature of placing one's faith in a figure who is unseen and disbelieved by most of the other characters. MacDonald's mode of nonsense thus corresponds with and anticipates the views of G.K. Chesterton or Anthony Burgess in which nonsense

---

36 Durham Peters, *Speaking into the Air*, 7, 9, 268.
37 Smith, *On Christian Teaching*, 56.
38 Diamond can never agree with North Wind that this act is justified, and North Wind's hurried response indicates her own uncertainty as to the justification for her actions; MacDonald, *North Wind*, 97.
39 See Jean-Jacques Lecercle, *Philosophy of Nonsense: The Intuitions of Victorian Nonsense Literature* (London and New York: Routledge, 1994); Eric Partridge, "The Nonsense Words of Edward Lear and Lewis Carroll", in *Here, There and Everywhere: Essays Upon Language* (London: Hamish Hamilton, 1950), 162–88; Elizabeth Sewell, *The Field of Nonsense* (London: Chatto and Windus, 1952).
40 Adam Walker, "Objects of Nonsense, Anarchy, and Order: Romantic Theology in Lewis Carroll's and George MacDonald's Nonsense Literature", *North Wind: A Journal of George MacDonald Studies* 37 (2018): 18.
41 George MacDonald, *The Princess and the Goblin* [1872] (London: Penguin, 1996).

is a "bizarre way of making sense" of the world in relation to the metaphysical.[42] Indeed, Josephine Gabelman's study of nonsense as a theological mode encapsulates MacDonald's sense of nonsense as a refusal to follow rational methods and logical sense to anticipate "[an] upside-down kingdom".[43]

Nonsense as Pedagogy: The "Wind from Behind"

It is now time to turn to the nonsense poem, which McGillis has helpfully described as the text that facilitates Diamond's transition into a poet who anticipates and communicates hope and poetry in working-class London.[44] The poem structurally transfers the reader from the world of Diamond's journeys with the mysterious North Wind into a more Dickensian London, replete with child crossing-sweeps, drunken cabmen, and families in financial precarity: yet the book refuses to abandon its fantastical element. During Diamond's time in London, the novel features an embedded fairytale, a curious episode where a horse claims to be an angel, and both Diamond and Nanny experience evocative North Wind-associated dreams. Such blending of fantasy and realism is typical in MacDonald's works,[45] forcing readers to grapple with the questions: what is real, and how should we respond to our perceived realities? After Diamond returns from his visit to the back of the North Wind, the reader learns that he has been extremely ill. Is North Wind real, then, or are we seeing merely the delusions of a dying boy? If both realities are true, what is the nature of the interaction between them?

At this point, Diamond and his mother, and subsequently, the book's readers, are solicited by – or subjected to – a poem that Diamond's mother labels "such nonsense!", although she goes on to read it at her son's urging.[46] MacDonald's subsequent presentation of the poem forces the reader to consider that the poem is more than space-filling drivel. Even if one skips the poem, one must flip several pages to get to the end of the chapter, suggesting the poem's physical and spatial claim to significance. Yet the context of the poem *does* appear nonsensical at face value, for it presents few ways forward for Diamond's family who are genuinely in a position of extreme financial insecurity. Diamond's father's employer has lost his wealth, forcing Diamond's family to relocate, and placing pressure on Diamond's father to find a new job. This context raises the question: how can the kind of relational knowledge that Diamond has gained in his sojourns with North Wind

---

42   G.K. Chesterton, "A Defence of Nonsense", *The Defendant*, 2nd ed. (London: R. Brimley Johnson, 1902), 42–50, and "Child Psychology and Nonsense", in *Collected Works* 32, ed. Lawrence J. Clipper (San Francisco: Ignatius Press, 1989); Anthony Burgess, "Nonsense", in *Explorations in the Field of Nonsense*, ed. Wim Tigges (Amsterdam: Rodopi, 1987), 17–22.
43   Josephine Gabelman, *A Theology of Nonsense* (Eugene, OR: Wipf and Stock Publishers, 2016), 206.
44   McGillis, "Language and Secret Knowledge", 123–6.
45   John Stuart Pridmore, "Transfiguring Fantasy: Spiritual Development in the Work of George MacDonald" (unpublished PhD dissertation: University of London, 2000).
46   MacDonald, *North Wind*, 138–9.

speak to the practical realities of living in a world of unstable jobs and scarce resources? Diamond's mother is understandably anxious about her family's financial situation. She laments, "your father has nothing to do, and we shall have nothing to eat by and by", with legitimate anxiety – her husband enters the gig economy, and the family, effectively living hand to mouth, run out of money when he falls ill, emphasising the practical realities of scarcity in daily life.[47]

What Diamond offers – and what the poem invites – is a way of seeing the world in terms of generativity and abundance, rather than competitive scarcity. Diamond points out that he and his mother have food in the basket and comments, when his mother likens him to a sparrow that does not consider the winter or frost, "But the birds get through the winter, don't they?" In response to his mother's observation that some die, Diamond says (not unreasonably), "They must die some time."[48] In what may seem a callous comment, he reveals an implicit wisdom in recognising that things need not look the same in different temporal stages, and his comments suggest a perception of peace that comes from seeing the world in terms of provision rather than lack. At this point the rustling book catches Diamond's attention. There is a purposiveness attributed to the poem: the narrator tells us that Diamond "seemed to be of the same mind as the wind", and in later chapters, when Diamond learns to read, he cannot find the poem, suggesting a supernatural, time-bound revelatory quality to the poem.[49] Yet to readers this poem bears the hallmarks of gossip: although the novel implies that North Wind has sent the poem, suggesting a testimonial quality, the reader never knows the sender or source. Moreover, the poem's dissemination feels like gossip rather than testimony delivered in a setting where receivers are primed to receive first-hand knowledge: the readers, like Diamond's mother, are plunged into a grammatically overwhelming set of images of plenitude and motion:

I know a river

whose waters run asleep

run run ever

singing in the shallows

dumb in the hollows[50]

The "genesis" moment of this poem is its declaration of personal knowledge. It is not a scientific knowledge of the river based on names, chemical components, or categories; it is a relational knowing based on the river's interactions with its surroundings. Notably, the river manifests itself differently in different regions,

---

47   MacDonald, *North Wind*, 201.
48   MacDonald, *North Wind*, 136.
49   MacDonald, *North Wind*, 138; also 175.
50   MacDonald, *North Wind*, 139.

singing in the shallows, silent in the hollows: it actively responds to different settings in specific ways. The river (redolent of the river of life in the Revelation of St John) blesses generations of creatures by its banks:

and all the swallows

that dip their feathers

in the hollows

or in the shallows

are the merriest swallows of all

for the nests they bake

with the clay they cake

with the water they shake

from their wings that rake

the water out of the shallows

or the hollows

will hold together

in any weather

and so the swallows

are the merriest fellows

and have the merriest children[51]

In some ways, it is hard to characterise this as a nonsense poem when it is possible, by chunking portions, to make sense of the images that layer one another. Grammatically speaking, the chief thing that makes this nonsensical is the extravagant length of the sentence. The entire poem is a sentence, overwhelming logical comprehension. This is, in large part, the poem's aim; flooding, as it does, the reader with visions of abundance of life to suggest that the logical portioning of experiences detracts from that true educational pursuit of being endlessly unsettled and perpetually seeking unattainable truths. The overflow of superlatives creates a current of words that attempts to divert logical thoughts. We are carried along by the patterns of assonance, the omission of punctuation marks, and the incessant use of "and", all of which distract readers from parsing the discrete images of the wildlife by the river. We are presented with incessant images of abundance and constant creation that crowd atop each other: because of the river, birds can transform mud into clay and can make nests. These practical acts of creation enable multigenerational blessing: the swallows' children are the "merriest children". The inextricable relationships between the river inhabitants and the river, which enable the growth of

---

51   MacDonald, *North Wind*, 139.

the swallows, the daisies, and the lambs alike, are reinforced by the way the images cluster in a single sentence. Find a source of relational knowledge, the poem implies, and this enables a generous, multigenerational way of being. This way of being provides a key to perceiving the world in a way that invites abundance and creativity, even if that creativity is as mundane as swallows making nests.

The poem ends not with the river, but with a gesture to a greater life-giving power, suggesting that the conduits for generative thinking – the river in the poem, the poem itself – depend on a practical hope in a goodness that is at work throughout the world:

for the wind that blows

is the river of life

flowing for ever […]

and it's all in the wind

that blows from behind.[52]

Almost abruptly, the physical river, with which we have been travelling for nearly two hundred lines, is displaced: the metaphorical river of life is the "wind that blows". With MacDonald's vocation as a preacher, it is impossible to read of "wind" without also hearing the Biblical pun on "Spirit" (exemplified with great clarity in the third chapter of the Gospel of John). But because MacDonald avoids Christian language, the identity of this divine, life-giving wind is obscured to include broader ways of thinking about hope in a life-giving source that enables generative patterns of behaviour. This practical hope in an overarching goodness that compels and underpins our behaviours in this world is, the poem concludes, what enables us to respond without submitting with pessimism to paradigms of scarcity.[53] Indeed, Diamond, after hearing this poem, responds practically and creatively to situations of great scarcity and anxiety, suggesting the usefulness as well as the beauty of this generative way of thinking. Practically, when his father is ill, he takes on his father's job as a cab driver, enabling his family to afford their daily needs; creatively, he effects a stronger transformation in an alcoholic cabbie by singing to the cabbie's infant and showcasing the potential for joy in the stress of poverty.

Crucially, Diamond's mother also demonstrates a greater openness to actions that do not make sense in a logic of scarcity, suggesting that the poem's dissemination amongst recipients who initially consider it nonsense can produce transformations within those once-resistant listeners. MacDonald's narrator tells us with certainty that she "couldn't find any sense in [the poem]",[54] indicating that

---

52 MacDonald, *North Wind*, 143.
53 For more on practical hope, see Adrienne Martin, *How We Hope: A Moral Psychology* (Princeton, NJ: Princeton University Press, 2014).
54 MacDonald, *North Wind*, 139.

Diamond's mother receives the poem only as a piece of meaningless gossip at the seaside. Yet she later shows an increased openness to act based on trust in the generosity of others. When Diamond's acquaintance Mr Raymond asks Diamond's parents to care for an orphaned crossing-sweep, Nanny, and to look after (and sometimes work) Mr Raymond's horse, Ruby, Diamond's father sees only the costs incurred by taking on more mouths to feed. Diamond's mother encourages him to accept the wager as she thinks with compassion on Nanny's needs.[55] When the wager does not seem to work and Diamond's father is pessimistic about whether Mr Raymond will provide sufficient recompense, labelling Mr Raymond a "hard man", Diamond's mother encourages her husband to hope in Mr Raymond's kindness – a hope justified when Mr Raymond offers Diamond's father a better-paid, more stable job.[56] While Diamond's mother's transformation is not as extreme as her son's – she still laughs at Mr Raymond's proposition of pairing Diamond-the-horse and Ruby in a double harness[57] – her willingness to think in terms of generosity indicates that she has been transformed by her encounter with the poem. Although she first received the poem as a piece of drivel, she increasingly acts in accordance with the poem's values because she has witnessed and been compelled by her son's actions and has allowed her perceptions of human nature to shift. Education, as MacDonald reminds us, is a process that unfolds relationally.

Although *At the Back of the North Wind* features moments of conventional learning (including a two-sentence summary of how Diamond learns to read[58]), the novel is most interested in pedagogy as a relationship based on trust. Diamond's trust in North Wind and acceptance that her way of seeing reality holds truth presents a dynamic pedagogy which, like the nonsense poem, trusts in goodness and delights in the generosity of others. This perception of the world as a place of abundance provides an alternative to the anxiety and scepticism that accompanies paradigms of scarcity. However, this requires trust, and the narrator's subjective sharing of Diamond's story creates an interpretive space into which we as readers are invited to respond, in trust or with doubt, to the second-hand knowledge encoded in the novel.

Bibliography

Primary

Barbauld, Anna Letitia. *Hymns in Prose for Children*. London: Printed for J. Johnson, 1781.
Barbauld, Anna Letitia. *Lessons for Children Aged Two to Three*. London: Printed for J. Johnson, 1778.

---

55   MacDonald, *North Wind*, 239.
56   MacDonald, *North Wind*, 262.
57   MacDonald, *North Wind*, 267.
58   MacDonald, *North Wind*, 175.

Bronfenbrenner, Urie. "Toward an experimental ecology of human development." *American Psychologist*, 32.7 (July 1977): 513–31.

Carroll, Lewis. *Through the Looking-Glass, and What Alice Found There*. London: Macmillan, 1872.

Chesterton, G.K. "A Defence of Nonsense." In *The Defendant*, 2nd ed., 42–50, London: R. Brimley Johnson, 1902.

Chesterton, G.K. "Child Psychology and Nonsense." In *Collected Works* 32. Ed. Lawrence J. Clipper. San Francisco: Ignatius Press, 1989.

Fenn, Lady Ellenor. *Cobwebs to Catch Flies: Or, Dialogues in Short Sentences, Adapted for Children from the Age of Three to Eight Years. In Two Volumes*. London: Printed by John Marshall, 1783. Eighteenth Century Collections Online, Gale Document CW3317078925.

Hughes, Thomas. *Tom Brown at Oxford* [1861]. London: Macmillan, 1889.

MacDonald, George. "The Fantastic Imagination". In *A Dish of Orts: Chiefly Papers on the Imagination, and on Shakespeare*, 222–8. Hamburg: Tredition Classics, 1893.

MacDonald, George. *At the Back of the North Wind*. Ed. Roderick McGillis and John Pennington. Ontario: Broadview, 2011.

MacDonald, George. *The Princess and the Goblin* [1872]. London: Penguin, 1996.

Pliny the Elder. *Natural History* vol. 4 of 10. Trans. H. Rackham. Cambridge, MA: Harvard University Press and London: William Heineman Ltd, 1938.

Secondary

Durham Peters, John. *Speaking into the Air: A History of the Idea of Communication*. Chicago, IL: University of Chicago Press, 1999.

Fricker, Elizabeth. "Second-Hand Knowledge." *Philosophy and Phenomenological Research* 73, no.3 (2006): 592–618.

Fujimura, Makoto. *Culture Care: Reconnecting With Beauty for our Common Life*. Lisle, IL: InterVarsity Press, 2017.

Gabelman, Josephine, *A Theology of Nonsense*. Eugene, OR: Wipf and Stock Publishers, 2016.

Gardiner, Bruce. "Christ's Parable of the Sower: Intellectual Property Rights in Gossip and Testimony." *Literature and Aesthetics*, 28 (2018): 193–221.

Green, Melody. "Death and Nonsense in the Poetry of George MacDonald's *At the Back of the North Wind* and Lewis Carroll's *Alice* Books." *North Wind: A Journal of George MacDonald Studies* 30 (2011): 38–49.

Haidt, Jonathan. *The Righteous Mind: Why Good People are Divided by Politics and Religion*. London: Penguin, 2013.

Jeffrey Johnson, Kirstin. "Rooted in All Its Story, More is Meant than Meets the Ear: A Study of the Relational and Revelational Nature of George MacDonald's Mythopoeic Art." Unpublished PhD dissertation: University of St Andrews, 2011.

Lecercle, Jean-Jacques. *Philosophy of Nonsense: The Intuitions of Victorian Nonsense Literature*. London: Routledge, 1994.

Leech, Geoffrey. *Principles of Pragmatics*. London: Longman, 1983.

Manlove, Colin. "A Reading of *At the Back of the North Wind*." *North Wind: A Journal of George MacDonald Studies* 27 (2008): 51–78.

Martin, Adrienne. *How We Hope: A Moral Psychology*. Princeton, NJ: Princeton University Press, 2014.

McGillis, Roderick. "Language and Secret Knowledge in *At the Back of the North Wind*." *Proceedings of the Seventh Annual Conference of the Children's Literature Association*. Ed. Priscilla Ord, 120–7. (1982).

Partridge, Eric. "The Nonsense Words of Edward Lear and Lewis Carroll." In *Here, There and Everywhere: Essays Upon Language*, 162–88. London: Hamish Hamilton, 1950.

Pridmore, John Stuart. "Transfiguring Fantasy: Spiritual Development in the Work of George MacDonald". Unpublished PhD dissertation: University of London, 2000.

Sewell, Elizabeth. *The Field of Nonsense*. London: Chatto and Windus, 1952.

Smith, David I. *On Christian Teaching: Practicing Faith in the Classroom*. Grand Rapids, MI: William B. Eerdmans, 2018.

Thomas Ankeny, Rebecca. "Teacher and Pupil: Reading, Ethics, and Human Dignity in George MacDonald's *Mary Marston*." *Studies in Scottish Literature*, 29 (1996): 227–37.

Thomas Ankeny, Rebecca. "The Mother Tongue: Acquiring Language and Being Human." In *Truth's Bright Embrace: Essays and Poems in Honor of Arthur O. Roberts*. Ed. Paul N. Anderson and Howard R. Macy, 223–37. Newberg, OR: George Fox University Press, 1996.

Walker, Adam. "Objects of Nonsense, Anarchy, and Order: Romantic Theology in Lewis Carroll's and George MacDonald's Nonsense Literature." *North Wind: A Journal of George MacDonald Studies* 37 (2018): 11–27.

Wood, Lisa. *Modes of Discipline: Women, Conservatism, and the Novel After the French Revolution*. Lewisburg, PA: Bucknell University Press, 2003.

20

Virtue or Villainy? Mrs. Grose in "The Turn of the Screw" and *The Haunting of Bly Manor*

Liz Shek-Noble

Henry James' novella, "The Turn of the Screw" (1898), begins with a description of a coterie gathered around a fire on Christmas Eve as they listen to a ghost story told by Griffin, a member of their party. The unnamed first-person narrator tells the reader that "The story had held us [...] sufficiently breathless";[1] the guests are equal parts thrilled and appalled by the "gruesome" tale of a child who has had the unfortunate fate of being visited by a ghost. Yet Griffin's story is but a prelude to the "quite too horrible" tale delivered by Douglas and which serves as the main narrative of the novella (116). Before Douglas can triumph against his would-be competitors in this arena of entertainment, he must first get the crowd on his side. First, Douglas sells the shock value and singularity of his narrative to his audience: "It's beyond everything. Nothing at all that I know touches it [... for] dreadfulness" and "for general uncanny ugliness and horror and pain" (116). He also makes use of his audience's need for immediate gratification by delaying the telling of his tale until four nights later. Rather indelicately, Douglas hints at an unrequited romance between the governess and the master of Bly, though "not in any literal vulgar way" (118). And so, Douglas' strategies of deferral, magnification and foreshadowing all work to create a highly anticipated story among his patient and eager audience: the "hushed little circle [...] compact and select [...] round the hearth" was "subject to a common thrill" (119).

I have started this chapter with the Prologue of "The Turn of the Screw" because its atmospherics, interpersonal dynamics and temporality capture my experiences listening to Bruce's lectures and seminars. No matter whether you were listening to Bruce in a lecture theatre or in his office, regardless of whether he was teaching in front of hundreds of students or just a select few, the effect was the same: you felt as if the story was being told only to you and for you:

---

1   Henry James, "The Turn of the Screw", in *The Turn of the Screw and Other Stories* (Oxford: Oxford University Press, 1992), Prologue, 115. Hereafter cited in the text as "Turn". All subsequent references are to this edition and cited in parentheses in the text.

"It was to me in particular that he appealed to propound this" (116). Intensity, immediacy and sociability characterised Bruce's teaching and are features that speak to his generosity as an educator. But I have also started with the Prologue because it highlights one of the most enduring qualities of Bruce's teaching – that is, its irresistible performativity. Putting aside the considerable pedagogical value of Bruce's teaching for a moment, I will always remember fondly how *exciting* Bruce's lectures and seminars were: like the narrator who pressures Douglas to retrieve the governess' manuscript post-haste and agree to an "early hearing" (116), it was difficult for me to wait patiently for Bruce's lecture or seminars to begin or continue into another week, as much as "it was just his scruples that charmed me" (116).

There is one final reason why "The Turn of the Screw" is the principal focus of this chapter. When I first learned about the *festschrift* for Bruce, his lecture on "The Turn of the Screw", delivered as part of the first-year undergraduate course, Reading English Texts (2014),[2] immediately sprang to mind. For within this lecture, Bruce's talent for offering contrary and unorthodox readings of canonical literature was on full display. Thomas M. Cranfill and Robert L. Clark, Jr. describe how "The Turn of the Screw" is "a source of endless inspiration and provocation"[3] among critics and artists alike. Bruce's lecture has taken as its starting point two significant and competing ways of viewing Mrs. Grose that were evident during the peak of criticism on "The Turn of the Screw":[4] either as an unintelligent, older and unattractive widow or as a villain who is intensely resentful of the governess for being given "supreme authority" at Bly (121). The former interpretation of Mrs. Grose is typified in Colm Tóibín's sniping remark that she is "deeply stupid",[5] whereas the latter has been pushed to absurdity in Eric Solomon's mock satirical essay, "The Return of the Screw". However, Bruce's lecture, in keeping with his "general fondness for underdogs"[6] in literature and culture, shows that Mrs. Grose

---

2   All subsequent references to Bruce's lecture on "The Turn of the Screw" will refer to those included as part of the course, ENGL1012: The Gothic Imagination (2014). Hereafter cited in the text as "Henry James".

3   Thomas M. Cranfill and Robert L. Clark, Jr., "The Provocativeness of *The Turn of the Screw*", *Texas Studies in Literature and Language* 12, no. 1 (1970): 93.

4   By "peak" I am referring to readings of "The Turn of the Screw" that engage directly with or have been retrospectively defined as taking part in the "pro-" versus "non-" apparitionist debate, that is, with determining whether the ghosts are "real" (the former) or the governess' hallucinations (the latter). Non-apparitionists have sometimes viewed the governess as on a religious mission to "save" the children's souls from evil (Heilman) or that her hallucinations stem from repressed sexual longing for her employer (Goddard; Wilson) or a Victorian anxiety towards the corruption of innocent children by immoral servants (Nardin). Robert B. Heilman, "The Freudian Reading of *The Turn of the Screw*", in Henry James, *The Turn of the Screw* [1898], ed. Deborah Esch and Jonathan Warren, 2nd ed. (New York: Norton, 1999), 177–84; Harold C. Goddard, "A Pre-Freudian Reading of *The Turn of the Screw*", *Nineteenth-Century Fiction* 12, no. 1 (1957): 1–36; Edmund Wilson, "The Ambiguity of Henry James", *Hound and Horn* (April 1934): 385–406; Jane Nardin, "'The Turn of the Screw': The Victorian Background", *Mosaic: An Interdisciplinary Critical Journal* 12, no. 1 (1978): 131–42.

5   Colm Tóibín, "Pure Evil: 'The Turn of the Screw'", *The Henry James Review* 30, no. 3 (2009): 239.

6   I would like to thank the anonymous reader of this chapter for their astute observation.

is far from being slow-witted or fiendish; in fact, she is highly skilled at interpreting and adjudging the governess' frenzied testimony. In this respect, Bruce's sympathetic reading of Mrs. Grose suggests continuity with Arthur Boardman's appraisal of this character. For Boardman, the answer to whether the ghosts are real or confected by the governess' imagination is definitively settled through "analysing the function in the work of Mrs. Grose".[7] Importantly, Boardman elevates Mrs. Grose to the position of being a "first reader of the governess' story" even though she is "illiterate".[8] That Boardman believes readers should through Mrs. Grose's judgement accept the governess' account as reasonable and true demonstrates admirable qualities of this character that have often been denied to her by other critics: she is reliable and honest, a "giver of hints" to the governess that things are awry at Bly, and most importantly, an incisive "first reader" of the governess whose judgement must be accepted because its logic stems from scepticism that has put the governess' account through a series of rhetorical twists and turns.[9]

This chapter will begin with an overview of the two interpretations that have informed Bruce's alternative reading of Mrs. Grose. This will be followed by a close analysis of Mrs. Grose's interactions with the governess as a means of demonstrating her facility to dissect, elucidate and parse the often-confused recollections of the governess. Finally, I will discuss *The Haunting of Bly Manor* (2020), a miniseries adaptation of "The Turn of the Screw" created by Mike Flanagan, which offers a fresh approach towards Mrs. Grose as compared to standard cinematic portrayals of her character.

"A Magnificent Monument to the Blessing of a Want of Imagination"

A key issue at stake in "The Turn of the Screw" is the question of what – or whom – is the subject of interpretation and interpretability. Bruce argues that Miles and Flora are the "text" that the governess must interpret and "from the outset she fears she misses, or doesn't catch, something in [them]" (Gardiner, "Henry James", 6–5). For Bruce and following on from Boardman, Mrs. Grose's role as the "first" reader of the governess' account[10] is an essential rhetorical feature of the novella that enables the young woman to perform the "interpretive labour" of psychologically "turning" over what she sees and hears at Bly (Gardiner, "Henry James", 6–5). Acting as the governess' only confidante during the time in which she held her post, Mrs. Grose routinely

---

7   Arthur Boardman, "Mrs. Grose's Reading of *The Turn of the Screw*", *Studies in English Literature, 1500–1900* 14, no. 4 (1974): 619.
8   Boardman, "Mrs. Grose's Reading", 619.
9   Boardman, "Mrs. Grose's Reading", 634.
10 Boardman writes of Mrs. Grose in the following way: "she is 'first' [reader] in that the governess constantly confides in her, and she is a 'reader' in that like us she knows [...] only what the governess tells her about what the governess experiences. Further, she is an informed 'reader', for she knows the characters in the governess' narrative first-hand, both the quick and the dead. And she is a critical 'reader', for she continually tests the governess' story." Boardman, 621.

subjects the governess to persistent, yet nonetheless equanimous, interrogation. This leads Bruce to label the pair as "one joint investigative team", where Mrs. Grose's main contribution is to act as a "countervailing power" to the governess by moderating the latter's conspiratorial inclination to view the children as willing accomplices in their corruption by the ghosts (Gardiner, "Henry James", 6–9). By midway through the narrative, the governess is convinced that the preternatural goodness and beauty of Miles and Flora are but "a policy and a fraud!", and moreover that the ghosts of Peter Quint and Miss Jessel are intent on manipulating the children: "They want to get to them […] For the love of all the evil that, in those dreadful days, the pair put into them. And to ply them with that evil still, […] is what brings the others back" (181). However, Mrs. Grose withholds her judgement until after she becomes an ear-witness to Flora's "appalling language" and concludes that Miles has been dismissed from school for stealing letters: "It strikes me that by this time your eyes are open even wider than mine" (221, 222).

Bruce's reading of Mrs. Grose runs contrary to common historical interpretations of this character as being a credulous and unintelligent woman.[11] Mrs. Grose's illiteracy is treated as a sign of her general lack of intelligence, even though common sense understands that books and schooling do not have a monopoly on the cultivation of human intelligence. N. Bryllion Fagin, for one, calls her "a simple [and…] undiscerning person";[12] this is echoed by Dennis Tredy in his appraisal of the housekeeper as "simple-minded".[13] In keeping with these less-than-sterling descriptions of her character, Robert B. Heilman calls Mrs. Grose "slow-witted",[14] while "highly unimaginative" springs forth from E.C. Curtsinger.[15]

On the other hand, Eric Solomon, C. Knight Aldrich and Helen Killoran have departed from this reading by regarding Mrs. Grose as the novella's primary antagonist.[16] Calling her one of the "most clever and desperate of Victorian

---

11   Recent scholarship, for example Priscilla L. Walton's feminist critique of the novella, has offered more nuanced appraisals of Mrs. Grose. In Walton's view, Mrs. Grose is the "proper" and "ineffectual" figure of the matron. For the governess to assume authority over the "I" of her/the narrative, she must find a way to escape from the "triptych of patriarchal feminine constructions", these being the mother (Mrs. Grose), whore (Miss Jessel), and the lunatic (herself, if her account of the ghosts is to be rejected). Ultimately, this endeavour proves impossible. Priscilla L. Walton, "'What then on earth was I?': Feminine Subjectivity and *The Turn of the Screw*", in *The Turn of the Screw: Complete, Authoritative Text with Biographical and Historical Contexts, Critical History, and Essays from Five Contemporary Critical Perspectives*, ed. Peter G. Beidler (Boston, MA: St. Martin's Press, 1995), 263, 257, 266.
12   N. Bryllion Fagin, "Another Reading of *The Turn of the Screw*", *Modern Language Notes* 56, no. 3 (1941): 157.
13   Dennis Tredy, "Shadows of Shadows – Techniques of Ambiguity in Three Film Adaptations of 'The Turn of the Screw': J. Clayton's *The Innocents* (1962), D. Curtis's *The Turn of the Screw* (1974), and A. Aloy's *Presence of Mind* (1999)", *Review électronique d'études sur le monde anglophone* 3, no. 2 (2005): n.p.
14   Heilman, "The Freudian Reading", 179.
15   E.C. Curtsinger, "'The Turn of the Screw' as Writer's Parable", *Studies in the Novel* 12, no. 4 (1980): 349.
16   Eric Solomon, "The Return of the Screw", *The University Review – Kansas City* 30 (1964): 205–11; C. Knight Aldrich, "Another Twist to 'The Turn of the Screw'", *Modern Fiction Studies*

villainesses", Solomon believes that Mrs. Grose is responsible for murdering Quint due to her deep possessiveness over Flora.[17] Solomon also proposes that Mrs. Grose displays a hidden cunning in exploiting the governess' willingness to view her as intellectually and socially inferior; once gaining the governess' trust, she can "cleverly [work...] on her victim's imagination" and drive her insane by telling her that the ghosts she has apparently seen are Quint and Miss Jessel.[18] Aldrich holds a similar interpretation of Mrs. Grose, believing that the housekeeper "hates the governess" and seeks to "destroy her".[19] To lend support to their argument, Aldrich directs the reader's attention to three main points: first, that Mrs. Grose discourages the governess from speaking to Miles or anyone else within the household to provide visual corroboration of Quint; second, that Mrs. Grose is the only person to hear Flora utter shocking language ("From that child – horrors! [...] On my honour, Miss, she says things –!" [James, "Turn", Chapter 21, 220]); and third, that Mrs. Grose is in fact Miles and Flora's biological mother.[20] For Aldrich, Mrs. Grose's resentment towards the governess is attributed to the latter being a potential maternal obstacle to the children's affections.[21] Meanwhile, Killoran's reading of "The Turn of the Screw" sees the governess and Mrs. Grose as being engaged in a "rivalry [...] for control of the children".[22] Miss Jessel is consequently regarded as a "psychological projection of the competition between herself and Mrs. Grose to 'get hold of' Flora".[23]

With respect to these interpretations of Mrs. Grose, there are moments in the governess' recollections of the housekeeper that lend support to an interpretation of her character as being impressionable and naive. The governess' first meeting with Mrs. Grose catches her off-guard due to the latter's submissive welcome; the housekeeper is said to have dropped the governess "as decent a curtsy as if I had been the mistress or a distinguished visitor" (123). Furthermore, the governess' private narration of Mrs. Grose suggests that she regards the housekeeper as a valuable ally, though never an equal, due to her lesser occupational status within the household and level of education.[24] According to the governess, Mrs. Grose was a "stout simple plain clean wholesome woman" prone to rash emotion ("with one of the quick turns of simple folk, she suddenly flamed up" [124, 126]) and parochial language ("'Laws!' said my friend under her breath. The exclamation was homely" [181–2]). Yet it is clear that critics, as well as the governess, do Mrs. Grose a "disservice" to name

---

13, no. 2 (1967): 167–78; and Helen Killoran, "The Governess, Mrs. Grose and 'The Poison of an Influence' in 'The Turn of the Screw'", *Modern Language Studies* 23, no. 2 (1993): 13–24.

17   Solomon, "Return", 211, 208.

18   Solomon, "Return", 207.

19   Aldrich, "Another Twist", 168.

20   Aldrich, "Another Twist", 170, 172, 175.

21   Aldrich, "Another Twist", 175.

22   Killoran, "The Governess", 13.

23   Killoran, "The Governess", 18.

24   The governess remarks in Chapter 6 that Mrs. Grose showed "a deference to my more than questionable privilege". James, "The Turn of the Screw", 148.

her virtue as "stupidity" (Gardiner, "Henry James", 6–9). According to Bruce, Mrs. Grose's main virtue is in fact "an amalgam of trust, charity, [and] hope" that is most apparent in her willingness to listen to the governess' allegations even as they strain credulity (Gardiner, "Henry James", 6–9). Moreover, Mrs. Grose's urge to remain loyal to the governess even when her eyewitness account differs from her companion's is apparent in two crucial moments. In Chapter 20, neither Mrs. Grose nor Flora allegedly sees the ghost of Miss Jessel at the lake; the governess notes that Mrs. Grose looked at her with a "sense, touching to me even then, that she would have backed me up if she had been able" (214). After Flora relocates to Mrs. Grose's bedroom, Mrs. Grose reports back to the governess that she now "believe[s]" the children are under the corrupting influence of Quint and Miss Jessel due to the child's "appalling language", language which she had previously heard while the other servants were still alive (221).

As much as Mrs. Grose can be said to be the governess' faithful and compassionate companion, it is also necessary to highlight how undue attention on her emotional generosity causes another kind of injury to her character. Bruce has argued that the general tendency to view the governess as a psychologically disturbed individual whose sanity and reliability must be questioned is evidence of a "critical narcissism" to disbelieve a narrator or writer solely because of their gender (Gardiner, "Henry James", 6–12). For Bruce, this "ad hominem fallacy" undergirds the more specific interpretive problem in "The Turn of the Screw" of whether the governess has authority over her own narrative, that is, whether she has in fact seen the ghosts of Quint and Jessel and that their intentions for the children are nefarious (Gardiner, "Henry James", 6–14). To my mind, there has been some critical tendency to view Mrs. Grose as an unthinking "tag along" to the governess,[25] yet such accounts fail to recognise how the housekeeper displays a range of interpretive skills that highlight an abundance of scepticism and restraint. Thus, like James W. Gargano, I view Mrs. Grose's lack of imagination as being the character's main virtue; as she is "incapable of seeing visions", the reader can depend on her to provide "unvarnished fact" rather than delusion.[26] Indeed, Mrs. Grose's hesitation to accept the governess' "eager" "theory of evil" is what leads C.B. Ives to call her "aggravatingly sane and unimaginative".[27] Moments in which the governess discloses her alleged encounters with the ghosts demonstrate that

---

25   Boardman's article on the housekeeper appears as one of the more thorough and positive examinations of this character, though Morgan Day Frank has similarly suggested that Mrs. Grose may be a "better reader" of the governess than the governess is of herself. Catherine Toal has also praised Mrs. Grose as "a source of vital factual information [who…] stands between the necessarily indispensable Mrs. Bread of *The American* and an even more earthily named successor, Fanny Assingham, of *The Golden Bowl*" (87). Frank, "Don't Read", *New Literary History* 51, no. 1 (2020): 45–66; and Catherine Toal, "Murder and 'Point of View'", in *The Entrapments of Form: Cruelty and Modern Literature* (New York: Fordham University Press, 2016), 66–93.

26   James W. Gargano, "*The Turn of the Screw*", *Western Humanities Review* 15, no. 2 (1961): 173.

27   C.B. Ives, "James's Ghosts in *The Turn of the Screw*", *Nineteenth-Century Fiction* 18, no. 2 (1963): 187.

Mrs. Grose's absence of imagination is a crucial counterweight to her companion's propensity to locate answers to material phenomena in the realm of the paranormal. Take, for instance, the governess' conversation with Mrs. Grose in Chapter 5 after her second encounter with Quint. Prior to this, the governess believes she has seen Quint on the tower and once again through the window of the dining room. The latter sighting leads the governess to formulate her theory that "it was not for me he [Quint] had come. He had come for someone else" (142). After an eerie moment of doubling wherein the governess assumes Quint's position on the lawn and Mrs. Grose her own in the dining room, the governess confesses that she has been visited by "an extraordinary man" on two occasions (144). The governess' and Mrs. Grose's conversation reveals the former's psychological propensity to grasp at conclusions drawn from limited eyewitness testimony. Mrs. Grose's questioning involves a careful dissection of what the governess has seen; through its focus on ascertaining concrete facts about Quint and the scene in which the supposed "crime" has taken place, Mrs. Grose aids in proving the veracity of the governess' account.

Mrs. Grose's "direct examination" of the governess involves a range of techniques, including questions that are open-ended; mirroring the governess' language for the purposes of clarification; and seeking to assemble a coherent timeline and visual identification of Quint. For example, Mrs. Grose asks the governess whether she has seen Quint before (144) and whether she believes there was any purpose or motivation behind his appearances: "What was he doing on the tower?" (145). Repetition of the governess' words is another technique employed by Mrs. Grose so that the former's recollections remain consistent under increasing scrutiny: "What extraordinary man?" (144). Furthermore, Mrs. Grose employs the use of clarifying and leading questions to extract further information from the governess. She asks whether the governess has seen Quint "nowhere but on the tower" and supposes that the governess is "afraid" of him not only for her own sake, but for the children's (144, 145). It is also notable that the housekeeper refrains from prematurely disclosing her hypothesis until after the governess has given her "perfectly precise, point-by-point" visual identification of Quint, a description that A.J.A. Waldock points out is of someone whom "she had never seen in her life and never heard of".[28] Although she had a "far-away faint glimmer of consciousness […] acute" (145), Mrs. Grose only accepts the veracity of the governess' account after she is satisfied that her younger companion has proven beyond all reasonable doubt that the intruder is Quint; in addition to giving a description of Quint's physical appearance, the governess also remarks on a supposed discrepancy between his social class and sartorial choices ("They're smart, but not his own" [147]), along with the possibility that he may be adept at deception ("He gives me a sort of sense of looking like an actor" [146]).

---

28   A.J.A. Waldock, "Mr. Edmund Wilson and *The Turn of the Screw*", *Modern Language Notes* 62, no. 5 (1947): 333, 334.

Following the appearance of an adult female apparition at the lake, the governess rushes to Mrs. Grose and makes three alarming proposals: the unknown person whom she has seen is the ghost of Miss Jessel; the children are fully aware of her and Quint's presence; and that Miss Jessel and Quint intend to harm the children. While monitoring Flora, the governess becomes aware that "There was an alien object in view – a figure whose right of presence I instantly and passionately questioned" (154). The governess' immediate fear of the mysterious figure necessarily intersects with her own rapid ascension to the head of Bly. Indeed, as a young and inexperienced woman whom Douglas calls "a fluttered anxious girl out of a Hampshire vicarage" (119), the governess' eagerness to assume her professional duties with the utmost competence means that any unexpected happenstance is registered as an incursion or even worse, as a threat. While the governess' immediate reaction to seeing the female figure at the lake is to "g[et] hold of" Mrs. Grose and provide "no intelligible account" of the matter, her older companion withholds any judgement until it is possible to construct a logical chain of reasoning out of the governess' jumbled thoughts (155). Notably, in the first half of Chapter 7, Mrs. Grose returns each of the governess' accusations with a question, thereby refusing to offer explicit agreement until receiving what she regards as an acceptable level of proof that the figure is indeed Miss Jessel. Until the governess provides a description of Miss Jessel's "infamous" and "wonderfully handsome" beauty, along with the way in which she gazed at Flora "with a kind of fury of intention" (158), Mrs. Grose's position is to remain suspicious of the governess' interpretive leaps. Mrs. Grose's scepticism is obvious in the abundant number of questions that she asks the governess,[29] as well as her use of imperative language to force the governess to engage in a self-examination of her beliefs:

"She has told you?"
"Then how do you know?"
"Do you mean aware of *him* [Quint]?"
"Came how – from where?"
"And without coming nearer?"
"Was she someone you've never seen?"
"Miss Jessel?"
"Ah how *can* you?"
"You mean you're afraid of seeing her again?"
"Isn't it just a proof of her [Flora's] blest innocence?"

---

29 Boardman has previously observed that Mrs. Grose's scepticism is evident in her repeated disinclination to accept the governess' testimony at face value ("How indeed does one know that another person one sees is looking for someone else?"). Although the housekeeper's behaviour is "tender and charitable and thus comforting" to the governess, her mode of listening is characterised by a civility in which she never outwardly rejects nor dismisses her companion's allegations. Readers should therefore take Mrs. Grose "as humoring the governess without openly accusing her of having lost her mind". Boardman, "Mrs. Grose's Reading", 626.

"At you, do you mean – so wickedly?"

"Fixed her [Flora]?"

"Do you mean of dislike?"

"Worse than dislike?"

"The person was in black, you say?"

"Tell me how you know." (James, "Turn", Chapter 7)

Interestingly, once Mrs. Grose surmises that the figure is Miss Jessel, the one-sidedness of their conversation – with Mrs. Grose assuming the role of "interrogator" and the governess her "suspect" – comes to an end. It is now the governess' turn to ask Mrs. Grose to let go of her "discreet sensitivity to everyone around her" (Gardiner, "Henry James", 6–10) and for the latter to "give [her] the whole thing" (159).[30] The governess applies pressure on Mrs. Grose to divulge the scandalous nature of Miss Jessel and Quint's relationship and the many liberties that the latter took with other members of the household. As Mrs. Grose confesses, "I've never seen one like him [Quint]. He did what he wished. […] With them all" (159).

The two examples above demonstrate that Mrs. Grose is far from being a character whose illiteracy renders her a poor "reader" of human psychology. In fact, Mrs. Grose's illiteracy enables her character's perceptions to be grounded in the mundane rather than the fantastical. Bruce has noted that "Mrs. Grose's illiteracy means she hasn't read [Anne] Radcliffe, [Jane] Austen, or the Brontës" (Gardiner, "Henry James", 6–10);[31] that Mrs. Grose is not susceptible to the kinds of sentimental Gothic romances of the nineteenth century favoured by the governess means that her interpretive tools are protected from literary suggestibility. Ultimately, like Bruce, I would pose the question, "who is to say" that Mrs. Grose "is not the *most* acute interpreter" in the narrative, considering that her illiteracy might in fact anchor the character's thoughts and actions to the material, not suprasensory, world? (Gardiner, "Henry James", 6–10)

---

30   Taeko Kitahara argues that Mrs. Grose's "lack of commentary" about Miss Jessel and Quint is a form of "inarticulacy" akin to silence. Unlike the children's "intentional silence", which for Kitahara suggests collusion with the ghosts, Mrs. Grose's "verbal inability to express herself" is a means of affirming the "unspeakability" of the ghosts' influence over the children. I am inclined, like Bruce, to view Mrs. Grose's reticence as a display of the character's prudence. Furthermore, nowhere in Mrs. Grose's conversations with the governess is it suggested that she is at a proverbial loss for words. Taeko Kitahara, "The Haunted Theater of Fiction: Silence and Sound in 'The Turn of the Screw'", in *The Sound of James: The Aural Dimension in Henry James's Work*, ed. Leonardo Buonomo (Trieste: Edizioni Università di Trieste, 2021), 89, 90.

31   While strolling around the grounds, the governess daydreams about a chance encounter with the master following her first sighting of Quint on the tower: "Was there a 'secret' at Bly – a mystery of Udolpho or an insane, an unmentionable relative kept in unsuspected confinement?" James, "Turn", Chapter 4, 138.

"It's Not the First Time I've Seen Things That Aren't There": Hannah Grose in *The Haunting of Bly Manor*

I would now like to focus on *The Haunting of Bly Manor* (hereafter *The Haunting*) and its portrayal of Mrs. Hannah Grose. Flanagan's recent miniseries is noted for being less tethered to its source material than earlier cinematic adaptations of "The Turn of the Screw". As a result, Mrs. Grose's role in resolving the epistemological uncertainty around the ghosts becomes even more prominent in *The Haunting* as compared to James' novella and previous adaptations. Critics such as Toíbín,[32] James W. Palmer,[33] Dennis Tredy[34] and Taeko Kitahara[35] have observed that *The Innocents* (1961) – perhaps the most well-known cinematic adaptation of "The Turn of the Screw" – preserves the original ambiguity of the novella by keeping open the possibility that the ghosts are real *and* that the governess' sanity cannot be taken for granted. The appearance of the ghosts onscreen might be interpreted as an inarguable display of (their) verisimilitude. Yet according to Palmer, *The Innocents* reintroduces ambiguity by questioning the objectivity of what the governess sees and hears; the film exploits the Freudian implications of the novella, and thus the interpretation of the governess as being sexually repressed, through phallic imagery, symbolic clothing and a combination of "subjective" and "objective" points of view and sounds.[36]

The central ambiguity of "The Turn of the Screw" is almost entirely removed from *The Haunting*. Unlike its source text, the miniseries does not prolong the viewer's uncertainty about the reality of the ghosts or the mental stability of the governess – refashioned as au pair Danielle "Dani" Clayton – for very long. By just over halfway through the miniseries (episode 5 of 9), epistemological clarity is achieved on several mysteries introduced in earlier episodes. First, viewers become aware that the ghosts of Peter Quint and Miss Jessel *are real*, and thus that Dani is not hallucinating *all of the time*. Viewers also come to distinguish between Dani's "objective" and "subjective" perspectives in terms of the nonhuman figures that intrude into her life: whereas Quint and Miss Jessel are ghosts who are "real" and "seen" by not only Dani but other staff members of Bly Manor, Dani's unexpected visions of her former fiancé are a mental projection of her guilt for disclosing her homosexuality minutes before his untimely death.[37] But perhaps the most important way that *The Haunting* promotes a "pro-apparitionist" interpretation of itself is in its transformation of Mrs. Grose's character. Viewers come to the

---

32 Toíbín, "Pure Evil".
33 James W. Palmer, "Cinematic Ambiguity: James's 'The Turn of the Screw' and Clayton's 'The Innocent'", *Literature/Film Quarterly* 5, no. 3 (1977): 198–215.
34 Tredy, "Shadows of Shadows".
35 Kitahara, "The Haunted Theater".
36 Palmer, "Cinematic Ambiguity", 200–2.
37 A comparable situation occurs with Miles and Flora's uncle, where his *doppelgänger* is a manifestation of the character's extreme self-loathing.

realisation that the ghosts are real because Mrs. Grose's trajectory within the miniseries involves her shocking recognition that she is in fact one of them. That Dani and other "living" characters including Flora and Miles, Owen the cook, and Jamie the housekeeper all interact with Mrs. Grose is the clearest indication that *The Haunting* exists in a world where the paranormal inserts itself into everyday life in seamless fashion.

If *The Haunting of Bly Manor* removes the essential ambiguity of "The Turn of the Screw", then what does it put in its place? I propose that *The Haunting* retains its audience's interest through the way it uses Mrs. Grose to propel an investigation into why the ghosts initially misrecognise themselves as being alive. Moreover, Mrs. Grose's revelation that she was murdered by Quint through his bodily possession of Miles provides a fascinating take on "The Turn of the Screw" in terms of what Quint and Miss Jessel wish to *do* with Miles and Flora once they "get to them" (181). While the governess in "The Turn of the Screw" fears that Quint and Miss Jessel wish to corrupt the children so that they "keep up the work of the demons" (181), *The Haunting* does not adopt a Judeo-Christian framework in which the governess is intent on saving the children's "souls" from "evil". In *The Haunting*, Quint and Miss Jessel's ability to possess the bodies of Miles and Flora springs from a desperation to escape Bly Manor and the horrifying inevitability that their faces and memories will deteriorate because of the "curse" initiated by Viola Willoughby-Lloyd, the original owner of the estate. Mrs. Grose's prominence in the episode "The Altar of the Dead"[38] introduces the problem that all people who die at Bly Manor are unable to escape its "invented gravity", even though the question of *why* will be answered in later episodes of the miniseries ("The Romance of Certain Old Clothes").

Visually speaking, Mrs. Grose in *The Haunting* is a far cry from the way this character has been physically portrayed in other television and cinematic adaptations. From *The Innocents* to more recent adaptations of "The Turn of the Screw" such as *Presence of Mind* (1999, dir. Aloy), *Ghost Story: The Turn of the Screw* (2009, dir. Fywell) and *The Turning* (2020, dir. Sigismondi), the casting of Mrs. Grose has followed the general critical reception of her character as being a middle-aged or senior woman who is by extension past her sexual prime. In his lecture, Bruce humorously rejects Malcolm Pittock's belief that Mrs. Grose "can act disinterestedly"[39] towards the children's supposed perversion by the ghosts

---

38   Flanagan makes several inside-jokes, as it were, to James' oeuvre and the adaptation history of "The Turn of the Screw". Dani's last name gives a nod to the director of *The Innocents*, while the song "O Willow Waly" features as a musical motif in *The Haunting*. It is also notable that flowers are a prominent motif in *The Haunting* in a similar way to *The Innocents*. All of the miniseries' episodes are named after short stories by James. Also, Dani's employer, the master of Bly Manor and both uncle and biological father to Miles and Flora, is Henry Wingrave. His last name recalls James' 1892 short story, "Owen Wingrave", and its eponymous character. The limits of this chapter do not allow for an analysis of how James' other short (ghost) stories have found their way into *The Haunting* beyond simple reference.

39   Malcom Pittock, "The Decadence of *The Turn of the Screw*", *Essays in Criticism* 55, no. 4 (2005): 340.

because she is neither sexually attracted towards the master nor the recipient of his affections (or anybody else's for that matter). "What utter nonsense!" Bruce proclaims, and in defence of Mrs. Grose he states that one must not suppose that "older women think clearly because they've passed menopause" (Gardiner, "Henry James", 6–9; 10). Film directors inspired by "The Turn of the Screw", however, have for the most part in their casting drawn a clear biological separation between the governess and Mrs. Grose. Invariably, Mrs. Grose has been portrayed by older female actors whose physique and style of dress set the character up as a matronly counterpart to the governess, even if her lack of sexual attractiveness and drive mean that her thoughts stay clear from being "riven with unsatisfied desire" (Gardiner, "Henry James", 6–9). Megs Jenkins (1917–1998), for example, played Mrs. Grose twice, the first time in *The Innocents* and then in the 1974 television film, *The Turn of the Screw*.[40] Sue Johnston, the actor who played Mrs. Sarah Grose in *Ghost Story*, was sixty-six years old when this television film was released. Barbara Marten in *The Turning* holds the title of being the oldest actor so far to play Mrs. Grose onscreen, being seventy-seven years of age at the time *The Turning* came to theatres, while Lauren Bacall comes a close second for her turn as Mado Remei in *Presence of Mind* (seventy-five years of age).

Mrs. Hannah Grose in *The Haunting* bucks this standard casting decision in several ways. Played by T'Nia Miller, a British actor of Jamaican heritage, Mrs. Grose appears as a woman in her mid-thirties who has a budding yet ultimately unfulfilled romantic relationship with Owen, the cook played by Rahul Kohli, a British actor of Indian Hindu heritage. Certainly, Miller and Kohli's casting reflects changes that Flanagan has made to the context in which *The Haunting* is set. The miniseries relocates the main narrative of "The Turn of the Screw" to 1987, thus reflecting the racial diversity of the United Kingdom of the late twentieth century as compared to Britain at the *fin-de-siècle*. Miller's comparatively youthful portrayal of *The Haunting* is important since her character is locked in a series of "dream-hops" in which Owen's projected form facilitates her eventual acknowledgement that she is no longer alive. "The Altar of the Dead" involves two key memories or dream-hops that Mrs. Grose returns to repeatedly. The first is a tender moment shared with Owen at a bonfire, in which he asks her to leave Bly Manor and go to Paris with him. The second is Mrs. Grose's memory of the first time she meets Owen when he interviews for the position of cook. Gradually, Mrs. Grose becomes aware that she has interviewed Owen several times: "haven't we already done this?" In subsequent repetitions of this dream-hop, Mrs. Grose and Owen deviate from the regular "script" of interviewer and interviewee; without telling Mrs. Grose explicitly that she is a ghost, Owen insinuates the terrible situation in which she – and other dead occupants of Bly – now find themselves:

---

40 *The Turn of the Screw*", TV movie, director Dan Curtis, ABC Television, 1974.

I'll be stuck in this glue trap of a town like everybody else. [...] That glue, setting in, before we really know it. That bottomless, icy terror realizing we may be stuck forever. [...] Do we realise when we're in the glue? Or when the water around us is boiling? Or do we sit there, saying this will be ok?

Together with the repetition of Mrs. Grose's memory of the bonfire, which has an outcome she is incapable of changing (Owen will not hear her when she finally agrees to leave with him for Paris), the dreaded weight of Owen's words forces Mrs. Grose to accept her shocking fate: that she is dead, was murdered by Miles/Quint, and that her body is at the bottom of a well. Moreover, "The Altar of the Dead" also begins the work of explaining the nature of Mrs. Grose's and Quint's mutual antipathy and how the latter came to die at Bly Manor. In "The Turn of the Screw", Mrs. Grose has a "dread of Quint when he was alive, a dread that lingers strongly in her memory".[41] Boardman refers to the fact that Mrs. Grose calls Quint "clever" and "deep", and that he took enormous liberties with everyone at Bly, including the master.[42] "The fellow was a hound," Mrs. Grose declares unabashedly (159). In "The Altar of the Dead", Mrs. Grose dream-hops to a memory in which she confronts Quint as he is stealing an heirloom owned by Flora and Miles' deceased mother, Charlotte Wingrave. Quint disabuses Mrs. Grose of her belief that the Wingraves are her family rather than her employers. "It's a mistake," he says, for Mrs. Grose to think that Bly Manor is her home. In a statement reminiscent of Douglas' comment to the unnamed narrator that Mrs. Grose was "head of the little establishment – but belowstairs only" (120), Quint reminds Mrs. Grose in *The Haunting* that "There's them, and then there's us [...]. We're 'the help'." Unruffled, Mrs. Grose demands that Quint leave the necklace in its rightful place, only for him to return later in the night to steal it. As Quint prepares to leave the house, Mrs. Grose, Flora and Miles witness the spectral incarnation of Viola Willoughby-Lloyd kill him and drag his body to the lake. As both an eyewitness to Quint's death and a ghost herself, Mrs. Grose drives the narrative of *The Haunting* towards resolving the complex mythology surrounding Bly Manor. Indeed, the reason why Mrs. Grose dream-hops is because memories are "a lie preferred to the truth [that she was dead] instead" ("The Romance of Certain Old Clothes"). Furthermore, in "The Altar of the Dead", viewers come to share Mrs. Grose's deep distrust of Quint, especially in terms of his influence over Miles. Indeed, only moments after he is murdered by Viola, Quint unexpectedly learns how to occupy Miles' body. This revelation will lead to his plan with Miss Jessel to possess Miles' and Flora's bodies respectively so that they may be able to leave Bly Manor forever.

---

41 Boardman, "Mrs. Grose's Reading", 624.
42 Boardman, "Mrs. Grose's Reading", 624.

Conclusion

In this chapter, I have taken Bruce's lecture on "The Turn of the Screw" as inspiration for a recuperative reading of Mrs. Grose in both James' novella and *The Haunting of Bly Manor*. Bruce's lecture cautions scholars to avoid leaping to premature conclusions about literary characters, for doing so may reveal more about our own prejudices and biases than we might think. Speaking about the governess, Bruce states that "We should – shouldn't we? – be most reluctant to make adverse findings about the autonomy, probity, and competence of a narrator – though there will be occasions of course, when we must make such adverse findings" (Gardiner, "Henry James", 6–12). Certainly, as much as the governess, Mrs. Grose has often been misunderstood in the critical reception history of "The Turn of the Screw". My aim in this chapter has thus been to advocate a reading of Mrs. Grose that foregrounds her intelligence, equanimity and perspicacity. In the same way that Bruce behoves us to "credit the teller of a tale with as much insight and truthfulness as conceivable" (Gardiner, "Henry James", 6–15), Mrs. Grose must be praised as a remarkably sharp "reader" of the governess and the unsettling events at Bly.

Bibliography

Aldrich, C. Knight. "Another Twist to 'The Turn of the Screw.'" *Modern Fiction Studies* 13, no. 2 (1967): 167–78.

Boardman, Arthur. "Mrs. Grose's Reading of *The Turn of the Screw*." *Studies in English Literature, 1500–1900* 14, no. 4 (1974): 619–35.

Cranfill, Thomas M., and Robert L. Clark, Jr. "The Provocativeness of *The Turn of the Screw*." *Texas Studies in Literature and Language* 12, no. 1 (1970): 93–100.

Curtsinger, E.C. "'The Turn of the Screw' as Writer's Parable." *Studies in the Novel* 12, no. 4, (1980): 344–58.

Fagin, N. Bryllion. "Another Reading of *The Turn of the Screw*." *Modern Language Notes* 56, no. 3 (1941): 196–202.

Frank, Morgan Day. "Don't Read." *New Literary History* 51, no. 1 (2020): 45–66.

Gardiner, Bruce. "Henry James: *The Turn of the Screw* (1889)." ENGL1012: The Gothic Imagination. First Semester 2014. The University of Sydney, Lecture.

Gargano, James W. "*The Turn of the Screw*." *Western Humanities Review* 15, no. 2 (1961): 173–9.

Ghost Story: The Turn of the Screw. Directed by Tim Fywell. BBC, 2009.

Goddard, Harold C. "A Pre-Freudian Reading of *The Turn of the Screw*." *Nineteenth-Century Fiction* 12, no. 1 (1957): 1–36.

The Haunting of Bly Manor. Directed by Mike Flanagan, Ciarán Foy, Liam Gavin, Yolanda Ramke and Ben Howling, Axelle Carolyn, and E.L. Katz. Intrepid Pictures, Amblin Television, and Paramount Television Studios, 2020.

Heilman, Robert B. "The Freudian Reading of *The Turn of the Screw*." In Henry James, *The Turn of the Screw*. 1898. Ed. Deborah Esch and Jonathan Warren. 2nd ed. New York: Norton, 1999, 177–84.

The Innocents. Directed by Jack Clayton. Achilles Film Production, 1961.

James, Henry. *The Turn of the Screw and Other Stories*. Ed. T.J. Lustig. Oxford: Oxford University Press, 1992.

Ives, C.B. "James's Ghosts in *The Turn of the Screw*." *Nineteenth-Century Fiction* 18, no. 2 (1963): 183–9.

Killoran, Helen. "The Governess, Mrs. Grose and 'The Poison of an Influence' in 'The Turn of the Screw'." *Modern Language Studies* 23, no. 2 (1993): 13–24.

Kitahara, Taeko. "The Haunted Theater of Fiction: Silence and Sound in 'The Turn of the Screw'." In *The Sound of James: The Aural Dimension in Henry James's Work. Papers from the 8th International Conference of the Henry James Society. Trieste, 4–6 July 2019*. Ed. Leonardo Buonomo. Trieste: Edizioni Università di Trieste, 2021, 85–103.

Nardin, Jane. "'The Turn of the Screw': The Victorian Background." *Mosaic: An Interdisciplinary Critical Journal* 12, no. 1 (1978): 131–42.

Palmer, James W. "Cinematic Ambiguity: James's 'The Turn of the Screw' and Clayton's 'The Innocents'." *Literature/Film Quarterly* 5, no. 3 (1977): 198–215.

Pittock, Malcolm. "The Decadence of *The Turn of the Screw*." *Essays in Criticism* 55, no. 4. (2005): 332–51.

Presence of Mind. Directed by Antoni Aloy. Enrique Cerezo PC, 1999.

Solomon, Eric. "The Return of the Screw." *The University Review – Kansas City* 30 (1964): 205–11.

Toal, Catherine. "Murder and 'Point of View'." In *The Entrapments of Form: Cruelty and Modern Literature*. New York: Fordham University Press, 2016, 66–93.

Toíbín, Colm. "Pure Evil: 'The Turn of the Screw'." *The Henry James Review* 30, no. 3 (2009): 237–40.

Tredy, Dennis. "Shadows of Shadows – Techniques of Ambiguity in Three Film Adaptations of 'The Turn of the Screw': J. Clayton's *The Innocents* (1962), D. Curtis's *The Turn of the Screw* (1974), and A. Aloy's *Presence of Mind* (1999)." *Review électronique d'études sur le monde anglophone* 3, no. 2 (2005): n.p.

The Turn of the Screw. Directed by Dan Curtis. ABC Television, 1974.

The Turning. Directed by Floria Sigismondi. DreamWorks Pictures, Amblin Entertainment, Vertigo Entertainment, Reliance Entertainment, and Chislehurst Entertainment, 2020.

Waldock, A.J.A. "Mr. Edmund Wilson and *The Turn of the Screw*." *Modern Language Notes* 62, no. 5 (1947): 331–4.

Walton, Priscilla L. "'What then on earth was I?': Feminine Subjectivity and *The Turn of the Screw*." In *The Turn of the Screw: Complete, Authoritative Text with Biographical and Historical Contexts, Critical History, and Essays from Five Contemporary Critical Perspectives*. Ed. Peter G. Beidler. New York: St. Martin's Press, 1995, 253–67.

Wilson, Edmund. "The Ambiguity of Henry James." *Hound and Horn* (April 1934): 385–406.

Djuna Barnes' Modernity: Addition, Subtraction, Failure, Fantasy

Melissa Hardie

1. Faithful Infidelity

When I was an undergraduate I wrote two essays for Bruce. The first, for a course called "Modes of the Gothic", sought to relate the concepts of the sublime and sublimation through a reading of Anne Radcliffe's *The Mysteries of Udolpho*, a novel Bruce lectured on with the electrifying relish that has always been a hallmark of his teaching style. I was taken with Edmund Burke's expository catalogue of sublime phenomena in *A Philosophical Enquiry into the Origin of Our Ideas of the Sublime and Beautiful* and equally with Radcliffe's aching dilatoriness; and with the course as a pretext for knitting these wayward instances of explanation together. The second essay was for a course Bruce taught with Penny Gay, called "Feminine and Masculine", and it attempted a reading of Hemingway's *Fiesta* alongside Foucault's *History of Sexuality Volume 1*. When I picked up my essay from the General Office I was agitated to see not only that I had misspelt the names of both Hemingway and Foucault in every instance of their usage (I still need to check "Hemingway" from time to time), but also that Bruce had put a line through the misspelt words every single time they occurred.

My essays were the first that I wrote on a typewriter (a Canon Typestar), rather than by hand, and the drumming persistence of my errors, and their correction, felt to me technologically assisted or even obscurely motivated. The modernist promise of the typewriter was to create more rapid, reliable, legible (if nondescript) text, and yet it revealed itself to be the means to compound rather than eradicate error and eccentricity. Between the books' covers and my typing hand a slip had occurred and become profusely visible across three thousand or so carefully scripted words: a parapraxis, *Fehlleistungen*. This term from Freud I was only to learn years later as a form of consolation for such moments of psychical betrayal, and reflecting on this episode I am struck by the way the *infidelity* of my typing was in fact also a form of *faithfulness*, as for Laplanche and Pontalis "it transpires that what appear to be bungled actions turn out in fact – on another level – to be quite successful ones, and that unconscious wishes are fulfilled by such behaviour in a manner that is often very plain to see".[1] These misspellings, unfaithful to the letter, were faithful instead as a successful redirection from purported to repressed goal, and in their reiteration a form of solidarity, or fidelity arose, as it did, too, from Bruce's painstaking corrections. Fidelity to meaning became a more obscure goal than might be supposed, if even the most patently "bungled" action of textual infidelity could be so tenaciously tied to another realm of interpretative possibility.

Nowhere else might the problem of indeterminate meaning better resolve into an encounter between infidelity and its surprising other, fidelity, than in characteristic strategies of literary interpretation where (for example) purported disciplinary innovation may in fact be faithful to (or worse, reducible to) earlier disciplinary norms. Reanimating this relation productively generates interpretative possibilities through precisely the irresolvable fact of their similarities and differences: their faithfulness and unfaithfulness. Heather Love opens her introduction to the *PMLA* issue on Queer Modernism, "Modernism by Night", by asking, "Is Queer Modernism simply another name for Modernism?"[2] Love's question, less or more than rhetorical, identifies less the way in which Modernist texts can be understood to identify "queer" as a central problematic and more the way in which the canon of writing about Modernism has been pressured by a "non-normative" imperative sufficiently dominant in the critical field that few Modernist texts, in her words, "appear to have stayed high and dry ... bad modernism, outsider modernism, and marginal modernism begin to look more and more like modernism itself".[3] Love argues that

> Of all the forms of marginal modernism that have surfaced in the past couple of decades, queer modernism seems particularly likely to merge into modernism proper. ... With the emergence of queer literary studies dating from the late 1980s and early 1990s, the specificity of same-sex identities or desires has not been an absolute criterion in tracing the queerness of a particular textual object, author, or set of relations.[4]

Instead, the very "pervasiveness" of non-normativity produced a state of "permission" where queer becomes the "uninvited guest, unexpected but not totally unwelcome, that shows up without visible relations or ties".[5]

In his essay on Djuna Barnes' *Nightwood* so introduced by Love, Brian Glavey lights on the phrase "queer ekphrasis" to situate *Nightwood* between recent

---

1   Jean Laplanche and Jean-Bertrand Pontalis, *The Language of Psycho-Analysis*, trans. Donald Nicholson-Smith (London: Karnac Books, 1988), 300.
2   Heather Love, "Modernism at Night", *PMLA* 124, no. 3 (2009): 744.
3   Love, "Modernism at Night", 744.
4   Love, "Modernism at Night", 745.
5   Love, "Modernism at Night", 744.

formulations of "queer indeterminacy". This it does by staging a rendezvous, if not reconciliation, between the current preoccupations of queer and an earlier aesthetic regime, one that sought to find formal expression for the novel's stylistic complexity in Joseph Frank's influential concept of "spatial form".[6] Glavey's phrase exemplifies what Heather Love calls a "merging", in this case of a revived, historical, formalist reading of the novel (Joseph Frank's 1945 coinage "spatial form") with the preoccupations of queer theory.[7] This reconciliation or "merging" performs at the level of a motivated textual analysis a move comparable to the one I will make here, merging "queer" with "adultery" through the singular marriage or "unexpected" reconciliation of the two in Barnes' novel. Where queer "shows up without visible relations or ties" (Love) in the Modernist novel (that is, with only a history of repressed or closeted representation), adultery constitutes precisely the opposite, the assertion of a visible relation through contracted fidelity and its equally visible disruption as evidence of contractual dereliction.[8] *Nightwood*, in fact, offers a way to think through the relation of the two, a faithful infidelity or "queer adultery" that also advances a way of thinking through late Modernism's interest in historicising the novel and in quelling the momentum of Modernist experimentation. Queer adultery, as it is formulated in *Nightwood*, facilitates the novel's formal project of considering history – what might be termed, after Love, "visible relations or ties" – as a context for its formal experimentation.

Of the many ways in which *Nightwood* has come to be regarded as a disruptive, late modern text, its formal eccentricity is never far from the front. The novel, whose plot mostly concerns a failed relationship between two women, Nora Flood and Robin Vote, begins with an extended historicising prologue that narrates the marriage and deaths of Robin Vote's husband's parents, Guido and Hedvig Volkbein. This narrative, given in a mock-genealogical form alongside a dense account of the material cultures of *fin-de-siècle* Vienna and 1920s Europe, is a puzzling one despite all the ways in which the novel has been close read over the decades. The marriages of the Volkbeins, father and son, progress the story only by moving us historically forward to the point where Robin, straying from her marriage – the adultress – comes into contact with Nora. The saga of the Volkbeins, senior and junior, stages adulterous transgressions in a "historicising" way, where marriage does the work Tony Tanner requires of it – stitching together social and affective obligations as they abide in descriptions of bourgeois domesticity. To quote Tanner:

> The most important mediation procedure that attempts to harmonize the natural, the familial, the social, and even the transcendental is, of course, marriage. Thus,

---

6   Brian Glavey, "Dazzling Estrangement: Modernism, Queer Ekphrasis, and the Spatial Form of *Nightwood*", *PMLA* 124, no. 3 (2009): 749–63.
7   Love, "Modernism at Night", 744.
8   Love, "Modernism at Night", 744.

in a marriage you may participate in nature's pattern of coupling and breeding; but this can be incorporated within the existing interfamilial patterns and validated contractually by society. It can also be sanctioned by the church. Ideally, then, marriage offers the perfect and total mediation between the patterns within which men and women live. ... If the mediation of marriage works, then everything is, as it were, at rest, all the patterns moving harmoniously together. It is the bourgeois ideal (an ideal that precludes the envisaging of possible patterns of *historical* and *political* change). But if something happens to disturb this mediation, or rather all the mediations that center on marriage, or to make them unacceptable or impossible, then a person involved may experience that anxiety or "unhappy consciousness" that is a result of feeling he or she is participating in two or more irreconcilable patterns, with no means of mediating them any longer.[9]

It is the failure of marital mediation that is generated by the topic of adultery, and consequent upon that the "possible patterns of *historical* and *political* change".[10] Adultery in that respect performs cognate service to queer, denaturing the "normative" indices brokered by any such social-cultural contract. Reading *Nightwood* under the rubric of adultery then offers a generic way to align its conventional disruption of norms through adultery with its unconventional disruption of norms through "queer", precisely as it sutures the two: its distended historical "prologue" presenting the Volkbeins and its revision in the "queer adultery" of Robin and Nora's relationship. Attending to its interest in adultery requires an historicised response to the generically conventional association between adultery and the novel, where the disruption of the contract of marriage threatens other kinds of social contracts, and where adultery becomes a generative *topos* for the making of novelistic stories *qua* stories. While substantial critical labour has been exerted to articulate the way in which *Nightwood* figures an isomorphism between non-normative sexual practice and experimental writing, its interest in marriage, class and adultery offers another way to articulate Barnes' relationship with, on the one hand, the realist novel, and on the other, convention and women's sexual sociality.

For all the ways in which queer readings of *Nightwood* have relied on a non-normative imperative – for example, in their contemplation of its highly eccentric formal properties – a same-sex relationship, that is a baldly queer thematic – constitutes its central object of analysis. At the same time, that relationship is bracketed from the novel's diffuse representation of social life in a cosmopolitan European demi-monde, but not therefore isolated. Instead, it is given infrastructural support by being textually generated through its interpellation as a family history *of* adultery. This thematic, rather than interpretative queer

---

9   Tony Tanner, *Adultery in the Novel: Contract and Transgression* (Baltimore, MD: Johns Hopkins University Press, 1979), 14–17, emphasis in original.

10   Tanner, *Adultery in the Novel*, 16–17.

"merging", sets the stage for a late Modern recontextualisation of the conventions of putatively transgressive adultery. Adultery could be understood as simply the most conventional of the various forms of errancy that destabilise bourgeois life in *Nightwood*. But what if adultery is, in fact, critical to the novel's experimentation with formal convention as much as its experimental representations of queer sexuality and unsettled domesticity? In this sense, adultery in its late Modern context offers a way to articulate relationships between realist and non-realist narrative structures.

Nightwood uses experimental representations of adultery as conventional trespass to frame an engagement with the history of the adulterous heroine in realist novels. In particular, the serially narrated carriage ride at the heart of *Nightwood*'s distortion of narrative temporal flow in favour of "spatial form" maps Emma Bovary's famous, adulterous carriage ride onto the novel's modernist timeline. Where *Madame Bovary*'s 1857 carriage ride facilitates a metaphorisation of adultery as a vehicle of a future-oriented momentum (plot progression), *Nightwood*'s serially narrated carriage ride – in which Robin Vote unlocks herself from the intimacy of her partnership with Nora to have a queerly adulterous liaison with Jenny Petherbridge inaugurated in the carriage and uncomfortably witnessed by a child – inhibits any similar sense that this transgression facilitates movement forward. The carriage ride produces the stasis of Frank's spatial form, an inset tableau of sexual action covert according to the prim realist conventions borrowed from Bovary (that is, only obliquely depicted), but inhibiting the temporal flow of the novel in favour of its spatial reorganisation.

Despite Tanner's framing of adultery athwart this magnificent instatement of "patterns" it is scarcely credible to see adultery as transgressive per se, given its centrality or even canonicity as novelistic *topos*. Although accounts of the novel and adultery are typically structured around generic and conventional claims regarding realism, it's no accident that the "major" novel of High Modernism, *Ulysses*, pivots its day around adultery in action or in report – Molly Bloom's adulterous liaison with Boylan. Adultery, far from simply indexing transgression, indexes formal convention and familiarity. Its citation in *Nightwood*, far from boding disruption, makes a more subtle engagement possible – it facilitates a queer "patterning" that both reproduces and departs from the patterns Tanner identifies, where Barnes formally and structurally argues equivalence between the adultery committed by Robin in her marriage to Felix and that performed in her relationship with Nora, a kind of argument, in "bad modernist" vocabulary, for a queer marriage equality.

Formally, then, such a pivot is instated by *Nightwood*'s otherwise inscrutable but dense contextualisation of its central story, the queer romance of Nora Flood and Robin Vote, with two heterosexual marriages: the first, of Guido Volkbein senior, in Schorskian *fin-de-siècle* Vienna, the second, of Robin Vote and Guido's son Felix.[11] The first marriage is not marked by adultery, but the second marriage, between Felix and Robin is, and the progressive decline of marital "mediation" between generations becomes a condition for the novel's account of its central relationship; it is only adulterously that Robin makes a partnership with Nora and it is queerly adulterously that she ends that relationship as well.

2. Museal Modernism

Nightwood's extended introduction of the Volkbein parents of Felix in its first chapter moves against the implicitly forward momentum of the novel. Between the Volkbein opening and the narration of Nora and Robin's love affair, no progress is made in the novel without an associated drag structured by reminiscence, allegorical anecdote, and other forms of situated quelling. Most distinctly this arrest and delay is personified in the figure of Matthew O'Connor, the doctor whose virtuosic anecdotes derail interpersonal transactions even as his "gynaecological" activities support them.[12] In its dilatory and dilettante prose *Nightwood* reframes late Modernism as a pivot towards historicising that Modernist drive by drawing attention instead to its recalcitrance. Given its centrality in an account of queer Modernism, *Nightwood*'s lapidary prose and dense description, its accumulation of ekphrastic passages with the momentum of molasses, and its circling, circuitous narrative contest the ethos of modernist representations of futurity itself as a discernible elsewhere in favour of an implicit injunction to read momentum as historical and driven by memory.

Nightwood's attention to the practice of recollection and its materialisation in objects that concretise or arrest memory provides a succinct example that demonstrates memory and repetition as the key alliance brokered between queer and adultery, fidelity and infidelity. Early in the description of the marriage of Hedvig and Guido Volkbein their house is described as "a fantastic museum of their encounter".[13] This "museum" forms a material hold or crypt for the objects that facilitate the marriage and also describes this vault in terms of display and spectacle, the show of the marriage. Its collection is made up of counterfeit and misrepresented items which Guido has used to generate a material context for his own prosperity. Later in the novel, the apartment that Nora buys for Robin is similarly described:

> In the passage of their lives together every object in the garden, every item in the house, every word they spoke, attested to their mutual love, the combining of their humours. There were circus chairs, wooden horses bought from a ring of an old merry-go-round, Venetian chandeliers from the Flea Fair, stage-drops from Munich, cherubim from Vienna, ecclesiastical hangings from Rome, a spinet from

---

11   Carl E. Schorske, *Fin-de-siècle Vienna: Politics and Culture* (New York: Alfred A. Knopf Inc., 1979). Bruce introduced me to Schorske.

12   O'Connor's "interest in gynaecology had driven him half around the world". Djuna Barnes, *Nightwood* (London: Faber, 1936), 44.

13   Barnes, *Nightwood*, 17.

England, and a miscellaneous collection of music boxes from many countries; such was the museum of their encounter, as Felix's hearsay house had been testimony of the age when his father had lived with his mother.[14]

These two premises are each described as a "museum of their encounter" with the unexpectedly pivotal word being "their". Here, it ambiguously encompasses all three couples: Guido and Hedvig, Felix and Robin, and Robin and Nora. Barnes' compression of these separate couples into two separate premises and one intact metaphor interlaces the sentimental adultery plot and the queer romance, a form of marriage equality *avant la lettre* that guides the extended Volkbein prelude.

One other effect of the novel's abutment of a story of marriage and adultery with its queer romance is that it encourages a desire to read its adulterous Volkbein prologue "historically", and the rest of the novel "affectively". In its pairing of the two, an extended historicising introduction "merges" with the narrative of queer devotion and infidelity to "merge" the adulterous and the queer as forms of historical transgression. Daniela Caselli writes:

> *Nightwood* is queer neither because it places centre stage a series of minoritised groups nor because it metonymically recuperates them as tropes of universal estrangement. Its queerness (never to be found ready-made, always to be recognised) can be read in its uniquely unrelenting distrust in mimesis, in its untrustworthy and manipulative seductiveness, and, importantly, in its skirting a little too close for comfort to what is possibly the biggest of Modernist no-nos: sentimentality.[15]

Caselli's take identifies the same problematic Love identifies in her *PMLA* introduction (published the same year); it displaces the centrality of the minoritised precisely while trying to analyse the queer effects of the novel. Here "distrust" in mimesis manifests itself in a prose style that analogises and extends into absurdity the functional value of analogy. At the same time, the claim that Barnes' circumlocution primarily rides on a distrust of mimesis has to reckon with Barnes' tactical interest in precise repetition and doubling, as for instance in the transposition of the phrase "museum of their encounter" across two generations of Volkbeins and into the domestic heart of the queer couple's home and hearth. Encounters across generations process the same sets of novelistic tropes even if, as Tyrus Miller says, these engagements generate "regressive unravelling" as a symptom of *Nightwood*'s "late" Modernity.[16] *Nightwood*'s merging of adultery and queer carries with it a significant set of encounters within and concerned with literary history as such. The first is between

---

14 Barnes, *Nightwood*, 85.
15 Daniela Caselli, *Improper Modernism: Djuna Barnes' Bewildering Corpus* (Farnham, Surrey: Ashgate, 2009), 175.
16 Tyrus Miller, *Late Modernism: Politics, Fiction, and the Arts Between the World Wars* (Berkeley: University of California Press, 1999), 62.

realism's fictional preoccupation with adultery as moral turpitude, and infidelity as excess and its distorted or "regressive" second order recurrence in (late) experimental Modernism. The second is between adultery as transgression of contract and adultery as compliance with convention. The third is late Modernism's critical engagement with the implicitly future-oriented fantasy of High Modernism's "make it new", where recourse to an earlier regime of conventional representation detours such a fantasy of forward momentum. The fourth is the coupling of historicist (realist, contractual) description with the lapidary prose of a text whose utter purpose would otherwise seem to be the entire occultation of historical context in favour of its flawed, unfaithful recollection. The last is a meta-textual arbitration of the grounds upon which adultery can encounter queer, where "strange museums of encounter" demonstrate that the non-normativity of Modernism's queer relies on something other than queer (its adulterous shadow) and with the drive to document queer adultery.

It is on a divan that Robin Vote is first encountered in *Nightwood*, when Dr Matthew O'Connor is called to a hotel to attend to her. O'Connor, who has been ensconced with Felix Volkbein for the duration of a lengthy monologue at *Café de la Mairie*, brings Volkbein with him as he takes a few steps to the *Hôtel Récamier*. By bringing Felix along he puts into motion the encounter between Felix and Robin that provides a point of contact between the 1880s history of the Volkbeins and 1920s Paris. Accompanying O'Connor, Felix arrives like the "uninvited guest" of queer, in Love's words, "unexpected but not totally unwelcome", and he "shows up without visible relations or ties".[17] Were it not for the careful foregrounding of similarity between his parents' marriage and his wife's later adulterous liaison with Nora the relation might remain more obscure, but the representation of these intimacies as "spatial" entities (museums), as visual and concrete representations of intersubjective "encounter", is proleptically installed by the description of Robin's chamber.

The proper noun *Récamier* identifies not only the hotel but also an association between the divan and David's 1800 portrait of *Madame Récamier*, although the sparseness of ornament in the painting is not reproduced in the description of Robin's bed. This extended ekphrasis figures the sight of Robin as a textual birth, within a prose figured precisely as a stylistic ornament, too much, "oversung":

> On a bed, surrounded by a confusion of potted plants, exotic palms and cut flowers, faintly oversung by the notes of unseen birds, which seemed to have been forgotten – left without the usual silencing cover, which, like cloaks on funeral urns, are cast over their cages at night by good housewives)[sic] – half flung off the support of the cushions from which, in a moment of threatened consciousness she had turned her head, lay the young woman, heavy and dishevelled.[18]

---

17 Love, "Modernism at Night", 745.
18 Barnes, *Nightwood*, 55.

In Barnes' description, the unconscious body "threatens consciousness" as the unremembered birds create "oversung" text, left uncovered, and thus unsilenced, a return of the repressed. The cloaking of songbirds is funereal in the passage's simile; the "unseen birds" are "forgotten" by the woman who even in her introduction promises to be a distracted *femme au foyer*, not merely (as she is evoked in the title of the chapter, *La Somnambule*) a sleepwalker but, more pertinently, inattentive. Robin's inattention is the symptom of her infidelity, where she roams and drifts in Paris apparently without a conscious drive for cohesive motion or interaction.

Robin's errancy is mimicked by the incorporation of an accidental, a stray closing parenthesis that like the birds is left without its "cover", the opening parenthesis that like the cover "seems" to have been forgotten. Or perhaps this stray random parenthesis, unfaithful to the text, is a parapraxis that instates the typesetter as also "inattentive" and "threatening consciousness" precisely in her or his unconscious slippage. This inexplicable, single parenthesis betrays the otherwise painstaking authorial stamp, as if to demonstrate that never-ended possibilities are, in fact, the consolation of writing and that errors or infelicities provide as Barthes writes "the site of fantasy";[19] writing of Flaubert he says:

> Flaubert subtracts, erases, constantly returns to zero, begins over again. Flaubertian sequestration has for its center (and its symbol) a piece of furniture which is not the desk but the divan: when the depths of agony are plumbed, Flaubert throws himself on his sofa: this is his "marinade," an ambiguous situation, in fact, for the sign of failure is also the site of fantasy, whence the work will gradually resume, giving Flaubert a new substance which he can erase anew.[20]

Barthes' formulation identifies failure and fantasy's interrelation as something that becomes in itself an intransitive grandiosity:

> Apparently, then, style engages the writer's entire existence, and for this reason it would be better to call it henceforth a *writing*: to write is to live ("*A book has always been for me,*" Flaubert says, "*a particular way of living*"), writing is the book's goal, not publication. This precellence, attested – or purchased – by the very sacrifice of a life, somewhat modifies the traditional conceptions of "writing well," ordinarily given as the final garment (the ornament) of ideas or passions.[21]

The divan is metonymy for a *writing* praxis which is inalienable from *living* as praxis, a writing not confined or oriented by publication – cessation – or by the notion of style as essentially finalising ("le mot juste"). That grandiosity, of the

---

19   Roland Barthes, "Flaubert and the Sentence", *New Critical Essays*, trans. Richard Howard (New York: Hill & Wang, 1980), 70.
20   Barthes, "Flaubert", 70.
21   Barthes, "Flaubert", 70.

writing life, describes Barnes' practice through her career but especially in her later years, when she devotes herself to the great work of what Scott Herring describes as a "geriatric avant-garde" full of erasure, addition, subtraction, failure and fantasy.[22] Editorial trespass is a way to keep alive, and also at bay, the prospect of publication as a form of "final word", one that must necessarily be both faithful to the prospect of the work's endurance and unfaithful to its capacity to "threaten" consciousness, the insistence of the potential to fulfil wishes rather than curtail them.

Such a writing praxis requires error, parapraxis, the very faithfulness to the inevitability of error and its correction as the "marinade" that defines a writing life. A writing life is the occasion for erroneous felicity, where faithfulness to a more subterranean end can only be encountered through unwitting reversals and infidelities. Bruce's chapter on *Creatures in an Alphabet*, Djuna Barnes' last book and as late as Modernism gets, opens by observing that "Some of its creatures are odder than odd".[23] The "odder than odd" is a paradoxical figure that neatly identifies the problem of unfaithfulness as itself a "marinade" or writing life, a sequestration that like Robin Vote on her couch at the *Hôtel Récamier* can grant the permeability of conscious states to their unconscious intruders. Such a state of abnegation is represented in Barnes' abecedarium by one of those "odder than odds" Bruce identifies, the letter X who "has crossed himself away".[24] This gesture remains one of fidelity to the task: of editing, correction, addition and subtraction, fidelity and infidelity.

Bibliography

Barnes, Djuna. *Creatures in an Alphabet*. New York: The Dial Press, 1982.

Barnes, Djuna. *Nightwood*. London: Faber and Faber, 1936.

Barthes, Roland. *New Critical Essays*. Trans. Richard Howard. New York: Hill & Wang, 1980.

Caselli, Daniela. *Improper Modernism: Djuna Barnes' Bewildering Corpus*. Farnham, Surrey: Ashgate, 2009.

Gardiner, Bruce. "Djuna Barnes's *Creatures in an Alphabet:* From A for Anecdotage to Z for Zoomancy." In *Shattered Objects: Djuna Barnes's Modernism*. Eds. Elizabeth Pender and Catherine Setz, 75–94. University Park, PA: The Penn State University Press, 2019.

Glavey, Brian. "Dazzling Estrangement: Modernism, Queer Ekphrasis, and the Spatial Form of *Nightwood*." *PMLA* 124, no. 3 (2009): 749–63.

Herring, Scott. "Djuna Barnes' Geriatric Avant-garde." *PMLA* 130, no. 1 (2015): 69–91.

Laplanche, Jean and Jean-Bertrand Pontalis. *The Language of Psycho-Analysis*. Trans. Donald Nicholson-Smith. London: Karnac Books, 1988.

Love, Heather. "Modernism at Night." *PMLA* 124, no. 3 (2009): 744–8.

---

22   Scott Herring, "Djuna Barnes and the Geriatric Avant-varde", *PMLA* 130, no. 1 (2015): 69–91.

23   Bruce Gardiner, "Djuna Barnes's *Creatures in an Alphabet:* From A for Anecdotage to Z for Zoomancy", in *Shattered Objects: Djuna Barnes's Modernism*, eds. Elizabeth Pender and Catherine Setz (University Park: The Penn State University Press, 2019), 75.

24   Djuna Barnes, *Creatures in an Alphabet* (New York: The Dial Press, 1982), n.p.

Miller, Tyrus. *Late Modernism: Politics, Fiction, and the Arts Between the World Wars*. Berkeley: University of California Press, 1999.

Schorske, Carl E. *Fin-de-siècle Vienna: Politics and Culture*. New York: Alfred A. Knopf Inc., 1979.

Tanner, Tony. *Adultery in the Novel: Contract and Transgression*. Baltimore, MD: Johns Hopkins University Press, 1979.

22

The Last Man: Literature and Survival

Peter J. Hutchings

S'il y a un rapport entre écriture et passivité, c'est que l'une et l'autre supposent l'effacement, l'exténuation du sujet: supposent un changement de temps: supposent qu'entre être et ne pas être quelque chose qui ne s'accomplit pas arrive cependant comme étant depuis toujours déjà survenu – les désœuvrement du neutre, la rupture silencieuse du fragmentaire.[1]

If there is a relation between writing and passivity, it is because both assume the effacement, the extenuation of the subject: both assume a change in time, and that between being and non-being, something which never yet takes place happens nonetheless, as having long since already happened. The unworking of the neuter, the silent rupture of the fragmentary.[2]

Mary Shelley's 1826 novel, *The Last Man*, tells the story of Lionel Verney, the survivor of a plague that has killed all humankind. Verney lives on in the libraries of Rome, dedicating himself to writing the history of the last man, a book addressed to the dead. Bruce Gardiner supervised my PhD, which read Shelley's book, among others, in consideration of modes of first person narrative and practices of writing. This essay is a meditation on the dynamics of literature, reading and survival, dedicated to a literary and personal survivor.

Two scenes of writing, and of reading. The first scene (and sequence will be challenging in this context), is in a cave, that of the Cumaean Sibyl in a description that is presented as an introduction to the work that follows. The second scene (and ultimate beyond the usual sense of an ending or finality), is in a library, in Rome, and comes at the climax of the novel.

---

1   Maurice Blanchot, *L'écriture du désastre* (Paris: Gallimard, 1980), 29–30.
2   Maurice Blanchot, *The Writing of the Disaster*, trans. Ann Smock (Lincoln and London: University of Nebraska Press, 1986), 14, translation modified.

In the Cave

So, to the first scene.

The "Author's Introduction" to *The Last Man*, while clearly an introduction, is not so clearly the account of an "author". Notions of authorship are complicated by a discourse that opens with an account of a visit to the Bay of Naples and the Baiae in December 1818:

> I visited Naples in the year 1818. On the 8th of December of that year, my companion and I crossed the Bay, to visit the antiquities which are scattered on the shores of Baiae.[3]

This account is to be contrasted with the impressions of this visit recorded in Mary's *Journal*:

> Tuesday, Dec. 8. – Go on the sea with Shelley. Visit Cape Miseno, the Elysian Fields, Avernus, Solfatara. The Bay of Baiae is beautiful; but we are disappointed by the various places we visit.[4]

The fact that this is all that is recorded there about this journey effectively functions to distance the more elaborate account of the "Introduction" from any relation to the events of December 1818, from History and from a Mary Shelley as Historical and Authorial Subject. However, at first the "Introduction's" account concurs with the *Journal*:

> We visited the so called Elysian Fields and Avernus: and wandered through various ruined temples, baths, and classic spots; at length we entered the gloomy cavern of the Cumaean Sibyl. Our Lazzeroni bore flaring torches, which shone red, and almost dusky, in the murky subterranean passages, whose darkness thirstily surrounding them, seemed eager to imbibe more and more of the element of light. We passed by a natural archway, leading to a second gallery, and enquired, if we could not enter there also. The guides pointed to the reflection of their torches on the water that paved it, leaving us to form our own conclusion; but adding it was a pity, for it led to the Sibyl's Cave. Our curiosity and enthusiasm were excited by this circumstance, and we insisted upon attempting the passage. As is usually the case in the prosecution of such enterprizes, the difficulties decreased on examination. We found, on each side of the humid pathway, "dry land for the sole of the foot." At length we arrived at a large, desert, dark cavern, which the Lazzeroni assured us was the Sibyl's Cave. We were sufficiently disappointed —[5]

---

3   Mary Shelley, *The Last Man*, ed. Hugh J. Luke, Jr. (Lincoln: University of Nebraska Press, 1965), 1.
4   Mary Shelley, *Mary Shelley's Journal*, ed. Frederick L. Jones (Norman: University of Oklahoma Press, 1947), 113.
5   Shelley, *The Last Man*, 1.

The account breaks off with a dash, and this is the point at which the "Introduction" is most in accord with the *Journal* account, in the noting of the disappointment the unnamed "Mary" and "Percy" felt in this place. The divergence between the two accounts then opens at exactly this point of identity and, following the dash, the account opens up the question of the processes of writing-reading in a certain allegorical mode – one that is itself involved in the oracular and apocalyptic genres – for what is figured here is a revelation of the oracular, apocalyptic texts that will then be the texts revealed in *The Last Man*, a text that will reveal the End of Man to come two centuries later, an Apocalypse Not Now, Not Yet.[6] There will be a revelation of the mode in which these revelations, apocalypses may be inscribed or intoned, a revelation of an answer to the question of the place of the writer, here a writer of the female gender operating within the bounds of late romanticism: within the closure of that romanticism, but at its limen, its threshold. The revelation, then, of how one may write at the End, of what can be written of the End.

After the dash – the account proceeds –

> Yet we examined it with care, as if its blank, rocky walls could still bear trace of celestial visitant. On one side there was a small opening. Whither does this lead? we asked: can we enter here? – *"Questo poi, no,"*[7] said the wild looking savage who held the torch; "you can advance but a short distance, and nobody visits it."[8]

The travellers then proceed through a number of narrow and difficult passages, finally reaching another cave, containing a raised stone seat and the "perfect snow-white skeleton of a goat", which has apparently fallen through the veiled aperture in the roof of the cavern. Mary Shelley continues this account by mentioning the other adornments of this space:

> The rest of the furniture of the cavern consisted of piles of leaves, fragments of bark, and a white filmy substance, resembling the inner part of the green hood which shelters the grain of the unripe Indian corn.[9]

So far, then, there is a succumbing to enthusiasm which leads to a further investigation of the passage leading to a second cavern – which is supposed to be the Sibyl's Cave and isn't – and then the investigation and penetration of another series of passages to the third cavern, one veiled by nature, containing leaves, bark, and corn hoods. Now the identity of this last cavern is revealed:

---

6   For Jacques Derrida's development of this pun in the context of a philosophical tradition of questions of apocalypse, see "No Apocalypse, Not Now (full speed ahead, seven missiles, seven missives)", trans. Catherine Porter and Philip Lewis, *Diacritics* 14 no.2 (Summer 1984): 20–31.
7   "That won't do."
8   Shelley, *The Last Man*, 1.
9   Shelley, *The Last Man*, 2.

At length my friend, who had taken up some of the leaves strewed about, exclaimed, "This *is* the Sibyl's Cave; these are Sibylline leaves." On examination, we found that all the leaves, bark, and other substances, were traced with written characters. What appeared to us more astonishing, was that these writings were expressed in various languages: some unknown to my companion, ancient Chaldee, and Egyptian hieroglyphics, old as the Pyramids. Stranger still, some were in modern dialects, English and Italian. We could make out little by the dim light, but they seemed to contain prophecies, detailed relations of events but lately passed; names, now well known, but of modern date; and often exclamations of exultation or woe, of victory or defeat, were traced on their scant pages. This was certainly the Sibyl's Cave; not indeed exactly as Vergil describes it; but the whole of this land had been so thoroughly convulsed by earthquake and volcano, that the change was not wonderful though the traces of ruin were effaced by time; and we probably owed the preservation of these leaves, to the accident which had closed the mouth of the cavern, and the swift-growing vegetation which had rendered its sole opening impervious to the storm. We made a hasty selection of such of the leaves, whose writing one at least of us could understand; and then, laden with our treasure, we bade adieu to the dim hypaethric cavern, and after much difficulty succeeded in rejoining our guides.

During our stay in Naples, we often returned to this cave, sometimes alone, skimming the sun-lit sea, and each time added to our store. Since that period, whenever the world's circumstance has not imperiously called me away, or the temper of my mind impeded such study, I have been employed in deciphering these sacred remains.[10]

Thus, the "real" cave, the last cave, of the Cumaean Sibyl is revealed, its veil undercut: a veiling previously made complete by nature after a moment of the "catastrophe" of the fall of the goat, but which is now rent again and revealed by enthusiasm, rather appropriately given that it is a Sibylline cave. Therein, the texts of various voices delivered through the Sibyl lie, texts ranging across History as the oracular utterances are fabled to have done, texts of voices requiring reinscription: requiring a Sibyl to render them intelligible again. Or for the first time. These are texts or voices whose origins it would be better for us not to inquire after; whose multiplicity and multivalency will intone the death knell of certain rules of discourse, and of concepts of an author, intoning a death knell for certain orders of Literature and Philosophy.

This "Author's Introduction" to *The Last Man* breaks the oracular mode free from the constraints of unintelligibility, and of the hermeneutic constraint which requires a translator for oracles and apocalyptic texts: a constraint no less incumbent upon masculine writers of apocalyptic texts than upon feminine writers,

---

10　Shelley, *The Last Man*, 2–3. The other "sacred remains" belonging to Mary Shelley might be recalled here: the heart of Percy, saved by Edward John Trelawny, and his literary remains.

as indicated by the critical history of commentaries upon John of Patmos' *Apocalypse*.[11] Where previously the oracular-oneiric or apocalyptic text required a masculine translator-priest for its intelligible inscription, this task now becomes a feminine one and, in terms of the structure of this sexual-hermeneutic economy, thus one belonging to the Sibyl herself.

> I present the public with my latest discoveries in the slight Sibylline pages. Scattered and unconnected as they were, I have been obliged to add links, and model the work into a consistent form. But the main substance rests on the truths contained in these poetic rhapsodies, and the divine intuition which the Cumaean damsel obtained from heaven.
>
> I have often wondered at the subject of her verses, and at the English dress of the Latin poet. Sometimes I have thought, that, obscure and chaotic as they are, they owe their present form to me, their decipherer. As if we should give to another artist, the painted fragments which form the mosaic copy of Raphael's Transfiguration in St. Peter's; he would put them together in a form, whose mode would be fashioned by his own peculiar mind and talent. Doubtless the leaves of the Cumaean Sibyl have suffered distortion and diminution of interest and excellence in my hands. My only excuse for thus transforming them, is that they were unintelligible in their pristine condition.
>
> My labours have cheered long hours of solitude, and taken me out of a world, which has averted its once benignant face from me, to one glowing with imagination and power. Will my readers ask how I could find solace from the narration of misery and woeful change? This is one of the mysteries of our nature, which holds full sway over me, and from whose influence I cannot escape. I confess, that I have not been unmoved by the development of the tale; and that I have been depressed, nay, agonized, at some parts of the recital, which I have faithfully transcribed from my materials. Yet such is human nature, that the excitement of mind was dear to me, and that the imagination, painter of tempest and earthquake, or, worse, the stormy and ruin-fraught passions of man, softened my real sorrows and endless regrets, by clothing these fictitious ones in that ideality, which takes the mortal sting from pain.
>
> I hardly know whether this apology is necessary. For the merits of my adaptation and translation must decide how far I have well bestowed my time and imperfect powers, in giving form and substance to the frail and attenuated Leaves of the Sibyl.[12]

Two points here: one, on the process of writing as transcription and decipherment; the other, on the consolations of the imagination of disaster. When Mary Shelley writes that "Yet such is human nature, that the excitement of mind was dear to

---

11   John of Patmos, *Apocalypse* (The Book of Revelation).
12   Shelley, *The Last Man*, 3–4.

me, and that the imagination, painter of tempest and earthquake, or, worse, the stormy and ruin-fraught passions of man, softened my real sorrows and endless regrets, by clothing these fictitious ones in that ideality, which takes the mortal sting from pain", she can be understood as stating that the thought of the death of all humanity offered solace for her loss of Percy Shelley, found in the process of writing (or transcribing) the Sibylline texts.

A play occurs here between the terms used to describe the appearance of this oracular text, its phenomenal appearance in the world *as* text, a movement between terming it a product of the revelation of the "divine intuition" of the Sibyl – implicitly linking it to a theory of genius and imagination – and terming the text a work of decipherment and translation, a work reading these texts and making them intelligible, legible. At first, the text is an inscription of certain "discoveries" in the Sibylline pages, resting upon them and upon "intuition". Then, it appears that there has been a "transformation" of those pages and not simply a decipherment, and this text finally appears as an "adaptation and translation" giving "form and substance" to those leaves and pages. There is also the matter – involving a theory of poetry and genre – of the transformation of *verse* into *prose*, one bound to retain the poetic quality of verse expression in the guise of unmetered language.

The fact that this priestly function of interpretation and decipherment is discharged by a female and feminine writer – one who thus shares some sexual identity with the Sibyl – raises a number of questions concerning the implications of this shift upon sexual-hermeneutic economies: does Mary Shelley become a "drag-priest", and what are the implications of such a discursive transvestism for writing-reading and Philosophy?[13] Does this conflation of roles put into question the categories of writer/decipherer, even announcing the Death of the Hermeneut?

This "Author's Introduction" is, then, an account of certain apocalypses leading to the genesis of an apocalyptic-eschatological text in which there is a concurrence, between and in the various shifts in the description of the inscriptive/hermeneutic operations occurring here – of the revelation of text(s) and the text(s) of revelation – a concurrence complicit with an activity of translation. An account in which an extreme position with regard to generic orders and laws of inscription is delineated: neither a text of direct experience, nor of personal vision, rather a hybrid of these, with all the hermaphroditism of hybrids.

In a Library in Rome

After the introduction, the novel begins. It is a first person narrative featuring Lionel Verney, a native of the British Isles, and is set in the late twenty-first century.

---

13 Transvestism's confusion and conflation of roles and genderings is further complicated here by the relation between the Sibyl and her inspiration: is her enthusiasm directed at being complicit with a god or a goddess?

It conjures a future barely different to the early nineteenth century, and hardly marked by the industrialisation which was occurring as it was written. Presciently, the throne is held by the House of Windsor, and balloon travel is the greatest advance on coaches and boats. Spread over three volumes, the narrative is far less remarkable than its framing: both the opening in the Sibyl's cave, and its ending in a deserted Rome. The major action involves a "PLAGUE" which sweeps through Europe from the Orient, and eludes the measures of medical science. Eventually, it kills all of humanity: Verney contracts the plague, but survives it, as an apparently sole survivor. In one of the many unexplained aspects of the plague's action, Verney wanders a depopulated Europe without encountering corpses: the dead apparently burying themselves, or vanishing.

He eventually arrives in Rome, where he spends time in its libraries, seeking solace from his sense of devastation after the loss of all his friends and family.

> I endeavoured to read. I visited the libraries of Rome. I selected a volume, and, choosing some sequestered, shady nook, on the banks of the Tiber, or opposite the fair temple in the Borghese Gardens, or under the old pyramid of Cestius, I endeavoured to conceal me from myself, and immerse myself in the subject traced on the pages before me. As if in the same soil you plant nightshade and a myrtle tree, they will each appropriate the mould, moisture, and air administered, for the fostering their several properties – so did my grief find sustenance, and power of existence, and growth, in what else had been divine manna, to feed radiant meditation.[14]

As a complement to the extreme position taken up in the "Author's Introduction", *The Last Man* takes up an extreme position as concerns Man and History in being the narrative of the LAST MAN, Lionel Verney: an exile from humanity and its History (and even from death). Its position of extremity is in being at the limits in a *liminal* position with regard to certain categories but yet included within them and bounded by them. Recalling Nietzsche's narrative of the *letzten Philosophen*, Verney's narrative is begun in Rome amidst the death of humanity from a strange PLAGUE, and the beginning gesture of this tale that is to become *The Last Man* – before any of these "events" occur – one recorded late in the tale's narrative order, is as follows:

> I was presented, meantime, with one other occupation, the one best fitted to discipline my melancholy thoughts, which strayed backwards, over many a ruin, and through many a flowery glade, even to the mountain recess, from which in early youth I had first emerged.
>
> During one of my rambles through the habitations of Rome, I found writing materials on a table in an author's study. Parts of a manuscript lay scattered about.

---

14   Shelley, *The Last Man*, 338–9.

It contained a learned disquisition on the Italian language; one page an unfinished dedication to posterity, for whose profit the writer had sifted and selected the niceties of this harmonious language – to whose everlasting benefit he bequeathed his labours.

I will also write a book, I cried – for whom to read? – to whom dedicated? And then with a silly flourish (what so capricious and childish as despair?) I wrote,

DEDICATION
TO THE ILLUSTRIOUS DEAD.
SHADOWS, ARISE, AND READ YOUR FALL!
BEHOLD THE HISTORY OF THE
LAST MAN.[15]

The logical problems and paradoxes of this inscription encapsulate the problems of the apocalyptic genre in general, particularly the temporal paradoxes involved: a text written at the End of History that is yet a self-proclaimed "HISTORY OF THE LAST MAN", dedicated to the dead, and without a reader other than its "author" – underlining the conflation of reading and writing in this text.

It also returns us to the "Author's Introduction", as writing occurs as both solace in loss, and as an activity of taking up discarded texts.

It is an extraordinarily striking and melancholic scenario, and prefigures Friedrich Nietzsche's reflections on the same trope in the figure of the last Philosopher, as a *Geschichte der Nachwelt* ("History of Posterity").

Ödipus.
Reden des letzten Philosophen mit sich selbst.

Ein fragment aus der Geschichte der Nachwelt.

Den letzten Philosophen nenne ich mich, denn ich bin der letzte Mensch. Niemand redet mir als ich selbst, und meine Stimme kommt wid die eines Sterbenden zu mir! Mit dir, dem letzten Errinerungshauch alles Menschenglücks, laß mich nur eine Stundenoch verkehren, durch dich täusche ich mir die Einsamkeit hinweg und lüge mich in die Vielheit und die Liebe hinein, denn mein Herz sträubt sich zu glauben, daß die Liebe todt sei, es ertägt den Schauder der einsamsten Einsamkeit nicht und zwingst mich zu reden, als ob ich Zwei wäre.

Höre ich dich noch, mein Stimme Du flücherst, indem du fluchst? Und doch sollte dein Fluch die Eingeweide dieser Welt zerbersten machen! Aber sie lebt noch und schaut mich nur noch glänzender und kälter mit ihren mitleidslosen Sternen an, sie lebt, so dumm und blind wie je vorher, un nur einer stirbt, der Mensch.[16]

---

15 Shelley, *The Last Man*, 339.
16 Friedrich Nietzsche, *Das Philosophenbuch* [1872–73/75], in *Nietzsche's Werke* X: *Nachgelaßene Werke* (Leipzig: C. G. Naumann, 1903), §87.

Oedipus.

Discourse of the last Philosopher with himself.

A Fragment from the History of Posterity.

I call myself the last Philosopher, because I am the last man. No one speaks with me but myself, and my voice comes to me like the voice of a dying man! Let me associate for but one hour more with you, dear voice, with you, the last trace of the memory of all human happiness. With you I escape loneliness through self-delusion and lie myself into multiplicity and love. For my heart resists the belief that love is dead. It cannot bear the shudder of the loneliest loneliness, and so it forces me to speak as if I were two persons.

Do I still hear you, my voice? Are you whispering as you curse? And yet your curses should cause the bowels of this earth to burst open! But the world continues to live and only stares at me even more glitteringly and coldly with its pitiless stars. It continues to live as dumbly and blindly as ever, and only one thing dies, Man.[17]

A discourse of the last man with himself, couched in the form of a fragment from a future history of posterity: this is an impossible discourse which fragments History, and has an eccentric relation to philosophic discourse. It raises the question of the discursive possibility of both History and Philosophy, of their laws of genre and generation. Nietzsche's schema perfectly fits *The Last Man* and the genre of the apocalyptic – a genre of texts with the project of a revelation of the last, the end. In its paradox, it shows the tenacious logic that if someone is talking to me (even if it is myself), I am not yet alone. For Shelley and Verney, if they are writing, then there is always the possibility of a reader, of another survivor to witness their survival.

Both Verney's Rome, and Nietzsche's "fragment from the history of posterity" share a scene of devastation in which loneliness is escaped through a self-delusion that opens up an impossible dialogue. For Nietzsche, this dialogue is at the end point of Philosophy, understood as a discourse involving a certain conception of humanity, which is said to have died while the world continues to live. It is a death on the other side of the pursuit of knowledge, which Nietzsche had analysed as being a dangerous encounter with dispelling all that kept humanity alive: a protective form of ignorance.[18]

For Mary Shelley or Lionel Verney, literature – its reading, its writing – offers a form of survival, in the face of bereavement and devastation. Literature becomes

---

17   Friedrich Nietzsche, *Philosophy and Truth: Selections from Nietzsche's Notebooks of the Early 1870s*, ed. and trans. Daniel Breazeale (Atlantic Highlands, NJ: Humanities Press, 1979), §87.

18   See Friedrich Nietzsche, "Über Wahrheit und Lüge im außermoralischen Sinne" [1873] in *Werke* III.2. *Nietzsche Werke: Kritische Gesamtausgabe*, ed. Giorgio Colli and Mazzino Montinari (Berlin: Walter de Gruyter, 1973); "On Truth and Lies in a Nonmoral Sense", in *Philosophy and Truth*, ed. and trans. Daniel Breazeale, 79–97.

a mode of living on, for both the survivors and the dead, even a literature that imagines the death of all as solace for the death of a few.

Modes of Reading: Modesty and Care

As noted in the epigraph from Maurice Blanchot, the writing of the disaster is structured by temporal rupture, and the effacement of the subject. As he puts it: "something which never yet takes place happens nonetheless, as having long since already happened", which he claims inheres in the relation between writing and passivity.

Familiarly, passivity is more associated with reading than with writing. Mary Shelley – in her "Author's Introduction" to *The Last Man* as well as in her more famous 1831 Preface to *Frankenstein; Or The Modern Prometheus* – positions writing as a form of reading, and as a product of the unknown known. Writing after *The Last Man*, Mary Shelley enlarges on the ghost story competition in the Byron–Shelley circle which led to *Frankenstein*, and Mary commences the account of her contribution as follows:

> I busied myself to *think of a story* – a story to rival those which had excited us to this task. One which would speak to the mysterious fears of our nature and awaken thrilling horror – one to make the reader dread to look round, to curdle the blood, and quicken the beatings of the heart. ... I thought and pondered – vainly. I felt that blank incapability of invention which is the greatest misery of authorship, when dull Nothing replies to our anxious *invocations*. "Have you thought of a story?" I was asked each morning, and each morning I was forced to reply with a mortifying negative.[19]

Thought is figured as being unproductive, a vain resource, particularly in terms of the writing of a story defined as speaking "to the mysterious fears of our nature". Thought having failed, there is an invocation – the voice's calling – of invention, with all its appropriate religious and oracular associations.

Mary Shelley then goes on to relate conversations between Byron and Percy Shelley concerning the principle of life and the possibility of reanimation, "to which I was a devout but *nearly silent* listener", and then narrates the night of her dream:

> Night waned upon this talk, and even the witching hour had gone by before we retired to rest. When I placed my head on my pillow, *I did not sleep, nor could I be said to think*. My imagination, *unbidden*, possessed and guided me, gifting the successive images that arose in my mind with a *vividness far beyond the usual*

---

19 Mary Shelley, *Frankenstein; Or, The Modern Prometheus: The 1818 Text*, ed. James Rieger (Chicago, IL: University of Chicago Press, 2nd ed., 1982), 226; emphasis added.

bounds of reverie. I saw – *with shut eyes, but acute mental vision* – I saw the pale student of the hallowed arts kneeling beside the thing he had put together. I saw the hideous phantasm of a man stretched out, and then, on the working of some powerful engine, show signs of life, and stir with an uneasy, half-vital motion. Frightful it must be; for supremely frightful would be the effect of any human endeavour to mock the stupendous mechanism of the Creator of the world.[20]

Almost as if in a riposte to Keats' question "Do I wake or sleep?" Mary Shelley writes that she does neither: "I did not sleep, nor could I be said to think." Imagination possesses the writer as if in a dream, but this reverie is already beyond itself: it is "far beyond the usual bounds of reverie". What is also beyond those "usual bounds" is the subject of those images itself: the "hideous phantasm". Haunting Mary's vision is a process of abjection: her vision comes to her in an abject manner with an image of an abject creation.

Like a Sibyl, the writer "sees" with her eyes closed, "seeing" beyond the bounds of what may normally be seen: she "sees" that which would mock God, and in this, that which would be "supremely frightful". The "stupendous mechanism of the Creator of the world", then, will not only be Man but also the system of concealment in which the Creator is figured, since the creation of Life and Man is the point at which the Creator is created as Creator. And this will be borne out in the various interchanges in the narrative between the roles of Creator/created, organised around readings of the Promethean myth and the Miltonic-Satanic myth: both Victor and the creature take on the roles of Creator and Man in relation to their contestation of the poles of a Master/Slave dialectic.

Yet, to return to the question of thought versus dream, there is a certain slippage in the difference between thought and non-thought argued here: not only are the usual bounds of reverie exceeded here, but also the difference – sketched by Mary Shelley – between what can be said to be "thought" (attached to some notion of will and voluntarism, such that it is solely an active process), and what is presented as other than thought. A slippage constituting the laws governing what may be thought, and how thought appears in writing. Further, a slippage legislating for the area whose bounds are exceeded: in this case, reverie. At first, "imagination" is used to distinguish this non-thought, but Mary will later announce that she "*had thought of a story*". She will also describe the product of her vision as an "idea":

The idea so possessed my mind that a thrill of fear ran through me, and I wished to exchange the ghastly image of my fancy for the realities around. I see them still: the very room, the dark parquet, the closed shutters with the moonlight struggling through, and the sense I had that the glassy lake and white high Alps were beyond. I could not so easily get rid of my hideous phantom; still it haunted me. I must try to think of something else. I recurred to my ghost story – My tiresome, unlucky

---

20   Shelley, *Frankenstein*, 227–228; emphases added.

ghost story! Oh! If I could only contrive one which would frighten my reader as I myself had been frightened that night!

Swift as light and as cheering was the idea that broke in upon me. "I have found it! What terrified me will terrify others; and I need only describe the spectre which had haunted my midnight pillow." On the morrow I announced that I had *thought of a story*.[21]

Again, there is a recurrence of the structure that might be referred to as the unknown-known, as writing-reading more than one knows. Before Mary knows it, before it has entered the realm or bounds of thought, she has solved the problem of the ghost story, but she does not realise this at first. The story – what she knows but does not know – haunts her. And, when she announces that she has thought of a story, a passage from a realm outside "thought" – from non-thought to thought – may be identified. In this passage the story traverses the distance between thought and its other, the story/idea has come forth into thought and into the world, but only after it had come to mind.

Thoughts unbidden, texts found, deciphered, transcribed and transposed: these are modes of reading and writing that are modest about claims of originality, and careful to preserve and cherish a wider body of literature. From the Sibyl's cave to the libraries of Rome, the reader and writer still proceeds with care.

Now, let us imagine the last Academic. A survivor, of plagues both literal and figurative, of the changing histories and practices of university teaching, research and administration. A person of modesty, and meticulousness, committed to reading and teaching as critical acts, a commitment borne with generosity and dedication.

Bibliography

Blanchot, Maurice. *L'écriture du désastre*. Paris: Gallimard, 1980.

Blanchot, Maurice. *The Writing of the Disaster*. Trans. Ann Smock. Lincoln: University of Nebraska Press, 1986.

Derrida, Jacques. "No Apocalypse, Not Now (full speed ahead, seven missiles, seven missives)." Trans. Catherine Porter and Philip Lewis, *Diacritics* 14 no.2 (Summer 1984), 20–31.

Nietzsche, Friedrich. *Das Philosophenbuch* [1872–73/75]. In *Nietzsche's Werke* X: *Nachgelaßene Werke*. Leipzig: C.G. Naumann, 1903.

Nietzsche, Friedrich. "On Truth and Lies in a Nonmoral Sense." In *Philosophy and Truth: Selections from Nietzsche's Notebooks of the early 1870s*. Ed. and trans. Daniel Breazeale. Atlantic Highlands, NJ: Humanities Press, 1979.

Nietzsche, Friedrich. *Philosophy and Truth: Selections from Nietzsche's Notebooks of the early 1870s*. Ed. and trans. Daniel Breazeale. Atlantic Highlands, NJ: Humanities Press, 1979.

Nietzsche, Friedrich. "Über Wahrheit und Lüge im außermoralischen Sinne" [1873]. In *Werke* III.2. *Nietzsche Werke: Kritische Gesamtausgabe*. Ed. Giorgio Colli and Mazzino Montinari. Berlin: Walter de Gruyter, 1973.

---

21   Shelley, *Frankenstein*, 228.

Shelley, Mary. *Frankenstein; Or, The Modern Prometheus: The 1818 Text*. Ed. James Rieger. Chicago, IL: University of Chicago Press, 2nd ed., 1982.

Shelley, Mary. *The Last Man*. Ed. Hugh J. Luke, Jr. Lincoln: University of Nebraska Press, 1965.

Shelley, Mary. *Mary Shelley's Journal*. Ed. Frederick L. Jones. Norman: University of Oklahoma Press, 1947.

Contributors

Peter Banki is founder and director of the Festival of Death and Dying and of Erotic Living. He has also been a member of the Philosophy Research Initiative at the University of Western Sydney, where he has lectured and tutored in the School of Humanities and Languages. He holds a PhD from New York University (2009). His book *The Forgiveness to Come: The Holocaust and the Hyper-Ethical* came out in 2018 with Fordham University Press. His research interests include the intersections between philosophy and sexuality, and the politics of reconciliation and forgiveness in relation to personal and cultural trauma.

A.J. Carruthers is a poet, literary critic and journalist. In 2024 he was the recipient of the Cy Twombly Award for Poetry from the Foundation for Contemporary Arts. He is author of *Literary History and Avant-Garde Poetics in the Antipodes: Languages of Invention* (Edinburgh University Press, 2024), *Stave Sightings: Notational Experiments in North American Long Poems* (Palgrave Macmillan, 2017), three volumes of a long poem: *Axis Z Book 3* (Cordite, 2023), *Axis Book 2* (Vagabond, 2019) and *Axis Book 1: 'Areal'* (Vagabond, 2014), and the sound poem *Consonata* (Cordite, 2019). He has worked as Lecturer at Shanghai University of International Business and Economics (SUIBE), Associate Professor at Nanjing University, and is currently a Visiting Fellow at the Australian National University.

Anthony Cordingley is Robinson Fellow at the University of Sydney, on secondment from the Université Paris 8, France, where he is Associate Professor in English and Translation. He was fortunate to be supervised by Bruce Gardiner for a PhD thesis, which was developed into *Samuel Beckett's* How It Is*: Philosophy in Translation* (Edinburgh University Press, 2018). He teaches across modernist literature, comparative literature, translation studies, and his work has appeared in journals such as *Comparative Literature*, *Modern Philology*, *PMLA*, *Twentieth-Century Literature* and *Translation Studies*. On the editorial board of *Samuel Beckett Today/Aujourd'hui* and an editor for the Beckett Digital Manuscripts Project (www.beckettarchive.org), he recently co-authored with Chris

Ackerley and Llewellyn Brown, *Samuel Beckett's* Comment c'est / How It Is*: Annotations* (Paris: Lettres Modernes Minard/Classiques Garnier, 2024). His work in translation studies includes the co-/edited volumes *Self-translation: Brokering Originality in Hybrid Culture* (Bloomsbury, 2013) and *Collaborative Translation: From the Renaissance to the Digital Age* (Bloomsbury, 2016). He recently completed a Marie Skłodowska-Curie Fellowship project, "Genetic Translation Studies" at the KU Leuven's Centre for Translation Studies, financed by the EU Horizon 2020 research and innovation program.

Jack Cox is the author of the novel *Dodge Rose* (Dalkey Archive, 2016).

Toby Fitch (he/they) is a leading Australian poet, editor, critic and teacher. He is poetry editor of *Overland*, a lecturer in creative writing at the University of Sydney and the author of eight collections of poetry, most recently *Sydney Spleen* (Giramondo, 2021) and *Object Permanence: Calligrammes* (Puncher & Wattmann, 2022). He is the editor of the anthologies *Best of Australian Poems 2021* (with Ellen van Neerven) and *Groundswell: The Overland Judith Wright Poetry Prize for New and Emerging Poets 2007–2020*. His poetry has been awarded the Grace Leven Prize and the Charles Rischbieth Jury Prize, while his PhD, consisting of a poetry book, *The Bloomin' Notions of Other & Beau*, and a thesis, "Themparks: Alternative Play in Contemporary Australian Poetry", won the University of Sydney's Dame Leonie Kramer Prize for Australian Poetry.

Adam Gall teaches Australian environmental history at NYU Sydney, and academic writing and research at the University of Sydney. He writes on Australian cinema, literature, and cultural politics, as well as investigating the relationship between mediated attachment and ethico-political commitment in settler-colonial city and suburban environments.

Bruce Gardiner's career summary, "Bruce Gardiner: Educational and Academic History", is found in Appendix 1 of this volume.

Peter Godfrey-Smith is an Australian philosopher of science and writer, who is currently Professor of History and Philosophy of Science at the University of Sydney. He works primarily in philosophy of biology and philosophy of mind, and also has interests in general philosophy of science, pragmatism (especially the work of John Dewey), and some parts of metaphysics and epistemology. Elected to the American Philosophical Society in 2022, Godfrey-Smith has taught at Harvard University, Stanford University, Australian National University and the CUNY Graduate Center. He was the recipient of the Lakatos Award for his 2009 book, *Darwinian Populations and Natural Selection* (Oxford University Press), which discusses the philosophical foundations of the theory of evolution. His most recent book is *Metazoa: Animal Life and the Birth of the Mind* (HarperCollins, 2020).

Melissa Hardie is Associate Professor in the School of Arts, Communication and English, University of Sydney. With Meaghan Morris and Kane Race she edited *The*

Year's Work in Showgirl Studies (Indiana University Press, 2024). That collection offers both a history of the reception of *Showgirls* and new angles on the film, and includes her new essay, "Fifty Shades of *Showgirls*". Recently she has published an article on Todd Field's *Tár* in *Film Quarterly*, on *Charlie's Angels* and blockchain in *Australian Humanities Review* and, with Amy Villarejo, on the 1970s drama *Family* and historical homophobia in *Television Studies in Queer Times* (Routledge, 2023). She is currently working on Patricia Nell Warren's 1970s bestselling gay trilogy *The Front Runner*, *The Fancy Dancer* and *The Beauty Queen*, and finishing a book about the closet and styles of its remediation.

Alexis Harley is the Graduate Research Coordinator for Creative Arts and English at La Trobe University, where she lectures in literary studies. She writes about the ways in which literary and aesthetic cultures have shaped scientific research, natural history writing, and the theorisation of nature itself, with particular focus on the long nineteenth century, a period of intensified literary, ecological and cultural change. This work ranges across subjects as diverse as literary influences on colonial specimen collecting practices, colonial representations of rabbits and the origins of invasion ecology, the ways in which Romantic aesthetic culture manifests in Charles Darwin's early writing, and how the poetics of the sublime influenced early nineteenth-century writing about geology and climate. She is the author of *Autobiologies: Charles Darwin and the Natural History of the Self* (Bucknell University Press 2014), recently co-edited *Bees, Science and Sex in the Literature of the Long Nineteenth Century* (Palgrave 2024), and is currently working with colleagues on an account of the complicated outworking of Romanticism in colonial Australia to the present day. Like so many of his students, Alexis Harley remains transfixed by the recollection of Bruce Gardiner's extraordinary teaching: by his daring, dazzling curricula; his inimitable textual analysis; by the care with which he treated students' ideas and writing. In 1998, Bruce referred to one of a then-undergraduate Alexis' sentences as a grenade. He went on to find in several of her subsidiary sentences the resultant "shrapnel". As she thought, then (and still), if anyone knows what it is to pull the safety pin on a sentence ...

Peter Hutchings (Emeritus Professor) – Bachelor of Arts (Hons), PhD, University of Sydney – was the Dean of the School of Humanities and Communication Arts at Western Sydney University from 2011 to 2021, and the Pro Vice-Chancellor of the Humanities and Social Sciences from 2020 to 2021. His career included positions at the University of Sydney (1988–91), Boston University in Sydney (1992), the University of Hong Kong (1992–95), and the Australian Learning and Teaching Council (2008–10). His research interests are in the arts, cinema, critical legal studies, cultural studies, literature and philosophy, as well as the history of Chinese migration and cultural exchange in Australia. His publications have appeared in Australian and international refereed journals and in the mainstream print media, and he is the author of *The Criminal Spectre in Law, Literature and Aesthetics:*

Incriminating Subjects (Routledge, 2001). Currently, he is researching issues of sovereignty and cinema in the post-9/11 period.

Michelle Kelly is a writer and administrator living on unceded Awabakal land. Her Honours thesis "Reading Smut: Anaïs Nin's Erotica on the Market" (2002) was supervised by Bruce Gardiner, as was her PhD thesis, "Library Encounters: Textuality and the Institution" (2012).

Kate Lilley is a poet and a scholar of queer, feminist textual history and theory from seventeenth-century women's writing to contemporary poetry and poetics. From 2013 to 2021, she directed the Creative Writing program at the University of Sydney, where she is now an Honorary Associate Professor. Lilley has published three books of poetry, *tilt* (Vagabond, 2018; winner of the Victorian Premier's Literary Awards, 2019), *Versary* (Salt, 2002; winner of the Grace Levin Prize, 2002) and *Ladylike* (University of Western Australia Publishing, 2012), as well as two Vagabond chapbooks, *Round Vienna* and *Realia*. She is the editor of *Margaret Cavendish: Blazing World and other writings* (Penguin Classics, 2014) and *Dorothy Hewett: Selected Poems* (University of Western Australia Publishing, 2010). Lilley is also the poetry editor of *Southerly*.

Jessica Lim teaches English at St Andrew's Cathedral School, Sydney. She previously supervised English literature at the University of Cambridge where she was a Director of Studies in English at Lucy Cavendish College. Her research centres on women's writing and children's literature from the eighteenth and nineteenth centuries, with a particular focus on theological and pedagogical concerns. Alongside Louise Joy, she co-edited *Women's Literary Education, 1690–1850* (Edinburgh University Press, 2023), and her work has appeared in *L. M. Montgomery's "Emily of New Moon": A Children's Classic at 100* (University Press of Mississippi, 2024), *Journal for Eighteenth Century Studies, The Charles Lamb Bulletin, Notes and Queries* and *Oxford Research in English*. Jessica was supervised by Bruce Gardiner during her Honours year at the University of Sydney (2013), where she composed her thesis on the works of George MacDonald.

Marc Mierowsky is a Lecturer and ARC DECRA Fellow in the School of Culture and Communication at the University of Melbourne. He is an associate editor of *The Cambridge Edition of the Correspondence of Daniel Defoe* (2022), and co-editor with Nicholas Seager of Defoe's *The Fortunate Mistress (Roxana)* (2024) for Oxford World's Classics. With Sarah Balkin, he is co-author of *Comedy and Controversy: Scripting Public Speech* (Cambridge University Press, 2024). His book *A Spy Amongst Us: Daniel Defoe's Secret Service and the Plot to End Scottish Independence* is forthcoming with Yale University Press.

Benjamin Miller is a Lecturer in English and Writing at the University of Sydney. He has published on representations of blackness and Aboriginality in US and Australian theatre, film, music and writing in journals such as *JASAL, Journal of*

Australian Studies and *Ab-Original*. His work explores the alternative modes of rhetoric used by Indigenous artists, from David Unaipon (Ngarrindjeri) to Adam Briggs (Yorta Yorta).

Brett Neilson is Professor and Deputy Director at the Institute for Culture and Society, Western Sydney University. With Sandro Mezzadra, he is author of *Border as Method, or, the Multiplication of Labor* (Duke University Press, 2013), *The Politics of Operations: Excavating Contemporary Capitalism* (Duke University Press, 2019) and *The Rest and the West: Capital and Power in a Multipolar World* (Verso Books, 2024).

Christopher Richardson has a Bachelor of Arts (Hons) in English literature from the University of Sydney. His Honours year was wisely spent under the supervision of Bruce Gardiner, exploring the nonsense verse of Edward Lear. Christopher attained a Master of International Security (with Merit) from the University of Sydney and Master of Teaching (Secondary) from the University of New England, Armidale. His PhD from the University of Sydney explored the childhood policies and practices of the Democratic People's Republic of Korea (North Korea). Christopher has taught English and IB Global Politics at Santa Sabina College in Strathfield since 2021. He is the author of seven published books for young readers, including the epic maritime fantasy novel *Empire of the Waves* (Penguin, 2015).

Nick Riemer is a Senior Lecturer in the department of English and Writing and of Linguistics at the University of Sydney, and a member of the Histoire des théories linguistiques laboratory, Université Paris Cité. His research is in semantics and the history and philosophy of the language "sciences". He is the author, among other books, of *L'emprise de la grammaire: Propositions épistémologiques pour une linguistique mineure* (ENS Éditions, 2021) and *Boycott Theory and the Struggle for Palestine: Universities, Intellectualism and Liberation* (Rowman & Littlefield, 2023).

Monique Rooney teaches US literature and television in the English Program at the Australian National University. She is the author of *Living Screens: Melodrama and Plasticity in Contemporary Film and Television* (Rowman & Littlefield, 2015), and her recent essays have appeared in *Textual Practice*, *New Review of Film and Television Studies* and *Angelaki*. Currently, she is working on two projects: preparing her second monograph, *Brow Work: Tastemaking and Networked Being in Contemporary Literature and Art* and researching the papers of Ruth Park in preparation for writing a literary biography.

Liz Shek-Noble is a researcher and educator specialising in disability studies and contemporary Australian literature. Her most recent appointment was at the University of Tokyo, where she was a Project Assistant Professor in the Center for Global Education. Her work has appeared in peer-reviewed publications including *Journal of Australian Studies*, *Genre* and *Journal of Postcolonial Writing*. She has served as a guest editor of *Antipodes* and *Journal of Literary and Cultural Disability*

Studies for its special issues on explorations of disability in Australian genre fiction and intersections between critical animal studies and disability studies respectively.

Rodney Taveira is Senior Lecturer in American Studies and Academic Director at the United States Studies Centre at the University of Sydney. His research on American fiction, television, art and cinema has appeared in *The Journal of Popular Culture*, *Cultural Studies Review*, *Comparative American Studies* and in edited collections. He writes popular pieces on American society and culture, and he has been interviewed on national television and radio. His current monograph, "The Cinematic Face of American Literature", argues that new critical perceptions on violence, sexuality, and the way writing makes meaning are observed in contemporary American fiction when it is read through the lens of visual culture. He directs the American Studies program at the University of Sydney.

Susan E. Thomas is the founder of the WRIT program and Writing Hub at the University of Sydney. Her research focuses primarily on theories of writing, grounded in cognitive rhetoric, with a particular interest in affect. She is also interested in life writing, feminist and global rhetorics, writing across the curriculum, and writing centres. Her work has appeared in *TEXT*, *Across the Disciplines*, *Rhetoric Review* and *Composition Studies*, and her current monograph *Navigating the Unexpected: Writers and Writing Programs in Times of Change* is forthcoming in 2024 by the University Press of Colorado. Susan currently directs the Student Writing Fellows Program in the Writing Hub and is past president of the American Council of Writing Program Administrators.

Appendix 1. Bruce Gardiner: Educational and Academic History

Bruce Gardiner (born 1953)

1958–1965 Belmore South Public School

- 1965 Dux

1966–1971 Kingsgrove North High School

- 1966–1969 School Certificate English, Latin, French, Mathematics, Science, Geography
- 1970–1971 Higher School Certificate English, Art, Mathematics, Science, Geography
- 1970 International Science School, University of Sydney
- 1971 National Mathematics Summer School, Australian National University
- 1971 Dux

I benefitted immensely from the Wyndham Scheme's 1962 transformation of NSW school curricula and from attending a non-selective, co-educational state high school staffed by teachers who ranged from the thoroughly competent to the brilliant. It was attended by many friendly and generous fellow students who achieved an exceptionally high matriculation rate, matching Joanna Mendelssohn's description of the school in *Which school?: Beyond Public versus Private* (North Melbourne: Pluto Press, 2007). The most inspiring classes I recall were those on the history of the English sonnet, Euclid's theorems, and projective geometry (in summer school); the most exciting excursions were those to a Hunter Valley sewage farm, contemporary art galleries in Paddington, and a 1970 performance of Tyrone

Guthrie's *King Oedipus*. I particularly relished studying Islamic art in the self-selected, self-directed component of the HSC Art syllabus. To my high school education, I owe the catholicity of intellectual interests I still pursue.

1972–1975 Undergraduate student at the University of Sydney

- 1972 English I, Pure and Applied Mathematics I, Geography I
- 1973 English II Course 1 Honours, English II Course 2, Thomas Henry Coulson Scholarship
- 1974 English III Course 1 Honours, English III Course 2, James Coutts Scholarship 1
- 1975 English IV Honours in English Literature since 1500, James Coutts Scholarship 2, NSW Institute of Journalists Prize
- 1976 awarded Bachelor of Arts English Honours Class I, University Medal (shared)

By and large, changes to state school curricula are well-founded and enduring whereas those at universities are arbitrary and fickle. So, I was lucky to study at the University of Sydney at the very beginning of a relatively brief period in which students in the Arts Faculty could take as many courses as they wanted in one subject and choose many optional components in them taught in small classes, an opportunity that most universities now deny their students. To study English literature exclusively for three years was an extraordinary opportunity that widened rather than narrowed my intellectual horizons. The dichotomy between specialist and generalist study is entirely false. To a handful of teachers, each teaching quite differently, I owe my greatest intellectual debt, particularly to Adrian Colman, Pamela Law, Bill Maidment, Simon Petch and Jim Tulip, and no less a debt to my fellow Honours students, whose intellectually invigorating company and encouragement sustained me for the last three years of my degree.

1976–1981 Doctoral candidate at Princeton University

- 1976–1981 Fulbright Scholarship
- 1976–1980 Princeton Tuition Scholarship
- 1976–1979 Arthur Macquarie Scholarship
- 1980 Frederick Elgar–Kathleen Karnaghan–A.J.A. Waldock Scholarship
- 1981 Preceptorship in English Composition and Modern Drama
- 1983 Doctor of Philosophy degree conferred after oral examination for a thesis on "The Rhymers' Club: A Social and Intellectual History" supervised by Samuel Hynes and later published under the same title among a series of volumes on American and English Literature edited by Stephen Orgel (New York: Garland, 1987).

My debts as a Princeton graduate student are in equal measure personal and institutional. Personally, I benefitted most from seminars taught by four eminent scholars – Hans Aarsleff, E.D.H. Johnson, Carol Kay, and D.W. Robertson, Jr. – and from the intellectual camaraderie of my peers, especially my housemates from 1978 through 1980 – musicologist Richard Agee (later at Colorado College, who died in 2023), political scientist John Burke (later at the University of Vermont) and American literature scholar Glen MacLeod (later at the University of Connecticut, Waterbury). Institutionally, I benefitted most from my several sponsors' generous financial support; the bounty of the university's Harvey S. Firestone Memorial Library; the university's proximity to New York City, enabling me to attend many classical music performances and visit innumerable modern art exhibitions, some under the exacting tutelage of James Mollison; and Freddie Laker's low-cost Transatlantic flights between John F. Kennedy and London Gatwick airports, enabling me to study at London's libraries and visit its museums and art collections, and enabling the university to fly me across the Atlantic for a job interview.

1981–2021 Academic staff member at the University of Sydney

- 1981–1992 Lectureship in English
- 1992–2021 Senior Lectureship in English
- 1988–1998 teaching in the Women's Studies Program
- 1988–1997 teaching in the Celtic Studies Program
- 2002–2008 English Honours coordinator
- 2008–2016 teaching in the United States [American] Studies Program
- 2010–2016 teaching in the International and Comparative Literature Program
- 2017 teaching in the Writing Studies Program

As honoured as I first was to become my former teachers' colleague, I was more honoured later as many former students one by one became mine. I am especially grateful to the colleagues who taught courses jointly with me, as Don Anderson did for fifteen years, until the university abolished the practice as extravagant, and those who helped me so much when I fell ill with HIV/AIDS in 1987, especially Gerry Wilkes for his administrative help and Don Anderson for his indefatigable practical help. And I am no less grateful to the students who enabled me to teach so many courses on so many subjects, all of which entirely depended on the bountiful resources of Fisher Library and the expertise and devotion of its staff. A full list of courses I taught and theses I supervised appears in Appendix 2. I append a photograph of me on my last day at work, about to set sail wearing a replica of the tie James Joyce designed to commemorate the publication of *Ulysses*.

Figure A.1 A photograph of Dr Bruce Gardiner on his last day at work, about to set sail wearing a replica of the tie James Joyce designed to commemorate the publication of *Ulysses*. Photo by Elizabeth Connor.

Appendix 2. Bruce Gardiner: Record of Teaching and Supervision, 1981–2021

Teaching

English I (lectures, unless noted otherwise)

- 1982–1984 Robert Browning, selected poems
- 1982, 1985–1986 Selected poets and novels, and Shakespeare (tutorials)
- 1983 Oscar Wilde, *The Importance of Being Earnest*
- 1985–1986 Literature, culture, and race: Shakespeare to V.S. Naipaul
- 1999–2000 Plagiarism and citation
- 2000 Victorian medievalist poetry, and Thomas Hardy, *Under the Greenwood Tree*
- 2000 Poe, Browning, and Whitman
- 2007 Modernist New York City poetry
- 2008–2010 H.D., Frank O'Hara, and the cinema
- 2012–2013 Prosopopoeia in Romantic, Victorian, and Modernist literary texts
- 2014 Henry James, *The Turn of the Screw*, and Herman Melville, *Billy Budd*
- 2018–2019 The Gothic Imagination: Goethe, Coleridge, Mary Shelley, Hawthorne, Poe, Dickinson, Le Fanu, Christina Rossetti, Gilman, Henry James, and Wharton (lectures and tutorials)
- 2019–2020 Modernist women poets and *haute couture*
- 2020 The poetry of Whitman, Dickinson, Stein, and Langston Hughes

English II and III (lectures, unless noted otherwise)

- 1981 Thomas Hardy, selected novels and poems (seminars)
- 1982–1983 Modes of the Gothic: Walpole to Maturin

- 1982–1984, 1992–1993 English III: selected nineteenth and twentieth-century poets and novels, and Shakespeare (tutorials)
- 1983–1985 Alfred Tennyson, selected poems
- 1983 English literature, 1900–1930: selected texts
- 1983 Victorian poets of faith and doubt (seminars)
- 1985 Ezra Pound, selected poems
- 1988 Irish Modernism [also for the Celtic Studies Program]
- 1988–1992 Women Writers, 1850–1930 [also for the Women's Studies Program]
- 1990–1991, 1993–1994, 1996–1997 W.B. Yeats and Irish poetry [also for the Celtic Studies Program]
- 1991–1998 "Sapphos in Poetry": women's writing, 1760–1960 (lectures, seminars, and tutorials) [also for the Women's Studies Program]
- 1995 Modernism, selected texts
- 1991–1998, 2000, 2002 American claims: Indian, settler, slave (lectures, seminars, and tutorials)
- 1998 Medieval themes in modern literature
- 1999 Yeats, Joyce, and Ireland (with Fiona Morrison) (lectures and seminars)
- 1999, 2002 Childhood Cultures (with Geoff Williams) (lectures and seminars)
- 2002 Marianne Moore and Frank O'Hara
- 2003, 2005, 2019–2020 The Tristan legend from Beroul and Thomas to du Maurier and Updike
- 2004, 2008, 2010 The poetry of W.B. Yeats
- 2005 The Bible in American literature
- 2005, 2007, 2009, 2011, 2017 Quotation, citation, and plagiarism (lectures and seminars) [in 2017 for the Writing Studies Program]
- 2005, 2007, 2009, 2011, 2013, 2016, 2018 Philosophies of language from Locke to Herder
- 2007, 2009 Victorian poetry
- 2009, 2011 James Joyce, *Ulysses*
- 2013 The literatures of the Iroquois and the Empire State
- 2014, 2016, 2018, 2020 Literary theory: an introduction (basic questions; textual, editorial, and bibliographical theory; aesthetics from Kant to Wilde) (lectures and tutorials)
- 2019 Reading poetry: Spenser, *The Faerie Queene*; the sonnet; Aboriginal and Anglo-Australian poetry (tutorials)
- 2020 Henry James, *The Portrait of a Lady*

English II and III Honours Prerequisites (seminars, unless noted otherwise)

- 1984–1986 Modern American poetry and painting (with Terry Smith and Jim Tulip)

- 1984–1986 Masculine and feminine: Whitman to Woolf (with Penny Gay)
- 1990–1994, 1996–1997 "Make It New", the American lyric: Pound, Moore, and O'Hara (with Don Anderson until 1992)
- 1995–1998 The literature of decadence
- 1998 Poetry and poetics
- 2003–2004 Canon, taste, and value (lectures)
- 2003–2004 The English language (tutorials)
- 2003 Literary criticism (tutorials)
- 2007–2009, 2011 Aesthetics and aestheticism: Kant to Wilde
- 2007 The English language and the English canon (tutorials)
- 2008 English research methods (lectures and tutorials)
- 2012 Literary theory: an introduction (lectures and tutorials)
- 2013–2017, 2019–2020 "The Literary in Theory": chiefly Heidegger, Lacan, Adorno, Irigaray, Spivak, and Butler

English IV Honours Seminars (with Don Anderson until 1996)

- 1982 Twentieth-century literature (also with Penny Gay)
- 1983–1985 Twentieth-century epics, parodies, and travesties
- 1988 Modernism and postmodernism
- 1992–1996 "Red, Black, Blond, and Olive": Meso-American, Native American, Anglo-American, and African American literatures
- 1999–2000 The literature of New York City and New Orleans
- 2002–2005, 2007–2008 Honours research workshops and colloquia
- 2002–2005 The learned and the literary: Bacon to Darwin
- 2009–2012, 2015, 2019 History writing in English: Bacon to Macaulay

Postgraduate English Seminars

- 1989 English literature from 1880 to 1920 (with Margaret Harris and Pamela Law)
- 1992 Literary research (with Brian Kiernan)
- 1995–2015 Occasional seminars on scholarly citation and research conduct
- 1996 New York City poetry
- 1999, 2003, 2005, 2007, 2009, 2011 New Orleans literature
- 1999 *Fin de siècle, fin du globe*: H.G. Wells and W.B. Yeats
- 2002 Jorge Luis Borges, selected stories, and Samuel Beckett, *Company*, *Ill Seen Ill Said*, and *Worstward Ho*
- 2003 English epics: Gibbon, Carlyle, and Joyce
- 2005 English epics: battle narratives from *The Battle of Maldon* to Macaulay

International and Comparative Literature Program Seminars

- 2010 James Joyce, *Ulysses* (great books)
- 2012 Frank O'Hara and New York School painting (words and pictures)
- 2012, 2015, 2020 New Orleans literature (cities of the world)
- 2013 Literary Orientalism: Herder to Said (what is literature?)
- 2014 Sexual farce: Wilde, Osbourne, and Orton (love in different languages)
- 2014, 2016 Jane Austen, *Mansfield Park*, and Emily Brontë, *Wuthering Heights* (great books)
- 2015 Oriental and Native American motifs in English literature (what is literature?)
- 2016 Gertrude Stein, Frank O'Hara, and Painting (words and pictures)

United States Studies Program lectures

- 2008–2016 Whitman, *Leaves of Grass*, and Harriet Jacobs, *Incidents in the Life of a Slave Girl* (American foundations)

Supervision

Honours and Coursework Masters supervisions (comprehensive but incomplete list of submitted theses, with cross-listings)

Poetry
- Christopher Marlowe
- William Shakespeare
- William Blake and Arthur Rimbaud
- William Blake and Vladimir Mayakovsky
- Percy Bysshe Shelley
- Alfred, Lord Tennyson
- Edward Lear
- Charles Baudelaire, T.S. Eliot, and Hart Crane
- Emily Dickinson (two theses)
- G.M. Hopkins
- G.M. Hopkins and Duns Scotus
- G.M. Hopkins and Stéphane Mallarmé
- W.B. Yeats (four theses)
- T.S. Eliot
- T.S. Eliot and Ludwig Wittgenstein
- ee cummings
- Nancy Cunard

- Langston Hughes
- Judith Wright
- Frank O'Hara (three theses)
- Kevin Hart and Martin Heidegger
- Simon Armitage
- Madness and poetry
- Objects and objectivity in poetry
- Rhetoric of Romantic poetry

Novels and Prose

- *One Thousand and One Nights*
- Sir Walter Ralegh and Captain John Smith
- Mary Lamb
- Edgar Allan Poe and Virginia Woolf
- Charles Dickens and Émile Zola
- George Eliot
- Herman Melville (two theses)
- Fyodor Dostoevsky and Joseph Conrad
- George MacDonald
- George MacDonald and Lewis Carroll
- George MacDonald and C.S. Lewis
- Lewis Carroll
- Henry James
- Henry James and F. Scott Fitzgerald
- Richard Jefferies
- Thomas Hardy (two theses)
- Guy de Maupassant and Kate Chopin
- Oscar Wilde
- Oscar Wilde and E.M. Forster
- Oscar Wilde, Bret Easton Ellis, and Will Self
- Olive Schreiner (two theses)
- Gertrude Atherton and Edith Wharton
- Marcel Proust and Vladimir Nabokov
- Gertrude Stein (two theses)
- Gertrude Stein and Pablo Picasso
- Gertrude Stein and Marguerite Duras
- James Joyce (seven theses)
- James Joyce and Djuna Barnes
- James Joyce and Samuel Beckett
- James Joyce and Stanley Cavell
- Wyndham Lewis
- Virginia Woolf

- D.H. Lawrence and Evelyn Waugh
- Djuna Barnes
- Ben Hecht
- Aldous Huxley
- Jean Toomer and Toni Morrison
- William Faulkner and Flannery O'Connor
- Jorge Luis Borges and Peter Carey
- Vladimir Nabokov
- Anaïs Nin and Pauline Réage
- Evelyn Waugh and Henry Green
- Samuel Beckett
- Jean Genet and James Baldwin
- Clarice Lispector
- William Styron
- Tayeb Salih
- E.L. Doctorow
- Toni Morrison
- Toni Morrison and her contemporaries
- Elena Ferrante and Luce Irigaray
- Paul Auster
- George R.R. Martin
- Catherynne Valente
- Autobiography
- Popular mythology and popular culture in post-war American fiction
- Representations of women in young adult fiction and video games
- Translation as a theme in fiction

Theatre, Performance, Visual, and Rhetorical Arts

- Rhetoric of Romantic poetry
- W.B. Yeats and Maurice Maeterlinck
- W.B. Yeats, Sean O'Casey, and Brian Friel
- Singers and singing in Gertrude Atherton and Edith Wharton
- Pablo Picasso and Gertrude Stein
- Edward Adams and Eugene O'Neill
- Letters and words in Jasper Johns
- J.F. Kennedy and Richard Nixon televised debates rhetoric
- Representations of women in video games and young adult fiction
- Reality television

Literary Theory and Philosophy

- Duns Scotus and G.M. Hopkins

- Francis Bacon
- Early Modern semiotics
- Martin Heidegger and Kevin Hart
- Ludwig Wittgenstein and T.S. Eliot
- Paul de Man
- Paul de Man and Jacques Derrida
- Gilles Deleuze and Félix Guattari
- Stanley Cavell and James Joyce
- Jacques Derrida
- Jacques Derrida and John Searle
- Luce Irigaray and Elena Ferrante
- Fredric Jameson
- George Lakoff and metaphor
- Objects and objectivity in poetry
- Contemporary aesthetics

Other Topics

- Clytemnestra and Salomé
- Don Juan and Don Giovanni
- Nineteenth-century Hellenism
- Oscar Wilde's parents' writings
- Aleister Crowley and Robert Graves

Research Masters and Doctoral supervisions (including only primary or ultimate supervision of awarded degrees)

- 1989. Peter J. Hutchings. "Grave Plots: Narrative, Genre, and Death, from Late Romanticism to Postmodernism." PhD.
- 1991. Judith Elen. "'These walls will fall and rest': House and Home in Women's Fiction." PhD.
- 1994. Jennifer Ann McDonell. "Victorian Polemic and the Poetics of the Feminine Subject: Robert Browning, Pompilia, and *The Ring and the Book*." PhD.
- 1995. Alex Houen. "Narrative, Ontology, Metaphor: A Literary Ethics; Forster, Woolf, Beckett, Ricoeur, Heidegger, Bergson, Spinoza, Deleuze." MPhil.
- 1997. Mark Byron. "Beckett's Later Short Prose Texts: *explicitus est liber* [the book is set in order, finished]." MPhil.
- 2001. Michael Stuart Lynch. "Desire in the Subject of Discourse: Faulkner, Heidegger, Lacan, Foucault." PhD.
- 2002. Vanessa Kirkpatrick. "'A subtle fire beneath the flesh': Representations of Pain in Women's Poetry, Medieval to Modern." PhD.

- 2003. Wayne Pickard. "Lexicology, Biblical Allusion, and Symbolism in the Poetry of Emily Dickinson." PhD.
- 2003. Sean Brendan Pryor. "Time and Poetry: Wallace Stevens and T.S. Eliot." MPhil.
- 2005. Catriona Jane Menzies-Pike. "The Composition of the Modernist Book: *Ulysses*, *A Draft of XXX Cantos*, and *The Making of Americans*." PhD.
- 2006. Simon Clarke. "The City in Blake's *Jerusalem*: Los's Work, the Intervolution of Jerusalem and Vala, and the Isolation of the Hermaphrodite." PhD.
- 2007. Andrew Court. "Darwin and Analogy in Late Nineteenth-Century Literary History." MPhil.
- 2007. Kai Chun Fung. "The Reception of Elizabethan and Jacobean Drama in the Romantic Period: The Case of John Ford." MA Research.
- 2008. Anthony Cordingley. "Samuel Beckett's *Comment c'est / How It Is*: A Philosophy of Composition." PhD.
- 2009. Amelia Fuqua. "Virginia Woolf, *The Waves*, and the Hindu Scriptures." MA Research.
- 2012. Michelle Kelly. "Library Encounters: Textuality and the Institution." PhD.
- 2012. Aaron Nyerges. "A Geography of Resistance." PhD.
- 2012. Elizabeth Sofatzis. "Theodicy and the Problem of Evil in the Poetry of Gerard Manley Hopkins and Three of his Contemporaries: Thomas Hardy, Christina Rossetti, and Robert Browning." PhD.
- 2013. Yuan Zhang. "The Story of Beauty: Edith Wharton's Aesthetic Views in First-Person Narratives." PhD.
- 2014. Elizabeth Shek-Noble. "'Any kind of outcast whatsoever': The Art and Politics of David Wojnarowicz." PhD.
- 2015. Mark Azzopardi. "Saul Bellow and Kurt Vonnegut: History, Politics, and American Fiction in the Cold War, 1944–1970." PhD.
- 2015. Siva Prashant Kumar. "Borges and Mathematics: *los juegos con el tiempo y con lo infinito* [games with time and infinity]." MA Research.
- 2016. Bushra Naz. "Henry James's Critique of Women's Judgment: Aesthetic and Ethical Autonomy in *The Portrait of a Lady*, *The Aspern Papers*, *The Spoils of Poynton*, and *The Outcry*." PhD.
- 2018. Carissa Ern Ai Chye. "Curating the Curator: The (Self-)Construction of Frank O'Hara as Myth." PhD.
- 2018. Alexandra Margaret Gallagher. "'Breathing for a while on our earth': Re-Reading S.T. Coleridge's 'Dejection: An Ode' and 'Letter to Asra' in Light of His Severe Rheumatic Fever." MA Research.
- 2019. David James Potter. "Ardor or Ada?: Authority, Artifice, and Ambivalence in Nabokov's *Ada, or Ardor*." MPhil.

Index

academic collaborations 45
Adorno, Theodor 118, 119
adultery 275
aesthetics 120, 152, 157, 158, 164, 179
  female aesthetes 160
Alter, Robert 230
amanuensis 68, 71
American literature 195
Aristotle 41, 44, 120
Auden, W.H. xi
Australian literature 187
Australian settler colonialism 195
authorship 284
autoethnography 37

Barbauld, Anna Letitia 243
Barnes, Djuna xxiii, 280
  Nightwood 272, 274, 275–277
Barthes, Roland 279
Baudelaire, Charles 75, 80, 85
Baudrillard, Jean 27
Bellow, Saul 228
Benjamin, Walter 75, 76–77, 80, 82
Berman, Marshall 85
Bible 217, 221
  literary analysis 230
Blake, William 19, 25, 142, 171
Blanchot, Maurice xxiii, 92
Bloom, Harold 231
Bourdieu, Pierre 42
Bourgeois, Louise 121
Brontë, Charlotte 172
Brontë, Emily 170, 173, 176, 177
Bulaitis, Zoe Hope 34

Burroughs, William 203
Butler, Judith 35, 121, 175

Carpenter, Humphrey 24
Carroll, Lewis 23
Cavafy, Constantine 170, 172, 177
Celan, Paul 93, 95
children's literature 23, 25, 239
Cixous, Hélène 174
colonisation 185
compassion 143
Cooper, James Fenimore 171
creative thinking 35
critical reflection 36
critical witnessing x
cultural rhetorics 36
Cunard, Nancy 75, 83

dandyism 80, 82–83
Darwin, Charles 68, 135
death 173
decadence 80, 82, 83
Derrida, Jacques 54–55, 91, 171
Dickinson, Emily xv, 113, 114, 120
Dryden, John xxi
  Religio Laici (poem) 218, 222
  Hind and the Panther 223–224, 226
dunamis x
DuPlessis, Rachel Blau 205

Eagleton, Terry 85
Echo 193
Edwards, Jonathan 220
elegies and elegiac poems 201, 208, 209

Eliot, T.S. 55
en acte x
energia x
epiphany 18
essentialism 175, 180

Felman, Shoshana 65
festschriften 21
Field, Michael 78
first person narrative 283
flapper 84
Flaubert, Gustave 279
flâneur 82, 83, 85
Fox, Mem 144, 145
Frank, Arthur 37
Frank, Joseph 273
Frow, John 65
Frye, Northrop 15

Gardiner, Bruce
  as a storyteller 38, 255
  breadth of works taught 9
  feedback on student work 8, 64, 73
  health 10
  interest in birds xx
  published works 67
  research-informed teaching 294
  student-centred 47, 48
  teaching style xviii, 8, 77, 200, 220, 236, 256, 271
Ginsberg, Allen xx, 201
  Howl (poem) 205
  Kaddish (poem) 210–211, 213–214
  obscenity trial
Ginsberg, Naomi 202, 206
"god professor" 3
Gornick, Vivian 228
Gould, John 191
  Birds of Australia 191

Hardy, Thomas 178
Harootunian, Harry 86, 87
Haussmann, Georges-Eugène 77
Heidegger, Martin 42, 93, 95, 146, 165, 173, 175, 179
Herder, Johann Gottfried von 137
hermeneutics 14
higher education 34
Higher School Certificate 53
HIV/AIDS 81
homophobia 82

Hopkins, Gerard Manley 170
Howe, Susan 113, 122–123
Hughes, Thomas 243
humanities education xii, 35
  value of 38
humanity 166
  human difference 166

Indigenous concept of time 194
Indigenous intellectual property rights 45
Indigenous philosophy 189
Irigaray, Luce xviii–xix, 165, 167, 171, 175, 179
irritation 123

James, Henry xxii, 255
  "The Turn of the Screw" 255, 257–263, 265
  The Haunting of Bly Manor 264–267
Joyce, James 63
  Ulysses 169

Kant, Immanuel 137
Kermode, Frank xi
knowledge and understanding 62

Lacan, Jacques 175
Laughton, Charles 142
Lear, Edward xi, 24, 26–27
Leavis, F.R. 186
literary criticism 14–17, 44, 236
literary decadence 79, 82
literary studies 76, 201, 222
  interpretation 217, 220, 223, 227, 272
literary theory 165
literature fosters liberalism 140
Love, Heather 272
Lowth, Robert 227–228
lyrebirds xx, 185, 190, 192
lyric poetry 139, 186

MacDonald, George xxii, 239, 245
  vision of education 251
managerialism 3, 4, 7, 9, 33
Mapplethorpe, Robert 121
masculinity 173
metaphor 136, 142
metrics 33
mimesis and mimicry 119, 186, 192
misogyny 159
modernism xxiii, 272
moral imagination 135
mortal meaning 136

Müller, Friedrich Max 71
Murray, Les 188

Native American literature 43
neoliberalism x, 3, 14, 33, 34, 35, 49, 200
Ngai, Sianne 123
nonsense literature 239, 246
nonsense poetry xxii
novels, modernist xxiii
Nussbaum, Martha xvii, 135, 139–142

originality 188
Owens, Rochelle 19
Ozick, Cynthia 229–236

parabasis 66
pedagogical influences xi, xiii, 62
pedagogical motifs xiii
pedagogy 239, 243
phenomenality 166, 169
philosophy 54
Picasso, Pablo 168, 178
Plato 62
    Theaetetus's Complaint 62–64
play xvi, 125
playful reading xvii
Poe, Edgar Allan 77
poetry xv, 89, 186, 227
    American poets 116
    criticism xxi
politics of citation 45
Poulet, Georges 29
Pound, Ezra 64
Powell, Malea 35
prosopopoeia 136, 142
publishing x, xiii
Pullman, George 44

queer ekphrasis 272
queer modernism 272
queer signification 210

Rajan, Tilottama xi
reading 76, 89, 221, 223, 226, 283
    close reading 76, 79, 116, 257, 258
    responses to 61
reading list 73
research-informed teaching 48
rhetoric 41–42, 46
    history of xii
rhythmical repetition 139

Rich, Adrienne 115
Robinson, Marilynne 22
Rodgers, Carolyn M. 167, 178
Romanticism 186, 188, 189
Rorty, Richard xiii, 54
Ruskin, John 153

sacred 128
Schleiermacher, Friedrich xi, 221
Schopenhauer, Arthur 152–153
Schwartz, Delmore 228
semiosis 186
Shakespeare, William 160
Shelley, Mary xxiii, 283, 292
    The Last Man 283
Shelley, Percy 212, 292
    Adonais (poem) 212
Shumway, David 34
Shōnagon, Sei 172
Simmel, Georg 77
Simon, Richard 221, 222
sleep 137
Smith, David I. 246
Snediker, Michael 200–201
social criticism xi
Socrates 62
Spivak, Gayatri 174
stars 136
Stein, Gertrude xv, 103, 172
Stevens, Wallace 168, 173
storytelling 36
Sydney Morning Herald 81

Taylor, Jane 135
teaching materials xii
Tennyson, Emily 26
Teuton, Chris 43
textual analysis 195, 273
theophany 18
theory of language 175
Tiedemann, Rolf 84
Todtnauberg 93
Trilling, Lionel 229
trust in education 243, 244, 251
twentieth century literature 199

undergraduate studies 22
university bureaucracy 200
university culture xi, 43, 200
university departments 5
university mission xi

unwritten knowledge 123

ways of learning xx
Whitman, Walt xi, 17
  American tradition 17
  poetics 17
  prophetism 17
Wilde, Oscar xvii
  Picture of Dorian Gray xvii, 151

Williams, William Carlos 205
Woolf, Virginia 178
Wright, Alexis 194
Wright, Judith 187

Yeats, William Butler 64

Zweig, Stefan 21

www.ingramcontent.com/pod-product-compliance
Lightning Source LLC
Chambersburg PA
CBHW041642010726
47507CB00012B/428